SETTING UP OF BUSINESS ENTITIES

A READY RECKONER

DR. PRATAP SIMHA NETAJI

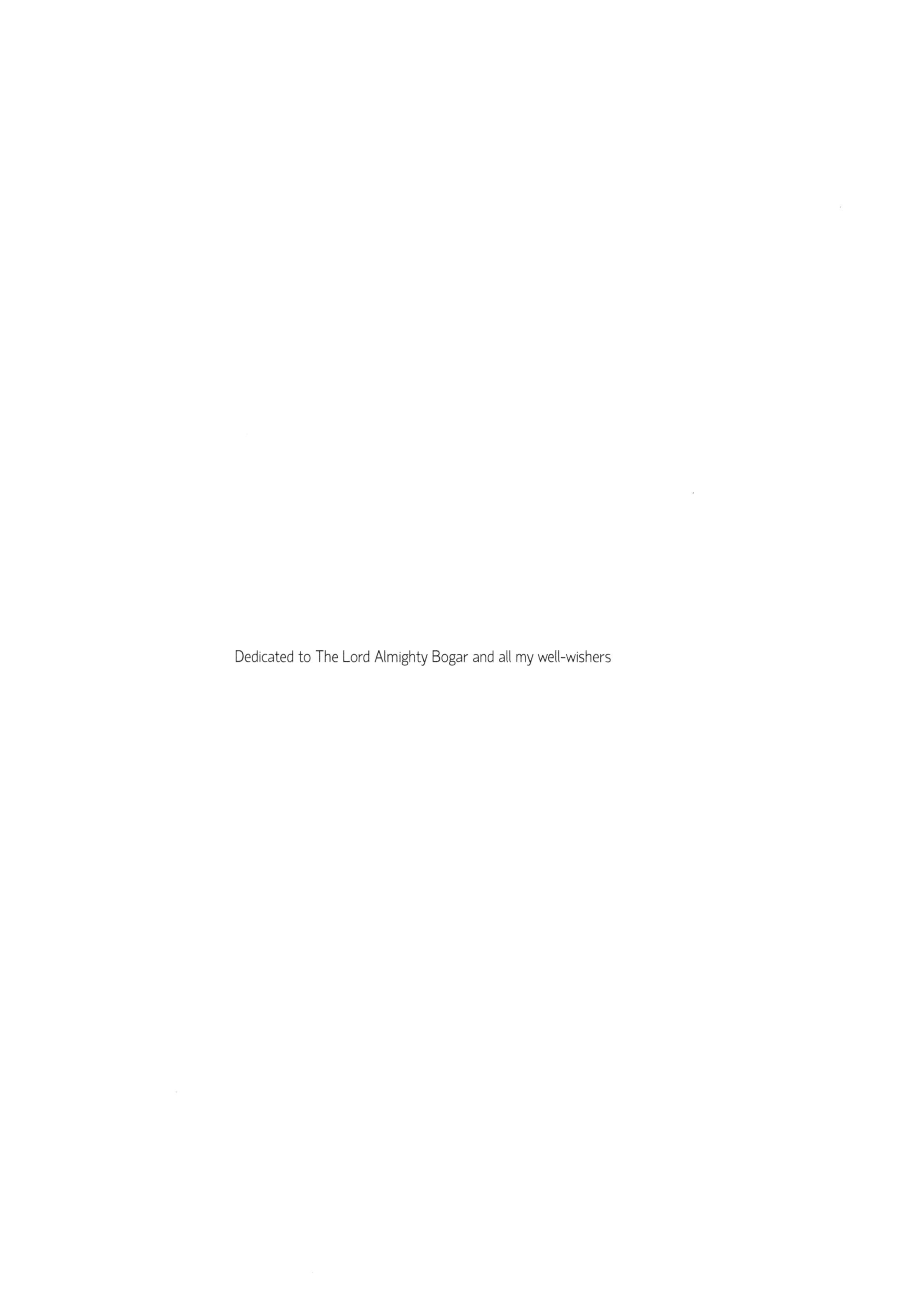

Dedicated to The Lord Almighty Bogar and all my well-wishers

Contents

Preface

The book titled "Setting up of Business entities" serves as an invaluable guide for entrepreneurs and business professionals seeking to navigate the intricate landscape of India's business environment. Authored with precision and comprehensive insight, the purpose of this book is to demystify the complexities inherent in establishing and running successful business entities in India.

One of the primary objectives of the book is to provide a thorough understanding of the regulatory framework governing business operations in the country. It meticulously outlines the legal procedures, compliance requirements, and bureaucratic processes that must be adhered to when setting up and operating a business in India. By offering a detailed roadmap through the bureaucratic maze, the book aims to empower readers with the knowledge necessary to navigate the legal landscape seamlessly.

Moreover, the book delves into the cultural and socio-economic nuances that shape the Indian business milieu. It sheds light on the unique challenges and opportunities that businesses may encounter, offering practical insights to help entrepreneurs adapt and thrive in this diverse and dynamic market. From market entry strategies to understanding consumer behavior, the book equips readers with the tools to make informed decisions and formulate effective business strategies.

"Setting up of Business entities" is a comprehensive resource designed to empower both novice and seasoned entrepreneurs with the knowledge and insights needed to establish and grow successful businesses in the vibrant and rapidly evolving Indian market.

TARGET AUDIENCE

"Embarking on the journey of setting up of business entities requires a nuanced understanding of the country's complex economic landscape. For post-graduate commerce students, management scholars and educators seeking comprehensive insights, the book 'Setting up of Business entities' serves as an invaluable guide. Tailored to meet the specific needs of this target audience, the book delves into the intricacies of India's business environment, offering a profound exploration of regulatory frameworks, market dynamics, and cultural nuances.

Post-graduate commerce students, with their academic foundation, will find the book to be a practical extension of their theoretical knowledge. Management students will appreciate the strategic perspectives woven into the narrative, providing them with a holistic understanding of business operations in the Indian context. As for educators, the book not only equips them with up-to-date information but also serves as a pedagogical tool to enhance classroom discussions and case studies.

The content is meticulously curated to bridge the gap between theory and real-world application, ensuring that readers gain actionable insights. By addressing the unique challenges and opportunities prevalent in India, this book becomes an indispensable resource for those aspiring to navigate the dynamic Indian business landscape. With its relevance and depth, 'Setting Up of Business entities' becomes an essential companion for post-graduate commerce students, management scholars, and educators seeking to impart practical knowledge in the ever-evolving field of business management.

Dt. Pratap Simha Netaji

Acknowledgements

I sincerely acknowledge the Almighty, my parents, family, and friends for helping my dream come true. This is my first publication as a book.

Prologue

The book titled "Setting up of Business entities" serves as a comprehensive guide that delves into the intricate landscape of establishing and running a business in one of the world's most dynamic and diverse economies. The book provides an insightful exploration of the multifaceted aspects that entrepreneurs and investors need to consider when navigating the Indian business environment.

The background of the book can be traced back to the increasing global interest in India as a key player in the international business arena. With its burgeoning population, rapidly expanding middle class, and a thriving market, India has become an attractive destination for both domestic and foreign businesses. However, the complexities of the Indian regulatory framework, cultural nuances, and diverse regional landscapes pose unique challenges for those seeking to establish and operate businesses within the country.

The authors of "Setting up of Business entities" bring to the forefront their extensive experience and expertise in the realms of Indian business, law, and economics. The book is meticulously crafted to cater to a wide audience, ranging from budding entrepreneurs to seasoned business professionals looking to venture into the Indian market. It serves as a valuable resource, offering a step-by-step guide to navigate the bureaucratic intricacies, legal requirements, and cultural considerations inherent in the process of setting up business entities.

The content of the book covers a broad spectrum, encompassing legal frameworks, regulatory compliance, tax implications, and strategic insights into market trends and consumer behavior. It also addresses the nuances of doing business in various sectors, considering the unique challenges and opportunities each presents. Real-world case studies and practical examples are interwoven throughout the book, providing readers with a practical understanding of the theoretical concepts discussed.

As India continues to evolve as a global economic powerhouse, "Setting up of Business entities" stands out as an indispensable tool for those seeking to capitalize on the vast potential offered by the Indian market. With its comprehensive coverage and practical approach, the book serves as a reliable companion for anyone navigating the complexities of establishing and managing a successful business venture in the diverse and dynamic landscape of India.

CHAPTER ONE

OVERVIEW

1.1 ECONOMIC OVERVIEW OF INDIA

India, with its vast and diverse economy, presents a promising landscape for those considering setting up of business entities in the country.

1.1.1 Macroeconomic Landscape:

India is one of the world's fastest-growing major economies, boasting a GDP that places it among the top economies globally. The country has a large and young population, which not only contributes to a sizable consumer market but also offers a robust labor force. However, it's important for businesses to navigate the diverse economic conditions across different states and regions.

1.1.2 Government Initiatives:

The Indian government has been actively promoting ease of doing business through various reforms. Initiatives such as "Make in India" and "Startup India" aim to attract foreign investment, boost manufacturing, and encourage entrepreneurship. These efforts have led to improvements in areas like company registration, obtaining permits, and resolving insolvency.

1.1.3 Challenges:

Despite the favorable aspects, businesses should be aware of certain challenges. Bureaucratic processes, complex tax structures, and varying regulations across states can pose hurdles. Infrastructure gaps, though improving, remain in some areas and may affect supply chains.

1.1.4 Digital Transformation:

India has witnessed a digital revolution, with increased internet penetration and widespread use of smartphones. This has opened up opportunities for businesses to leverage technology for growth. E-commerce, fintech, and other digital services are burgeoning sectors, indicating a shift in consumer behavior.

1.1.5 Sectors of Opportunity:

Several sectors in India hold significant promise. Information Technology, pharmaceuticals, renewable energy, and healthcare are witnessing substantial growth. Additionally, the government's focus on sustainability and environmental initiatives creates opportunities in the green and clean energy sectors.

1.1.6 Cultural Considerations:

Understanding the cultural nuances and local preferences is important for success in the Indian market. India is a diverse country with different languages, customs, and traditions. Adapting business strategies to local tastes and preferences can be a key factor in building a successful enterprise.

India's economic overview for setting up business entities is filled with opportunities, but it requires a strategic and well-informed approach. Businesses should be adaptable, stay updated on regulatory changes, and leverage the growing digital landscape. While challenges exist, the potential rewards in this dynamic and rapidly evolving market make India an enticing destination for those looking to establish a presence in South Asia.

1.2 BUSINESS OPPORTUNITIES IN INDIA

India presents a myriad of business opportunities for entrepreneurs and investors looking to establish a foothold in one of the world's fastest-growing economies. With a population exceeding 1.4 billion and a rapidly expanding middle class, the Indian market offers a vast consumer base for a wide range of products and services.

One of the key sectors with immense potential is the technology industry. India has emerged as a global hub for information technology and software services, providing a fertile ground for tech startups and multinational corporations alike. The country's skilled workforce, cost-effective labor, and a supportive ecosystem make it an attractive destination for businesses looking to innovate and capitalize on the digital revolution.

Additionally, the renewable energy sector in India is gaining prominence as the government focuses on sustainable development and reducing dependence on traditional sources. Entrepreneurs venturing into solar, wind, and other renewable energy projects can benefit from government incentives and a growing market demand for clean energy solutions.

The healthcare industry in India is another promising arena for business ventures. With a growing awareness of health and wellness, there is a rising demand for quality healthcare services, pharmaceuticals, and medical technologies. Entrepreneurs can explore opportunities in areas such as telemedicine, healthtech startups, and innovative healthcare solutions to cater to the evolving needs of the Indian population.

Furthermore, the e-commerce sector in India has witnessed exponential growth in recent years. The increasing penetration of the internet and smartphones has transformed the way consumers shop, providing a fertile ground for online retail businesses. From e-commerce platforms to logistics and digital payment solutions, there are numerous avenues for entrepreneurs to tap into the thriving e-commerce ecosystem.

Despite the vast opportunities, setting up of business entities in India requires a nuanced understanding of the local market dynamics, regulatory environment, and cultural nuances. Entrepreneurs should conduct thorough market research, establish strong local partnerships, and navigate the regulatory landscape to ensure a successful and sustainable business operation.

India's diverse and dynamic business landscape offers a wealth of opportunities for those willing to explore and invest in the country. Whether in technology, renewable energy, healthcare, or e-commerce, entrepreneurs can capitalize on the burgeoning market and contribute to the economic growth of one of the world's most promising economies.

1.3 REGULATORY ENVIRONMENT

The regulatory environment in India plays a crucial role in shaping the landscape for businesses looking to establish themselves in the country. India, being a diverse and rapidly growing economy, has implemented a range of regulations to govern various aspects of business operations. Navigating this regulatory framework is a key consideration for entrepreneurs and corporations seeking to set up and operate business entities in India.

One of the primary aspects of the regulatory environment in India is compliance with company registration and incorporation procedures. The Ministry of Corporate Affairs oversees these processes, and business entities must adhere to the Companies Act, which outlines the legal requirements for forming and managing companies. This involves obtaining necessary approvals, submitting documentation, and adhering to timelines specified by the authorities.

Taxation is another important aspect of the regulatory landscape in India. The Goods and Services Tax (GST), introduced in 2017, has streamlined the indirect tax structure, making it more uniform across the country. Understanding and adhering to the GST regulations is imperative for businesses to avoid legal complications. Additionally, businesses must comply with the Income Tax Act and other direct tax regulations, which can vary depending on the nature and scale of operations.

Labor laws and regulations in India are essential considerations for businesses intending to set up operations. The country has a complex set of labor laws that govern aspects such as employment contracts, working conditions, and employee benefits. Ensuring compliance with these regulations is crucial to maintain a harmonious employer-employee relationship and avoid legal disputes.

Foreign Direct Investment (FDI) policies also play a significant role in the regulatory environment. The Indian government has periodically revised and liberalized FDI norms to attract foreign investments across various sectors. Understanding the sector-specific FDI regulations is essential for foreign investors to make informed decisions about their investments in India.

Environmental regulations have gained prominence as sustainability becomes a global priority. Businesses must adhere to environmental laws and obtain necessary clearances for activities that may impact the environment. The Ministry of Environment, Forest and Climate Change regulates environmental clearances and compliance.

Navigating the regulatory environment in India requires a thorough understanding of these diverse and dynamic regulations. Seeking professional advice and establishing a strong legal and compliance framework are important steps for businesses to thrive in the Indian market. Despite the complexities, India's business environment offers immense opportunities, and successful navigation of the regulatory landscape can lead to sustainable and profitable ventures.

1.4 BENEFITS OF SETTING UP OF BUSINESS ENTITIES IN INDIA

Setting up of business entities in India offers a myriad of benefits that attract entrepreneurs and corporations alike. The country, known for its diverse culture, rich history, and burgeoning economy, has become a global hub for investment.

1.4.1 Advantages of Establishing a Business in India:

1. Vast Consumer Market: India boasts a massive and diverse consumer market with a population exceeding 1.4 billion. This vast demographic difference presents unparalleled opportunities for businesses to tap into various industries, from consumer goods to services, and cater to a wide range of needs.

2. Economic Growth Potential: India has consistently demonstrated strong economic growth, making it one of the fastest-growing major economies in the world. The government's initiatives to promote 'Make in India' and various economic reforms have further enhanced the ease of doing business, fostering an environment condusive to growth and development.

3. Skilled Workforce: India is home to a large pool of skilled and educated professionals, particularly in fields such as information technology, engineering, medicine, and management. This skilled workforce provides businesses with the necessary human capital to innovate, drive productivity, and stay competitive on a global scale.

4. Cost-Effective Labor: The cost of labor in India is relatively lower compared to many developed countries. This cost advantage enables businesses to reduce operational expenses, making it an attractive destination for manufacturing, outsourcing, and other labor-intensive industries.

5. Government Incentives and Policies: The Indian government actively promotes foreign direct investment (FDI) through various incentives and policies. Schemes like the Goods and Services Tax (GST) and the implementation of the Insolvency and Bankruptcy Code have streamlined business processes, making it easier for companies to operate efficiently.

6. Strategic Location: India's geographical location makes it an ideal base for businesses looking to expand into the Asian market. Its proximity to major economies in the Middle East and Southeast Asia facilitates easier trade and logistics.

7. Technological Advancements: India has made significant strides in technology and innovation. With a thriving startup ecosystem and a focus on digital transformation, businesses in India can leverage cutting-edge technologies and advancements to enhance their operations and stay ahead in the global marketplace.

8. Cultural Diversity and Market Insights: The diverse cultural landscape of India provides businesses with unique market insights. Understanding and respecting local cultures and preferences is crucial for success, and businesses can use this knowledge to tailor their products and services to meet the specific needs of the Indian consumer.

9. Stable Political Environment: India has a stable and democratic political system, offering a secure environment for businesses to thrive. The government's commitment to economic reforms and infrastructure development contributes to a condusive atmosphere for investment and growth.

Setting up of business entities in India offers a wealth of opportunities, from accessing a vast consumer market to tapping into a skilled workforce and benefiting from favorable government policies. As the country continues to evolve and embrace global economic trends, it stands as an attractive destination for businesses seeking sustainable growth and success

CHAPTER TWO

UNDERSTANDING THE INDIAN BUSINESS LANDSCAPE

2.1 HISTORICAL PERSPECTIVE

Understanding the historical perspective of setting up businesses in India involves tracing the evolution of the Indian business landscape through various phases.

2.1.1 Brief Overview:

1. Pre-Independence Era (Before 1947):

During British colonial rule, India's economy was largely agrarian, with limited industrialization. The business environment was influenced by British policies, and Indian entrepreneurs faced various restrictions and limitations.

2. Post- Independence (1947- 1991):

After gaining independence in 1947, India adopted a mixed economy model, with a focus on socialism and central planning. The government played a significant role in various sectors through FiveYear Plans, and private entrepreneurship was limited. Industrial licensing and controls were introduced, leading to a highly regulated business environment.

3. Liberalization (1991 Onwards):

In 1991, India initiated economic reforms to liberalize its economy, moving away from the socialist model. The government introduced measures to encourage foreign direct investment (FDI), reduced trade barriers, and dismantled the License Raj (industrial licensing system). This period marked a significant shift towards a marketoriented economy, promoting entrepreneurship and private sector participation.

4. Information Technology (IT) Boom:

In the late 1990s and early 2000s, India witnessed a boom in the IT and software services industry. Companies like Infosys, TCS, and Wipro emerged as global players, contributing significantly to India's economic growth.

5. Retail and Services Expansion:

The 2000s saw the expansion of retail and service sectors, with the growth of companies like Reliance, Tata, and others in various industries. The rise of ecommerce platforms further transformed the retail landscape.

6. Ease of Doing Business Reforms:

In recent years, the Indian government has been focusing on improving the ease of doing business by implementing various reforms. Initiatives like the Goods and Services Tax (GST), Insolvency and Bankruptcy Code (IBC), and Make in India campaign aim to create a more businessfriendly environment.

7. Challenges and Opportunities:

While there have been significant improvements, challenges persist, such as bureaucratic hurdles, complex regulations, and infrastructure bottlenecks. Opportunities arise from India's large consumer base, growing middle class, and the potential for innovation and technology driven sectors. Understanding the historical context is important for businesses looking to navigate the Indian market. Despite challenges, India's business landscape continues to evolve, presenting opportunities for both domestic and international entrepreneurs.

2.2 EVOLUTION OF INDIAN ECONOMY

The evolution of the Indian economy has been a fascinating journey, marked by significant transformations and milestones that have shaped the landscape for setting up businesses in the country. From its early days of agrarian dominance to the present era of technology-driven growth, India has undergone a remarkable economic metamorphosis.

In the pre-independence era, the Indian economy was largely agrarian, with agriculture contributing a substantial portion to the GDP. The industrial sector was nascent, and business opportunities were limited. However, with the winds of change blowing after gaining independence in 1947, India embarked on a path of economic development. The first few decades saw a focus on import substitution industrialization, aiming to reduce dependency on foreign goods and create a self-sufficient economy.

The 1991 economic reforms marked a watershed moment in the evolution of the Indian economy. The country opened its doors to globalization, liberalizing its markets and dismantling trade barriers. This era of economic liberalization paved the way for increased foreign direct investment (FDI) and the establishment of multinational corporations in India. The business environment became more competitive, with a surge in entrepreneurship and the emergence of a vibrant private sector.

The Information Technology (IT) revolution in the late 20th century played a important role in transforming India into a global hub for technology and business process outsourcing. Cities like Bangalore and Hyderabad became synonymous with innovation and technological prowess. The outsourcing boom not only contributed significantly to the GDP but also attracted international businesses to set up operations in India.

As the 21st century unfolded, the Indian economy continued its upward trajectory, diversifying into various sectors such as pharmaceuticals, renewable energy, and e-commerce. Government initiatives like 'Make in India' aimed at promoting manufacturing and 'Digital India' focused on harnessing technology for inclusive growth have further fueled the entrepreneurial spirit in the country.

However, challenges persist. Despite progress, bureaucratic red tape, and regulatory complexities can still pose hurdles for businesses. Infrastructure gaps and regional disparities also need attention. Nevertheless, the Indian government remains committed to economic reforms, aiming to create a more business-friendly environment.

The evolution of the Indian economy has been characterized by resilience, adaptability, and a commitment to growth. Setting up businesses in India today offers a diverse and dynamic market with vast potential. As the country continues to navigate the complexities of a globalized world, opportunities for entrepreneurs and businesses are abundant, making India an exciting destination for those looking to be a part of its economic journey.

2.3 MAJOR ECONOMIC REFORMS

India has embarked on a transformative journey with major economic reforms aimed at fostering a more condusive environment for setting up businesses. These initiatives reflect the government's commitment to enhance ease of doing business, attract foreign investments, and propel economic growth. The multifaceted reforms encompass various aspects of the business ecosystem, ranging from regulatory frameworks to administrative procedures, with the overarching goal of promoting entrepreneurship and job creation.

One of the important reforms has been the simplification and streamlining of regulatory processes. The introduction of a unified online portal for business registration, licensing, and compliance has significantly reduced bureaucratic hurdles. Entrepreneurs can now navigate through the intricacies of establishing a business more efficiently, minimizing delays and administrative bottlenecks. This digitalization of processes not only enhances transparency but also mitigates corruption risks, fostering a business-friendly environment.

Furthermore, the Indian government has been proactive in rationalizing and simplifying the tax regime. The Goods and Services Tax (GST), introduced as a comprehensive indirect tax reform, has replaced a complex web of multiple taxes. This has not only streamlined the taxation structure but also facilitated a seamless flow of goods and services across state borders, creating a unified national market. The simplification of tax procedures has been particularly beneficial for businesses, reducing compliance burdens and promoting a more predictable and investor-friendly tax environment.

In parallel, efforts to strengthen the financial ecosystem have been underway. The introduction of Insolvency and Bankruptcy Code (IBC) has bolstered the resolution framework for distressed businesses, promoting a more efficient and time-bound process for debt recovery. This has instilled confidence among investors and lenders, as they can now rely on a robust legal framework to address financial distress, thereby encouraging greater participation in the Indian business landscape.

The liberalization of foreign direct investment (FDI) norms is another important aspect of India's economic reforms. The government has progressively eased restrictions on foreign investments across various sectors, encouraging global players to explore opportunities in the Indian market. This has not only infused capital but also brought in advanced technologies and managerial practices, contributing to the overall development of the business ecosystem.

India's major economic reforms in setting up businesses signify a paradigm shift towards a more progressive and investor-friendly landscape. The concerted efforts to simplify regulatory processes, rationalize taxation, strengthen the financial framework, and liberalize foreign investments collectively aim to position India as a global business hub. As these reforms continue to unfold, they are expected to catalyze economic growth, foster innovation, and create a dynamic business environment for both domestic and international entrepreneurs.

2.4 CURRENT BUSINESS SCENARIO

In recent years, India has been recognized as a promising destination for setting up businesses due to its rapidly growing economy, large consumer base, and various government initiatives aimed at promoting ease of doing business. The business environment in India is dynamic and diverse, offering both opportunities and challenges.

One of the notable initiatives is the "Make in India" campaign, which encourages domestic and foreign companies to manufacture their products within the country. The government has implemented several reforms to simplify regulatory processes, reduce bureaucratic hurdles, and create a more business-friendly environment. The Goods and Services Tax (GST) implementation in 2017 was a significant step towards creating a unified tax system, streamlining taxation, and fostering a seamless market.

However, setting up a business in India comes with its share of challenges. Navigating through complex regulatory frameworks, bureaucratic procedures, and diverse cultural landscapes can be daunting. Understanding and complying with local laws, taxation policies, and labor regulations are important for a successful venture. Infrastructure challenges in some regions, especially in terms of logistics and transportation, may also pose hurdles.

Foreign investors are increasingly showing interest in sectors such as technology, renewable energy, healthcare, and e commerce. The startup ecosystem in India has witnessed significant growth, with a surge in innovative ventures across various industries. The government has launched initiatives like "Startup India" to support entrepreneurship and facilitate the growth of startups through funding and mentorship programs.

Despite the challenges, the Indian market's sheer size and potential make it an attractive destination for businesses seeking growth opportunities. The ongoing digital transformation and advancements in technology have further accelerated business innovation and expansion.

The current business scenario in setting up a business in India reflects a mix of opportunities and challenges. Government initiatives, regulatory reforms, and a burgeoning consumer market contribute to the country's appeal for businesses, while navigating through regulatory complexities and infrastructure limitations remains important for success. As the business landscape evolves, staying informed about the latest developments and adapting strategies accordingly is essential for businesses aiming to thrive in the dynamic Indian market.

2.5 KEY INDUSTRIES

In the current business scenario in India, several key industries play important roles in attracting entrepreneurs and fostering economic growth. India's diverse and dynamic market offers numerous opportunities for setting up businesses across various sectors. Some key industries that stand out in this regard include Information Technology (IT), Pharmaceuticals, Renewable Energy, E-commerce, and Manufacturing.

The Information Technology sector has been a driving force in India's economic landscape for decades. With a vast pool of skilled IT professionals and a growing demand for digital solutions globally, India remains a favorable destination for IT businesses. The government's initiatives like "Digital India" campaign support the growth of the IT industry, making it an attractive choice for entrepreneurs.

The Pharmaceuticals industry in India has witnessed substantial growth, fueled by a large population and increasing healthcare needs. The country has emerged as a pharmaceutical hub, not only catering to the domestic market but also exporting to various countries. Favorable government policies, a robust regulatory framework, and a cost-effective manufacturing environment contribute to the industry's success.

Renewable Energy is gaining prominence as India endeavors to meet its energy needs sustainably. The government's emphasis on clean energy initiatives and the push towards reducing dependence on fossil fuels create significant opportunities for entrepreneurs in the renewable energy sector. Solar and wind power projects, in particular, are experiencing a surge in investments and business activities.

E-commerce has witnessed exponential growth in India, driven by increasing internet penetration and changing consumer preferences. The rise of online marketplaces and digital payment systems has created a condusive environment for e-commerce businesses. The government's push for a digital economy further supports the growth of this sector.

The Manufacturing sector continues to be a cornerstone of India's economy. The 'Make in India' initiative, aimed at promoting domestic manufacturing and attracting foreign investments, has bolstered the sector. With a focus on ease of doing business and infrastructure development, setting up manufacturing units in India has become more attractive for entrepreneurs.

In addition to these key industries, sectors like Healthcare, Education, and Agriculture also present significant opportunities for business setups. The government's proactive measures, such as GST implementation and regulatory reforms, contribute to creating a business-friendly environment.

Despite these opportunities, entrepreneurs need to navigate challenges such as bureaucratic hurdles, infrastructure gaps, and regulatory complexities. Nevertheless, the overall business climate in India is optimistic, with a young and dynamic workforce, a burgeoning consumer market, and a government committed to economic reforms. Entrepreneurs exploring business ventures in India find a fertile ground where innovation, resilience, and strategic planning can lead to success in the diverse and ever-evolving Indian market.

2.6 EMERGING SECTORS

In the dynamic landscape of the Indian economy, the emergence of new sectors has become a prominent feature, offering unprecedented opportunities for entrepreneurs and investors alike. The current business scenario in India reflects a diversification of traditional industries and the rise of innovative sectors that harness the power of technology and changing consumer preferences.

One of the notable emerging sectors is the technology-driven startup ecosystem. India has witnessed a surge in the number of startups, particularly in areas such as fintech, healthtech, edtech, and agritech. The government's initiatives, such as "Startup India," have played an important role in fostering a condusive environment for entrepreneurs, providing them with financial support, mentorship, and regulatory ease. The young and vibrant demographic of the country, coupled with increasing digital penetration, has created a fertile ground for these startups to flourish.

Another significant domain experiencing rapid growth is renewable energy. With a heightened focus on sustainability and environmental conservation, there has been a substantial shift towards renewable energy sources like solar and wind power. The Indian government's ambitious targets for clean energy production and various incentives for businesses in this sector have led to increased investments and collaborations. Entrepreneurs venturing into renewable energy not only contribute to the country's energy transition but also position themselves in a sector with long-term sustainability.

The healthcare sector has also undergone a transformation, especially with the advent of telemedicine and digital health solutions. The global health crisis has accelerated the adoption of technology in healthcare delivery, making it an attractive space for business development. Entrepreneurs are exploring opportunities to create innovative solutions, ranging from remote patient monitoring to AI-driven diagnostics, to address the evolving healthcare needs of the population.

E-commerce continues to be a powerhouse in the Indian business landscape, but its dynamics are constantly evolving. Beyond the traditional e-commerce platforms, there is a surge in niche and specialized e-commerce ventures catering to specific consumer segments. Additionally, the integration of technology, artificial intelligence, and data analytics is reshaping the online retail experience, offering personalized recommendations and enhancing customer engagement.

The current business scenario in India is marked by the rise of diverse and innovative sectors. Entrepreneurs entering the market are capitalizing on technological advancements, changing consumer behavior, and government support to carve a niche for them. The key to success lies in adaptability, agility, and a keen understanding of the evolving market dynamics. As India continues its journey towards economic growth, these emerging sectors present exciting opportunities for those looking to set up and thrive in the ever-changing business landscape.

2.7 MARKET TRENDS

In the dynamic landscape of the Indian business scenario, several market trends are shaping the setting up of businesses, reflecting the evolving economic and regulatory environment. These trends underscore the opportunities and challenges that entrepreneurs face as they navigate the complexities of establishing and growing their ventures in the country.

One prominent trend is the increasing emphasis on digitalization. The Indian government's push towards a digital economy has led to a surge in online businesses and technology-driven solutions. E-commerce, digital payments, and fintech are witnessing unprecedented growth, creating a condusive environment for entrepreneurs to explore innovative business models.

Another noteworthy trend is the focus on sustainability and social responsibility. As global awareness of environmental issues rises, Indian consumers are becoming more conscious of their choices. Businesses that integrate sustainable practices and demonstrate a commitment to social responsibility are gaining favor in the market. Entrepreneurs are recognizing the importance of aligning their business strategies with environmental and social goals to appeal to the discerning Indian consumer.

The regulatory landscape in India is also undergoing significant changes, aimed at simplifying processes and fostering a more business-friendly environment. Initiatives like the 'Make in India' campaign and various economic reforms are attracting both domestic and foreign investments. Streamlined procedures for company registration, ease of compliance, and incentives for specific industries are contributing to a more condusive atmosphere for business setup.

In the post-pandemic era, remote work and digital connectivity have become integral to business operations. Many entrepreneurs are capitalizing on the flexibility offered by remote work models, leading to the rise of virtual teams and distributed enterprises. This trend not only allows for cost savings but also enables businesses to tap into a diverse talent pool across geographical boundaries.

Despite these positive trends, challenges persist. Infrastructure bottlenecks, bureaucratic hurdles, and complex tax structures remain obstacles for entrepreneurs. Additionally, fierce competition in certain sectors requires businesses to differentiate themselves through innovation, quality, and customer-centric approaches.

The market trends in setting up businesses in India reflect a dynamic and evolving landscape. Entrepreneurs need to stay agile, embrace digitalization, prioritize sustainability, and navigate regulatory changes to capitalize on the abundant opportunities presented by the Indian market. As the business environment continues to transform, those who adeptly align their strategies with emerging trends are likely to thrive in the vibrant and ever-changing Indian market.

2.8 CULTURAL AND SOCIAL FACTORS

Setting up a business in India requires a nuanced understanding of the cultural and social factors that significantly influence the business environment. India is a diverse and multi-cultural country with a rich tapestry of traditions, languages, and customs. Navigating through these intricacies is crucial for the success of any business venture.

Cultural factors play a pivotal role in shaping the business landscape in India. The concept of 'Jugaad,' which refers to innovative and frugal solutions to problems, is deeply ingrained in the Indian ethos. Entrepreneurs often need to be adaptable and resourceful to thrive in this environment. Additionally, the hierarchical structure prevalent in Indian society is reflected in business relationships. Respect for authority and age, as well as a strong emphasis on personal relationships, are crucial in establishing and maintaining business connections.

Social factors also influence business operations in India. The caste system, though officially abolished, still influences social interactions to some extent. Understanding these dynamics is essential for building effective teams and fostering a harmonious workplace. Moreover, India places a strong emphasis on family values, and businesses often need to acknowledge and accommodate these values in their corporate culture.

Language is another significant factor in the Indian business landscape. While English is widely spoken, especially in business and urban settings, regional languages can be crucial for effective communication, especially when dealing with local markets. Employing individuals who are fluent in local languages can be an asset in establishing connections with diverse consumer bases.

Religious diversity also shapes business practices in India. Understanding and respecting various religious festivals and holidays is crucial for scheduling business activities. Many businesses adapt their marketing strategies and product launches to align with religious and cultural celebrations, which can significantly impact consumer behavior.

Moreover, India's collectivist culture places importance on group harmony and consensus decision-making. Building a collaborative work environment and engaging in social activities can contribute to a positive company image and enhance employee satisfaction.

A deep appreciation for the cultural and social fabric of India is indispensable for any business looking to establish itself in this vibrant and diverse market. Entrepreneurs must navigate these factors with sensitivity and flexibility, recognizing that success lies not just in the products or services offered but in the ability to integrate with and contribute to the broader cultural and social landscape of the country.

2.9 BUSINESS ETIQUETTE

Setting up a business in India requires a nuanced understanding of the cultural and business etiquette prevalent in the country. India, with its rich history and diverse population, boasts a unique business environment where relationships and etiquette play aimportant role. Adhering to these cultural norms can significantly enhance the chances of success and foster positive business interactions.

First and foremost, establishing trust is paramount in Indian business culture. Building relationships takes precedence over immediate transactions. Therefore, investing time in getting to know your potential business partners, clients, and associates on a personal level is essential. Engaging in casual conversations, expressing genuine interest in their culture, and participating in social events contribute to fostering trust and long-lasting connections.

Communication in India often involves a more indirect and nuanced approach. While English is widely spoken in business settings, it is important to be mindful of the cultural nuances in communication. Politeness, humility, and a diplomatic tone are highly valued. It is advisable to avoid confrontational or aggressive communication styles, as they may be perceived as disrespectful.

Punctuality is appreciated, but flexibility is equally important. Business meetings may not always adhere strictly to schedules, and it is advisable to be patient and adaptable. In Indian culture, relationships take precedence over deadlines, and negotiations may extend beyond the initially allocated time. Demonstrating patience and understanding during such situations will reflect positively on your professionalism.

Understanding the hierarchical structure within Indian businesses is important. Respect for authority and seniority is deeply ingrained in the culture. It is customary to address individuals by their titles and use appropriate honorifics. Additionally, decision-making processes may involve multiple levels of approval, so patience is key when awaiting responses or decisions.

Gift-giving is a common practice in Indian business circles and is considered a gesture of goodwill. When presenting gifts, it is essential to choose items that align with the recipient's cultural and personal preferences. Additionally, offering and receiving gifts with both hands is a sign of respect.

Lastly, being aware of religious and cultural sensitivities is fundamental. India is a melting pot of diverse religions and traditions. Avoiding sensitive topics and demonstrating respect for cultural differences will contribute to a harmonious and successful business relationship. Establishing a business in India requires a deep appreciation for its cultural intricacies. By prioritizing relationship-building, practicing effective communication, demonstrating patience, respecting hierarchies, and acknowledging cultural diversity, businesses can navigate the Indian business landscape with grace and foster enduring partnerships.

2.10 UNDERSTANDING LOCAL CUSTOMS

Setting up a business in a new location involves more than just understanding the legal and economic aspects; it requires a deep appreciation for the local customs and cultural nuances that shape the business landscape. Recognizing and respecting these customs is not merely a courtesy, but a strategic imperative that can significantly impact the success or failure of a venture.

One of the key aspects of understanding local customs is appreciating the cultural values that influence business interactions. Different societies have distinct communication styles, levels of formality, and expectations when it comes to professional relationships. For instance, in some cultures, building personal connections before diving into business discussions is important, while in others, a more direct and results-oriented approach may be preferred. Being attuned to these preferences can help establish rapport and trust with local partners, clients, and stakeholders.

Moreover, being aware of local traditions and etiquettes is essential in fostering positive relationships. In many cultures, the exchange of gifts or participation in local celebrations may be seen as a gesture of goodwill. Conversely, overlooking or disregarding these traditions may lead to misunderstandings and strained relations. Taking the time to learn about and participate in local customs demonstrates a commitment to integration and a genuine interest in the community, enhancing the business's reputation and credibility.

Understanding the local business etiquette also involves grasping the concept of time and punctuality. Some cultures place a high value on punctuality and efficient use of time, while others prioritize a more relaxed and flexible approach. Adhering to local expectations regarding meetings and deadlines reflects a respect for the local rhythm and can contribute to smoother business operations.

In addition, navigating the regulatory landscape requires an understanding of the unwritten rules that govern business conduct in a particular region. This includes comprehending the importance of relationships, hierarchy, and the influence of family connections in decision-making processes. Failure to acknowledge and respect these dynamics may hinder progress and impede the establishment of a successful business presence.

Ultimately, recognizing and embracing local customs is not just a matter of compliance; it is an integral part of building a sustainable and mutually beneficial business relationship. It goes beyond language proficiency and legal acumen to encompass a holistic understanding of the social fabric in which the business operates. By appreciating and adapting to local customs, businesses can foster positive connections, build a strong reputation, and lay the groundwork for long-term success in a new and diverse market.

2.10 QUESTIONS

1. What do you mean by understanding local customs?
2. Explain the evolution of Indian economy?
3. What are the major economic reforms for setting up of business in India?
4. Explain the evolution of Indian economy?
5. What are the emerging sectors in India for setting up of business?
6. Explain the current senario for setting up of business in India?

CHAPTER THREE

INTRODUCTION TO BUSINESS SETUP

3.1 DEFINITION AND CONCEPT OF BUSINESS

Business is a multifaceted and dynamic concept that has been explored and defined by various scholars and thinkers throughout history. At its core, business encompasses the activities and processes involved in the production, exchange, and distribution of goods and services to meet the needs and wants of society. Scholars from different disciplines have contributed to the understanding of business, offering diverse perspectives on its nature and role in the socio-economic landscape.

One influential perspective on the definition of business comes from the renowned economist Milton Friedman. In his seminal work, "Capitalism and Freedom," Friedman emphasized the primary objective of business as profit maximization. According to Friedman, businesses exist to generate profits for their shareholders within the bounds of legal and ethical standards. This perspective highlights the importance of economic efficiency and the pursuit of self-interest in the business context.

On the other hand, Peter Drucker, a management guru and author of "The Practice of Management," provided a broader and more holistic view of business. Drucker argued that the purpose of a business is to create and satisfy customers. He emphasized the significance of understanding customer needs and continuously innovating to meet those needs effectively. Drucker's perspective underscores the customer-centric nature of successful businesses and the importance of adaptability in a rapidly changing market environment.

In the realm of organizational behavior, Chester Barnard, in his work "The Functions of the Executive," focused on the concept of cooperation within a business. Barnard believed that the success of an organization depends on the willingness of individuals to work together towards common goals. His perspective highlights the social and interpersonal aspects of business, emphasizing the role of effective communication and collaboration in achieving organizational objectives.

The concept of business has also been explored from a strategic management standpoint. Michael Porter, in his book "Competitive Strategy," introduced the idea of competitive advantage. According to Porter, businesses must create a sustainable competitive advantage by being a cost leader, differentiating their products, or focusing on a niche market. This strategic perspective emphasizes the importance of positioning and differentiation in achieving long-term success.

The concept of business is rich and multifaceted, with scholars offering diverse definitions and perspectives. From the profit-centric views of Friedman to the customer-centric approach of Drucker, and the emphasis on cooperation by Barnard, each perspective contributes to a comprehensive understanding of the complex world of business. These varied viewpoints highlight the interdisciplinary nature of business studies, drawing on economics, management, and organizational behavior to capture the essence of this crucial societal institution.

3.2 IMPORTANCE OF SETTING UP BUSINESS ENTITIES

Setting up of business entities is an important endeavor that not only fuels economic growth but also plays an important role in shaping the social fabric of communities. The importance of establishing businesses transcends mere financial gains, extending its impact to the very core of our societies.

From an economic perspective, businesses serve as the backbone of a thriving economy. They generate employment opportunities, providing individuals with a means to support themselves and their families. As businesses expand, so does the demand for skilled and unskilled labor, creating a ripple effect that stimulates economic activity. Additionally, the creation of new enterprises fosters innovation and competition, driving productivity and efficiency in various sectors.

The economic significance of setting up a business is further underscored by its contribution to wealth creation. Entrepreneurs, driven by their vision and determination, not only build personal prosperity but also contribute to the overall prosperity of the community and nation. Successful businesses generate tax revenues, which fund essential public services such as education, healthcare, and infrastructure, thereby enhancing the quality of life for all citizens.

Beyond economic considerations, businesses play a important role in shaping the social landscape. They serve as catalysts for community development by fostering a sense of identity and pride. Local businesses become integral parts of the social tapestry, supporting local events, sponsoring sports teams, and contributing to charitable causes. This active involvement strengthens the social bonds within a community, creating a sense of belonging and shared responsibility.

Moreover, businesses can act as agents of positive change by promoting diversity, inclusivity, and ethical practices. As drivers of employment, they have the power to empower individuals from various backgrounds, promoting social mobility and reducing inequality. Ethical business practices not only contribute to a positive corporate culture but also set a standard for responsible behavior that resonates throughout society.

The importance of setting up a business extends far beyond profit margins and financial success. Businesses are integral to the economic vitality of nations, driving job creation, innovation, and wealth generation. Simultaneously, they contribute to the social fabric by fostering community development, promoting inclusivity, and championing ethical practices. Embracing the establishment and growth of businesses is essential for a robust and interconnected society that thrives both economically and socially.

3.3 ROLE OF ENTREPRENEURS IN BUSINESS ESTABLISHMENT

Entrepreneurs play an important role in the establishment and growth of businesses, contributing significantly to economic development and innovation. Their responsibilities extend beyond mere business ownership to encompass a range of critical functions that drive success. The characteristics of entrepreneurs set them apart as dynamic individuals capable of navigating the challenges inherent in the competitive business landscape.

One of the primary responsibilities of entrepreneurs is to identify viable business opportunities. This involves keen market analysis, identifying gaps or unmet needs, and envisioning innovative solutions. Entrepreneurs must possess a forward-thinking mindset, constantly seeking ways to stay ahead of market trends and emerging technologies.

Once a business idea is conceptualized, entrepreneurs assume the responsibility of assembling a capable and motivated team. Leadership skills are paramount in creating a cohesive and high-performing workforce. Entrepreneurs inspire and guide their team, fostering a collaborative environment that encourages creativity and problem-solving.

Financial management is another critical aspect of an entrepreneur's role. From securing initial funding to budgeting, resource allocation, and monitoring financial performance, entrepreneurs must navigate the complexities of fiscal responsibility. This demands a combination of financial acumen, risk management, and adaptability to changing economic conditions.

Entrepreneurs are also the driving force behind the development of a business strategy. Crafting a clear vision and mission, setting achievable goals, and devising a roadmap for success are essential components of strategic planning. Entrepreneurs must possess strategic thinking skills, allowing them to anticipate challenges, identify opportunities, and adapt their approach accordingly.

Adaptability and resilience are characteristic traits that set successful entrepreneurs apart. The business landscape is dynamic and subject to rapid changes. Entrepreneurs must be agile, able to pivot when necessary, and resilient in the face of setbacks. A positive mindset and the ability to learn from failures contribute to long-term success.

Innovation is at the core of entrepreneurial endeavors. Entrepreneurs strive to create value by introducing new products, services, or processes. Creativity, curiosity, and a willingness to take calculated risks characterize their approach to innovation.

Moreover, ethical conduct and social responsibility are becoming increasingly important for entrepreneurs. A commitment to ethical business practices and a consideration of the social and environmental impact of their ventures contribute to long-term sustainability and positive corporate citizenship.

The role of entrepreneurs in business establishment is multifaceted, encompassing responsibilities that range from identifying opportunities and assembling teams to strategic planning and financial management. The characteristics of successful entrepreneurs include leadership, adaptability, resilience, innovation, and a commitment to ethical practices. As drivers of economic growth and agents of change, entrepreneurs play a important role in shaping the business landscape and fostering innovation.

3.4 FACTOR INFLUENCING BUSINESS SETUP

Setting up a business involves a complex interplay of internal and external factors that significantly impact the decision-making process. These factors play an important role in shaping the strategic direction, feasibility, and overall success of a business venture.

3.4.1 INTERNAL FACTORS:

1. Organizational Culture: The internal culture of a business, including its values, beliefs, and practices, profoundly influences decision-making. A culture that encourages innovation and risk-taking may lead to more ambitious business setups, while a conservative culture may result in cautious decisions.
2. Leadership and Management: The skills and decisions of leaders and managers are critical internal factors. Effective leadership can steer the business through challenges, while poor leadership may hinder growth and sustainability.
3. Resources and Capabilities: The internal resources, such as financial capital, human capital, and technological infrastructure, directly impact business decisions. The availability of skilled personnel, adequate funding, and advanced technology can influence the scale and scope of the business.
4. Organizational Structure:The structure of the organization, including hierarchies, communication channels and decision-making processes, affects how decisions are made. A flexible and adaptive structure may facilitate quicker and more effective decision-making.
5. Financial Position:The financial health of a business is an important internal factor. The availability of funds, profitability, and financial stability influence decisions related to investments, expansions, and day-to-day operations.

3.7 EXTERNAL FACTORS:

1. Economic Conditions: The overall economic climate, including factors like inflation, interest rates, and market trends, significantly affects business decisions. Economic downturns may lead to more conservative decisions, while periods of growth may encourage expansion
2. Market Trends and Competition: Understanding market trends and the competitive landscape is vital for setting up a successful business. External factors such as consumer preferences, industry trends, and the actions of competitors impact product development, pricing, and marketing strategies.

3. Legal and Regulatory Environment: Laws and regulations imposed by governments and regulatory bodies influence business decisions. Compliance with legal requirements, industry standards, and ethical considerations is important for long-term success.
4. Technological Advancements: The rapid pace of technological innovation can present both opportunities and challenges. Adopting new technologies can enhance efficiency and competitiveness, but failing to keep up with advancements may lead to obsolescence.
5. Social and Cultural Factors: Societal and cultural influences shape consumer behavior and preferences. Understanding and adapting to cultural nuances can impact marketing strategies and product positioning.
6. Environmental Sustainability: Increasing awareness of environmental issues has led businesses to consider sustainability in decision-making. Factors such as environmental regulations, consumer preferences for eco-friendly products, and the overall impact on the environment can affect business choices.

The successful establishment of a business requires a comprehensive analysis of both internal and external factors. A holistic approach that considers these various elements helps businesses make informed decisions, navigate uncertainties, and position themselves for long-term success in a dynamic and competitive business environment.

3.5 QUESTIONS

1. What are the FACTOR INFLUENCING BUSINESS SETUP
2. Explain the importance of setting up of business in India?
3. Write short notes on the concept of setting up of business?
4. Role of Entrepreneurs in Business Establishment. ? Explain.
5. Explain the difference types of companies?

CHAPTER FOUR

TYPES OF BUSINESS ENTITIES

4.1 BUSINESS STRUCTURES IN INDIA

Setting up a business in India involves navigating a diverse and dynamic economic landscape, with various business structures available to entrepreneurs. India offers several options for organizing and operating businesses, each with its own set of advantages and considerations. The choice of business structure plays a crucial role in determining the legal, financial, and operational aspects of the venture.

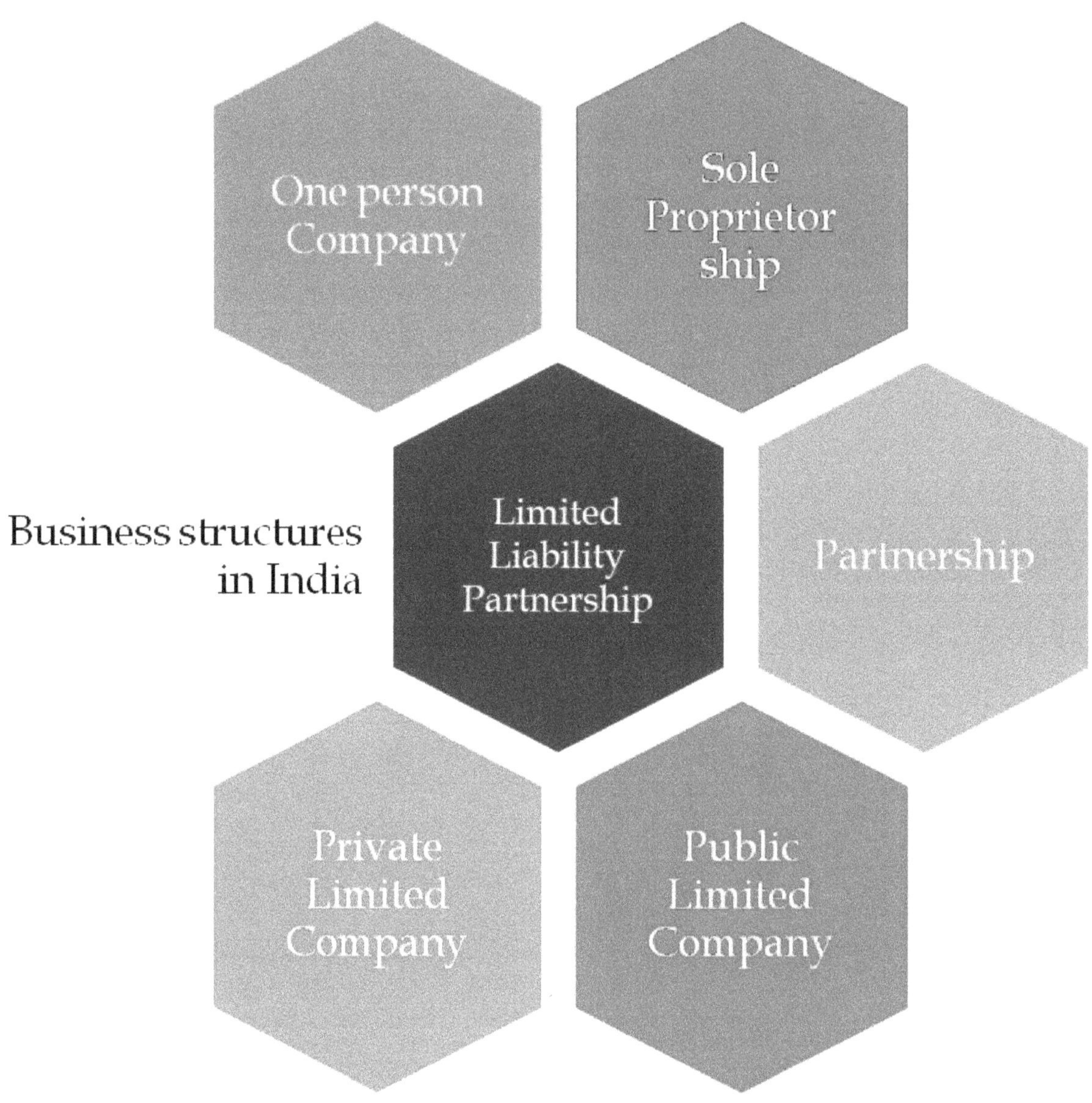

Enter Caption

4.2 COMMON BUSINESS STRUCTURES IN INDIA

1. Sole Proprietorship:

A sole proprietorship is the simplest form of business organization, where a single individual owns and manages the business. This structure is easy to set up and has minimal compliance requirements. However, the owner has unlimited personal liability, and the business and personal assets are not separate entities.

2. Partnership:

Partnerships are formed by two or more individuals who agree to share profits and losses. There are two types of partnerships: general partnerships and limited liability partnerships (LLPs). In a general partnership, partners have unlimited liability, while LLPs provide a level of protection to partners' personal assets. Partnerships are suitable for small and medium-sized enterprises (SMEs) and professional services.

3. Private Limited Company:

Private Limited Companies are the most prevalent form of business entities in India. They offer limited liability to shareholders, which mean their personal assets are not at risk for the company's debts. Private Limited Companies have a separate legal identity, making it easier to raise capital through the issuance of shares. However, they have stricter regulatory compliance and reporting requirements compared to sole proprietorships and partnerships.

4. Public Limited Company:

Public Limited Companies are suitable for larger businesses intending to raise capital from the public through the sale of shares on the stock exchange. These companies have more stringent regulatory requirements, including periodic financial disclosures and a higher level of corporate governance. The liability of shareholders is limited to their share capital.

5. Limited Liability Partnership (LLP):

An LLP combines the flexibility of a partnership with the limited liability of a company. It is a popular choice for professionals such as lawyers, accountants, and consultants. LLPs have a separate legal entity and require less compliance compared to companies, making them an attractive option for certain businesses.

6. One Person Company (OPC):

Introduced to support solo entrepreneurs, an OPC allows a single person to establish a company with limited liability. The owner is the sole shareholder and director. OPCs provide the advantages of a company structure without the need for multiple directors or shareholders.

When setting up a business in India, entrepreneurs must carefully consider their business goals, scale, and the level of regulatory compliance they are willing to undertake. Consulting with legal and financial professionals is crucial to making an informed decision based on the specific requirements and nature of the business. India's business structures offer a diverse range of options, allowing entrepreneurs to find the most suitable framework for their ventures.

4.3 COMPANY REGISTRATION

Setting up a business in India involves several important steps, and one of the fundamental aspects is the registration process. The procedures and documentation required for company registration play an important role in ensuring compliance with Indian laws and regulations.

1. Choose the Type of Company: The first step in the company registration process is to determine the type of company you want to establish. In India, you can opt for a Private Limited Company, Public Limited Company, Limited Liability Partnership (LLP), or One Person Company (OPC). Each type has its own set of rules and regulations.

2. Obtain Digital Signature Certificate (DSC):

Digital Signature Certificates (DSC) is mandatory for filing online applications with the Ministry of Corporate Affairs (MCA). Each director and subscriber must obtain a DSC from authorized certifying agencies.

3. Director Identification Number (DIN):

Directors of the proposed company need to obtain a unique Director Identification Number (DIN) from the MCA. This can be done by filing an online application with the necessary documents, such as identity proof and address proof.

4. Name Reservation:

Choose a unique and suitable name for your company and apply for name reservation with the Registrar of Companies (RoC). The name should comply with the Companies Act, 2013, and the rules specified by the MCA. Once approved, the name is reserved for 20 days.

5. Prepare Memorandum and Articles of Association:

Draft the Memorandum of Association (MoA) and Articles of Association (AoA) for the company. These documents outline the company's objectives, capital structure, and internal regulations. Ensure compliance with the Companies Act, 2013.

6. Filing Incorporation Documents:

Prepare and file the incorporation documents, including the MoA, AoA, and other necessary forms, with the RoC. This can be done online through the MCA portal. Along with the documents, submit the requisite fees based on the authorized capital of the company.

7. PAN and TAN Application:

After incorporation, apply for a Permanent Account Number (PAN) and Tax Deduction and Collection Account Number (TAN) for the company. These are essential for financial transactions and tax compliance.

8. Obtain Certificate of Incorporation:

Once the RoC verifies the documents and approves the application, a Certificate of Incorporation is issued. This document signifies the legal existence of the company.

9. Post-Incorporation Compliance:

After obtaining the Certificate of Incorporation, fulfill post-incorporation compliance requirements. This includes opening a bank account, obtaining GST registration (if applicable), and adhering to other regulatory obligations.

10. Maintain Ongoing Compliance:

Comply with ongoing statutory requirements, such as filing annual returns, conducting board meetings, and maintaining proper books of accounts. Non-compliance may result in penalties and legal consequences.

4.4 TAXATION SYSTEM

In India, the taxation system for corporate entities plays an important role in shaping the business landscape and influencing investment decisions. The corporate tax structure is designed to strike a balance between promoting economic growth and ensuring fiscal sustainability. Understanding the intricacies of the taxation system is important for entrepreneurs and businesses looking to set up operations in the country.

India has undergone significant changes in its corporate tax regime. The government introduced a landmark reform in 2019 by slashing the corporate tax rate to attract foreign investments and stimulate domestic economic growth. The reduced tax rate is applicable to both existing companies and new manufacturing entities, providing a competitive edge on the global stage.

The corporate tax rate is categorized into two brackets: one for domestic companies and another for new manufacturing companies. Domestic companies typically pay a base rate, while new manufacturing entities enjoy a lower rate as part of the government's "Make in India" initiative, aimed at boosting local production and employment.

It's essential for businesses planning to establish a presence in India to consider various aspects of the taxation system. The concept of Minimum Alternate Tax (MAT) is a significant consideration. MAT ensures that companies, despite availing various exemptions and deductions, contribute a minimum percentage of their book profits as tax.

Additionally, businesses need to comprehend the Goods and Services Tax (GST), a comprehensive indirect tax levied on the supply of goods and services. GST has replaced multiple indirect taxes, simplifying the tax structure and fostering a unified national market.

Entrepreneurs should also be aware of Transfer Pricing Regulations, as transactions between related entities, both domestic and international, are subject to scrutiny to prevent tax evasion through manipulation of prices.

To ease compliance and streamline procedures, the government has been actively working on digital initiatives. The introduction of the Goods and Services Tax Network (GSTN) and the e-filing system for income tax returns have simplified the tax filing process, making it more transparent and efficient.

While India offers a vast market and growth opportunities, businesses should carefully navigate the taxation landscape to ensure compliance and optimize their financial strategies. Staying informed about regulatory updates and seeking professional advice can significantly contribute to the success of enterprises venturing into the dynamic Indian business environment.

Goods and Services Tax (GST) plays a pivotal role in the setting up of businesses in India across various entities. Introduced in July 2017, GST is a comprehensive indirect tax that has replaced a complex structure of multiple taxes such as Value Added Tax (VAT), central excise duty, and service tax. This unified taxation system has streamlined the business environment, making it more transparent and efficient for various entities.

For businesses in India, irrespective of their size and nature, understanding and adhering to the GST regulations is crucial. One of the significant advantages of GST is the elimination of cascading taxes, which allows businesses to claim input tax credit on the taxes paid on their purchases. This ensures a more seamless flow of credit throughout the supply chain, promoting efficiency and reducing the overall tax burden.

In the context of setting up a business, GST compliance is mandatory for entities with a turnover exceeding the prescribed threshold limit. This threshold varies for goods and service providers, ensuring that even small businesses are brought under the GST ambit. The registration process involves obtaining a unique Goods and Services Tax Identification Number (GSTIN), which is essential for carrying out business transactions.

GST also has implications for different business structures, such as sole proprietorships, partnerships, and corporations. Each entity needs to understand how GST impacts its operations and compliance requirements. For example, while a sole proprietor may have relatively simpler compliance obligations, a corporation with pan-India operations may need to navigate through complex multi-state tax regulations.

Moreover, GST has facilitated the ease of doing business by providing a unified platform for tax filing through the Goods and Services Tax Network (GSTN). Businesses can file their returns, claim input tax credits, and fulfill other compliance obligations online, reducing paperwork and administrative hassles.

Setting up a business in India entails navigating a complex regulatory landscape, and one important aspect that demands attention is customs duty. Customs duty is a tax imposed by the government on the import and export of goods. In the context of establishing a business in India, understanding the implications of customs duty is imperative for various entities, including sole proprietors, partnerships, and corporations.

For foreign entities looking to invest in India, customs duty plays an important role in determining the cost-effectiveness of importing goods and services. The Indian government has established a structured customs duty framework that encompasses both basic customs duty and additional duties such as Countervailing Duty (CVD) and Special Additional Duty (SAD). These duties are levied based on the nature of the goods, their classification under the Harmonized System of Nomenclature (HSN), and any applicable trade agreements.

Sole proprietors embarking on business ventures in India must meticulously assess the customs duty implications, as this directly impacts the pricing and competitiveness of imported goods. Partnering with reliable customs consultants can provide valuable insights and assist in optimizing duty payments.

Partnerships, on the other hand, may need to align their business strategies with the prevailing customs duty rates to ensure cost-effective importation of raw materials or finished products. This collaborative approach helps in streamlining logistics and avoiding any unexpected financial burdens.

Corporations setting up operations in India must conduct a comprehensive analysis of customs duty implications to formulate an effective supply chain strategy. Adhering to the regulatory requirements and staying abreast of changes in customs policies is crucial for maintaining compliance and avoiding any legal repercussions.

The Indian government has taken significant steps in recent years to simplify customs procedures through the implementation of digital platforms like the Customs Electronic Commerce/Trade (ICEGATE) portal. This initiative aims to facilitate smoother clearance processes, reducing the bureaucratic hurdles for businesses.

Understanding customs duty is indispensable for entities setting up business operations in India. Navigating the intricate customs regulations requires diligence, strategic planning, and often collaboration with customs experts to ensure seamless import and export activities. Adapting to the dynamic customs environment is vital for the success and sustainability of businesses operating in the Indian market.

4.5 INTELLECTUAL PROPERTY RIGHTS

Intellectual Property Rights

4.5.1 Trademarks - Procedure and Registration for Setting Up Business

In the vibrant landscape of India's business environment, establishing a distinctive brand identity is crucial for success. Trademarks play a important role in safeguarding this identity, providing legal protection for businesses and ensuring that consumers can identify and trust their preferred products or services. The procedure and registration of trademarks in India involve a systematic approach designed to accommodate various entities, fostering a fair and competitive business environment.

The first step in the process is to conduct a comprehensive trademark search to ensure that the proposed mark is unique and not already in use. This search helps businesses avoid potential conflicts and infringement issues. Following a successful search, the next step is to file a trademark application with the appropriate authorities, namely the Controller General of Patents, Designs, and Trademarks (CGPDTM) in India.

Entities looking to register trademarks in India include individuals, proprietorships, partnerships, companies, and foreign entities. Each category has its own set of requirements and considerations. For individual and proprietorship registrations, the applicant's personal details and a representation of the proposed trademark are submitted. In the case of partnerships, the application includes the partnership deed along with the individual details. For company registrations, the Memorandum of Association and Articles of Association, along with individual details, are necessary.

Foreign entities seeking trademark registration in India follow a slightly different procedure. Typically, they need to appoint an authorized agent or attorney in India to represent them during the application process. Additionally, a proof of use or intent to use the trademark in India is required. This ensures that the trademark registration process aligns with the principles of fairness and reciprocity.

The registration process involves a thorough examination of the trademark application by the Trademarks Registry. Once approved, the tra demark is published in the Trademarks Journal, allowing for a 4-month window for any interested party to raise objections. If no objections are raised, or if successfully resolved, the trademark is registered, providing the owner with exclusive rights to use the mark in connection with the registered goods or services.

Post-registration, it is essential for businesses to actively protect and enforce their trademark rights. Regular monitoring, taking prompt legal action against infringement, and renewing registrations at the appropriate intervals are integral components of a robust trademark strategy.

4.5.2 Patents:

In India, the process of obtaining patents is a crucial aspect for businesses looking to protect their intellectual property. The patent system is governed by the Indian Patent Act, which provides a framework for the grant and registration of patents. This legal mechanism ensures that innovators and businesses receive exclusive rights to their inventions, fostering innovation and economic growth.

To initiate the process of obtaining a patent in India, businesses must first conduct a comprehensive search to determine if a similar invention already exists. This step helps in avoiding duplication and ensures that the proposed invention is novel and non-obvious. Subsequently, a detailed patent application must be prepared, including a thorough description of the invention, along with drawings and other necessary documents.

The patent application is then filed with the Indian Patent Office, which has regional branches across the country. The application undergoes a thorough examination process to assess the novelty, inventive step, and industrial applicability of the invention. This examination is conducted by patent examiners who assess the application against the criteria set out in the Patent Act.

Once the examination process is complete, and the invention is found to meet the statutory requirements, the patent is granted. The granted patent provides the business with exclusive rights to make, use, sell, and import the patented invention for a specific period, typically 20 years from the date of filing the application.

In the context of setting up a business in India, the protection of intellectual property through patents becomes even more significant. Entrepreneurs and entities involved in diverse sectors, such as technology, pharmaceuticals, and manufacturing, rely on the patent system to safeguard their innovations and maintain a competitive edge in the market.

Various entities, including individuals, startups, small and medium enterprises (SMEs), and large corporations, can participate in the patent registration process. The Indian government encourages and supports innovation by providing specific incentives and fee structures for startups and SMEs, making it more accessible for them to protect their intellectual property.

In conclusion, the patent procedure and registration for setting up a business in India involve a systematic approach that begins with a thorough search and culminates in the grant of exclusive rights. Businesses of all sizes and types can leverage the patent system to safeguard their innovations, foster creativity, and contribute to the overall growth of the Indian economy.

4.5.3 Copy rights:

Copyrights play a crucial role in protecting intellectual property, ensuring that creators are granted exclusive rights to their original works. In the context of setting up a business in India, understanding the procedures and registration requirements related to copyrights is essential for various entities.

In India, the copyright registration process is governed by the Copyright Act, 1957. Any original work, whether literary, artistic, musical, or dramatic, is eligible for copyright protection. The registration of copyrights provides creators with legal evidence and a public record of their ownership, making it easier to enforce their rights in case of infringement.

To initiate the copyright registration process, businesses and individuals need to submit an application to the Copyright Office along with the requisite fees. The application should include details such as the nature of the work, the author or creator's particulars, and a copy of the work itself. While registration is not mandatory, it is highly recommended, as it strengthens the legal position in case of disputes and enables the copyright owner to seek statutory damages and attorney fees.

Different entities, such as sole proprietorships, partnerships, and companies, may have distinct considerations when it comes to copyright registration. For instance, in the case of a business setup with multiple partners, it's crucial to establish clear agreements regarding the ownership and use of copyrights. Companies, on the other hand, must ensure that copyrights are appropriately assigned or licensed for any works created by employees in the course of their employment.

In addition to copyright registration, businesses in India should also be aware of the evolving landscape of intellectual property rights. Regular audits of intellectual property portfolios can help identify potential infringements, allowing entities to take timely legal action. Moreover, staying informed about updates to copyright laws and engaging in continuous education on intellectual property matters is crucial for maintaining a strong and enforceable position in the competitive business environment.

In conclusion, copyrights are integral to protecting the creative works of businesses and individuals alike. Understanding the procedures and registration requirements for copyright in the context of setting up a business in India is vital for safeguarding intellectual property and ensuring a robust legal foundation for the entity. As the business landscape continues to evolve, staying vigilant and proactive in managing copyrights will contribute to long-term success and innovation.

4.6 QUESTIONS:

1. What is the different type of business structures in India?
2. Write short notes on (a) trade mark. (b) Patents (c)copy rights
3. Explain the taxation system in India?
4. Explain the procedures for company registration?
5. What is one person company?

MARKET RESEARCH AND FEASIBILITY ANALYSIS

In today's dynamic and highly competitive business landscape, understanding consumer behavior, market trends, and competitor strategies is imperative for success. This is where marketing research emerges as a cornerstone of strategic decision-making for businesses across industries. Marketing research serves as a compass, guiding organizations to navigate through the complexities of the market by providing important insights that empower them to make informed decisions, develop effective marketing strategies, launch successful products, and ultimately, sustainably grow their businesses.

Marketing research plays a crucial role in setting up a business in India, as it provides valuable insights that can inform strategic decision-making and increase the chances of success.

5.1 IMPORTANCE OF MARKET RESEARCH

1. Understanding the Market Landscape: India is a diverse country with varying consumer preferences, cultural nuances, and economic conditions across different regions. Marketing research helps businesses gain a deeper understanding of the local market dynamics, including consumer behavior, purchasing patterns, competition, and regulatory environment.
2. Identifying Opportunities and Threats: Through comprehensive market research, businesses can identify emerging opportunities and potential threats in the Indian market. This allows them to capitalize on untapped market segments, anticipate competitive challenges, and adapt their strategies accordingly.
3. Tailoring Products and Services: By gathering insights into consumer needs, preferences, and pain points, businesses can tailor their products or services to better meet the demands of the Indian market. This customization enhances the relevance and appeal of offerings, increasing the likelihood of acceptance and adoption by target customers.
4. Pricing Strategy: Pricing is a important aspect of marketing strategy, especially in a price-sensitive market like India. Market research helps businesses understand the price elasticity of demand, competitive pricing benchmarks, and willingness to pay of Indian consumers. This enables them to develop optimal pricing strategies that balance profitability with affordability.
5. Marketing Communication and Branding: Effective communication and branding are essential for building brand awareness, credibility, and loyalty in the Indian market. Marketing research provides insights into consumer preferences regarding advertising channels, messaging, and branding elements. This enables businesses to craft compelling marketing campaigns that resonate with their target audience and drive engagement.
6. Market Entry and Expansion: For businesses entering or expanding into the Indian market, conducting thorough market research is essential for making informed strategic decisions. It helps assess the feasibility of market entry, identify entry barriers, evaluate potential distribution channels, and localize business operations to align with Indian consumer preferences and cultural norms.

7. Risk Mitigation: By conducting market research, businesses can mitigate the risks associated with market uncertainties and make more informed investment decisions. It allows them to identify potential pitfalls, assess market volatility, and anticipate changes in consumer behavior or regulatory landscape, thereby minimizing the likelihood of costly mistakes.

5.2 ROLE OF MARKET RESEARCH IN BUSINESS DECISION-MAKING.

Market research plays a important role in informing and guiding various aspects of business decision-making, particularly in the setup phase of a new venture.

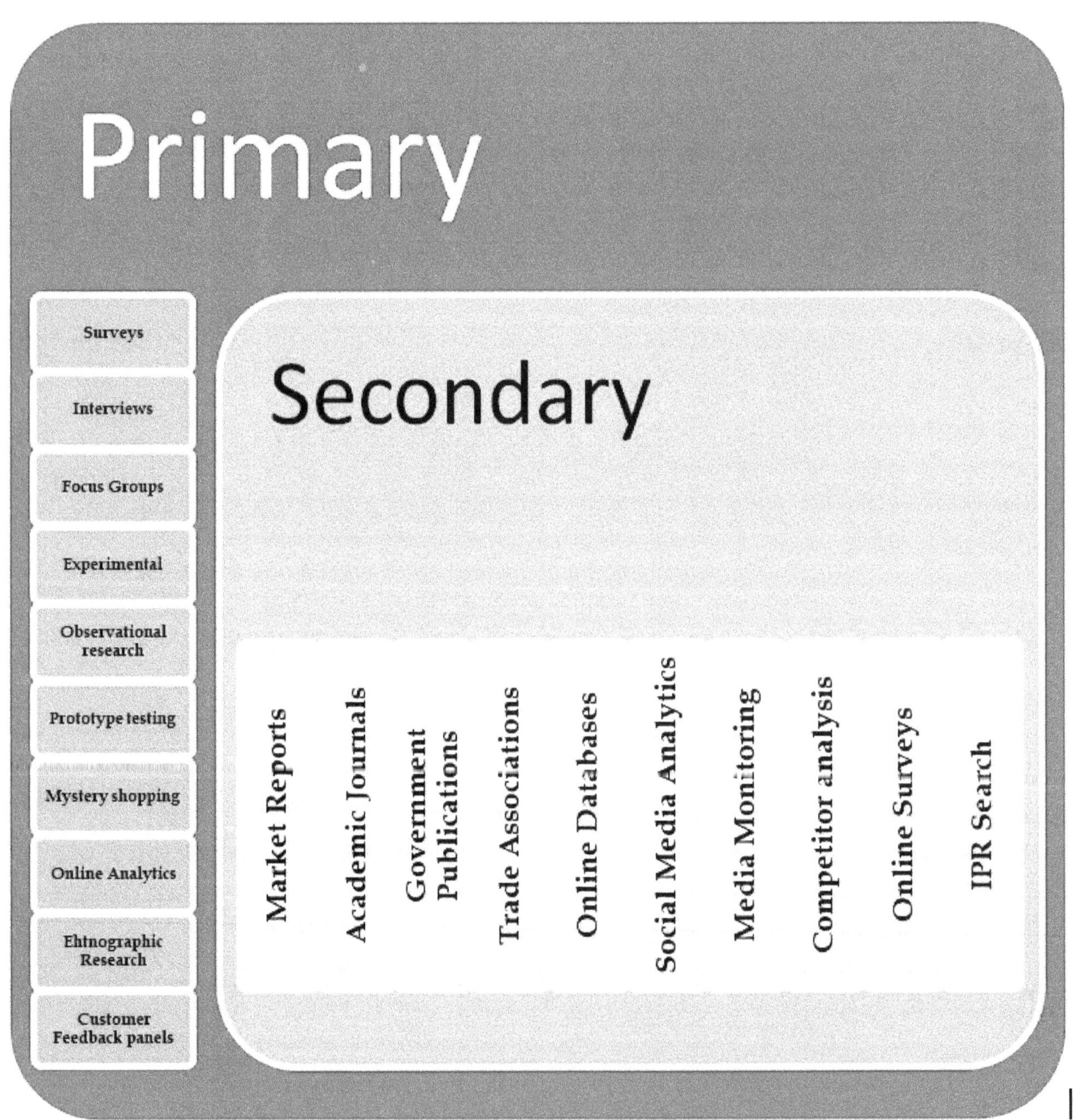

Methods of Marketing Research

5.2.1 ROLE OF MARKETING RESEARCH

1. Understanding Customer Needs and Preferences: Market research helps businesses gain insights into the needs, preferences, and behaviors of their target audience. By conducting surveys, focus groups, and analyzing existing data, entrepreneurs can identify gaps in the market, understand what customers are looking for, and tailor their offerings accordingly.
2. Assessing Market Demand: Before setting up of a business, it is essential to assess the demand for the product or service that is being offered. Market research helps in estimating the size of the target market, determining the level of demand, and identifying potential growth opportunities. This information is important for making decisions related to production levels, pricing strategies, and market positioning.
3. Competitive Analysis: Understanding the competitive landscape is vital for the success of any business. Market research allows entrepreneurs to analyze their competitors, including their strengths, weaknesses, pricing strategies, and market share. This knowledge enables businesses to differentiate themselves, identify areas for improvement, and develop strategies to gain a competitive advantage.
4. Identifying Market Trends: Markets are constantly evolving, driven by changes in consumer preferences, technology, regulations, and other factors. Market research helps businesses stay informed about emerging trends and shifts in the industry landscape. By staying ahead of these trends, entrepreneurs can adapt their business strategies accordingly, seize new opportunities, and mitigate potential risks.
5. Risk Mitigation: Starting a new business involves inherent risks, such as market volatility, changing consumer behavior, and unexpected challenges. Market research provides valuable data and insights that can help entrepreneurs identify and mitigate potential risks. By understanding market dynamics and customer preferences, businesses can make more informed decisions, reduce uncertainty, and improve their chances of success.
6. Optimizing Marketing Strategies: Effective marketing is essential for attracting customers and generating sales. Market research helps businesses understand which marketing channels are most effective for reaching their target audience, what messaging resonates with customers, and how to allocate resources efficiently. By optimizing their marketing strategies based on market research findings, businesses can maximize their return on investment and improve overall marketing effectiveness.
7. Informing Business Planning and Strategy: Market research serves as a foundation for strategic planning and decision-making throughout the business lifecycle. By providing data-driven insights into market dynamics, customer behavior, and competitive landscape, market research informs key business decisions such as product development, pricing strategies, distribution channels, and expansion opportunities. This ensures that businesses are aligned with market demands and positioned for long-term success.

5.2.2 PRIMARY AND SECONDARY RESEARCH METHODS

Setting up a business requires a comprehensive understanding of the market, target audience, competitors, and various other factors. Primary and secondary research methods serve as essential tools in gathering relevant information to make informed decisions.

5.2.2.1 PRIMARY RESEARCH METHODS:

- SURVEYS:

Surveys involve collecting data directly from respondents through questionnaires, interviews, or online forms. They provide insights into customer preferences, opinions, and behaviors.

Advantages:

1. Direct feedback from target audience.

2. Customizable questions to suit specific research objectives.

Disadvantages:

1. Potential for bias in responses.
2. Time-consuming and resource-intensive.

- INTERVIEWS:

Conducting one-on-one interviews allows for in-depth exploration of customer needs, preferences, and pain points.
Advantages:

1. Detailed insights into individual perspectives.
2. Opportunity for probing and clarification.

Disadvantages:

1. Limited sample size.
2. Requires skilled interviewers for accurate data collection.

- FOCUS GROUPS:

Focus groups bring together a small group of individuals to discuss specific topics, providing qualitative data and insights.
Advantages:

1. Stimulates discussion and idea generation.
2. Allows for observation of group dynamics.

Disadvantages:

1. Groupthink may skew results.
2. Participants may not represent the broader target market.

- OBSERVATIONAL RESEARCH:

This method involves directly observing consumer behavior in real-life settings, such as retail stores or online platforms.
Advantages:

1. Provides firsthand insights into actual behavior.
2. Minimizes bias associated with self-reporting.

Disadvantages:

1. Limited to observable behaviors.
2. Ethical considerations regarding privacy and consent.

- EXPERIMENTS:

Experiments involve manipulating variables to observe their effects on consumer behavior or product performance.
Advantages:

1. Allows for causal inference.
2. Control over variables for accurate testing.

Disadvantages:

1. Resource-intensive and time-consuming.
2. Results may not always generalize to real-world scenarios.

- PROTOTYPE TESTING:

Testing prototypes with potential customers helps gather feedback on product features, usability, and overall satisfaction.
Advantages:

1. Early identification of design flaws.
2. Iterative improvement based on user feedback.

Disadvantages:

1. Requires development of prototypes.
2. Feedback may vary based on prototype fidelity.

- MYSTERY SHOPPING:

This involves hiring individuals to pose as customers and evaluate the quality of service and customer experience.
Advantages:

1. Provides insights into competitor offerings.
2. Evaluates customer service from the user perspective.

Disadvantages:

1. Limited to observable aspects of service.
2. Requires careful selection and training of mystery shoppers.

- ONLINE ANALYTICS:

Analyzing website traffic, user engagement metrics, and online interactions provides valuable insights into customer behavior and preferences.
Advantages:

1. Real-time data collection.

2. Quantitative metrics for analysis.

Disadvantages:

1. Limited to online interactions.
2. May not capture offline customer behavior.

- ETHNOGRAPHIC RESEARCH:

Immersing researchers in the natural environment of the target audience helps understand cultural norms, values, and behaviors.
Advantages:

1. Deep understanding of cultural context.
2. Reveals implicit needs and preferences.

Disadvantages:

1. Time-consuming and expensive.
2. Requires cultural sensitivity and rapport-building.

- CUSTOMER FEEDBACK PANELS:

Establishing panels of loyal customers who provide ongoing feedback on products and services helps in continuous improvement efforts.
Advantages:

1. Builds customer loyalty and engagement.
2. Provides actionable insights for product refinement.

Disadvantages:

1. Limited to existing customer base.
2. Potential bias from overly positive feedback.

5.2.2.2 SECONDARY RESEARCH METHODS:

1. MARKET REPORTS:

Accessing existing market reports and industry analyses provides valuable data on market size, trends, and competitors.
Advantages:

1. Cost-effective compared to primary research.
2. Comprehensive coverage of industry landscape.

Disadvantages:

1. May lack specificity for niche markets.
2. Data may be outdated or generalized.

2. ACADEMIC JOURNALS:

Reviewing academic literature related to the industry or market segment can offer insights into consumer behavior, market dynamics, and emerging trends.
Advantages:

1. Rigorous and credible sources of information.
2. Access to cutting-edge research findings.

Disadvantages:

1. Limited accessibility to non-academic audiences.
2. May not directly address business concerns.

3. GOVERNMENT PUBLICATIONS:

Government agencies often publish data on demographics, economic indicators, and regulatory frameworks that are relevant to businesses.
Advantages:

1. Reliable and authoritative sources of information.
2. Free or low-cost access to data.

Disadvantages:

1. Data may be outdated or aggregated.
2. Limited customization for specific research needs.

4. TRADE ASSOCIATIONS:

Industry-specific trade associations often collect and disseminate data on market trends, consumer preferences, and regulatory changes.
Advantages:

1. Industry-specific insights and expertise.
2. Networking opportunities with industry professionals.

Disadvantages:

1. Membership fees may be required.
2. Potential bias towards industry interests.

5. ONLINE DTABASES:

Accessing online databases such as market research firms' repositories or academic libraries provides a wealth of secondary data.

Advantages:

1. Wide range of data sources and formats.
2. Searchable and easily accessible platforms.

Disadvantages:

1. Costly subscription fees for premium databases.
2. Quality and reliability of data may vary.

6. SOCIAL MEDIA ANALYSIS:

Analyzing social media platforms for mentions, sentiment, and engagement related to the industry or brand provides insights into consumer perceptions and trends.

Advantages:

1. Real-time data on consumer sentiment.
2. Access to unfiltered opinions and feedback.

Disadvantages:

1. Requires specialized tools for analysis.
2. Limited control over data collection.

7. COMPETITOR ANALYSIS:

Studying competitors' websites, marketing strategies and product offerings helps identify market gaps and competitive advantages.

Advantages:

1. Benchmarking against industry peers.
2. Identifying opportunities for differentiation.

Disadvantages:

1. Limited access to proprietary information.
2. Competitor actions may change rapidly.

8. MEDIA MONITORING:

Monitoring news articles, press releases, and industry publications provides insights into market trends, public opinion, and competitive developments.

Advantages:

1. Timely updates on industry news.
2. Identifying emerging issues and opportunities.

Disadvantages:

1. Information overloads from vast media sources.
2. Difficulty in filtering relevant information.

9. ONLINE SURVEYS AND PANELS:

Accessing existing online survey platforms or panels allows for quick and cost-effective data collection from a large sample of respondents.
Advantages:

1. Rapid data collection and analysis.
2. Access to diverse respondent demographics.

Disadvantages:

1. Limited customization of survey questions.
2. Potential for sample bias in online panels.

10. PATENT AND INTELLECTUAL PROPERTY SEARCH:

Reviewing patents and intellectual property filings related to the industry or technology provides insights into innovation trends and potential areas of differentiation.
Advantages:

1. Identifying opportunities for product innovation.
2. Assessing competitive threats and barriers to entry.

Disadvantages:

1. Time-consuming and complex search processes.
2. Limited information on commercialization and market impact.

Both primary and secondary research methods offer valuable insights for setting up a business. While primary research provides direct and specific data tailored to the research objectives, secondary research offers a broader perspective and can complement primary findings. By leveraging a combination of these methods, businesses can make informed decisions and gain a competitive edge in their respective markets.

5.2.3 CONDUCTING MARKET SURVEY

Conducting market surveys is a vital step for any entrepreneur or business looking to establish a presence in India. With its diverse demographics, complex consumer behaviors, and rapidly evolving market trends, India offers immense opportunities but also challenges for businesses. A thorough understanding of the market landscape is essential to make informed decisions and devise effective strategies.

First and foremost, market surveys help in gaining insights into the preferences, needs, and purchasing behaviors of the target audience. India's vast population comprises various demographic segments with distinct preferences and purchasing power. A comprehensive survey helps in identifying these segments and understanding their demands, thereby enabling businesses to tailor their products or services accordingly.

Moreover, market surveys provide valuable information about the competitive landscape. India's business environment is highly competitive, with both domestic players and international brands vying for market share. By conducting surveys, businesses can assess the strengths and weaknesses of competitors, identify market gaps, and formulate strategies to gain a competitive edge.

Furthermore, market surveys aid in evaluating the feasibility of business ideas and assessing market demand. India's market dynamics are constantly evolving due to factors such as changing consumer preferences, technological advancements, and regulatory changes. Through surveys, businesses can gauge the demand for their offerings, assess market saturation, and identify emerging trends that could influence their success.

Additionally, market surveys help in understanding regulatory requirements, cultural nuances, and local business practices. India is a diverse country with varied cultural norms and regulatory frameworks across states and regions. Conducting surveys helps businesses navigate these complexities and ensure compliance with applicable laws and regulations.

Conducting comprehensive market surveys is an important component in the establishment of any business. These surveys provide important insights into the market landscape, customer preferences, and potential competitors, enabling entrepreneurs to make informed decisions and develop effective strategies.

5.2.4 PROCESS INVOLVED IN CONDUCTING MARKET SURVEYS FOR SETTING UP A BUSINESS:

1. Defining Objectives: The first step is to clearly outline the objectives of the market survey. Whether it's understanding customer needs, assessing market demand, or identifying key competitors, having well-defined goals will guide the entire survey process.

2. Identifying Target Audience: Next, it's essential to identify the target audience for the survey. This involves determining the demographic, geographic, and psychographic characteristics of the potential customers who are likely to engage with the business. Understanding the target audience ensures that the survey questions are tailored to their specific needs and preferences.

3. Designing Survey Instruments: Once the target audience is identified, the next step is to design the survey instruments, such as questionnaires or interviews. These instruments should be carefully crafted to elicit relevant information while being easy to understand and complete for respondents. It's crucial to include a mix of closed-ended and open-ended questions to gather both quantitative and qualitative data.

4. Selecting Data Collection Methods: There are various methods for collecting survey data, including online surveys, telephone interviews, focus groups, and in-person interactions. The choice of data collection method depends on factors such as the target audience, budget, and time constraints. Selecting the most appropriate method ensures maximum participation and reliable data collection.

5. Sampling Technique: Determining the sampling technique is crucial for ensuring the representativeness of the survey results. Whether using random sampling, stratified sampling, or convenience sampling, the method chosen should accurately reflect the characteristics of the target population. A well-designed sampling strategy minimizes bias and enhances the validity of the survey findings.

6. Implementing the Survey: With the survey instruments and data collection methods in place, it's time to implement the survey. This involves reaching out to the target audience through various channels, such as email, social media, or direct mail. Clear instructions and incentives may be provided to encourage participation and maximize response rates.

7. Analyzing Survey Data: Once the survey responses are collected, the next step is to analyze the data. This involves organizing, cleaning, and statistically analyzing the data to uncover meaningful insights. Data analysis techniques such as descriptive statistics, regression analysis, and cluster analysis may be employed to identify patterns and trends within the data.

8. Interpreting Results: After analyzing the data, the findings need to be interpreted in the context of the business objectives. This involves extracting actionable insights and implications from the survey results. By understanding the key findings, entrepreneurs can make informed decisions regarding product development, marketing strategies, and business expansion.

9. Iterative Process: Market surveys are often iterative, meaning that the process may need to be repeated or refined based on the initial findings. Continuous feedback and adjustments ensure that the business stays responsive to changing market dynamics and customer preferences.

10. Reporting and Presentation: Finally, the results of the market survey should be documented and presented in a clear and concise manner. This could take the form of a written report, presentation slides, or interactive dashboards. Communicating the findings effectively facilitates informed decision-making and aligns stakeholders towards common goals.

By following these steps and executing the market survey process diligently, businesses can gain valuable insights into the market landscape and position themselves for success in their respective industries.

5.3 CUSTOMER FEEDBACK

Customer feedback is the heartbeat of any successful business, providing invaluable insights into the satisfaction levels, preferences, and needs of the clientele. Analyzing the importance of customer feedback reveals a myriad of benefits that extend far beyond mere satisfaction ratings.

First and foremost, customer feedback serves as compass guiding businesses in the right direction. It offers a direct line of communication from the consumers to the company, allowing organizations to understand what they're doing well and where they need improvement. By actively listening to feedback, businesses can identify pain points, address issues, and refine their products or services to better meet customer expectations.

Moreover, customer feedback fosters a sense of trust and loyalty. When customers feel heard and valued, they're more likely to develop a strong affinity for the brand and become repeat purchasers. By acknowledging feedback and taking appropriate action, businesses demonstrate their commitment to customer satisfaction, which in turn cultivates long-term relationships and positive word-of-mouth referrals.

Furthermore, analyzing customer feedback provides businesses with a competitive edge in the market. In today's hyper-competitive landscape, understanding the evolving needs and desires of consumers is important for staying ahead of the curve. By staying attuned to customer feedback, companies can anticipate market trends, innovate proactively, and differentiate themselves from competitors, thus solidifying their position in the industry.

Additionally, customer feedback serves as a catalyst for continuous improvement. By soliciting feedback at various touchpoints along the customer journey, businesses can identify areas for enhancement and implement iterative changes to enhance the overall experience. Whether it's streamlining processes, enhancing product features, or refining customer service protocols, every piece of feedback offers an opportunity for growth and refinement.

In conclusion, the importance of customer feedback cannot be overstated. It is a powerful tool that enables businesses to enhance customer satisfaction, build trust and loyalty, gain a competitive edge, and drive continuous improvement. By prioritizing the collection and analysis of customer feedback, organizations can unlock invaluable insights that fuel success and longevity in today's dynamic marketplace.

Customer feedback is invaluable for businesses across industries as it provides important insights into customer satisfaction, preferences, and areas for improvement. Analyzing customer feedback allows businesses to make informed decisions and enhance various aspects of their products, services, and overall customer experience.

5.4 REASONS HIGHLIGHTING THE IMPORTANCE OF CUSTOMER FEEDBACK ANALYSIS:

1. Identifying Pain Points: Customer feedback helps businesses identify pain points in their products or services. By understanding what customers find frustrating or unsatisfactory, businesses can address these issues promptly, improving overall satisfaction and loyalty.

2. Improving Product Development: Customer feedback provides valuable input for product development. By listening to customer suggestions and complaints, businesses can prioritize enhancements and new features that align with customer needs and preferences, leading to more competitive and appealing offerings.

3. Enhancing Customer Experience: Analyzing feedback allows businesses to understand the customer journey better. This insight enables them to streamline processes, eliminate bottlenecks, and create more seamless interactions, ultimately leading to improved customer experience and retention.

4. Building Customer Loyalty: When customers feel heard and valued, they are more likely to remain loyal to a brand. By acting on feedback and demonstrating a commitment to addressing customer concerns, businesses can foster stronger relationships with their customers, leading to increased loyalty and advocacy.

5. Staying Competitive: In today's competitive landscape, businesses must continually evolve to meet changing customer expectations. Analyzing customer feedback provides valuable intelligence about competitors' strengths and weaknesses, enabling businesses to identify opportunities for differentiation and maintain a competitive edge.

6. Driving Innovation: Customer feedback often contains ideas and suggestions for innovative solutions or products. By carefully analyzing this feedback, businesses can uncover opportunities for innovation and stay ahead of market trends, driving continuous improvement and growth.

7. Informing Marketing Strategies: Understanding customers' likes, dislikes, and preferences can significantly impact marketing strategies. By leveraging insights from feedback analysis, businesses can tailor their messaging, targeting, and channels to resonate more effectively with their target audience, maximizing the return on marketing investment.

8. Mitigating Risk: Ignoring customer feedback can lead to reputational damage and lost revenue. By proactively addressing customer concerns and issues highlighted in feedback, businesses can mitigate risks associated with negative publicity, customer churn, and brand erosion.

5.5 FEASIBILITY ANALYSIS FOR BUSINESS VENTURES

In the dynamic landscape of modern business, embarking on a new venture requires thorough scrutiny and evaluation to ascertain its feasibility. Feasibility analysis serves as a cornerstone in the decision-making process, enabling entrepreneurs and business leaders to assess the viability of their ideas before committing resources. This comprehensive examination encompasses various dimensions including market potential, financial viability, operational feasibility, and regulatory compliance.

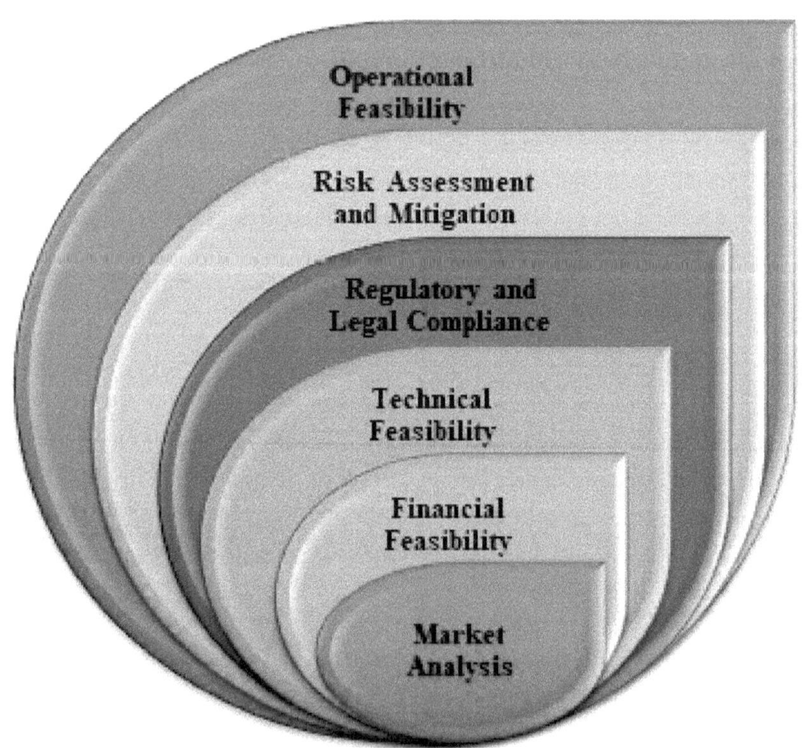

Feasibility Analysis for Business Ventures

5.5.1 Market Analysis:

At the heart of any feasibility analysis lies the evaluation of the market landscape. Understanding the demand-supply dynamics, consumer preferences, and industry trends is imperative in gauging the feasibility of a business venture. Market research methodologies such as surveys, interviews, and data analysis are employed to gather insights into target demographics, competitors, and market size. By identifying niche opportunities and potential barriers to entry, entrepreneurs can make informed decisions regarding market entry strategies and positioning.

5.5.2 Financial Feasibility:

Financial viability is a important aspect of feasibility analysis, as it determines the sustainability and profitability of the proposed venture. This entails conducting a thorough assessment of the project's costs, revenue projections, and return on investment. Financial modeling techniques such as discounted cash flow analysis, breakeven analysis, and sensitivity analysis are utilized to forecast future cash flows and assess the venture's financial viability under different scenarios. Additionally, securing adequate funding and ensuring a realistic budget allocation are paramount in mitigating financial risks and achieving long-term success.

5.5.3 Operational Feasibility:

Operational feasibility examines the practicality and efficiency of implementing the proposed venture within the existing infrastructure and resources. This involves evaluating factors such as production processes, supply chain logistics, human resource capabilities, and technological requirements. By conducting feasibility studies on operational aspects, businesses can identify potential bottlenecks, streamline workflows, and optimize resource utilization. Moreover, assessing the scalability of operations enables entrepreneurs to anticipate future growth and adapt their strategies accordingly.

5.5.4 Technical Feasibility:

In the digital age, technological feasibility plays a pivotal role in the success of business ventures. This entails assessing the compatibility of technology solutions with the intended objectives and operational requirements of the venture. From software platforms and hardware infrastructure to cybersecurity measures and data management systems, technical feasibility analysis ensures that the chosen technologies are robust, reliable, and aligned with the business goals. Moreover, staying abreast of technological advancements and industry best practices enables businesses to leverage innovation as a competitive advantage.

5.5.5 Regulatory and Legal Compliance:

Navigating the regulatory landscape is essential for ensuring compliance and mitigating legal risks associated with business ventures. This involves conducting thorough research on industry regulations, licensing requirements, zoning laws, environmental regulations, and taxation policies. By engaging legal experts and regulatory consultants, businesses can identify potential compliance issues and develop strategies to address them proactively. Moreover, maintaining transparency and ethical standards in business practices not only fosters trust among stakeholders but also safeguards the reputation and longevity of the venture.

5.5.6 Risk Assessment and Mitigation:

Feasibility analysis inherently involves assessing and mitigating risks that may impede the success of the venture. This requires identifying potential threats and vulnerabilities across various dimensions including market volatility, financial instability, operational challenges, technological disruptions, and regulatory changes. By conducting risk assessments and developing contingency plans, businesses can anticipate challenges and implement proactive measures to mitigate their impact. Additionally, diversifying revenue streams, building strategic partnerships, and maintaining a robust risk management framework are essential strategies for safeguarding against unforeseen contingencies.

5.5.7 Conclusion:

In conclusion, feasibility analysis serves as a cornerstone in the decision-making process for business ventures, enabling entrepreneurs and business leaders to evaluate the viability and potential risks associated with their ideas. By conducting comprehensive assessments across market, financial, operational, technical, and regulatory dimensions, businesses can make informed decisions and optimize their chances of success. Moreover, continuous monitoring and adaptation to changing market dynamics ensure the resilience and sustainability of the venture in the long run. Ultimately, feasibility analysis empowers businesses to navigate uncertainty with confidence and seize opportunities for growth and innovation.

5.6 COMPONENTS OF FEASIBILITY ANALYSIS:

Feasibility analysis is a systematic assessment of the practicality and viability of a proposed project or initiative. It involves evaluating various factors to determine whether the project is feasible to pursue, considering factors such as economic, technical, legal, operational, and scheduling constraints. The primary purpose of feasibility analysis is to provide decision-makers with the necessary information to determine whether to proceed with the project, modify it, or abandon it altogether.

1. Market Feasibility: This aspect examines the demand for the product or service the project aims to offer. It involves analyzing market trends, customer needs, competition, and potential market size. Market feasibility helps assess whether there is a sufficient market opportunity to support the project's success.

2. Technical Feasibility: Technical feasibility assesses whether the proposed project can be implemented using available technology and resources. It examines factors such as technology readiness, required expertise, infrastructure availability, and potential technical challenges. Technical feasibility helps determine whether the project can be realistically developed and deployed.

3. Financial Feasibility: Financial feasibility evaluates the project's economic viability by assessing its costs and potential returns. It involves estimating the initial investment required, ongoing operational expenses, revenue projections, and potential profitability. Financial feasibility helps determine whether the project can generate adequate returns to justify the investment.

4. Legal and Regulatory Feasibility: Legal and regulatory feasibility involves examining the legal and regulatory environment in which the project will operate. It assesses compliance requirements, permits, licenses, zoning laws, and potential legal risks. Legal and regulatory feasibility helps ensure that the project can be implemented without encountering legal obstacles.

5. Operational Feasibility: Operational feasibility evaluates whether the project can be effectively implemented and integrated into existing operations. It considers factors such as organizational capabilities, resource availability, workflow impact, and potential disruptions. Operational feasibility helps assess whether the project can be successfully executed within the organization's operational constraints.

By conducting a comprehensive feasibility analysis, stakeholders can identify potential risks, opportunities, and challenges associated with the project. This information allows decision-makers to make informed choices about whether to proceed with the project, modify its scope, or explore alternative options. Feasibility analysis helps minimize the likelihood of investing resources into projects that are unlikely to succeed and maximizes the chances of achieving project objectives.

5.7 SWOT ANALYSIS

SWOT analysis is a strategic planning tool that helps organizations identify their strengths, weaknesses, opportunities, and threats. By evaluating these internal and external factors, SWOT analysis provides valuable insights that inform strategic decisions in several ways:

1. Identifying Strengths: SWOT analysis helps organizations recognize their internal strengths, such as valuable resources, capabilities, or competitive advantages. Knowing their strengths enables organizations to leverage them effectively in strategic planning, whether it's by capitalizing on core competencies, enhancing existing capabilities, or differentiating them in the market.

2. Highlighting Weaknesses: Identifying weaknesses is crucial for organizations to address areas of improvement. By understanding internal weaknesses, such as operational inefficiencies, lack of resources, or skills gaps, organizations can develop strategies to overcome these challenges. This might involve investing in training programs, restructuring processes, or seeking partnerships to bolster areas of weakness.

3. Assessing Opportunities: SWOT analysis helps organizations recognize external opportunities in the market or industry. These opportunities could include emerging markets, technological advancements, changing consumer trends, or gaps in the competition. By identifying opportunities, organizations can develop strategies to capitalize on them, such as entering new markets, launching innovative products or services, or expanding existing offerings.

4. Identifying Threats: Understanding external threats is essential for organizations to mitigate risks and protect their interests. Threats could include competitive pressures, changes in regulations, economic downturns, or shifts in consumer preferences. By identifying threats early on, organizations can develop contingency plans, diversify their offerings, or strengthen their competitive positioning to minimize the impact of potential risks.

5. Informing Strategic Decisions: Overall, SWOT analysis provides a comprehensive overview of the internal and external factors that influence an organization's strategic position. By synthesizing this information, organizations can make informed decisions about their future direction, whether it's developing new products, entering new markets, optimizing operations, or addressing competitive challenges. SWOT analysis serves as a foundation for strategic planning, helping organizations align their resources, capabilities, and goals to achieve sustainable competitive advantage and long-term success.

5.8 SWOT ANALYSIS – GUIDELINES

5.8.1 Strengths:

1. Strong brand reputation and recognition in the market.
2. High-quality products or services.
3. Efficient and skilled workforce.
4. Robust financial performance and stable cash flow.
5. Advanced technology and infrastructure.
6. Competitive advantage in terms of pricing or unique selling proposition (USP).
7. Effective marketing strategies and customer loyalty programs.
8. Strong distribution network and partnerships.
9. Well-established customer base.
10. Adaptability to changing market trends and consumer preferences.

5.8.2 Weaknesses:

1. Limited product/service offerings compared to competitors.
2. Dependence on a few key customers for a significant portion of revenue.
3. Inadequate resources for research and development (R&D).
4. High production costs leading to narrow profit margins.
5. Lack of brand awareness or visibility in certain markets.
6. Poor inventory management leading to stockouts or excess inventory.
7. Weak online presence or digital marketing capabilities.
8. Internal conflicts or issues within the organization.
9. Vulnerability to external factors such as economic downturns or regulatory changes.

10. Inefficient business processes or outdated technology infrastructure.

5.8.3 Opportunities:

1. Expansion into new markets or geographical regions.
2. Diversification of product/service offerings to cater to emerging trends.
3. Strategic partnerships or collaborations with other businesses.
4. Acquisition of competitors to gain market share.
5. Introduction of innovative products or services.
6. Capitalizing on technological advancements for efficiency and productivity.
7. Growing demand for environmentally sustainable products or services.
8. Changes in consumer behavior offering new sales channels or revenue streams.
9. Emerging markets with untapped potential.
10. Changes in regulations creating new business opportunities.

5.8.4 Threats:

1. Intense competition from established players or new entrants.
2. Economic downturns impacting consumer spending.
3. Rapid technological advancements making current products or services obsolete.
4. Price wars initiated by competitors.
5. Supply chain disruptions or raw material shortages.
6. Legal or regulatory changes affecting business operations.
7. Negative publicity or brand damage due to scandals or controversies.
8. Shifting consumer preferences away from existing products or services.
9. Currency fluctuations impacting international operations.
10. Natural disasters or unforeseen events disrupting business continuity.

5.9 UTILIZING SWOT ANALYSIS IN BUSINESS DECISION MAKING FOR SETTING UP A BUSINESS IN INDIA

India, with its burgeoning economy and diverse market opportunities, presents an attractive landscape for entrepreneurs and businesses looking to establish a presence. However, entering this dynamic market requires careful consideration and strategic planning. One tool that can aid in this process is the SWOT analysis, which assesses the strengths, weaknesses, opportunities, and threats associated with a business venture.

5.10 OVERVIEW OF SWOT ANALYSIS

SWOT analysis is a strategic planning technique used to identify internal strengths and weaknesses, as well as external opportunities and threats facing a business or project. It involves a systematic assessment of various factors that can influence the success or failure of a venture.

5.10 SWOT ANALYSIS FOR SETTING UP A BUSINESS IN INDIA

5.10.1 STRENGTHS:

India offers several strengths that can be advantageous for businesses:

1. Large Market Potential: With a population of over 1.3 billion people, India represents a massive consumer base across various industries.
2. Skilled Workforce: India boasts a vast pool of educated and skilled professionals, particularly in IT, engineering, and management sectors, offering a competitive advantage in terms of talent acquisition.
3. Growing Economy: India's economy has been experiencing steady growth, presenting numerous opportunities for businesses to thrive.

5.10.2 WEAKNESSES:

However, there are also challenges and weaknesses that businesses need to navigate:

1. Complex Regulatory Environment: India's regulatory landscape can be intricate and bureaucratic, posing challenges in terms of navigating legal and administrative procedures.
2. Infrastructure Gaps: While India has made significant strides in infrastructure development, there are still gaps in areas such as transportation, logistics, and power supply, which can impact business operations.
3. Cultural and Linguistic Diversity: India's diverse cultural and linguistic landscape may require businesses to tailor their strategies and approaches to different regions and demographics, adding complexity to market penetration.

5.10.3 OPPORTUNITIES:

There are several promising opportunities for businesses looking to enter or expand in the Indian market:

1. Rapid Urbanization: India is witnessing rapid urbanization, creating demand for various goods and services in sectors such as real estate, retail, healthcare, and infrastructure development.
2. Emerging Technologies: With the rise of digitalization and technological innovation, there are opportunities for businesses to leverage emerging technologies such as e-commerce, fintech, and renewable energy solutions.
3. Government Initiatives: The Indian government has launched various initiatives to promote foreign investment, entrepreneurship, and industry-specific growth, offering incentives and support to businesses.

5.10.4 THREATS:

Despite the opportunities, businesses must also be mindful of potential threats:

1. Political Instability: Political volatility and policy changes can create uncertainty for businesses operating in India, impacting investment decisions and market stability.
2. Market Competition: India's market can be highly competitive, with both domestic and international players vying for market share across industries.
3. Economic Volatility: While India's economy has been growing, it is also susceptible to global economic fluctuations, currency fluctuations, inflation, and other macroeconomic factors that can impact business operations.

Conducting a SWOT analysis can be instrumental in informing strategic decision-making for businesses looking to establish or expand their presence in India. By carefully assessing the internal strengths and weaknesses, as well as external opportunities and threats, businesses can develop robust strategies to mitigate risks, capitalize on opportunities, and achieve sustainable growth in the Indian market. However, it is essential to continuously monitor and adapt to changes in the business environment to remain competitive and successful in the long term.

5.10.5 RECOMMENDATIONS

Based on the SWOT analysis, the following recommendations are proposed for businesses planning to enter the Indian market:

1. Conduct thorough market research to understand consumer preferences, market dynamics, and regulatory requirements.
2. Develop strategic partnerships with local stakeholders, suppliers, and distributors to navigate the complexities of the Indian market.
3. Invest in building strong relationships with government agencies, industry associations, and regulatory bodies to stay updated on policy changes and leverage available incentives.
4. Implement robust risk management strategies to mitigate potential threats and capitalize on emerging opportunities in the Indian market.
5. Continuously monitor and evaluate the business environment to adapt strategies and tactics accordingly, ensuring agility and resilience in the face of evolving challenges and opportunities.

5.11 QUESTIONS

1. Explain the importance of market research?
2. Explain Feasibility Analysis for Business Ventures?
3. Write short notes on customer feed back?
4. Explain the process of conducting market surveys.
5. Explain SWOT Analysis in Business Decision Making

BUSINESS PLANNING AND STRATEGY

6.1 BUSINESS PLAN - COMPONENTS

Setting up a business in India requires careful planning and execution. A comprehensive business plan should encompass various key elements to ensure success.

IMPORTANT COMPONENTS OF A BUSINESS PLAN:

1. Executive Summary: This section provides an overview of your business idea, goals, target market, competitive advantage, and financial projections. It should be concise yet compelling, enticing investors or stakeholders to delve deeper into your plan.

2. Business Description and Mission Statement: Outline your business concept, its purpose, and the problem it solves. Define your mission statement, encapsulating the core values and objectives of your venture.

3. Market Analysis: Conduct thorough research on the Indian market, including its size, growth potential, trends, and dynamics. Identify your target audience, their needs, preferences, and buying behavior. Analyze your competitors, their strengths, weaknesses, and market positioning.

4. Products or Services: Describe in detail the products or services you plan to offer. Highlight their unique features, benefits, and value proposition. Discuss any intellectual property rights or technological innovations that differentiate your offerings.

5. Marketing and Sales Strategy: Develop a comprehensive marketing plan to reach your target customers effectively. Outline your pricing strategy, distribution channels, promotional activities, and sales tactics. Consider the cultural and regional nuances of the Indian market in devising your marketing approach.

6. Operational Plan: Define the operational aspects of your business, including location, facilities, equipment, suppliers, and logistics. Discuss your production process, quality control measures, and regulatory compliance requirements.

7. Management and Organization: Introduce the key members of your management team and their roles. Outline the organizational structure, governance policies, and decision-making processes. Highlight any relevant experience, expertise, or credentials that demonstrate the team's capability to execute the business plan.

8. Financial Projections: Present detailed financial forecasts, including income statements, cash flow projections, and balance sheets. Estimate startup costs, operating expenses, revenue streams, and profitability over the short and long term. Provide assumptions and sensitivity analyses to support your projections.

9. Funding Requirements: Specify the amount of capital needed to launch and operate the business successfully. Identify potential sources of funding, such as equity investment, loans, grants, or partnerships. Discuss your strategy for managing finances and mitigating financial risks.

10. Risk Management Plan: Identify potential risks and challenges that could impact your business operations or objectives. Develop strategies to mitigate these risks, such as diversification, insurance coverage, or contingency plans. Address legal, regulatory, geopolitical, and macroeconomic factors that may affect your business in India.

11. Legal and Regulatory Considerations: Understand the legal and regulatory framework governing businesses in India. Ensure compliance with company registration, taxation, licensing, labor laws, intellectual property rights, and other relevant regulations. Seek legal counsel to navigate any complexities or uncertainties.

12. Sustainability and Corporate Social Responsibility (CSR): Incorporate sustainability practices and CSR initiatives into your business model. Demonstrate your commitment to environmental stewardship, social impact, ethical business practices, and community engagement. Align your values with the expectations of Indian consumers and stakeholders.

By addressing these key elements in your business plan, you can create a robust roadmap for setting up and operating a successful business in India. Flexibility and adaptability are essential as you navigate the dynamic business landscape and capitalize on emerging opportunities.

6.2 TEMPLATE FOR CREATING A BUSINESS PLAN.

Creating a business plan is important for setting up a business in India or anywhere else. It serves as a roadmap outlining your business goals, strategies, operations, and financial projections.

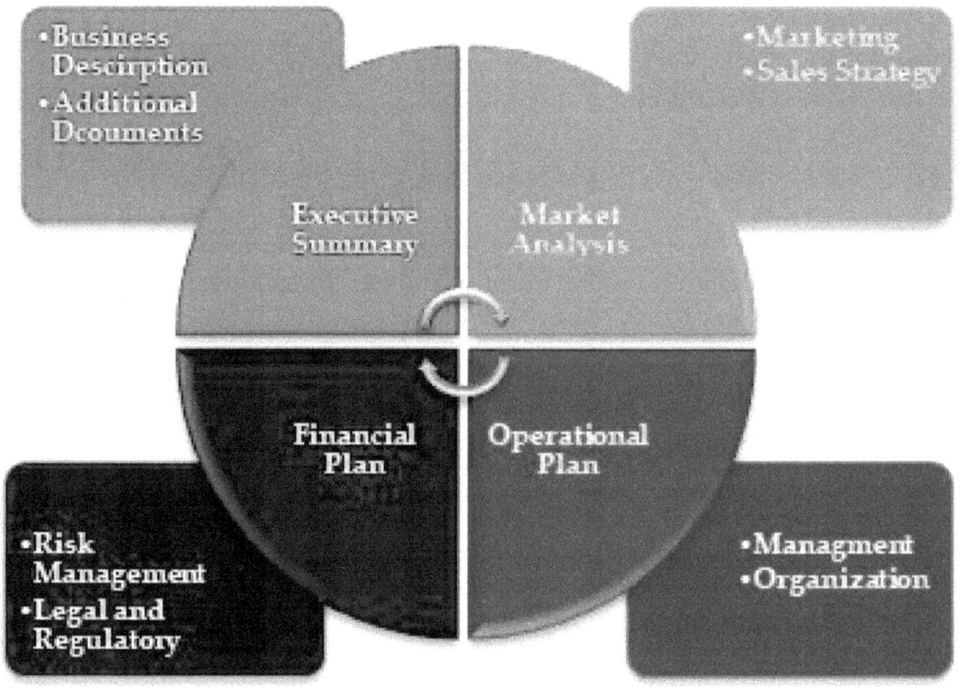

Template for creating business plan

1. Executive Summary:

a. Brief overview of your business concept.
b. Mission statement.
c. Business objectives.

2. Business Description:

a. Detailed description of your business idea.
b. Unique selling proposition (USP).
c. Legal structure (sole proprietorship, partnership, corporation, etc.).
d. Location of the business.

3. Market Analysis:

a. Overview of the industry in India.
b. Target market demographics.
c. Analysis of competitors.
d. SWOT analysis (Strengths, Weaknesses, Opportunities, Threats).

4. Marketing and Sales Strategy:

a. Marketing plan (online, offline, social media, etc.).
b. Sales strategy.
c. Pricing strategy.
d. Distribution channels.

5. Operational Plan:

a. Description of day –to-day operations.
b. Supply chain management.
c. Production process (if applicable).
d. Technology requirements.

6. Management and Organization:

a. Management team bios.
b. Organizational structure.
c. Roles and responsibilities.

7. Financial Plan:

a. Startup costs and funding requirements.
b. Revenue projections.
c. Break-even analysis.
d. Cash flow projections.
e. Profit and loss statement.
f. Balance sheet.
g. Financing options (if needed).

8. Risk Management:

a. Identification of potential risks.
b. Strategies for mitigating risks.
c. Contingency plans.

9. Legal and Regulatory Requirements:

a. Permits and licenses required.
b. Tax obligations.
c. Employment laws.

d. Intellectual property rights.

10. Appendix: Additional documents such as resumes of key team members, market research data, legal documents, etc.

6.3 STRATEGIC PLANNING

In the ever-evolving landscape of business, the path to success is often paved through careful planning and strategic foresight. Strategic planning serves as the compass guiding organizations towards their goals, providing a roadmap that navigates through uncertainties and challenges while leveraging opportunities for growth. At its core, strategic planning is not merely a process; it is a mindset that cultivates a proactive approach to decision-making, ensuring alignment between organizational objectives and the means to achieve them. In this introductory exploration, we delve into the significance of strategic planning in the establishment of businesses, unraveling its fundamental principles and highlighting its important role in shaping sustainable ventures amidst dynamic market dynamics. From defining mission statements to crafting actionable strategies, strategic planning empowers entrepreneurs to chart a course towards success, enabling them to adapt, innovate, and thrive in an ever-changing economic landscape.

Strategic planning is important for setting up a business in India for several reasons:

1. Understanding the Market:

Strategic planning helps in comprehensively understanding the Indian market, including consumer preferences, cultural nuances, regulatory environment, and competition. This understanding is vital for tailoring products or services to meet the needs of the local market effectively.

1. Risk Management:

India presents unique risks such as regulatory complexities, bureaucratic hurdles, and market volatility. Strategic planning enables businesses to anticipate and mitigate these risks by devising contingency plans and risk management strategies.

3. Resource Allocation:

Effective strategic planning assists in allocating resources efficiently. Whether it's capital investment, human resources, or technology, a well-thought-out plan ensures optimal utilization of resources, thereby maximizing returns on investment.

4. Long-term Vision:

Setting up a business in India requires a long-term vision. Strategic planning helps in defining clear business goals and objectives for the future, guiding decision-making processes and ensuring alignment with the company's vision.

5. Adaptability and Flexibility:

India's business landscape is dynamic and subject to rapid changes influenced by economic, political, and social factors. A strategic plan provides a framework for adapting to changing circumstances while staying focused on long-term objectives.

6. Legal and Regulatory Compliance:

India has complex legal and regulatory requirements that businesses must adhere to. Strategic planning involves understanding and complying with these regulations, reducing the risk of legal issues and ensuring smooth operations.

7. Market Penetration Strategies:

Strategic planning helps in devising effective market penetration strategies tailored to the Indian market. This includes decisions on pricing, distribution channels, marketing campaigns, and partnerships that can enhance the company's competitiveness and market share.

8. Building Partnerships and Alliances:

India offers opportunities for strategic partnerships and alliances with local businesses, government agencies, and other stakeholders. Strategic planning identifies potential partners and helps in building strong relationships for mutual benefit.

6.4 STRATEGIC PLANNING FOR LONG -TERM SUCCESS

Setting up a business in India can be a rewarding endeavor given its growing economy and vast market potential. To ensure long-term success, it's important to develop a strategic plan that addresses various aspects of the business.
1. Market Research and Analysis:

1. Understand the Indian market, including consumer behavior, trends, competitors, and regulatory environment.
2. Identify niche markets or unmet needs that your business can address.
3. Conduct thorough market research to gauge demand and assess market potential.

2. Legal and Regulatory Compliance:

1. Familiarize yourself with the legal and regulatory framework governing businesses in India, including company registration, taxation, labor laws, and intellectual property rights.
2. Seek professional legal advice to ensure compliance with all regulations and requirements.

3. Business Model Development:

1. Define your business model, including revenue streams, target customer segments, pricing strategy, and distribution channels.
2. Consider the scalability and adaptability of your business model to suit the Indian market dynamics.

4. Financial Planning and Budgeting:

1. Develop a detailed financial plan, including startup costs, operating expenses, revenue projections, and funding requirements.
2. Explore financing options such as bank loans, venture capital, angel investors, or government schemes.
3. Implement robust financial controls and budgeting processes to manage cash flow effectively.

5. Operational Setup:

1. Establish a physical presence in India, which may involve setting up an office, manufacturing facility, or distribution network.
2. Hire qualified personnel with local expertise who can navigate the cultural, linguistic, and business landscape effectively.
3. Invest in technology and infrastructure to support your operations efficiently.

6. Marketing and Branding:

1. Develop a comprehensive marketing strategy tailored to the Indian market, including digital marketing, social media, and traditional advertising channels.
2. Build brand awareness and credibility through targeted campaigns and strategic partnerships.
3. Adapt your messaging and branding to resonate with the cultural preferences and values of Indian consumers.

7. Customer Relationship Management:

1. Focus on building strong relationships with customers through excellent service, personalized experiences, and ongoing communication.
2. Leverage customer feedback and data analytics to continuously improve products and services.
3. Invest in customer retention strategies to foster loyalty and repeat business.

8. Risk Management:

1. Identify potential risks and challenges associated with operating in India, such as regulatory changes, political instability, currency fluctuations, or supply chain disruptions.
2. Develop contingency plans and risk mitigation strategies to minimize exposure and ensure business continuity.
3. Obtain appropriate insurance coverage to protect against unforeseen events.

9. Sustainability and Corporate Social Responsibility (CSR):

1. Integrate sustainability practices and CSR initiatives into your business operations, aligning with local environmental and social priorities.
2. Engage with local communities and stakeholders to build trust and goodwill.
3. Demonstrate your commitment to responsible business practices, which can enhance your brand reputation and long-term viability.

10. Continuous Monitoring and Adaptation:

1. Regularly monitor key performance indicators (KPIs) and metrics to track progress towards business goals.
2. Stay agile and responsive to market changes, customer feedback, and emerging opportunities.
3. Continuously iterate and refine your strategic plan based on lessons learned and evolving market conditions.

6.5 DEVELOPING LONG-TERM GOALS AND OBJECTIVES FOR SETTING UP A BUSINESS

Developing long-term goals and objectives for setting up a business requires careful consideration of various factors including market dynamics, regulatory environment, cultural nuances, and economic trends.
LONG-TERM GOALS AND OBJECTIVES FOR BUSINESS

1. Market Analysis: Conduct a thorough analysis of the Indian market to understand its size, growth potential, competitive landscape, consumer preferences, and trends. Consider factors such as demographics, income levels, urbanization, and technological advancements.
2. Regulatory Environment: Familiarize yourself with the regulatory framework governing businesses in India. Understand the legal requirements for registration, taxation, licensing, permits, and compliance with labor laws. Consider how these regulations may impact your business operations and long-term sustainability.
3. Cultural Considerations: Recognize the cultural diversity within India and how it may influence consumer behavior, marketing strategies, and employee relations. Adapt your business model, products, and services to resonate with the local culture while maintaining your brand identity.
4. SWOT Analysis: Conduct a SWOT (Strengths, Weaknesses, Opportunities, Threats) analysis to assess the internal and external factors that may affect your business in the Indian market. Identify your strengths to leverage, weaknesses to mitigate, opportunities to capitalize on, and threats to mitigate.
5. Financial Projections: Develop realistic financial projections for your business in India, considering factors such as startup costs, operating expenses, revenue forecasts, profit margins, and cash flow management. Evaluate the potential return on investment (ROI) and assess the financial feasibility of your long-term goals.
6. Market Entry Strategy: Determine the most suitable market entry strategy based on your goals, resources, and market conditions. Options may include establishing a wholly-owned subsidiary, forming a joint venture, partnering with local distributors or franchisees, or entering through mergers and acquisitions.
7. Sustainability and Corporate Social Responsibility (CSR): Integrate sustainability and CSR initiatives into your long-term goals and objectives. Consider the environmental, social, and governance (ESG) factors relevant to your business operations in India and outline strategies to contribute positively to the local community and environment.
8. Scalability and Flexibility: Design your long-term goals and objectives with scalability and flexibility in mind. Anticipate future growth opportunities and challenges, and ensure that your business model and strategies can adapt to changing market dynamics and emerging trends.
9. Talent Acquisition and Development: Develop a plan for recruiting, training, and retaining talent in India. Identify the skills and expertise required for your business operations and establishes initiatives for employee development, engagement, and succession planning.
10. Risk Management: Implement risk management strategies to mitigate potential risks and uncertainties associated with operating a business in India. Identify key risks such as political instability, economic fluctuations, legal disputes, cybersecurity threats, and supply chain disruptions, and develop contingency plans to address them.

6.6 FINANCIAL PLANNING PROCESS

Setting up a business in India involves various financial planning steps to ensure its success and sustainability.
1. Assessment of Business Idea:

1. Evaluate the viability and potential profitability of the business idea.
2. Conduct market research to understand the demand, competition, and target audience.

2. Setting Financial Goals:

1. Define short-term and long-term financial goals for the business.
2. Determine the amount of initial investment required to launch the business and sustain operations until it becomes profitable.

3. Budgeting:

1. Develop a detailed budget outlining the expenses required to establish and run the business.
2. Allocate funds for various expenses such as infrastructure, equipment, licenses, permits, marketing, and staffing.

4. Funding Strategy:

1. Explore different funding options such as personal savings, loans, venture capital, angel investors, or government schemes.
2. Decide on the most suitable funding sources based on the business's financial needs, risk tolerance, and growth prospects.

5. Legal and Regulatory Compliance:

1. Understand the legal and regulatory requirements for starting a business in India.
2. Allocate funds for registration fees, licenses, permits, and compliance with tax laws, labor laws, and other regulations.

6. Financial Projections:

1. Prepare financial projections including income statements, cash flow statements, and balance sheets.
2. Forecast revenues, expenses, and profits for the first few years of operation.

7. Risk Management:

1. Identify potential financial risks such as market fluctuations, competition, regulatory changes, and operational issues.
2. Develop risk mitigation strategies and allocate funds for contingency planning.

8. Tax Planning:

1. Consult with tax advisors to understand the tax implications of the business structure and operations.
2. Implement tax planning strategies to minimize tax liabilities and maximize tax benefits.

9. Financial Monitoring and Control:

1. Implement financial systems and processes for monitoring expenses, revenues, and cash flows.
2. Regularly review financial performance against budgeted targets and make necessary adjustments to ensure financial sustainability.

10. Exit Strategy:

1. Develop an exit strategy outlining options for exiting the business such as selling the company, merger, acquisition, or liquidation.
2. Plan for the financial implications of the exit strategy and ensure a smooth transition.

11. Continuous Financial Planning:

1. Regularly review and update the financial plan to reflect changes in the business environment, market conditions, and strategic objectives.

2. Stay informed about economic trends, regulatory changes, and industry developments that may impact the business's financial health.

By following these steps, businesses can effectively plan their finances and increase their chances of success in the Indian market. It's essential to seek professional advice from financial advisors, accountants, and legal experts to navigate the complexities of financial planning in India.

6.7 EFFECTIVE BUDGETING, FORECASTING AND AND FINANCIAL MANAGEMENT

Setting up a business in India requires careful consideration of budgeting, forecasting, and financial management.
1. Budgeting:

1. Budgeting is the process of estimating the company's future financial performance based on its objectives and available resources. It involves allocating resources to different activities within the organization.
2. When setting up a business in India, budgeting should encompass various aspects such as initial capital investment, operating expenses, marketing costs, regulatory compliance expenses, and contingencies.
3. Understanding the local market conditions, tax regulations, labor costs, and infrastructure expenses is crucial for creating an accurate budget.
4. It's essential to create both short-term and long-term budgets to effectively manage cash flow and ensure sustainability.

2. Forecasting:

1. Forecasting involves predicting future trends and outcomes based on historical data and current market conditions.
2. For a business in India, forecasting should take into account factors such as economic growth projections, consumer behavior, industry trends, and regulatory changes.
3. Utilizing tools like market research, trend analysis, and financial modeling can help in making more accurate forecasts.
4. Regularly reviewing and updating forecasts is important to adapt to changing market dynamics and mitigate risks.

3. Financial Management:

1. Financial management involves planning, organizing, directing, and controlling the financial activities of a business to achieve its objectives.
2. In the context of setting up a business in India, financial management includes managing working capital, optimizing cash flow, controlling costs, and maximizing profitability.
3. It's essential to comply with Indian accounting standards and tax regulations while managing finances.
4. Implementing robust financial reporting systems and internal controls is crucial for transparency and accountability.
5. Additionally, businesses should consider factors like foreign exchange risk management, access to financing options, and potential government incentives or subsidies.

Effective budgeting, forecasting, and financial management are essential for the successful establishment and operation of a business in India. By carefully planning and monitoring finances, businesses can navigate challenges, capitalize on opportunities, and achieve long-term growth and profitability in the Indian market.

Risk management is a important aspect of setting up a business as it involves identifying, assessing, and mitigating potential risks that could impact the success and sustainability of the business venture.

1. Regulatory Environment: Understanding the complex regulatory landscape in India is paramount. This includes company laws, taxation policies, foreign investment regulations, labor laws, environmental regulations, etc. Non-compliance can lead to penalties, fines, or even business closure.

2. Political and Economic Stability: India's political landscape can sometimes be volatile, with changes in government policies impacting businesses. Economic stability, inflation rates, currency fluctuations, and interest rates should also be evaluated for potential risks.

3. Market Risks: Market dynamics such as competition, consumer behavior, and market trends need careful analysis. Factors such as demand-supply gaps, changing consumer preferences, and technological disruptions can pose risks to business viability.

4. Legal and Contractual Risks: Drafting robust contracts and agreements is essential to protect the interests of the business. Legal disputes, intellectual property infringement, breach of contract, and litigation risks should be mitigated through proper legal counsel and documentation.

5. Operational Risks: Operational risks encompass a wide range of factors, including supply chain disruptions, logistics challenges, infrastructure inadequacies, and workforce issues. Developing contingency plans and implementing efficient operational processes can help mitigate these risks.

6. Financial Risks: Financial risks involve factors such as access to capital, liquidity management, exchange rate fluctuations, credit risks, and financial frauds. Maintaining sound financial management practices and diversifying financial resources can help mitigate these risks.

7. Cultural and Social Risks: Cultural nuances and social factors can significantly impact business operations in India. Understanding local customs, traditions, and societal norms is crucial for building strong relationships with customers, suppliers, and employees.

8. Security Risks: Cybersecurity threats, theft, vandalism, and other security risks should not be overlooked. Implementing robust security measures, data protection policies, and insurance coverage can help mitigate these risks.

9. Environmental Risks: With growing environmental awareness and stricter regulations, businesses need to consider environmental risks such as pollution, resource depletion, and climate change impacts. Adopting sustainable practices and complying with environmental standards can mitigate these risks.

10. Pandemic and Health Risks: Recent events like the COVID-19 pandemic have highlighted the importance of preparing for health-related risks. Businesses should have contingency plans in place to address pandemics, epidemics, and other health emergencies.

Effective risk management involves a systematic approach of identifying, assessing, prioritizing, and mitigating risks while also leveraging opportunities. By proactively addressing potential risks, businesses can enhance their resilience and increase their chances of success in the Indian market.

6.8 STRATEGIES FOR IDENTIFYING AND MITIGATING BUSINESS RISKS.

Setting up a business in India, like anywhere else, involves a variety of risks. Identifying and mitigating these risks is crucial for ensuring the success and sustainability of your venture. Here are some strategies for identifying and mitigating business risks when setting up a business in India:

1. Market Research and Analysis: Conduct thorough market research to understand the demand for your product or service in India. Analyze the competitive landscape, consumer behavior, regulatory environment, and cultural nuances to identify potential risks.

2. Regulatory Compliance: Understand the legal and regulatory framework governing businesses in India. Ensure compliance with all applicable laws, including company registration, taxation, labor laws, and any industry-specific regulations. Engage legal experts to navigate complex regulatory requirements.

3. Political and Economic Stability: Monitor political and economic developments in India to assess stability and potential risks. Changes in government policies, taxation, or economic conditions can impact businesses

significantly. Diversify investments and have contingency plans to mitigate such risks.

4. Local Partnerships and Networks: Build strong partnerships and networks with local businesses, suppliers, distributors, and government agencies. Local partners can provide valuable insights, access to resources, and help navigate bureaucratic processes, reducing operational risks.

5. Cultural Understanding: Understand the cultural nuances and business etiquette prevalent in India. Cultural differences can affect communication, negotiations, and relationship-building. Invest in cultural training for your team to minimize misunderstandings and foster positive relationships with stakeholders.

6. Financial Risks: Assess and manage financial risks, including currency fluctuations, inflation, and access to capital. Maintain sufficient liquidity, hedge currency risks where possible, and establish robust financial controls to mitigate financial risks.

7. Security and Infrastructure: Evaluate security risks related to physical infrastructure, cybersecurity, intellectual property protection, and supply chain vulnerabilities. Invest in secure infrastructure, data protection measures, and insurance coverage to safeguard against potential threats.

8. Talent Acquisition and Retention: Identify risks associated with talent acquisition, retention, and skills shortages in the Indian market. Develop strategies for recruiting and retaining skilled employees, including competitive compensation, training programs, and employee engagement initiatives.

9. Market Volatility and Competition: Anticipate market volatility and intense competition in India's dynamic business environment. Stay agile, monitor market trends, and continuously innovate to adapt to changing customer preferences and competitive pressures.

10. Contingency Planning: Develop comprehensive contingency plans to address potential risks and crises, such as natural disasters, political unrest, or market downturns. Establish clear protocols for risk assessment, crisis management, and business continuity to minimize disruptions to operations.

By implementing these strategies and staying vigilant, you can identify and mitigate business risks effectively when setting up a business in India, increasing the likelihood of success and long-term sustainability.

6.9 QUESTIONS

1. What is strategic planning?
2. Explain business plan and its components?
3. Draft a business plan template?
4. Explain the development of long-term goals and objectives for business?
5. Explain the risk management in business?
6. What are the strategies for identifying and mitigating business risks?

CHAPTER SEVEN

FINANCIAL PLANNING AND FUNDING THE BUSINESS

7.1 SOURCES OF BUSINESS FINANCE

Setting up a business requires adequate financing, and there are several potential sources entrepreneurs can explore.

1. Bootstrapping: This involves using personal savings or funds from friends and family to finance the business. It's one of the most common ways to start a business, especially for small ventures.
2. Bank Loans: Banks in India offer various loan products specifically tailored for business purposes, such as term loans, working capital loans, and loans against property. These loans usually require collateral and have specific terms and conditions.
3. Government Schemes: The Indian government often launches schemes to support entrepreneurship and small businesses. These schemes may offer subsidies, grants, or low-interest loans to eligible entrepreneurs. Some popular schemes include Startup India, Standup India, and Mudra Yojana.
4. Venture Capital and Private Equity: Venture capital (VC) and private equity (PE) firms provide funding to startups and growing businesses in exchange for equity ownership. They typically invest in high-growth potential ventures.
5. Angel Investors: Angel investors are affluent individuals who provide capital to startups in exchange for ownership equity or convertible debt. They often offer not only funding but also mentorship and industry connections.
6. Crowdfunding: Platforms like Kickstarter, Indiegogo, and Ketto enable entrepreneurs to raise funds from a large number of individuals, often in exchange for rewards or equity.
7. Non-Banking Financial Companies (NBFCs): NBFCs in India provide various financial services, including business loans, equipment financing, and invoice financing. They may have more flexible eligibility criteria compared to traditional banks.
8. Trade Credit: Suppliers may offer trade credit to businesses, allowing them to purchase goods or services on credit terms, typically with a specified payment period.
9. Microfinance Institutions (MFIs): MFIs provide small loans to entrepreneurs, particularly in rural and underserved areas. These loans are often aimed at microenterprises and self-employed individuals.
10. Initial Public Offering (IPO): Once a business reaches a certain size and profitability, it may choose to go public by offering shares to the public through an IPO. This can provide a significant source of capital for further expansion.
11. Grants and Subsidies: Certain industries or regions may offer grants and subsidies for business development, innovation, or job creation. These can be sourced from government bodies, industry associations, or non-profit organizations.
12. Corporate Partnerships and Joint Ventures: Collaborating with established companies through partnerships or joint ventures can provide access to funding, resources, and market opportunities.

7.2 INTERNAL AND EXTERNAL FINANCING OPTIONS.

Setting up a business requires careful consideration of various financing options, both internal and external, to ensure its successful establishment and growth. Internal financing involves utilizing resources within the business itself, such as retained earnings, while external financing involves seeking funds from outside sources like banks, investors, or government schemes.

7.2.1 Internal Financing:

1. Retained Earnings:

Retained earnings are profits accumulated by a business that are reinvested rather than distributed to shareholders as dividends. Utilizing retained earnings for setting up a business in India offers several advantages. Firstly, it doesn't incur any interest or repayment obligations, thus reducing financial strain. Secondly, it reflects the company's ability to generate profits, enhancing its credibility among stakeholders. However, the availability of retained earnings depends on the profitability and financial health of the business, which may limit the amount accessible for investment.

2. Personal Savings:

Entrepreneurs often utilize personal savings to finance their ventures. This method provides autonomy and flexibility in decision-making since there's no obligation to repay loans or share profits with external parties. However, it also involves personal financial risk, especially if the business encounters challenges. Moreover, the amount available for investment may be limited, potentially restricting the scale of the business.

7.2.2 External Financing

1. Bank Loans:

Bank loans are a common external financing option for businesses in India. Banks offer various loan products tailored to meet the diverse needs of entrepreneurs, such as term loans, working capital loans, and overdraft facilities. These loans typically require collateral and involve interest payments and repayment schedules. While bank loans provide immediate access to funds, they also entail financial obligations and the risk of default, which may lead to asset seizure or legal consequences.

2. Venture Capital and Angel Investors:

Venture capital firms and angel investors provide equity financing to startups and high-growth businesses in exchange for ownership stakes. In India, the startup ecosystem has witnessed significant growth, attracting investments from domestic and international venture capitalists. Partnering with venture capitalists or angel investors not only injects capital into the business but also provides strategic guidance and industry connections. However, entrepreneurs must be prepared to relinquish a portion of their ownership and align with investors' objectives, which may include rapid growth and eventual exit strategies.

3. Government Schemes and Grants:

The Indian government offers various schemes, grants, and subsidies to support entrepreneurship and business development across different sectors. These initiatives aim to foster innovation, create employment opportunities, and stimulate economic growth. Entrepreneurs can leverage government schemes for financial assistance, technical support, and infrastructure development. Examples include the Start-Up India initiative, Mudra Yojana, and various state-specific schemes. Accessing government support requires thorough research, compliance with eligibility criteria, and documentation procedures.

Both internal and external financing options play important roles in setting up a business in India. While internal financing offers autonomy and financial stability, external financing provides access to additional capital, expertise, and resources. Entrepreneurs must carefully evaluate their financing needs, assess the risks and benefits associated with each option, and develop a comprehensive financial strategy to support their business objectives effectively.

7.3 DEBT vs. EQUITY FINANCING

In the vibrant landscape of entrepreneurship in India, one of the fundamental decisions for aspiring business owners revolves around the choice between debt and equity financing. This decision is important as it not only shapes the financial structure of the enterprise but also influences its growth trajectory, risk profile, and ownership dynamics. Understanding the nuances of debt and equity financing is important for making informed decisions that align with the specific needs and goals of the business.

Debt financing involves raising capital by borrowing funds from external sources, such as banks, financial institutions, or private lenders, with a promise to repay the principal amount along with interest within a specified period. In the Indian context, debt financing offers several advantages for entrepreneurs. Firstly, it allows businesses to maintain full ownership and control over their operations since lenders do not acquire any equity stake or voting rights. This autonomy can be particularly appealing for founders who wish to retain decision-making authority. Additionally, interest payments on debt are typically tax-deductible, providing a cost-effective means of raising capital.

However, debt financing also carries inherent risks and limitations. The most obvious concern is the obligation to repay the borrowed amount, regardless of the business's performance. This can impose a significant financial burden, especially during periods of economic downturn or unforeseen challenges. Moreover, excessive leverage can strain the company's cash flow and limit its ability to invest in growth initiatives or navigate market fluctuations. In India, stringent regulatory frameworks and collateral requirements imposed by lenders further underscore the importance of prudent debt management practices.

On the other hand, equity financing involves selling ownership stakes in the business to external investors, such as venture capitalists, angel investors, or private equity firms, in exchange for capital infusion. Unlike debt financing, equity financing does not entail any repayment obligations, as investors assume the risk of potential losses in exchange for a share of future profits and ownership rights. In India's burgeoning startup ecosystem, equity financing has emerged as a preferred avenue for fueling growth and innovation, particularly in high-growth sectors such as technology, e-commerce, and fintech.

Equity financing offers several strategic advantages for entrepreneurs. Firstly, it provides access to substantial capital without incurring debt, enabling businesses to pursue ambitious expansion plans, research and development initiatives, and market penetration strategies. Moreover, equity investors often bring valuable expertise, networks, and industry insights to the table, which can complement the founder's vision and accelerate business growth. Additionally, since equity investors share the risks and rewards of the venture, they are incentivized to actively support its success through mentorship, strategic guidance, and operational support.

However, equity financing also entails certain trade-offs and considerations. Perhaps the most significant is the dilution of ownership and control, as each round of equity funding results in the issuance of new shares and a proportional reduction in the founder's ownership stake. This can lead to potential conflicts of interest, divergent priorities, and decision-making challenges as the business scales and attracts multiple investors. Furthermore, negotiating favorable terms with equity investors, such as valuation, governance rights, and exit strategies, requires careful deliberation and legal expertise to safeguard the founder's interests and preserve long-term value.

The choice between debt and equity financing for setting up a business in India is a multifaceted decision that hinges on various factors, including the company's growth stage, capital requirements, risk tolerance, and strategic objectives. While debt financing offers autonomy and tax benefits, it carries repayment obligations and financial constraints. Conversely, equity financing provides access to substantial capital, expertise, and support but entails ownership dilution and governance complexities. Ultimately, entrepreneurs must assess their unique circumstances, seek professional advice, and weigh the pros and cons of each financing option to chart a sustainable and successful path forward for their ventures in the dynamic Indian business landscape.

7.3.1 ADVANTAGES AND DISADVANTAGES OF DEBT AND EQUITY FINANCING

Debt and equity financing represent two fundamental methods through which businesses can raise capital to fund their operations, expansion, or other financial needs. Each approach carries its own set of advantages and disadvantages, influencing how businesses strategize their financial structure and decision-making. Understanding the implications of debt and equity financing is important for businesses to make informed choices aligned with their long-term objectives and risk tolerance.

ADVANTAGES OF DEBT FINANCING:

1. Interest Deductibility:One significant advantage of debt financing is the tax deductibility of interest payments. Interest on debt is often tax-deductible, reducing the overall tax burden on the business and improving its cash flow.
2. Maintaining Control:Unlike equity financing, debt financing does not dilute ownership or control of the business. Owners retain full ownership and decision-making authority, allowing them to maintain their vision and strategic direction.
3. Predictable Payments:Debt financing typically involves regular, fixed payments over a specified period, providing predictability and stability in cash flow management. This predictability facilitates better budgeting and financial planning.
4. Leverage:Debt allows businesses to leverage their assets and generate higher returns on equity. By borrowing funds, businesses can amplify their investment potential and pursue growth opportunities that may otherwise be out of reach.

DISADVANTAGES OF DEBT FINANCING:

1. Financial Risk: Debt introduces financial risk, as businesses are obligated to repay borrowed funds regardless of their financial performance. Failure to meet debt obligations can lead to severe consequences, including bankruptcy or loss of assets.
2. Interest Costs: While interest payments are tax-deductible, they still represent a fixed cost that must be paid regardless of business performance. High-interest rates or unfavorable loan terms can strain cash flow and diminish profitability.
3. Lack of Flexibility: Debt agreements often come with restrictive covenants and conditions imposed by lenders, limiting the flexibility of businesses to adapt to changing market conditions or pursue new opportunities.
4. Debt Overhang: Accumulating too much debt can create a burden known as debt overhang, where future earnings are allocated primarily to debt repayment rather than reinvestment in the business. This can hinder growth and innovation.

ADVANTAGES OF EQUITY FINANCING:

1. No Repayment Obligations: Unlike debt, equity financing does not require businesses to make regular interest or principal payments. Investors provide funds in exchange for ownership stakes, and returns are typically tied to the business's performance.
2. Shared Risk: Equity investors share the financial risk with business owners. If the business fails, investors may lose their investment, but they are not entitled to repayment like debt holders. This shared risk can provide a cushion during challenging times.
3. Long-Term Capital: Equity financing can provide access to long-term capital without the burden of debt repayment. This capital can be used to fuel growth initiatives, research and development, or other strategic endeavors.
4. Strategic Partnerships: Equity investors often bring valuable expertise, networks, and resources to the table, beyond just financial capital. Strategic partnerships with investors can open doors to new markets, customers, and opportunities for collaboration.

DISADVANTAGES OF EQUITY FINANCING:

1. Ownership Dilution: Equity financing entails diluting ownership and control of the business. As investors acquire ownership stakes, business owners relinquish some decision-making authority and may face conflicts of interest.
2. Profit Sharing: Equity investors are entitled to a share of the business's profits through dividends or capital appreciation. While this aligns interests between investors and owners, it reduces the proportion of profits retained by the business for reinvestment.
3. Potential for Disagreements: Differences in strategic vision, risk tolerance, or management style between owners and investors can lead to conflicts and disagreements, potentially disrupting business operations.
4. Information Disclosure: Equity financing often requires businesses to disclose sensitive financial and operational information to investors, increasing transparency but also exposing proprietary information to competitors or the public.

7.4 IMPLICATIONS FOR BUSINESS:

The choice between debt and equity financing has profound implications for a business's financial health, risk profile, and strategic direction. Businesses must carefully evaluate their capital needs, risk tolerance, and growth objectives to determine the most appropriate financing mix.

For established businesses with stable cash flows and collateral, debt financing may offer an efficient way to leverage assets and minimize ownership dilution. Conversely, startups or high-growth ventures may prefer equity financing to access capital without incurring debt obligations or sacrificing control.

Ultimately, the optimal financing strategy often involves a combination of debt and equity, tailored to the unique circumstances and objectives of the business. By understanding the advantages and disadvantages of each approach, businesses can make informed decisions that support their long-term success and sustainability.

7.5 GOVERNMENT SCHEMES AND SUBSIDIES FOR ENTREPRENEURS

In India, fostering entrepreneurship is a key priority for the government, recognizing its important role in economic growth, job creation, and innovation. To support aspiring entrepreneurs, various government schemes and subsidies have been introduced, aimed at easing the process of setting up and scaling businesses across different sectors. These initiatives encompass financial assistance, mentorship, skill development, and infrastructure support, among other facets, empowering individuals to realize their entrepreneurial dreams.

1. STARTUP INDIA:

Launched in 2016, Startup India is a flagship initiative by the Government of India aimed at fostering a condusive ecosystem for startups to thrive. It offers a plethora of benefits including tax exemptions, self-certification compliance, funding support through various channels such as funds of funds, and a dedicated Startup India Hub for networking and mentorship. Additionally, the scheme provides access to incubators and accelerators, simplification of patent filing processes, and relaxation in public procurement norms for startups.

2. MUDRA YOJANA:

The Pradhan Mantri MUDRA Yojana (Micro Units Development and Refinance Agency) aims to provide financial support to micro-enterprises in the form of loans up to Rs. 10 lakhs. These loans are categorized into three segments – Shishu (up to Rs. 50,000), Kishor (Rs. 50,001 to Rs. 5 lakhs), and Tarun (Rs. 5,00,001 to Rs. 10 lakhs), catering to entrepreneurs at different stages of business growth. The scheme facilitates access to credit without collateral, enabling aspiring entrepreneurs to initiate and expand their ventures.

3. STAND-UP INDIA:

Stand-Up India is an initiative targeted at promoting entrepreneurship among women, Scheduled Castes (SCs), and Scheduled Tribes (STs). Under this scheme, bank loans ranging from Rs. 10 lakhs to Rs. 1 crore are extended to at least one woman entrepreneur and one entrepreneur from either SC or ST category per bank branch for setting up greenfield enterprises. The scheme aims to empower underprivileged sections of society by providing them with financial assistance and handholding support through the entrepreneurial journey.

4. TECHNOLOGY DEVELOPMENT BOARD (TDB):

The Technology Development Board, under the Department of Science and Technology, offers financial assistance for commercializing indigenous technologies. It provides funding support for prototype development, technology demonstration, and market promotion, fostering innovation-driven entrepreneurship. The TDB plays a pivotal role in bridging the gap between research and commercialization, thereby facilitating the growth of technology-based startups in India.

5. PRADHAN MANTRI EMPLOYMENT GENERATION PROGRAMME (PMEGP):

PMEGP is a credit-linked subsidy scheme administered by the Ministry of Micro, Small & Medium Enterprises (MSME) to generate employment opportunities through entrepreneurship. It provides financial assistance in the form of margin money subsidy for setting up new micro-enterprises or expanding existing ones in the manufacturing and service sectors. The scheme aims to create sustainable livelihoods by promoting self-employment and entrepreneurship at the grassroots level.

6. INDUSTRIAL SUBSIDY AND INCENTIVE SCHEMES:

Various state governments offer sector-specific subsidies and incentives to attract investments and promote industrial development. These schemes encompass benefits such as capital subsidies, interest subsidies, power tariff subsidies, land allotment at concessional rates, and reimbursement of infrastructure development costs. Entrepreneurs can leverage these incentives to mitigate initial capital expenditure and enhance the viability of their ventures.

Government schemes and subsidies play a important role in nurturing entrepreneurship and fostering economic growth in India. By providing financial assistance, regulatory support, and infrastructure facilitation, these initiatives empower aspiring entrepreneurs to overcome initial hurdles and embark on their entrepreneurial journey with confidence. However, effective implementation, awareness dissemination, and continuous evaluation are imperative to ensure that these schemes reach their intended beneficiaries and catalyze the emergence of a vibrant startup ecosystem condusive to innovation, job creation, and inclusive development.

7.6 GOVERNMENT INITIATIVES SUPPORTING ENTREPRENEURS

GOVERNMENT INITIATIVES SUPPORTING ENTREPRENEURS - ELIGIBILITY CRITERIA AND APPLICATION PROCESS

Highlighting government initiatives supporting entrepreneurs is important for fostering innovation, economic growth, and job creation.

INITIATIVES GOVERNMENTS MAY IMPLEMENT, ALONG WITH TYPICAL ELIGIBILITY CRITERIA AND APPLICATION PROCESSES:

1. Small Business Grants and Loans:

- Eligibility Criteria: Generally, small businesses meeting specific criteria such as size, revenue, and industry focus may qualify. This could include factors like being a minority-owned business, a woman-owned business, or operating in certain economically disadvantaged areas.

- Application Process: Typically involves filling out an application form, providing business plans, financial statements, and demonstrating how the funds will be utilized.

2. Business Incubators and Accelerators:

- Eligibility Criteria: Usually targeted towards early-stage startups with high growth potential. Criteria might include the innovation of the business idea, scalability, and the potential for job creation.   ·

- Application Process: Startups typically apply to join an incubator or accelerator by submitting an application online. The application may require details about the business idea, the team, market analysis, and potential growth plans.

3. Tax Incentives and Credits:

- Eligibility Criteria: Businesses may qualify based on factors such as size, industry, location, or investment in research and development.

- Application Process: Businesses usually claim tax incentives or credits by including them in their annual tax filings. Some tax incentives may require advance registration or certification from relevant government agencies.

4. Government Contracts and Procurement Opportunities:

- Eligibility Criteria: Typically open to businesses meeting certain size standards and legal requirements. Some contracts may be specifically reserved for minority-owned, women-owned, or veteran-owned businesses.

- Application Process: Businesses can usually find contract opportunities through government procurement websites or by registering with relevant procurement agencies. The application process may involve submitting bids or proposals in response to specific solicitations.

5. Training and Mentorship Programs:

- Eligibility Criteria: Generally open to entrepreneurs at various stages of business development. Criteria may include willingness to participate, commitment to growth, and alignment with program objectives.

- Application Process: Entrepreneurs can apply to training and mentorship programs by completing an application form, providing information about their business, and sometimes attending interviews or information sessions.

6. Export Assistance Programs.

- Eligibility Criteria: Usually open to businesses interested in exporting their products or services. Criteria may include export readiness, market potential, and compliance with trade regulations.

- Application Process: Businesses can apply for export assistance programs by contacting relevant government agencies or trade promotion organizations. The application process may involve submitting export plans, attending training workshops, and meeting with export advisors.

It's essential for entrepreneurs to thoroughly research each initiative, understand the eligibility criteria, and follow the application process carefully to maximize their chances of success. Additionally, governments should strive to make these initiatives accessible and transparent to ensure that all eligible entrepreneurs have the opportunity to benefit from them.

7.7 CROWDFUNDING AND VENTURE CAPITAL

Setting up a business can be facilitated through various funding options, including crowdfunding and venture capital.

1. Crowdfunding:

Crowdfunding has gained popularity as a means of raising capital for startups and small businesses. In India, there are platforms like Ketto, Wishberry, and Fueladream that facilitate crowdfunding campaigns.

WORKING OF CROWDFUNDING:

Equity Crowdfunding: Investors provide funding in exchange for equity in the company. However, Equity crowdfunding is relatively new in India and has regulatory constraints.

1. Reward-based Crowdfunding: Backers contribute funds in exchange for rewards or early access to products or services.
2. Donation-based Crowdfunding: Individuals donate money to support a cause or project without expecting anything in return.

Advantages of crowdfunding include:

1. Access to capital without giving up equity
2. Validation of product or service idea through market demand
3. Building a community of supporters and potential customers

However, it's essential to note that crowdfunding success depends on effectively marketing your campaign and engaging with potential backers.

2. Venture Capital:

Venture capital (VC) involves investors providing capital to startups and small businesses in exchange for equity ownership. In India, the venture capital ecosystem has been growing rapidly, with numerous VC firms and angel investors actively seeking investment opportunities.

WORKING OF VENTURE CAPITAL:

- Seed stage:

Venture capital firms or angel investors provide funding to startups in the early stages of development, typically in exchange for equity.

- Early Stage:

Funding is provided to startups that have progressed beyond the initial stages but still require capital to scale their operations.

- Growth Stage:

Venture capital firms invest in companies that have demonstrated market traction and are poised for rapid growth. Advantages of venture capital include:

1. Access to substantial capital for scaling operations
2. Expertise and mentorship from experienced investors
3. Networking opportunities within the Venture capital ecosystem

However, securing venture capital can be challenging, as investors often look for startups with high growth potential, a strong team, and a scalable business model.

When considering crowdfunding or venture capital for setting up a business in India, it's important to thoroughly research and understand the requirements, regulations, and implications associated with each funding option. Additionally, having a solid business plan, a compelling value proposition, and a clear strategy for growth will increase your chances of attracting funding from investors or backers. Consulting with financial advisors or professionals experienced in startup funding can also provide valuable insights and guidance.

7.7.1 CROWD-FUNDING - DIFFERENT MODELS

Crowdfunding is a method of raising capital through the collective effort of a large number of individuals, typically via the internet. It's particularly useful for startups and small businesses looking for funding, as it allows them to bypass traditional financial intermediaries like banks or venture capitalists. In India, crowdfunding has gained popularity as a viable alternative for raising capital due to its accessibility and potential for widespread reach. There are several models of crowdfunding, each with its own characteristics and suitability for different types of projects or businesses.

1. Donation-Based Crowdfunding:

1. In this model, individuals contribute money to a project or cause without expecting anything tangible in return.
2. Commonly used for charitable causes, community projects, or social initiatives.
3. Contributors are driven by altruism or a belief in the project's mission.
4. Platforms like Milaap, Ketto, and ImpactGuru are popular for donation-based crowdfunding in India.

2. Reward-Based Crowdfunding:

1. In reward-based crowdfunding, backers contribute funds to a project in exchange for non-financial rewards or perks.
2. These rewards can vary from early access to the product, exclusive merchandise, or experiences related to the project.
3. This model is suitable for creative projects, product launches, or initiatives with a strong value proposition for backers.
4. Platforms like Kickstarter and Indiegogo offer reward-based crowdfunding options for businesses in India.

3. Equity Crowdfunding:

1. Equity crowdfunding involves investors providing capital to a business in exchange for equity ownership.
2. It allows businesses to raise funds by selling shares or ownership stakes to a large number of investors.
3. Investors stand to gain financially through dividends or capital appreciation if the business succeeds.
4. Equity crowdfunding platforms in India include LetsVenture, AngelList, and SeedInvest.

4. Debt Crowdfunding (Peer-to-Peer lending):

1. Debt crowdfunding, also known as peer-to-peer lending, involves individuals lending money to businesses or individuals in need of capital.
2. The borrowing entity repays the loan amount with interest over a specified period.
3. This model provides an alternative to traditional bank loans, especially for businesses with limited access to credit.
4. Platforms like Faircent and LenDenClub facilitate peer-to-peer lending in India.

5. Real Estate Crowdfunding:

1. Real estate crowdfunding enables investors to pool their resources to invest in real estate projects.
2. Investors can participate in property development, rental income, or property flipping without directly owning the property.
3. This model offers opportunities for diversification and access to real estate investments with lower capital requirements.
4. Indian platforms like PropShare and RealX facilitate real estate crowdfunding opportunities.

When setting up a business in India, it's essential to choose the crowdfunding model that aligns with your project's goals, funding requirements, and target audience. Additionally, ensure compliance with relevant regulations and guidelines set by regulatory authorities such as the Securities and Exchange Board of India (SEBI) to conduct crowdfunding activities legally and ethically. Consulting with legal and financial experts familiar with Indian regulations can help navigate the complexities of crowdfunding and ensure compliance with local laws.

7.7.2 ROLE OF VENTURE CAPITAL IN BUSINESS FINANCING.

Venture capital plays a important role in the financing landscape, particularly for startups and early-stage companies with high growth potential but limited access to traditional funding sources like bank loans or public markets.

1. Seed Funding: Venture capital often provides seed funding to startups in exchange for an equity stake in the company. This initial investment helps entrepreneurs develop their ideas, build prototypes, and conduct market research.

2. Early-Stage Financing: As startups progress beyond the seed stage, they may require additional capital to scale their operations, develop their products or services, and expand their market reach. Venture capital firms specialize in providing this early-stage financing to help companies grow rapidly.

3. Expertise and Guidance: Beyond just providing capital, venture capitalists often bring valuable expertise, industry connections, and strategic guidance to the companies they invest in. This support can help startups navigate challenges, make key business decisions, and accelerate their growth trajectory.

4. Risk Capital: Venture capital is inherently risky, as many startups fail to achieve success. However, venture capitalists are willing to take on this risk in exchange for the potential of high returns on their investments. This risk capital is essential for fostering innovation and entrepreneurship in the economy.

5. Long-Term Focus: Unlike traditional lenders or public investors, venture capitalists typically have a longer time horizon for their investments. They understand that it may take several years for a startup to reach its full potential and are willing to remain invested for the long term to maximize returns.

6. Catalyst for Innovation: Venture capital plays a critical role in driving innovation by funding groundbreaking technologies, disruptive business models, and novel solutions to pressing problems. Many of the world's most successful and transformative companies, such as Google, Facebook, and Amazon, have relied on venture capital to fuel their growth.

7. Economic Growth: By supporting the growth of high-potential startups, venture capital contributes to job creation, economic expansion, and wealth generation in society. Successful startups often spawn new industries, attract talent and investment, and stimulate further innovation across the economy.

8. Global Reach: Venture capital is a global phenomenon, with hubs of innovation and investment located in major cities around the world, such as Silicon Valley, New York, London, and Beijing. This global network enables startups to access funding, expertise, and markets on a worldwide scale.

Venture capital plays a vital role in the business financing ecosystem by providing capital, expertise, and support to startups and early-stage companies with high growth potential. Its ability to take on risk, foster innovation, and drive economic growth makes it a cornerstone of entrepreneurial ecosystems worldwide.

7.8 QUESTIONS

1. What are the Sources of Business Finance?
2. Explain the internal and external financing options.
3. Write in detail the advantages and disadvantages of debt and equity financing.
4. Distinguish between Debts vs. Equity Financing.
5. Government Schemes and Subsidies for Entrepreneurs Explain?
6. Write short notes on crowdfunding and venture capital?
7. Explain the different models of crowdfunding?
8. Explain the role of venture capital in business financing.

CHAPTER EIGHT

REAL ESTATE AND INFRA-STRUCTURE

8.1 CHOOSING A BUSINESS LOCATION

Choosing the right location for setting up a business in India is a important decision that can significantly impact the success and growth of the venture. Several factors need to be carefully considered to ensure that the chosen location aligns with the business objectives and operational requirements.

One of the primary considerations when selecting a business location in India is proximity to target markets and customers. Understanding the demographics and preferences of the target audience can help in identifying areas with high demand for the products or services offered by the business. Additionally, being close to suppliers, distributors, and other stakeholders can streamline operations and reduce logistical costs.

Infrastructure and transportation networks play a crucial role in determining the accessibility and connectivity of a business location. Opting for areas with well-developed roads, railways, ports, and airports can facilitate the movement of goods and people, enabling efficient distribution and access to markets both domestically and internationally.

Moreover, the availability of utilities such as electricity, water, and telecommunications infrastructure is essential for smooth business operations. Access to reliable and affordable utilities can minimize operational disruptions and ensure continuity in production and service delivery.

The regulatory and business environment of a particular location also needs to be evaluated before making a decision. Factors such as tax incentives, government policies, licensing requirements, and regulatory compliance can vary across states and regions in India. Choosing a location with a favorable regulatory environment and supportive government policies can reduce bureaucratic hurdles and enhance the ease of doing business.

Furthermore, considering the availability of skilled labor and workforce demographics is crucial for businesses that rely on human capital. Selecting locations with access to a skilled and educated workforce can contribute to productivity, innovation, and competitiveness.

Cultural and social factors should also be taken into account, especially for businesses catering to specific demographics or industries. Understanding local customs, preferences, and consumer behavior can help in tailoring products and services to meet the needs of the target market effectively.

8.2 SPECIAL ECONOMIC ZONES

Special Economic Zones (SEZs) represent an important aspect of India's economic landscape, providing a condusive environment for businesses to thrive and contribute significantly to the nation's growth trajectory. Established with the objective of boosting exports, generating employment, and attracting foreign investment, SEZs have emerged as vibrant hubs of industrial activity, innovation, and economic dynamism.

At their core, SEZs offer a range of fiscal and regulatory incentives aimed at enhancing the ease of doing business. These incentives include tax holidays, duty-free import of capital goods and raw materials, streamlined customs procedures, relaxed labor regulations, and infrastructure support. Such favorable conditions not only lower the operational costs for businesses but also foster an atmosphere condusive to rapid industrialization and technological advancement.

One of the most compelling aspects of SEZs is their role in driving exports. By facilitating the clustering of export-oriented industries, SEZs enable companies to leverage economies of scale, access international markets, and compete more effectively on the global stage. This, in turn, augments foreign exchange earnings and bolsters India's trade balance.

Moreover, SEZs serve as catalysts for regional development, particularly in areas that were previously underserved or marginalized. By catalyzing infrastructural development and creating employment opportunities, SEZs contribute to poverty alleviation, skill enhancement, and overall socio-economic upliftment of the surrounding communities.

The success of SEZs in India can be attributed to the synergy between government initiatives and private sector participation. While the government provides the necessary policy framework and infrastructure support, private enterprises drive innovation, investment, and job creation within these designated zones. This partnership underscores the collaborative approach required for sustainable economic development.

However, the concept of SEZs is not without its challenges. Criticisms often center on issues such as land acquisition, environmental concerns, labor exploitation, and the potential for tax evasion. Addressing these challenges requires a balanced approach that prioritizes socio-economic inclusivity, environmental sustainability, and regulatory compliance while preserving the competitive advantages of SEZs.

Special Economic Zones play an important role in India's economic growth story, offering a strategic platform for businesses to flourish, innovate, and contribute to national development. By harnessing the synergies between government policy, private enterprise, and global market dynamics, SEZs have the potential to drive India's journey towards becoming a global economic powerhouse while fostering inclusive and sustainable growth across regions.

8.3 INDUSTRIAL PARKS

Industrial parks in India serve as vital infrastructural hubs for businesses, offering a condusive environment for manufacturing, processing, and other industrial activities. These parks are strategically designed and developed to meet the needs of various industries, providing essential facilities and amenities to support business operations efficiently.

8.3.1 INDUSTRIAL PARKS IN INDIA AND WHY THEY ARE AN ATTRACTIVE SETTING FOR BUSINESSES:

1. Infrastructure and Facilities:

Industrial parks in India boast robust infrastructure, including well-planned layouts, roads, drainage systems, and utilities such as water, electricity, and telecommunications. These parks are equipped with modern amenities like warehouses, storage facilities, and transportation services to facilitate smooth logistics operations.

2. Government Support and Incentives:

The Indian government provides various incentives and support schemes to attract businesses to industrial parks. These incentives may include tax breaks, subsidies, reduced tariffs on imports and exports, and streamlined regulatory processes. Additionally, initiatives like the Make in India campaign aim to promote manufacturing activities and foster a condusive business environment.

3. Cluster Development:

Industrial parks often encourage the clustering of related industries, creating synergies and economies of scale. This clustering effect leads to increased collaboration, knowledge sharing, and supply chain efficiencies. For example, automotive manufacturers may cluster together in a specific industrial park, leading to the development of a robust automotive ecosystem with suppliers, service providers, and research institutions.

4. Access to Skilled Labor:

Industrial parks are typically located in areas with access to a skilled workforce. Proximity to educational institutions, vocational training centers, and residential areas ensures a steady supply of skilled labor for businesses operating within the park. Moreover, industrial training programs and skill development initiatives are often organized in collaboration with the government and industry associations to meet specific skill requirements.

5. Connectivity and Accessibility:

Industrial parks are strategically located near major transportation hubs such as airports, seaports, and highways, ensuring seamless connectivity for both domestic and international trade. This strategic positioning facilitates efficient movement of raw materials, finished goods, and personnel, reducing transportation costs and lead times for businesses.

6. Environmental Sustainability:

With growing awareness about environmental sustainability, many industrial parks in India are adopting eco-friendly practices and green technologies. Measures such as waste recycling, energy-efficient infrastructure, and green building certifications contribute to reducing environmental impact and enhancing the overall sustainability of industrial operations.

7. Customized Solutions and Flexibility:

Industrial parks offer flexibility in terms of plot sizes, lease agreements, and customization options to meet the diverse needs of businesses. Whether it's a small-scale manufacturing unit or a large multinational corporation, industrial parks can provide tailored solutions to accommodate various business requirements and expansion plans.

Industrial parks in India serve as dynamic ecosystems that foster innovation, collaboration, and growth for businesses across diverse sectors. With robust infrastructure, government support, skilled labor pool, and strategic connectivity, these parks offer an ideal setting for companies to establish and expand their operations, driving economic development and prosperity in the region.

8.4 REAL ESTATE REGULATIONS AND DOCUMENTATION

Setting up a business in India entails navigating a labyrinth of regulations and documentation, particularly in the realm of real estate. Real estate regulations play an important role in establishing a firm footing for any entrepreneurial venture, as they dictate the permissible uses of land, construction norms, and property ownership rights. Understanding and adhering to these regulations is important to ensure legal compliance, mitigate risks, and foster a condusive business environment.

One of the primary considerations for businesses is the acquisition or leasing of suitable commercial space. In India, this process involves meticulous scrutiny of land titles, zoning regulations, building codes, and environmental clearances. Engaging legal experts proficient in Indian real estate law is essential to conduct due diligence and verify the authenticity of property documents. Any discrepancies or ambiguities in land titles or ownership can impede the establishment of the business and lead to protracted legal disputes.

Moreover, businesses must comply with local municipal regulations pertaining to land use, building permits, and occupancy certificates. These regulations vary across different states and municipalities, adding another layer of complexity to the process. Obtaining necessary approvals and clearances from relevant authorities is imperative to commence construction or renovation activities smoothly.

Documentation plays an important role in the real estate transactions associated with setting up a business in India. It includes drafting and executing lease agreements, sale deeds, Memorandums of Understanding (MoUs), and other legal contracts. These documents delineate the rights and obligations of the parties involved, including landlords, tenants, developers, and regulatory authorities. Thorough review and negotiation of these agreements arc essential to safeguard the interests of the business and ensure clarity regarding terms such as rent, duration, maintenance responsibilities, and exit clauses.

Furthermore, businesses must comply with taxation laws applicable to real estate transactions, such as stamp duty, Goods and Services Tax (GST), and capital gains tax. Failure to adhere to tax regulations can lead to financial penalties and legal repercussions, underscoring the importance of seeking expert advice to optimize tax planning strategies.

In recent years, the Indian government has introduced several reforms aimed at streamlining the real estate sector and enhancing transparency. Initiatives like Real Estate (Regulation and Development) Act, 2016 (RERA) aim to protect the interests of property buyers and promote accountability among developers. Compliance with RERA provisions, including project registration, disclosure of project details, and adherence to timelines, is essential for businesses involved in real state development.

Navigating real estate regulations and documentation is an indispensable aspect of setting up a business in India. Diligent adherence to legal requirements, meticulous due diligence, and proactive engagement with legal and regulatory authorities are vital to ensure a smooth and legally compliant establishment of a business venture. By prioritizing regulatory compliance and documentation integrity, businesses can mitigate risks and lay a solid foundation for long-term success in the dynamic Indian market.

8.5 LAND ACQUISITION

In India, the acquisition of land for business purposes is regulated by various laws and procedures aimed at balancing the interests of landowners, investors, and the public. The primary legislation governing land acquisition is the Right to Fair Compensation and Transparency in Land Acquisition, Rehabilitation, and Resettlement Act of 2013 (RFCTLARR Act). This act replaced the archaic Land Acquisition Act of 1894 and introduced significant changes to the process of land acquisition, emphasizing fair compensation, rehabilitation, and resettlement of affected persons.

The procedure for land acquisition under the RFCTLARR Act involves several steps. Firstly, the acquiring authority must conduct a social impact assessment to evaluate the potential effects of the proposed acquisition on the affected communities. This assessment aims to ensure that the acquisition serves a public purpose and that adequate compensation and rehabilitation measures are put in place for those affected.

Once the social impact assessment is completed, the acquiring authority must issue a preliminary notification stating its intention to acquire the land. This notification must be published in local newspapers and prominently displayed in the affected area to inform the landowners and other stakeholders about the proposed acquisition.

Following the preliminary notification, the acquiring authority conducts a survey of the land to determine its boundaries and assess its value. Landowners are given an opportunity to raise objections or provide feedback during this stage.

After considering any objections and feedback received, the acquiring authority issues a final notification declaring its intention to acquire the land. Upon issuance of the final notification, the land is deemed to be vested in the government and the process of compensation and rehabilitation begins.

Under the RFCTLARR Act, landowners are entitled to receive compensation at market rates, along with additional benefits such as rehabilitation and resettlement assistance. The Act also specifies timelines for the payment of compensation and mandates the establishment of grievance redressal mechanisms to address any disputes or concerns raised by affected persons.

In addition to the RFCTLARR Act, businesses looking to acquire land in India must also comply with various state-specific laws and regulations governing land use, zoning, and environmental protection. Depending on the nature of the business and the location of the proposed project, additional approvals may be required from local authorities and government agencies.

Overall, while the process of land acquisition for business purposes in India can be complex and time-consuming, adherence to the relevant laws and procedures is essential to ensure transparency, fairness, and equitable treatment of all stakeholders involved. By following the prescribed regulatory framework and engaging with affected communities in a meaningful manner, businesses can establish a solid foundation for their operations while respecting the rights and interests of the local population.

8.6 LEASE AGREEMENTS

Lease agreements play an important role in the establishment and operation of businesses in India, serving as the cornerstone of property arrangements between landlords and tenants. The regulation and procedures governing lease agreements in India are primarily governed by the Transfer of Property Act, 1882, as well as various state-specific laws and regulations. Understanding these legal frameworks is important for businesses aiming to secure suitable premises for their operations.

In India, the process of setting up a business involves several procedural steps, and obtaining a lease agreement is among the initial and important stages. Businesses must identify suitable premises that align with their operational requirements and budgetary constraints. Once a suitable property is identified, negotiations between the landlord and the tenant ensue, during which the terms and conditions of the lease agreement are determined.

The lease agreement typically outlines key aspects such as the duration of the lease, rental amount, and mode of payment, maintenance responsibilities, and clauses pertaining to renewal, termination, and eviction. It is imperative for both parties to thoroughly review and understand the terms laid out in the lease agreement to avoid any future disputes or misunderstandings.

From a regulatory standpoint, businesses must ensure compliance with local laws and regulations governing property transactions. This may involve obtaining necessary approvals or permits from local authorities, adhering to zoning regulations, and fulfilling any statutory requirements mandated by the concerned jurisdiction.

Additionally, businesses should exercise due diligence in verifying the legal title and ownership of the property, ensuring that the landlord possesses the requisite rights to lease the premises. Engaging legal counsel or real estate professionals can provide valuable guidance throughout the lease negotiation and execution process, safeguarding the interests of both parties and facilitating a smooth transaction.

Furthermore, businesses operating in specialized sectors or industries may be subject to specific regulatory requirements or restrictions pertaining to the type of premises they can occupy. For instance, businesses in the food and beverage sector may need to comply with hygiene and safety standards prescribed by regulatory authorities.

8.7 QUESTIONS

1. Explain Choosing a Business Location?
2. Write a shart note on Special economic zone?
3. Explain industrial parks?
4. Explain real estate regulations and documentations?
5. Explain land acquisition for business?
6. What do you mean by lease agreements?

CHAPTER NINE

HUMAN RESOURCES AND LABOUR LAWS

9.1 HIRING AND RECRUITMENT

Hiring and recruitment are foundational elements of any organization's success, serving as the critical gateway through which businesses identify, attract, and ultimately select the best-suited talent to fulfill their objectives. In today's dynamic and competitive landscape, characterized by rapid technological advancements and shifting market demands, effective hiring practices have become paramount for companies striving to maintain a competitive edge. From attracting top-tier candidates to navigating complex selection processes, the realm of hiring and recruitment encompasses a diverse array of strategies, methodologies, and challenges.

Setting up a business involves various steps, and hiring and recruitment are important aspects, Understanding Indian Labor Laws:

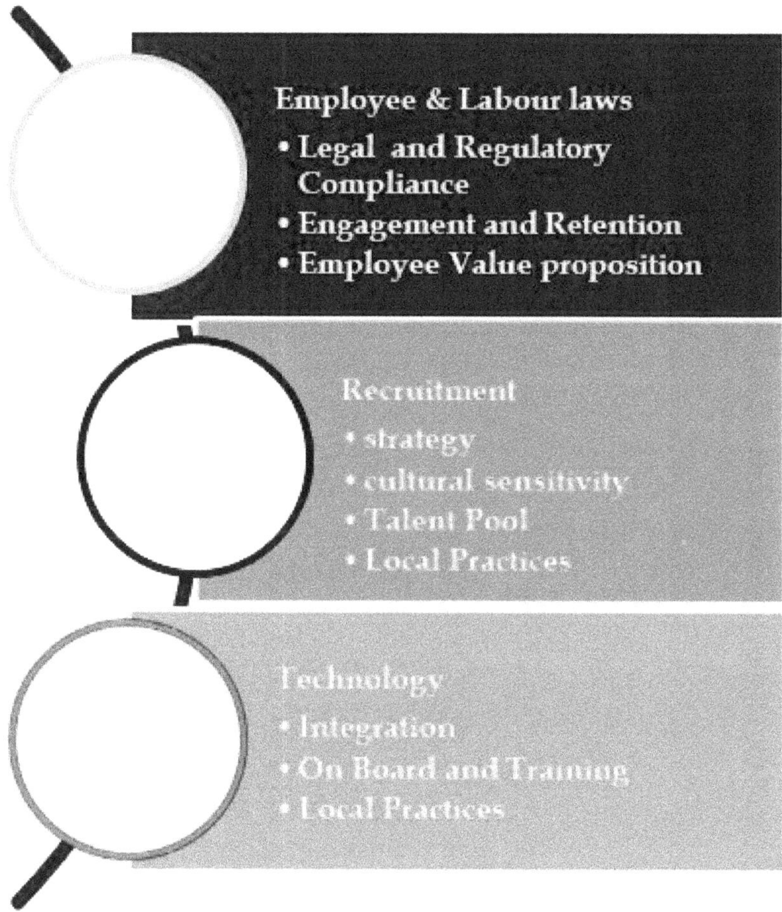

Important Aspects of Hiring and Recruitment

Familiarize yourself with Indian labor laws, including those related to employment contracts, minimum wages, working hours, and benefits such as provident fund and gratuity. Compliance with these laws is essential to avoid legal issues in the future.

1. Recruitment Strategy:

Develop a recruitment strategy tailored to the Indian market. Determine whether you'll hire locally or internationally and whether you'll use recruitment agencies, online job portals, or direct advertising to attract talent. Networking and leveraging personal connections can also be effective in India.

1. Cultural Sensitivity:

India is a diverse country with various cultures, languages, and customs. Understanding and respecting cultural differences is crucial in the hiring process. Consider factors like regional preferences, religious holidays, and communication styles when interacting with potential candidates.

3. Talent Pool:

Assess the availability of talent in the industry and location where you're setting up your business. India has a large and diverse talent pool across various sectors, but competition for skilled professionals can be intense, particularly in sectors like IT, engineering, and healthcare.

4. Technology Integration:

Leverage technology in your recruitment process. India has a significant tech-savvy population, and online recruitment platforms, applicant tracking systems (ATS), and video interviewing tools are widely used. Integrating these technologies can streamline your hiring process and reach a broader audience.

5. Employee Value Proposition (EVP):

Develop a compelling EVP to attract and retain top talent. In addition to competitive salaries, consider offering benefits such as flexible work arrangements, career development opportunities, and a positive work culture. Highlighting your company's mission, values, and impact can also appeal to Indian candidates.

6. Onboarding and Training:

Once you've hired employees, invest in their onboarding and training to ensure a smooth transition into their roles. Provide cultural orientation, job-specific training, and ongoing support to help employees succeed in their positions.

7. Employee Engagement and Retention:

Employee engagement is crucial for retention in the competitive Indian job market. Regularly solicit feedback from employees, recognize their contributions, and provide opportunities for growth and advancement within the organization.

8. Adapting to Local Practices:

Be prepared to adapt your HR policies and practices to align with local norms and regulations. This may include aspects such as performance appraisal systems, leave policies, and disciplinary procedures.

9. Legal and Regulatory Compliance:

Ensure compliance with all relevant labor laws and regulations in India. This includes obtaining necessary permits and registrations, adhering to tax obligations, and maintaining accurate records of employment-related documentation.

Hiring and recruitment are important processes for any organization to attract and select the best candidates for available positions.

A brief overview of the important steps involved:

1. Identifying Hiring Needs:

This involves understanding the organization's current and future requirements in terms of skills, experience, and roles.

2. Job Description Creation:

Develop clear and concise job descriptions outlining the responsibilities, requirements, and expectations for the role.

3. Advertising the Position:

Utilize various channels such as job boards, social media, company websites, and professional networks to reach potential candidates.

4. Screening Resumes/CVs:

Reviewing received applications to shortlist candidates who meet the specified criteria.

5. Initial Screening:

Conducting initial interviews, either through phone calls, video interviews, or screening questionnaires, to further assess candidates' qualifications and fit for the role.

6. Interviewing:

Organize in-depth interviews with shortlisted candidates to evaluate their skills, experience, cultural fit, and potential contributions to the organization.

7. Assessment and Testing:

Administer relevant assessments, tests or tasks to evaluate candidate's technical skills, cognitive abilities or personality traits etc.

8. Background Checks:

Conduct reference checks, verifying employment history, and performing background checks to ensure the authenticity of candidates' credentials.

9. Offering the Position:

Extend a formal job offer to the selected candidate with details such as salary, benefits, start date and any other relevant terms.

10. Onboarding:

Assist the new hire with the transition into their new role, providing necessary training, orientation, and support to help them integrate smoothly into the organization.

Throughout the hiring process, it's essential to maintain clear communication with candidates, provide a positive candidate experience, and adhere to legal and ethical standards to ensure fairness and compliance.

Organizations may leverage technology such as applicant tracking systems (ATS), video interviewing platforms, and online assessment tools to streamline and enhance the efficiency of their recruitment processes.

9.2 EMPLOYMENT CONTRACTS

Employment contracts serve as the cornerstone of the relationship between employers and employees, delineating the rights, responsibilities, and expectations of both parties. These legally binding agreements provide a framework for employment terms, covering essential aspects such as job duties, compensation, benefits, working hours, termination clauses, and confidentiality agreements. In today's dynamic and complex work environment, employment contracts play a pivotal role in safeguarding the interests of employers and employees, ensuring clarity, fairness, and compliance with relevant laws and regulations.

When setting up a business in India, employment contracts play a important role in establishing the terms and conditions of employment between the employer and employees.

9.2. IMPORTANT POINTS TO CONSIDER REGARDING EMPLOYMENT CONTRACTS:

1. Types of Contracts: In India, employment contracts can be either written or oral. However, it's always recommended to have written contracts to avoid misunderstandings.

2. Content of Contracts: The contract should clearly outline terms such as job responsibilities, salary, benefits, working hours, leave policies, termination clauses, non-compete clauses (if applicable), and any other relevant terms and conditions.

3. Legal Requirements: Employment contracts in India must comply with various labor laws and regulations, including but not limited to the Industrial Disputes Act, Minimum Wages Act, Payment of Gratuity Act, and the Employees' Provident Fund and Miscellaneous Provisions Act.

4. Offer Letters and Appointment Letters: Typically, job offers are extended through offer letters, and upon acceptance, formal appointment letters are issued. These documents should include details about the position, compensation, start date, and other relevant terms.

5. Probation Period: It's common for Indian companies to have a probationary period for new employees. The terms and conditions of the probation period should be clearly stated in the employment contract.

6. Confidentiality and Non-Disclosure: Employment contracts often include clauses related to confidentiality and non-disclosure of proprietary information to protect the employer's interests.

7. Notice Period: Both the employer and the employee are usually required to provide a notice period before terminating the employment contract. The duration of the notice period should be specified in the contract.

8. Dispute Resolution: Contracts may include clauses specifying the method of dispute resolution, such as arbitration or mediation, in case of any conflicts between the employer and employee.

9. Compliance with Local Laws: It's essential to ensure that employment contracts comply with the specific laws and regulations applicable to the state or region where the business operates in India.

10. Consultation with Legal Experts: Given the complexity of labor laws in India, it's advisable for employers to seek legal advice and consultation when drafting employment contracts to ensure compliance and mitigate legal risks.

Overall, employment contracts are vital documents that govern the relationship between employers and employees in India, and careful consideration should be given to drafting them to protect the interests of both parties and ensure compliance with relevant laws and regulations.

9.3 WORK PERMITS FOR EXPATRIATES

In an increasingly interconnected world, the movement of skilled professionals across borders has become a vital aspect of global business operations. Expatriates, individuals employed in a foreign country, bring with them specialized expertise, diverse perspectives, and invaluable contributions to the host nations' economies. However, navigating the complexities of international employment often hinges upon obtaining the necessary work permits. These permits serve as legal authorization for expatriates to work within a specific country, outlining the terms and conditions under which they may contribute to the workforce. Understanding the intricacies of work permits for expatriates is essential for both employers seeking to recruit talent globally and for expatriates themselves, as compliance with immigration laws is paramount in ensuring smooth transitions and productive engagements abroad. This introduction explores the fundamental concepts surrounding work permits for expatriates, shedding light on their significance, application processes, and the evolving landscape of global mobility.

In the context of human resource management and setting up a business in India, obtaining work permits for expatriates is an essential aspect. Here's an overview of the process and considerations:

1. Understanding Work Permit Categories: India offers various categories of work permits depending on the nature of the employment. These can include employment visas, business visas, project visas, etc. Each has its own specific requirements and limitations.

2. Employment Visa: For expatriates intending to work in India, an employment visa is typically required. This visa is issued to skilled professionals, managers, or executives being employed by an Indian company.

3. Eligibility Criteria: The eligibility criteria for obtaining an employment visa may vary based on factors such as the nature of the job, qualifications, experience, and the employing company's credibility. The Indian government may have specific requirements regarding minimum salary, qualifications, etc.

4. Employer's Responsibility: The employer in India usually plays a crucial role in facilitating the work permit process for expatriates. This includes providing necessary documents, sponsorship, and adhering to the legal obligations.

5. Documentation: Expatriates need to submit various documents as part of the visa application process. This may include a valid passport, employment contract, proof of qualifications, medical certificates, etc.

6. Duration and Renewal: Employment visas are typically issued for a specific duration, often corresponding to the duration of the employment contract. Renewal processes must be initiated in advance to ensure continuous legal status for the expatriate employee.

7. Compliance and Regulations: Employers must ensure compliance with all relevant immigration laws and regulations. This includes adhering to visa conditions, reporting requirements, and any changes in employment status.

8. Local Laws and Customs: It's crucial for expatriates to familiarize themselves with local laws, customs, and cultural sensitivities to ensure smooth integration into the workplace and society.

9. Consulting Legal Experts: Given the complexity of immigration laws and regulations, it's advisable for both employers and expatriates to seek guidance from legal experts specializing in immigration and employment law.

10. Ongoing Support and Integration: HR departments should provide ongoing support to expatriate employees to facilitate their integration into the workplace and local community. This can include assistance with housing, healthcare, schooling for dependents, language training, etc.

By addressing these considerations and navigating the work permit process effectively, businesses can successfully recruit and integrate expatriate talent into their operations in India, contributing to their overall success and growth.

9.4 STEPS INVOLVED IN RECRUITMENT AND HIRING PROCESS

Setting up a business involves several steps in the recruitment and hiring process.

1. Identifying Staffing Needs:

Determine the positions that need to be filled based on the business requirements, projected growth, and organizational structure.

2. Job Analysis and Description:

Conduct a thorough job analysis to understand the roles and responsibilities. Create job descriptions outlining qualifications, skills, and experience required for each position.

3. Recruitment Strategy:

Develop a recruitment strategy outlining the methods and channels for sourcing candidates. This can include online job portals, social media, recruitment agencies, job fairs, and employee referrals.

4. Advertising Job Openings:

Post job advertisements on relevant platforms and channels as per the recruitment strategy. Ensure compliance with local labor laws regarding job postings.

5. Screening Resumes:

Review resumes and applications received to shortlist candidates who meet the job requirements.

6. Conducting Interviews:

Schedule interviews with the shortlisted candidates. Depending on the role, interviews may include multiple rounds, such as telephonic interviews, video interviews, technical interviews, and face-to-face interviews.

7. Assessment and Evaluation:

Assess candidates through various methods, including skills tests, psychometric assessments, and behavioral interviews. Evaluate candidates based on their qualifications, experience, cultural fit, and potential for growth within the organization.

8. Background Verification:

Conduct background checks on the final candidates to verify employment history, educational qualifications, and any criminal records as per local regulations.

9. Offer Negotiation:

Extend job offers to selected candidates, including details such as compensation, benefits, job responsibilities, and start date. Negotiate terms if necessary to finalize the offer.

10. Offer Acceptance and Onboarding:

Once the offer is accepted, initiate the onboarding process, which includes completing necessary paperwork, providing orientation, training, and introducing the new hire to the team and company culture.

11. Legal Compliance:

Ensure compliance with labor laws, taxation regulations, and other legal requirements related to employment in India. This includes obtaining necessary permissions or registrations for hiring foreign nationals if applicable.

12. Probation Period:

Monitor the performance of new hires during the probation period and provide necessary support and feedback to facilitate their integration into the organization.

By following these steps, businesses can effectively recruit and hire talent in India while ensuring compliance with local regulations and fostering a positive employee experience.

9.5 STRATEGIES FOR ATTRACTING AND RETAINING TALENT.

In today's fiercely competitive global marketplace, businesses are increasingly recognizing theimportant l role of talent in driving organizational success. As companies navigate through the complexities of a dynamic workforce landscape, devising effective strategies for attracting and retaining top-tier talent has become a cornerstone of sustainable growth and innovation. In this ever-evolving landscape, where skilled individuals are the most prized asset, organizations must deploy comprehensive and adaptive approaches to not only attract but also retain talent. From fostering an enticing company culture to offering compelling career development opportunities, the pursuit of talent acquisition and retention has evolved into a multifaceted endeavor that demands strategic vision, agility, and creativity.

STRATEGIES FOR ATTRACTING AND RETAINING TALENT.

1. Create a Compelling Employer Brand:

Develop a strong brand identity that highlights your company's culture, values, and mission. Potential employees are often attracted to companies with a clear and inspiring vision.

2. Offer Competitive Compensation and Benefits:

Conduct research to ensure your salary and benefits packages are competitive within your industry and region. Consider offering additional perks such as flexible work schedules, remote work options, wellness programs, and professional development opportunities.

3. Provide Opportunities for Growth and Advancement:

Employees are more likely to stay with a company that offers opportunities for career advancement and skill development. Implement mentorship programs, training sessions, and career path planning to help employees grow within the organization.

4. Foster a Positive Work Environment:

Create a supportive and inclusive workplace culture where employees feel valued, respected, and motivated. Encourage open communication, recognize and reward achievements, and promote work-life balance.

5. Emphasize Work-Life Balance:

Offer flexible work arrangements, such as remote work options or flexible hours, to help employees balance their personal and professional lives. Respect employees' time off and encourage them to prioritize their well-being.

6. Build Strong Relationships with Employees:

Invest time in building strong relationships with your employees. Get to know them personally, listen to their feedback, and address any concerns they may have promptly.

7. Provide Meaningful Work: Employees are more likely to stay with a company that offers meaningful and fulfilling work. Ensure that employees understand how their role contributes to the overall success of the company and provide opportunities for them to make a difference.

8. Encourage Collaboration and Teamwork:

Foster a collaborative work environment where employees can work together to solve problems and achieve common goals. Encourage teamwork through team-building activities, cross-functional projects, and collaborative tools.

9. Offer Employee Recognition and Rewards:

Recognize and reward employees for their hard work and contributions to the company. This can include bonuses, promotions, awards, and public recognition in meetings or newsletters.

10. Conduct Exit Interviews and Act on Feedback:

When employees leave the company, conduct exit interviews to gather feedback on their experience. Use this feedback to identify areas for improvement and make necessary changes to enhance employee satisfaction and retention.

By implementing these strategies, one can attract top talent to their business and create an environment where employees are motivated to stay and contribute to the company's success.

9.6 COMPLIANCE WITH LABOR LAWS

Compliance with labor laws is an important aspect to consider when setting up a business in India. The country boasts a comprehensive legal framework governing labor rights, working conditions, and employment practices aimed at safeguarding the interests of both employees and employers. Adherence to these laws not only ensures ethical business practices but also fosters a conducive environment for sustainable growth and development.

India's labor laws cover a wide array of areas, including minimum wages, working hours, safety standards, social security, and employment contracts. Understanding and complying with these regulations is paramount to avoid legal repercussions and maintain harmonious employer-employee relations.

One of the fundamental aspects of labor law compliance in India is adhering to minimum wage requirements. Employers are obligated to pay their employees a minimum wage set by the respective state governments, ensuring fair compensation for their work. Failure to comply with these regulations can lead to fines, legal penalties, and damage to the company's reputation.

Furthermore, businesses must comply with regulations concerning working hours and overtime compensation. The law stipulates the maximum number of working hours per day and week, along with provisions for overtime pay beyond the prescribed limits. Ensuring proper scheduling and compensation not only promotes employee well-being but also mitigates the risk of labor disputes and litigation.

Safety and health standards in the workplace are another critical aspect of labor law compliance. Employers are required to provide a safe working environment, implement necessary safety measures, and provide training to employees on occupational hazards and safety protocols. Non-compliance with these regulations can result in accidents, injuries, and legal liabilities, undermining both employee welfare and business operations.

compliance with social security provisions such as provident fund contributions, employee insurance, and gratuity benefits is essential. These regulations aim to provide financial security and welfare benefits to employees, thereby fostering loyalty and productivity in the workforce.

In conclusion, adherence to labor laws is indispensable for businesses intending to operate in India. By prioritizing compliance with regulations governing wages, working conditions, safety standards, and social security, businesses can build a reputation as responsible corporate entities, foster employee trust and loyalty, and contribute to sustainable economic growth.

MINIMUM WAGES

The Minimum Wages Act in India stands as a cornerstone of labor legislation, playing an important role in regulating wages and ensuring fair compensation for workers across various industries. Enacted in 1948, the Act was formulated with the primary objective of safeguarding the interests of workers by establishing minimum wage standards, thereby preventing exploitation and promoting social justice. From the perspective of Human Resource Management (HRM), understanding the intricacies of the Minimum Wages Act is imperative for businesses planning to establish operations in India. This legislation directly impacts HR practices, requiring meticulous compliance to avoid legal repercussions and foster harmonious employer-employee relations.

In this context, comprehending the nuances of the Minimum Wages Act becomes essential for businesses navigating the dynamic landscape of HRM in India.

The Minimum Wages Act, 1948 is an Indian legislation enacted to safeguard the interests of workers by ensuring they receive fair wages for their labor. The Act applies to various industries and sectors, both in the organized and unorganized sectors.

9.7 RULES AND REGULATIONS UNDER THE MINIMUM WAGES ACT IN INDIA:

1. Fixation of Minimum Wages:

The Act mandates that both the Central and State Governments fix and revise the minimum rates of wages at regular intervals. These rates vary across different categories of employment, such as skilled, semi-skilled, and unskilled labor, as well as across different regions.

2. Coverage:

The Act applies to all employees engaged in scheduled employments, which are specific industries or sectors notified by the respective State Governments. These employments include sectors like agriculture, construction, manufacturing, hospitality, etc.

3. Wage Periods:

Wages must be paid at intervals not exceeding one month, typically before the expiry of the seventh day after the end of the wage period.

4. Payment of Minimum Wages:

Employers are required to pay wages to workers not less than the minimum rates fixed by the government, either in cash or through checks or bank transfers.

5. Overtime Wages:

In cases where employees work beyond the normal working hours, they are entitled to overtime wages, which are usually higher than the normal wages.

6. Deductions:

Employers are permitted to make certain deductions from the wages of employees, but these deductions should not exceed the limits specified under the Act.

7. Maintenance of Registers and Records:

Employers are required to maintain registers and records containing details such as the number of hours worked by each employee, wages paid, deductions made, etc.

8. Inspections and Penalties:

The Act empowers labor inspectors to conduct inspections of establishments to ensure compliance with the provisions of the Act. Employers found violating the provisions of the Act are liable to penalties, which may include fines or imprisonment.

9. Revision of Minimum Wages:

The minimum wages are subject to revision by the appropriate government at regular intervals, taking into account factors such as inflation, cost of living, etc.

It's important to note that while the Minimum Wages Act lays down the basic framework, the specific rules and regulations may vary from state to state in India as labor is a subject under the concurrent list of the Indian Constitution, allowing both the Central and State Governments to legislate on it.

9.8 WORKING HOURS AND OVERTIME

In India, working hours and overtime are governed by various labor laws and regulations, with the primary aim of ensuring fair treatment of employees and protecting their rights.

Concept of working hours and overtime in India:

1. Working Hours:

The standard working hours in India typically range from 8 to 9 hours per day and 48 to 54 hours per week, depending on the industry and state-specific regulations. For example, as per the Factories Act, 1948, the standard working hours for adult workers in a factory are 9 hours a day and 48 hours a week. However, some industries or establishments may have different norms regarding working hours, often influenced by industry practices, collective bargaining agreements, or company policies.

2. Overtime:

Overtime refers to the additional hours worked by an employee beyond the standard working hours, typically defined by law or contract. In India, the Payment of Wages Act, 1936, mandates that employees must be compensated at a higher rate for overtime work. The rate of overtime pay is usually 1.5 times the regular hourly wage rate for each hour of overtime worked. However, this rate may vary based on industry norms, collective agreements, or company policies. The Factories Act and the Shops and Establishments Act in various states provide guidelines regarding overtime regulations for workers in factories, shops, and other establishments.

3. Regulations and Compliance:

Employers are required to adhere to the applicable labor laws and regulations regarding working hours and overtime to ensure compliance and avoid legal repercussions. Non-compliance with overtime regulations can lead to penalties, fines, or legal action against the employer. It's essential for employers to maintain accurate records of employee working hours, including overtime hours worked and the corresponding compensation provided.

4. Employee Rights:

Employees have the right to refuse to work overtime if it exceeds the legal limits or poses a risk to their health and safety. They are entitled to receive proper compensation for any overtime worked, as per the prevailing regulations. Employers should communicate overtime policies clearly to employees and ensure transparency in overtime-related matters.

5. Exceptions and Special Circumstances:

Some industries or professions may have exemptions or special provisions regarding working hours and overtime, such as emergency services, transportation, healthcare, etc. Collective agreements between employers and trade unions may also outline specific provisions for working hours and overtime for unionized workers. Overall, working hours and overtime regulations in India aim to balance the needs of employers and employees while ensuring fair compensation and promoting a safe and healthy work environment. Employers should stay informed about relevant labor laws and uphold the rights of their employees regarding working hours and overtime.

9.9 EMPLOYEE TRAINING AND DEVELOPMENT

Employee training and development play a important role in shaping the workforce landscape of India, a dynamic and rapidly evolving economy. With a burgeoning population and a diverse labor force, India stands as one of the world's largest and most promising markets for businesses across various sectors. In this landscape, the effective training and development of employees emerge as essential pillars for organizational success, driving productivity, innovation, and competitiveness. As India continues its journey towards becoming a global economic powerhouse, the significance of investing in human capital through robust training and development initiatives becomes increasingly evident.

Setting up a business in India requires a comprehensive understanding of the local market, including its regulations, culture, and workforce. Employee training and development play a important role in this process.

1. Understanding Local Laws and Regulations: Before initiating any training program, it's essential to familiarize oneself with India's labor laws and regulations. These include employment contracts, minimum wage laws, working hour regulations, and other legal requirements related to employee training and development.

2. Cultural Sensitivity Training: India is a culturally diverse country with various languages, traditions, and customs. Conduct cultural sensitivity training to help the employees understand and respect these differences. This training can cover topics such as communication styles, hierarchy in the workplace, and religious sensitivities.

3. Language Training: If the business operates in English but the employees are not proficient, consider providing language training. English is widely spoken in the Indian business environment, but proficiency levels can vary. Language training can enhance communication skills and improve employee confidence.

4. Technical and Job-specific Training: Depending on the business sector, provide technical and job-specific training to the employees. This could include training on industry-specific tools, software systems, or processes relevant to the business operations.

5. Compliance and Ethics Training: Educate the employees on compliance standards, ethical guidelines, and company policies. This training should cover areas such as data privacy, anti-corruption laws, and workplace conduct to ensure that employees adhere to legal and ethical standards.

6. Leadership Development: Invest in leadership development programs to nurture future leaders within the organization. Provide training on leadership skills, conflict resolution, decision-making, and team management to empower employees to take on leadership roles.

7. Soft Skills Training: Soft skills such as communication, teamwork, problem-solving, and adaptability are essential for success in the workplace. Offer training programs that focus on developing these skills to enhance employee effectiveness and productivity.

8. Employee Wellness Programs: Promote employee well-being by implementing wellness programs that focus on physical, mental, and emotional health. Offer activities such as yoga classes, stress management workshops, and employee assistance programs to support the workforce.

9. Performance Management Training: Train managers and supervisors on effective performance management techniques, including goal setting, feedback delivery, and performance appraisal processes. This will help create a culture of continuous feedback and improvement within the organization.

10. Evaluation and Feedback Mechanisms: Continuously assess the effectiveness of the training programs through employee feedback, performance metrics, and other evaluation methods. Use this feedback to make necessary adjustments and improvements to the training initiatives.

By prioritizing employee training and development in the context of human resource management, one can effectively prepare the workforce for the challenges and opportunities of setting up a business in India. This investment in the employees will not only enhance their skills and capabilities but also contribute to the long-term success and sustainability of the business operations in the Indian market.

9.10 EMPLOYEE DEVELOPMENT

In the dynamic landscape of contemporary business, where innovation is the key to sustainability and growth, the role of human resource management (HRM) has evolved significantly. Among the myriad responsibilities entrusted to HR professionals, perhaps none is as critical as fostering ongoing employee development. In an era where talent is a prime differentiator, organizations must recognize that investing in their workforce is not just a discretionary expense but a strategic imperative.

Employee development encompasses a broad spectrum of activities aimed at enhancing an individual's skills, knowledge, and capabilities to perform current and future roles effectively. This process is not limited to formal training sessions or academic qualifications; rather, it encompasses a holistic approach that nurtures talent at every stage of the employee lifecycle.

in today's hypercompetitive environment, the adage "knowledge is power" holds more truth than ever before. Organizations that embrace a culture of ongoing employee development are better positioned to adapt to market fluctuations, drive innovation, and retain top talent. Through strategic investment in their human capital, companies can transcend challenges, capitalize on opportunities, and chart a course towards sustained success.

1. Skill Enhancement: India's workforce is diverse and dynamic. Continuous learning ensures employees stay updated with the latest industry trends, technologies, and best practices, enhancing their skill set and employability.

2. Global Competitiveness: With India's increasing integration into the global economy, employees need to possess competitive skills to thrive in the international marketplace. Ongoing development programs help Indian workers remain competitive on a global scale.

3. Innovation and Adaptability: Continuous learning fosters innovation and adaptability among employees. In rapidly changing industries such as technology and finance, the ability to innovate and adapt is essential for business success.

4. Employee Engagement and Retention: Investing in employee development demonstrates a commitment to their growth and career progression. This, in turn, boosts morale, increases job satisfaction, and reduces turnover rates, saving costs associated with recruitment and training.

5. Leadership Development: India's burgeoning economy requires effective leaders at all levels. Ongoing development programs help identify and nurture leadership talent within organizations, ensuring a pipeline of capable leaders for the future.

6. Compliance and Regulatory Requirements: Many industries in India are subject to stringent regulatory and compliance standards. Continuous training helps employees stay abreast of these requirements, reducing the risk of non-compliance and associated penalties.

7. Cultural Sensitivity and Diversity Training: In a country as diverse as India, with multiple languages, cultures, and traditions, ongoing training in cultural sensitivity and diversity is essential to foster a harmonious and inclusive work environment.

8. Digital Transformation: As India undergoes digital transformation across various sectors, employees need to acquire digital skills to remain relevant. Ongoing development programs can help bridge the digital skills gap and facilitate a smooth transition to the digital economy.

9.11 TRAINING PROGRAMS AND OPPORTUNITIES.

In today's rapidly evolving world, the demand for skilled professionals is constantly on the rise. Whether you're a recent graduate, a seasoned professional looking to upskill, or someone seeking a career change, investing in training programs and opportunities has become essential for staying competitive in the job market.

Training programs offer individuals the chance to acquire new skills, deepen their knowledge in specific areas, and adapt to the ever-changing demands of various industries. These programs come in various forms, ranging from traditional classroom-based courses to online workshops, bootcamps, and self-paced learning modules.

Whether you're aiming to enhance your expertise in a particular field, advance your career prospects, or simply stay updated with the latest trends and technologies, understanding the landscape of training programs and opportunities is important for personal and professional growth.

1. Cultural Awareness and Sensitivity Training: India is a culturally diverse country with different languages, customs, and traditions across regions. Training programs should emphasize cultural awareness and sensitivity to ensure effective communication and collaboration within the workforce.

2. Technical Skills Training: India boasts a large pool of skilled talent, especially in fields like technology, engineering, and finance. Training programs should focus on enhancing technical skills relevant to the specific industry or sector in which the business operates.

3. Compliance and Regulatory Training: India has complex labor laws and regulations that businesses need to comply with. HRM training programs should cover topics such as labor laws, taxation, intellectual property rights, and other regulatory requirements to ensure legal compliance and mitigate risks.

4. Entrepreneurship Development Programs: Setting up a business in India requires a deep understanding of the local market dynamics, regulatory environment, and business practices. Entrepreneurship development programs can provide aspiring entrepreneurs with the knowledge and skills needed to navigate the complexities of starting and running a business in India.

5. Soft Skills Development: In addition to technical skills, soft skills such as communication, leadership, teamwork, and problem-solving are essential for success in the Indian business environment. HRM training programs should focus on developing these skills among employees to enhance their effectiveness and productivity.

6. Language Training: English is widely spoken in Indian business circles, but proficiency in local languages can be advantageous, especially when dealing with customers, suppliers, and employees from diverse linguistic backgrounds. Language training programs can help employees develop proficiency in local languages, thereby improving communication and relationship-building efforts.

7. Cross-Cultural Training: India is a melting pot of cultures, and businesses often operate across different states with distinct cultural norms. Cross-cultural training programs can help employees understand and appreciate cultural differences, fostering a more inclusive and harmonious work environment.

8. Continuous Learning and Development: The business landscape in India is constantly evolving, driven by technological advancements, changing consumer preferences, and regulatory reforms. HRM should prioritize continuous learning and development initiatives to ensure that employees stay updated with the latest industry trends and developments.

By investing in comprehensive training programs and opportunities, businesses can effectively harness the potential of India's workforce and position themselves for long-term success in the dynamic Indian market.

9.12 POSITIVE WORK ENVIRONMENT

A positive work environment is not merely a buzzword but a important aspect of any thriving organization. It encompasses the atmosphere, culture, and relationships within a workplace that contribute to the overall well-being, satisfaction, and productivity of employees. In today's competitive landscape, fostering a positive work environment isn't just a nice-to-have; it's a strategic imperative for organizations aiming to attract, retain, and nurture top talent while maximizing performance and innovation.

At its core, a positive work environment is built on a foundation of respect, trust, communication, and inclusivity. It's where individuals feel valued, supported, and empowered to bring their authentic selves to work each day. In such an environment, collaboration flourishes, morale is high, and employees are motivated to go above and beyond in their roles.

Creating a positive work environment is important for any business, regardless of the location. However, when setting up a business in India, there are some cultural nuances and specific strategies that can help foster positivity and productivity among employees.

1. Respect for Hierarchical Structure:

In Indian culture, hierarchical structures are often respected. Maintain clear lines of authority and ensure that employees feel respected within their roles.

1. Open Communication Channels: Encourage open communication among employees and between employees and management. Provide avenues for feedback and suggestions, and ensure that employees feel heard and valued.

2. Promote Work-Life Balance: Indians value family and personal time. Offer flexible work arrangements when possible and encourage employees to maintain a healthy work-life balance.

3. Recognize and Reward Achievements: Acknowledge the hard work and achievements of employees regularly. This could be through public recognition, bonuses, or other incentives.

4. Encourage Collaboration and Teamwork: Foster a collaborative work environment where teamwork is encouraged. Encourage employees to work together towards common goals and celebrate team successes.

5. Provide Opportunities for Growth and Development: Invest in employee training and development programs to help employees enhance their skills and grow within the organization. This can include mentorship programs,

workshops, or access to online courses.

6. Promote Diversity and Inclusion: India is a diverse country with various languages, cultures, and backgrounds. Embrace diversity and ensure that all employees feel included and valued regardless of their backgrounds.
7. Create a Comfortable Physical Environment: Ensure that the workplace is comfortable and conducive to productivity. This includes providing ergonomic furniture, proper lighting, and a clean and organized workspace.
8. Offer Employee Benefits and Wellness Programs: Provide benefits such as health insurance, retirement plans, and wellness programs to support employee well-being.
9. Lead by Example: Finally, leadership plays a important role in shaping the work environment. Lead by example by demonstrating positivity, integrity, and a strong work ethic.

By implementing these strategies, one can create a positive work environment for their business in India, fostering employee satisfaction, productivity, and retention.

9.13 POSITIVE WORK PLACE CULTURE

In the modern landscape of business, fostering a positive workplace culture has emerged as a important factor for organizational success and employee satisfaction. A positive workplace culture encompasses a variety of elements that collectively contribute to creating an environment where employees feel valued, motivated, and engaged. From effective communication to recognition of achievements, from inclusivity to a sense of purpose, each element plays a vital role in shaping the overall culture within an organization.

Exploring the fundamental elements that constitute a positive workplace culture and delve into why they are essential for promoting productivity, creativity, and overall well-being among employees. By understanding these elements, organizations can cultivate an environment where individuals thrive, leading to improved performance, higher retention rates, and a stronger sense of community.

Creating a positive workplace culture is essential for the success and sustainability of any business, including those established in India.

Positive workplace culture:

1. Inclusive Environment: India is a diverse country with various languages, cultures, and backgrounds. Embrace this diversity and create an inclusive environment where everyone feels valued and respected regardless of their differences.
2. Clear Communication: Establish open lines of communication where employees feel comfortable expressing their ideas, concerns, and feedback. Encourage transparency and ensure that information flows freely across all levels of the organization.
3. Empowerment and Autonomy: Provide employees with the autonomy to make decisions and take ownership of their work. Empower them to contribute meaningfully to the company's goals and objectives.
4. Work-Life Balance: Recognize the importance of work-life balance and promote policies that support it. Encourage flexible work arrangements, offer wellness programs, and ensure that employees have time to recharge outside of work.
5. Recognition and Appreciation: Regularly recognize and appreciate employees for their hard work and contributions. Celebrate achievements, milestones, and successes as a team.
6. Professional Development: Invest in the professional development of your employees by providing training, mentorship programs, and opportunities for growth. Support them in advancing their skills and knowledge.
7. Fairness and Equity: Ensure fairness and equity in all aspects of the workplace, including hiring, promotions, and compensation. Implement clear policies and procedures to prevent discrimination and bias.

8. Social Responsibility: Demonstrate a commitment to social responsibility by engaging in initiatives that benefit the community and society at large. Encourage employee participation in volunteer activities and charitable causes.

9. Leadership and Role Modeling: Leadership plays a crucial role in shaping workplace culture. Lead by example and embody the values and principles you wish to instill in your organization. Foster a culture of integrity, accountability, and ethical behavior.

10. Continuous Improvement: Cultivate a culture of continuous improvement where employees are encouraged to seek out new ideas, experiment with innovative approaches, and learn from both successes and failures.

By prioritizing these elements, businesses can create a positive workplace culture that fosters employee engagement, satisfaction, and productivity, ultimately contributing to long-term success and growth in the Indian market.

9.14 ROLE OF LEADERSHIP

Leadership plays a crucial role in shaping the culture and atmosphere within any organization. A positive work environment is not merely a luxury; it's a necessity for productivity, employee satisfaction, and overall success. In today's dynamic and competitive landscape, leaders must understand the significant impact their actions and behaviors have on the morale and motivation of their teams.

Effective leadership goes beyond simply overseeing tasks and delegating responsibilities. It involves cultivating an environment where individuals feel valued, respected, and motivated to contribute their best efforts. This requires leaders to possess a combination of interpersonal skills, emotional intelligence, and a deep understanding of organizational dynamics.

Leadership plays a important role in fostering a positive environment, especially in the setting up of a business in India.

1. Vision and Direction: Effective leadership provides a clear vision and direction for the business. In the context of setting up a business in India, leaders need to articulate a vision that aligns with the cultural, social, and economic landscape of the country. This vision serves as a guiding light for employees and stakeholders, instilling a sense of purpose and direction.

2. Cultural Sensitivity: India is a diverse country with various cultural nuances. Leadership that is culturally sensitive can bridge gaps and create an inclusive environment where all employees feel valued and respected. Understanding and respecting cultural differences can enhance teamwork, communication, and collaboration.

3. Motivation and Inspiration: Leaders have the responsibility to motivate and inspire their teams, especially during the challenging phases of setting up a business. In India, where bureaucratic hurdles, regulatory complexities, and infrastructure challenges are prevalent, inspirational leadership can keep morale high and drive individuals and teams to overcome obstacles.

4. Adaptability and Flexibility: The business landscape in India is dynamic and often unpredictable. Effective leaders possess adaptability and flexibility to navigate through changing circumstances. They encourage innovation and experimentation, fostering an environment where employees feel empowered to adapt to evolving market conditions and seize new opportunities.

5. Ethical Standards: Integrity and ethical conduct are essential for building trust and credibility, both internally and externally. Leaders set the tone for ethical behavior within the organization, ensuring compliance with laws and regulations while upholding moral values. This is particularly important in India, where ethical considerations hold significant weight in business dealings.

6. Communication Skills: Clear and transparent communication is vital for building trust and alignment within the organization. Leaders must effectively communicate goals, expectations, and feedback to ensure everyone is on the same page. In a diverse country like India, where language and communication styles vary across regions,

strong communication skills become even more critical.

7. Empowerment and Development: Great leaders empower their teams by delegating authority and fostering a culture of autonomy and accountability. In the context of setting up a business in India, leaders should invest in the development of their employees, providing training and growth opportunities that align with the local context and market demands.

8. Risk Management: Leadership involves making tough decisions and managing risks effectively. In India, where regulatory frameworks and market dynamics can be challenging, leaders need to assess risks diligently and implement strategies to mitigate them. This requires a balance between boldness and prudence, with a focus on long-term sustainability.

9.15 LEGAL ASPECTS OF HUMAN RESOURCE MANAGEMENT

Setting up a business in India involves various legal aspects of human resource management.

IMPORTANT CONSIDERATIONS:

1. Employment Laws: India has numerous laws governing employment, including the Industrial Disputes Act, the Factories Act, the Shops and Establishments Act, and the Minimum Wages Act. These laws cover aspects such as working hours, wages, safety standards, and dispute resolution.

2. Contractual Agreements: It's essential to draft comprehensive employment contracts that comply with Indian laws. These contracts should outline terms of employment, including job roles, responsibilities, compensation, benefits, confidentiality clauses, termination procedures, and non-compete agreements.

3. Equal Opportunity and Anti-discrimination Laws: India has laws prohibiting discrimination based on gender, religion, caste, or disability. Employers must ensure their hiring practices, promotions, and treatment of employees adhere to these laws.

4. Labour Relations and Trade Unions: Employers need to understand the rights of employees to form trade unions and engage in collective bargaining. The Trade Unions Act, 1926, governs the formation and functioning of trade unions.

5. Social Security and Benefits: Compliance with social security obligations such as provident fund, employee state insurance, gratuity, and maternity benefits is mandatory for employers. These laws provide financial protection and benefits to employees in case of contingencies like illness, disability, or retirement.

6. Taxation and Payroll Compliance: Employers must comply with tax regulations related to payroll, including income tax deductions at source (TDS), professional tax, and goods and services tax (GST) on employee benefits.

7. Health and Safety Regulations: The Occupational Safety and Health (OSH) Act and related regulations mandate employers to provide a safe working environment, conduct regular safety audits, and implement measures to prevent workplace accidents and hazards.

8. Data Privacy and Confidentiality: Employers must adhere to data protection laws when handling employee information. The Personal Data Protection Bill, once enacted, will impose stricter regulations on the collection, storage, and processing of personal data.

9. Termination and Redundancy: Indian labour laws govern the procedures for termination of employment, including notice periods, severance pay, and compliance with due process to avoid legal disputes.

10. Compliance Reporting and Record-Keeping: Employers must maintain accurate records and regularly submit reports to regulatory authorities to demonstrate compliance with labour laws.

It's important for businesses to seek legal counsel or consult with HR professionals well-versed in Indian employment laws to ensure compliance and mitigate legal risks when setting up and managing human resources in

India.

Setting up a business in India requires compliance with various employment laws and regulations to ensure a fair and legally compliant work environment.

9.16 EMPLOYMENT LAWS AND REGULATIONS

1. The Shops and Establishments Act: Each state in India has its own version of this act, which governs the working conditions of employees in shops, commercial establishments, and other workplaces. It covers aspects such as working hours, holidays, and conditions of work.

2. Minimum Wages Act: This act sets the minimum wages that must be paid to various categories of workers. Employers are required to pay wages higher than the minimum wages specified by the state government.

3. Employees' Provident Funds and Miscellaneous Provisions Act (EPF): This act mandates the establishment of provident fund for employees and provides for retirement benefits such as pension, insurance, and deposits for housing.

4. Employees' State Insurance Act (ESI): The ESI Act provides for certain benefits to employees in case of sickness, maternity, injury, or death while on the job. Employers and employees contribute to the ESI fund, and the scheme is administered by the Employee State Insurance Corporation (ESIC).

5. Payment of Gratuity Act: This act mandates the payment of gratuity to employees who have completed at least five years of continuous service with an employer. It applies to establishments with ten or more employees.

6. Industrial Disputes Act: This act regulates the resolution of industrial disputes and governs aspects such as layoffs, retrenchment, and closure of establishments. It also provides for the mechanism of dispute resolution through conciliation, arbitration, and adjudication.

7. Maternity Benefit Act: This act provides maternity leave and other maternity benefits to women employees. It mandates a minimum of 26 weeks of maternity leave for pregnant women.

8. Equal Remuneration Act: This act prohibits discrimination in remuneration on the basis of gender and ensures equal pay for equal work.

9. Factories Act: This act regulates the working conditions in factories and covers aspects such as health, safety, welfare, working hours, and leave provisions for workers employed in factories.

10. Contract Labour (Regulation and Abolition) Act: This act regulates the employment of contract labor and provides for their welfare and working conditions. It applies to establishments engaging a specified minimum number of contract workers.

11. Sexual Harassment of Women at Workplace (Prevention, Prohibition, and Redressal) Act: This act requires employers to provide a safe working environment for women and mandates the establishment of Internal Complaints Committees (ICCs) to address complaints of sexual harassment at the workplace.

9.17 Implications of Human Resource Management

Setting up a business in India can have significant implications for human resource management (HRM) due to various factors including cultural differences, legal requirements, talent availability, and labor market dynamics.

1. Cultural Understanding: India is a diverse country with a rich tapestry of cultures, languages, and traditions. Understanding and respecting these cultural nuances is crucial for effective HRM. For instance, hierarchical structures are often respected in Indian workplaces, and maintaining harmony within teams is highly valued. HR practices need to align with these cultural norms to foster a positive work environment.

2. Labor Laws and Regulations: India has a complex regulatory framework governing employment and labor relations. HR managers need to ensure compliance with laws related to employment contracts, minimum wages, working hours, benefits, and workplace safety. Failure to adhere to these regulations can result in legal complications and reputational damage for the business.

3. Talent Acquisition and Retention: India is home to a large and diverse talent pool, including skilled professionals in various industries. However, competition for top talent can be intense, particularly in sectors such as technology, finance, and healthcare. HRM strategies should focus on effective recruitment, onboarding, and retention practices to attract and retain the best employees.

4. Skills Development and Training: Investing in employee training and development is essential for building a skilled workforce and driving business growth. HR managers should design training programs that address the specific needs of employees and align with the company's objectives. Additionally, leveraging government initiatives such as Skill India can help bridge skill gaps and enhance the employability of the workforce.

5. Performance Management: Establishing robust performance management systems is crucial for evaluating employee performance, providing feedback, and identifying areas for improvement. HR managers should implement fair and transparent performance appraisal processes to motivate employees and foster a culture of continuous learning and development.

6. Employee Relations and Engagement: Building strong employee relations and fostering a positive work culture are essential for employee satisfaction and productivity. HR managers should promote open communication, address grievances promptly, and create opportunities for employee engagement and feedback. Initiatives such as employee recognition programs, team-building activities, and employee wellness programs can enhance morale and job satisfaction.

7. Adapting to Remote Work: With the increasing trend towards remote work, especially in the wake of the COVID-19 pandemic, HR managers need to adapt their policies and practices to support remote and hybrid work arrangements. This may involve implementing flexible work policies, providing the necessary technology infrastructure, and ensuring effective communication and collaboration among remote teams.

Setting up a business in India requires careful consideration of various HRM factors to ensure compliance with local regulations, attract and retain top talent, and foster a positive work culture conducive to business success. By understanding the unique challenges and opportunities in the Indian market, HR managers can develop effective strategies to effectively manage human resources and drive organizational growth.

9.18 QUESTION

1. Explain Legal Aspects of Human Resource Management?
2. What are the employment laws and regulations
3. Explain the steps involved in recruitment and hiring process?
4. Explain the strategies for attracting and retaining talent.?
5. Explain employee trainning and development?
6. Explain training programs and opportunities?
7. Write short notes on minimum wages?
8. Explain the role of leadership in fostering a positive environment.

IMPORTANCE OF MARKETING IN BUSINESS

10.1 IMPORTANCE OF MARKETING

Marketing plays a important role in the success of any business, serving as the driving force behind the creation, promotion, and distribution of products or services. It is the strategic process of identifying, anticipating, and satisfying customer needs and wants while achieving organizational objectives. In today's competitive landscape, where consumers are inundated with choices, effective marketing is essential for businesses to differentiate themselves, attract customers, and foster long-term relationships.

Role of Market Research in Business Decision Making

1. Building Brand Awareness. Marketing initiatives help businesses establish and enhance brand awareness. Through targeted messaging and communication channels, companies can increase their visibility among potential customers. Consistent branding efforts create recognition and trust, leading to a competitive advantage in the market.

2. Driving Sales and Revenue: Effective marketing campaigns generate leads, drive conversions, and ultimately boost sales and revenue. By understanding consumer preferences and behavior, businesses can tailor their offerings and promotional strategies to meet market demand, resulting in increased profitability.

3. Market Expansion and Growth: Marketing facilitates market expansion by identifying new opportunities and segments for business growth. Through market research and analysis, companies can identify untapped markets, develop innovative products or services, and expand their customer base domestically and internationally.

4. Building Customer Relationships: Marketing fosters meaningful relationships with customers through personalized experiences and engagement strategies. By listening to customer feedback, addressing concerns, and delivering value-added solutions, businesses can cultivate loyalty and advocacy, leading to repeat purchases and referrals.

5. Competitive Advantage: In a saturated marketplace, effective marketing strategies provide a competitive edge by differentiating products or services from competitors. Whether through product innovation, pricing strategies, or superior customer service, businesses can position themselves as industry leaders and capture market share.

6. Adaptation to Market Dynamics: Marketing enables businesses to adapt to changing market dynamics and consumer preferences. By staying informed about industry trends, competitors' strategies, and emerging technologies, companies can pivot their marketing efforts to stay relevant and capitalize on new opportunities.

7. Financial Performance and Sustainability: Marketing investments contribute to long-term financial performance and sustainability by driving revenue growth and profitability. A well-executed marketing plan aligns with business objectives, maximizes return on investment, and ensures continued success in the marketplace.

Marketing plays an important role in setting up a business in India, Reasons why marketing is important for business establishment:

1. Market Understanding: Marketing helps in understanding the Indian market dynamics, including consumer behavior, preferences, and cultural nuances. This understanding is vital for tailoring products or services to meet the specific needs of Indian consumers.

2. Building Brand Awareness: Effective marketing campaigns help in creating brand awareness among the target audience in India. Building a strong brand presence is essential for gaining credibility and trust, especially in a competitive market like India.

3. Market Penetration: Marketing strategies assist in penetrating the Indian market by identifying target segments and positioning products or services accordingly. This helps in reaching out to potential customers and expanding the customer base.

4. Competitive Advantage: Marketing enables businesses to differentiate themselves from competitors by highlighting unique selling propositions (USPs) and communicating the value proposition to customers effectively. This competitive advantage is important for success in the Indian market.

5. Customer Engagement and Relationship Building: Marketing facilitates engagement with customers through various channels such as social media, email marketing, and advertising. Building strong relationships with customers fosters loyalty and encourages repeat business in the Indian context.

6. Adaptation to Local Trends: Indian market trends and preferences are constantly evolving. Effective marketing strategies enable businesses to adapt to these changes promptly and stay relevant in the market.

7. Regulatory Compliance: Marketing activities need to comply with various regulations and guidelines in India. Understanding these regulations and ensuring compliance is essential for avoiding legal issues and maintaining the reputation of the business.

8. Entry into New Markets: For businesses looking to expand into different regions or states within India, marketing plays a important role in facilitating market entry strategies, including identifying new opportunities and reaching out to local customers effectively.

9. Product Localization: Marketing helps in customizing products or services to suit the preferences and requirements of the Indian market. This may involve adapting product features, pricing strategies, or promotional tactics to resonate with Indian consumers.

10. Long-Term Sustainability: Sustainable business growth in India requires continuous marketing efforts to stay competitive, relevant, and connected with customers. Marketing contributes to the long-term sustainability and success of businesses operating in the Indian market.

10.2 ROLE OF MARKETING IN CREATING AWARENESS AND DRIVING SALES.

Marketing plays an important role in creating awareness and driving sales for businesses in India, as it does in any other part of the world.

Objectives:

1. Creating Awareness: In a diverse and competitive market like India, creating awareness about your brand, products, or services is essential. Marketing strategies such as advertising, public relations, social media campaigns, and content marketing help in reaching out to the target audience and making them aware of what your business offers. This is particularly important for new businesses entering the market, as they need to establish their presence and differentiate themselves from established competitors.

2. Understanding the Market: Before entering the Indian market, it's important to understand the local nuances, cultural sensitivities, and consumer preferences. Market research and analysis are integral parts of marketing that help businesses gain insights into the needs and behaviors of the target audience. By understanding the market dynamics, businesses can tailor their marketing strategies to resonate with the Indian consumers, thus increasing the chances of success.

3. Building Brand Equity: Marketing plays a significant role in building and strengthening the brand equity of a business. Through consistent messaging, branding initiatives, and delivering quality products or services, businesses can build trust and credibility among Indian consumers. A strong brand presence not only attracts customers but also fosters loyalty, leading to repeat purchases and positive word-of-mouth recommendations.

4. Driving Sales: Ultimately, the primary goal of marketing is to drive sales and generate revenue for the business. By effectively communicating the value proposition and benefits of their offerings, businesses can influence purchase decisions and stimulate demand. Marketing tactics such as promotions, discounts, and targeted advertising campaigns can help in converting leads into customers and boosting sales in the Indian market.

5. Adapting to Digital Trends: With the increasing penetration of smartphones and internet connectivity, digital marketing has become indispensable for businesses in India. Leveraging platforms such as social media, search engines, and e-commerce websites, businesses can reach a wider audience, engage with potential customers, and drive online sales. Investing in digital marketing capabilities is important for staying competitive and maximizing growth opportunities in the rapidly evolving Indian market.

10.3 MARKETING MIX AND ITS COMPONENTS

Setting up a business in India requires a comprehensive understanding of the marketing mix and its components to effectively penetrate the market. The marketing mix, often referred to as the 4Ps (Product, Price, Place, Promotion), provides a framework for businesses to tailor their strategies and offerings to meet the needs of their target audience.

1. Product:

1. Understanding the Indian market's preferences, culture, and needs is important for developing products that resonate with consumers.
2. Adaptation and localization of products may be necessary to suit the unique tastes and requirements of Indian consumers.
3. Emphasize quality, affordability, and functionality to cater to the diverse socioeconomic segments prevalent in the Indian market.

2. Price:

1. Pricing strategies must consider the purchasing power of different consumer segments in India.
2. Employing competitive pricing while maintaining profitability is essential in a price-sensitive market like India.
3. Offering discounts, promotions, and installment payment options can appeal to Indian consumers accustomed to seeking value for money.

3. Place:

1. Distribution channels play a significant role in reaching consumers across India's vast geographic expanse.
2. Establishing a robust distribution network, including partnerships with local distributors and retailers, is essential for widespread availability.
3. E-commerce platforms have gained significant traction in India, presenting an opportunity for businesses to expand their reach beyond traditional brick-and-mortar stores.

4. Promotion:

1. Cultural sensitivity and localization are paramount when developing promotional campaigns in India.
2. Leveraging digital marketing channels such as social media, search engine optimization (SEO), and influencer marketing can effectively target India's tech-savvy population.
3. Traditional advertising mediums like television, radio, and print media still hold sway in reaching certain demographics in India and should not be overlooked.

Additionally, for businesses setting up in India, it's important to consider regulatory compliance, market research, and building strong partnerships with local stakeholders. Understanding the nuances of the Indian market, including consumer behavior, cultural diversity, and regional variations, will be instrumental in devising a successful marketing mix tailored to the Indian context. Flexibility, adaptability, and a customer-centric approach are key to navigating the dynamic landscape of business in India.

10.4 DEVELOPING A MARKETING STRATEGY

Developing a marketing strategy for setting up a business requires a comprehensive understanding of the diverse market landscape, cultural nuances, and regulatory frameworks prevalent in the country. India, with its vast population and rapidly evolving economy, offers immense opportunities for businesses across various sectors. However, navigating through its dynamic market requires a well-thought-out marketing strategy tailored to the unique characteristics of the Indian market.

The first step in crafting a successful marketing strategy is conducting thorough market research. This involves analyzing market trends, consumer behavior, competitive landscape, and potential demand for the product or service being offered. Understanding the needs and preferences of the Indian consumer base is important for identifying target segments and positioning the business effectively.

Localization is the key in India's diverse market environment. The country is home to a multitude of languages, cultures, and socio-economic backgrounds. Adapting marketing messages, branding, and product offerings to resonate with local preferences can significantly enhance the relevance and appeal of the business to Indian consumers. Moreover, establishing strong relationships with local suppliers, distributors, and partners can facilitate smoother market entry and expansion.

Navigating regulatory requirements is essential for ensuring compliance and mitigating operational risks. India has a complex regulatory environment governing various aspects of business operations, including taxation, intellectual property rights, and foreign investment norms. Collaborating with legal experts and consultants familiar with Indian laws can help in navigating these regulatory hurdles and ensuring legal compliance.

Digital marketing plays an important role in reaching and engaging with Indian consumers, given the country's growing internet penetration and smartphone adoption. Leveraging social media platforms, search engine optimization (SEO), and targeted online advertising can help in building brand awareness, driving website traffic, and generating leads. Additionally, incorporating localized content and leveraging regional influencers can further enhance the effectiveness of digital marketing efforts.

Building a strong brand presence is essential for long-term success in the Indian market. Investing in brand building activities such as advertising campaigns, sponsorships, and experiential marketing can help in creating brand recall and loyalty among Indian consumers. Moreover, delivering high-quality products or services and providing excellent customer service are important for building trust and credibility in the market.

Continuous monitoring and adaptation are essential components of a successful marketing strategy in India. The market dynamics and consumer preferences are constantly evolving, necessitating regular assessment and adjustment of marketing tactics and strategies. By staying agile and responsive to market changes, businesses can maximize their chances of success and capitalize on the vast opportunities offered by the Indian market.

10.5 STEPS IN DEVELOPING A COMPREHENSIVE MARKETING STRATEGY.

Developing a comprehensive marketing strategy for setting up a business in India involves several steps.

1. Market Research and Analysis:

1. Identify the target market segments in India.
2. Understand consumer preferences, behaviors, and buying patterns.
3. Analyze competitors operating in the Indian market.
4. Assess market trends, opportunities, and potential challenges.

2. Define Objectives:

1. Clearly define the goals and objectives of your marketing strategy.
2. Ensure that objectives are specific, measurable, achievable, relevant, and time-bound (SMART).

3. Segmentation, Targeting, and Positioning (STP):

1. Segment the Indian market based on factors such as demographics, psychographics, geography, and behavior.
2. Select target segments that align with your business objectives and capabilities.
3. Develop a unique value proposition and positioning strategy to differentiate your brand in the Indian market.

4. Product or Service Offering:

1. Adapt your product or service offerings to meet the needs and preferences of Indian consumers.
2. Consider localization, customization, or product modifications if necessary.
3. Ensure compliance with local regulations and standards.

5. Marketing Mix (4Ps):

1. Product: Determine the features, packaging, branding, and quality of your offering.

2. Price: Set competitive pricing strategies considering local market dynamics, purchasing power, and pricing sensitivity.
3. Place: Determine distribution channels, retail partnerships, and logistics for reaching customers effectively.
4. Promotion: Develop integrated marketing communication strategies including advertising, public relations, sales promotions, digital marketing, and social media.

6. Budget Allocation:

1. Allocate resources for marketing activities based on the objectives, market potential, and expected returns.
2. Consider costs associated with market entry, advertising, promotion, sales efforts, and ongoing marketing operations.

7. Implementation Plan:

1. Develop a detailed timeline and action plan for executing marketing initiatives.
2. Assign responsibilities to team members or external agencies.
3. Monitor progress and adjust strategies as needed.

8. Evaluation and Control:

1. Establish metrics and key performance indicators (KPIs) to measure the effectiveness of marketing efforts.
2. Regularly track and analyze marketing performance against objectives.
3. Implement corrective actions or optimizations based on performance insights.

9. Legal and Regulatory Compliance:

1. Ensure compliance with Indian laws and regulations related to marketing, advertising, labeling, and consumer protection.
2. Obtain necessary licenses or permits for conducting marketing activities.

10. Cultural Sensitivity and Adaptation:

1. Understand cultural nuances and sensitivities in India to ensure that marketing messages resonate with the target audience.
2. Avoid cultural misinterpretations or offensive content that could damage brand reputation.

By following these steps, one can develop a comprehensive marketing strategy tailored to the Indian market, setting up the business for success.

10.6 TARGET AUDIENCE IDENTIFICATION AND SEGMENTATION.

Identifying and segmenting the target audience is an important step in setting up a business in India, or any other market for that matter. India is a diverse country with a vast population, varied cultures, languages, and socioeconomic backgrounds.

1. Market Research: Conduct thorough market research to understand the Indian market landscape. This should include demographic, geographic, psychographic, and behavioral factors. Understand the needs, preferences, and purchasing behaviors of different consumer segments.

2. Demographic Segmentation: Segment the market based on demographic factors such as age, gender, income, education, occupation, family size, and marital status. For example, a company selling luxury goods might target affluent consumers in metropolitan cities like Mumbai and Delhi.

3. Geographic Segmentation: Consider the geographical diversity of India and segment the market based on location. India can be segmented into regions such as North, South, East, and West, each with its own cultural nuances and consumer preferences.

4. Psychographic Segmentation: Understand the lifestyle, values, beliefs, interests, and attitudes of the target audience. This can help tailor marketing messages and product offerings to resonate with specific consumer segments. For instance, a health and wellness brand might target health-conscious urban professionals who prioritize fitness and well-being.

5. Behavioral Segmentation: Analyze consumer behavior and segment the market based on usage patterns, brand loyalty, purchase frequency, and benefits sought. This can help identify loyal customers, as well as potential opportunities for product diversification or market expansion.

6. Cultural Sensitivity: India is a culturally rich and diverse country with multiple languages, religions, and traditions. It's essential to understand and respect the cultural nuances of different regions while crafting marketing strategies and communication messages.

7. Digital Literacy and Accessibility: With the increasing penetration of smartphones and internet connectivity, digital marketing channels offer significant opportunities to reach target audiences in India. Consider factors such as internet usage patterns, social media preferences, and digital literacy levels while formulating your marketing strategy.

8. Adaptability: Be prepared to adapt your products, services, and marketing strategies based on the evolving needs and preferences of the Indian market. Consumer trends and preferences may vary over time, so staying agile and responsive is the key to maintaining relevance and competitiveness.

10.7 DIGITAL MARKETING AND ONLINE PRESENCE

Setting up a business requires a robust digital marketing strategy and a strong online presence due to the country's rapidly growing digital landscape.

1. Website Development: A professional and user-friendly website is essential for any business. Ensure your website is mobile-responsive, as a significant portion of internet users in India access the web through mobile devices.

2. Search Engine Optimization (SEO): Implement SEO techniques to improve your website's visibility in search engine results. This includes optimizing keywords relevant to your business, creating quality content, and building backlinks.

3. Social Media Marketing: India has a massive user base on social media platforms like Facebook, Instagram, Twitter, and LinkedIn. Create engaging content tailored to each platform to connect with your target audience and increase brand awareness.

4. Content Marketing: Content marketing plays a crucial role in building brand authority and attracting potential customers. Consider creating blogs, videos, infographics, and other types of content relevant to your industry to educate and engage your audience.

5. Email Marketing: Build an email list and leverage email marketing campaigns to nurture leads and drive conversions. Personalize your emails based on user behavior and interests to increase engagement.

6. Online Advertising: Utilize online advertising platforms like Google Ads, Facebook Ads, and LinkedIn Ads to reach your target audience effectively. Invest in pay-per-click (PPC) campaigns to drive traffic to your website and generate leads.

7. Local SEO: If your business caters to a specific geographical area, focus on local SEO strategies to improve your visibility in local search results. This includes optimizing your Google My Business listing, obtaining local

citations, and encouraging customer reviews.

8. E-commerce Platforms: If you're selling products online, consider leveraging popular e-commerce platforms like Amazon, Flipkart, and Shopify to reach a broader audience and streamline the selling process.
9. Mobile Apps: Developing a mobile app can provide a more personalized and convenient experience for your customers. Ensure your app is well-designed, intuitive, and offers valuable features to keep users engaged.
10. Analytics and Measurement: Regularly monitor and analyze your digital marketing efforts using tools like Google Analytics. Track key metrics such as website traffic, conversion rates, and social media engagement to assess the effectiveness of your strategies and make necessary adjustments.

By implementing these digital marketing strategies and establishing a strong online presence, one can effectively promote their business in India and drive growth in a competitive market.

10.8 IMPORTANCE OF DIGITAL MARKETING

Digital marketing plays an important role in the modern business landscape due to its ability to reach a vast audience, engage customers, and drive conversions effectively.

REASONS WHY DIGITAL MARKETING IS IMPORTANT:

1. Wide Reach: With the proliferation of the internet and the increasing usage of smartphones and other digital devices, digital marketing enables businesses to reach a global audience regardless of geographical boundaries. This level of reach is unparalleled compared to traditional marketing methods.
2. Targeted Advertising: Digital marketing allows businesses to target specific demographics, interests, behaviors, and even location, ensuring that marketing efforts are directed towards the most relevant audience. This targeted approach increases the chances of engaging potential customers and driving conversions.
3. Cost-Effective: Digital marketing often offers a higher return on investment (ROI) compared to traditional marketing channels. With tools like pay-per-click (PPC) advertising, businesses can allocate their budget efficiently and track the performance of their campaigns in real-time, allowing for better optimization and cost-effectiveness.
4. Data Analytics and Insights: One of the significant advantages of digital marketing is the ability to track and analyze the performance of marketing campaigns in real-time. Businesses can gather valuable insights into customer behavior, preferences, and trends, which can inform future marketing strategies and improve overall effectiveness.
5. Increased Engagement: Through various digital channels such as social media, email, and content marketing, businesses can actively engage with their audience, build relationships, and foster brand loyalty. Interactive content formats like quizzes, polls, and contests further enhance engagement levels.
6. Personalization: Digital marketing enables businesses to personalize their messaging and content based on individual customer preferences and behavior. Personalized marketing efforts are more likely to resonate with customers and drive meaningful interactions, leading to higher conversion rates.
7. Brand Visibility and Authority: Consistent and strategic digital marketing efforts can enhance a brand's visibility and establish it as an authority in its industry. Through content marketing, social media presence, and search engine optimization (SEO), businesses can position themselves as thought leaders and influencers within their niche.
8. Adaptability and Agility: In the rapidly evolving digital landscape, businesses need to be agile and adaptable to changes in consumer behavior, market trends, and technology. Digital marketing allows for quick adjustments to strategies and tactics, ensuring that businesses stay relevant and competitive

10.9 STRATEGIES FOR BUILDING AND MANAGING ONLINE PRESENCE

Building and managing an online presence for a business requires a well-thought-out strategy
IMPORTANT STEPS AND STRATEGIES

1. Define Your Goals: Start by defining what you want to achieve with your online presence. Whether it's increasing brand awareness, driving sales, or providing customer support, having clear goals will guide your strategy.
2. Identify Your Target Audience: Understand your target audience's demographics, preferences, and online behavior. This will help tailor your content and marketing efforts to effectively reach and engage them.
3. Create a Professional Website: Invest in creating a professional, user-friendly website that reflects your brand identity and provides a seamless browsing experience. Make sure your website is mobile-responsive, as mobile usage is high in India.
4. Search Engine Optimization (SEO): Optimize your website for search engines to improve its visibility in search results. This includes keyword research, optimizing meta tags and descriptions, creating quality content, and building backlinks.
5. Content Marketing: Develop a content strategy to provide value to your audience through blogs, articles, videos, infographics, etc. Create content that addresses your audience's pain points, interests, and questions.
6. Social Media Marketing: Leverage popular social media platforms like Facebook, Instagram, Twitter, and LinkedIn to connect with your audience, build relationships, and promote your products or services. Tailor your content to each platform and engage with your followers regularly.
7. Local SEO and Listings: Ensure your business is listed accurately on local directories, Google My Business, and other online listings. This helps improve your visibility in local searches, especially important for brick-and-mortar businesses targeting local customers.
8. Online Advertising: Consider using online advertising platforms like Google Ads, Facebook Ads, and LinkedIn Ads to reach your target audience and drive traffic to your website or landing pages. Monitor and optimize your campaigns for better ROI.
9. Email Marketing: Build an email list of leads and customers and send them targeted email campaigns to nurture relationships, promote new products or offers, and drive sales. Personalize your emails and segment your audience for better results.
10. Monitor and Analyze Performance: Use analytics tools like Google Analytics, social media insights, and email marketing metrics to track the performance of your online efforts. Analyze data regularly to identify what's working well and areas for improvement.
11. Adapt and Evolve: The digital landscape is constantly evolving, so be prepared to adapt your strategies accordingly. Stay updated with the latest trends, technologies, and consumer behaviors to remain competitive in the online space.

10.10 BRAND BUILDING AND CUSTOMER RELATIONSHIP MANAGEMENT (CRM)

Brand building and customer relationship management (CRM) are paramount aspects for establishing a successful business in India, a diverse and rapidly growing market. In this dynamic landscape, where competition is fierce and consumer preferences constantly evolve, creating a strong brand identity and nurturing lasting relationships with customers are key strategies for sustainable growth.

Brand building begins with defining a clear and compelling brand proposition that resonates with the target audience. This involves understanding the unique needs, values, and aspirations of Indian consumers across different demographics, regions, and socio-economic segments. By conducting thorough market research and leveraging cultural insights, businesses can craft brand messaging and positioning that effectively communicates their value proposition and sets them apart from competitors.

In India, where brand loyalty is often influenced by factors such as tradition, reputation, and emotional connections, building trust and credibility are crucial. Consistency in branding across various touchpoints, including advertising, packaging, and customer interactions, helps reinforce brand identity and foster trust among consumers. Additionally, investing in quality products or services, delivering exceptional customer experiences, and upholding ethical business practices further enhance brand reputation and loyalty.

Effective CRM complements brand building by nurturing long-term relationships with customers and maximizing their lifetime value. In a diverse market like India, where personal relationships and word-of-mouth referrals hold significant influence, personalized communication and attentive customer service are essential. Implementing CRM systems and technologies to capture customer data, analyze buying patterns, and tailor marketing efforts enables businesses to anticipate and meet the unique needs of individual customers.

Furthermore, actively engaging with customers through multiple channels, including social media, email marketing, and loyalty programs, facilitates ongoing dialogue and strengthens brand-customer relationships. By soliciting feedback, addressing concerns promptly, and rewarding customer loyalty, businesses can demonstrate their commitment to customer satisfaction and foster a loyal customer base.

Brand building and CRM are integral to the success of any business venture in India. By investing in building a strong brand identity and cultivating meaningful relationships with customers, businesses can establish a competitive edge, drive growth, and thrive in the dynamic Indian market landscape.

10.11 SIGNIFICANCE OF BRAND BUILDING.

Brand building holds immense significance for businesses looking to establish themselves in India's diverse and competitive market landscape. In a country where myriad options vie for consumer attention, crafting a distinct brand identity is paramount for long-term success and sustainability.

First and foremost, effective brand building fosters trust and credibility among consumers. In a market where brand loyalty is increasingly valued, establishing a reputable brand image becomes instrumental in attracting and retaining customers. By consistently delivering quality products or services, a brand can earn the trust of consumers, leading to repeat purchases and positive word-of-mouth recommendations.

Moreover, in a culturally rich and diverse nation like India, brands need to navigate a plethora of languages, customs, and traditions. Building a strong brand identity that resonates with the local populace is crucial for gaining acceptance and relevance in various regions across the country. Tailoring marketing strategies and messaging to suit the cultural sensitivities and preferences of different demographics can significantly enhance brand appeal and penetration.

Furthermore, brand building facilitates differentiation in a crowded marketplace. With numerous competitors vying for market share, establishing a unique value proposition sets a brand apart and enables it to carve out its niche. Whether through product innovation, superior customer service, or compelling storytelling, brands that stand out are more likely to capture consumer attention and command premium pricing

Additionally, a well-established brand serves as a powerful asset in attracting investment and forging strategic partnerships. Investors and collaborators are often drawn to brands with a strong market presence and growth potential, viewing them as safer bets for long-term returns. A robust brand image can thus open doors to funding opportunities, joint ventures, and alliances that fuel business expansion and innovation.

Furthermore, in the digital age, brand building extends beyond traditional advertising channels to encompass online platforms and social media. Leveraging digital marketing tools and technologies allows brands to reach a wider audience, engage with consumers in real-time, and gather valuable insights for refining their strategies. Building a strong online presence not only enhances brand visibility but also enables brands to foster direct relationships with customers, driving loyalty and advocacy.

10.12 IMPORTANCE OF CUSTOMER RELATIONSHIP MANAGEMENT.

Customer Relationship Management (CRM) holds significant importance for setting up a business in India, just as it does in any other part of the world. In the Indian business landscape, where competition is fierce and customer expectations are continually evolving, effective CRM practices can be instrumental for success.

Cultural Diversity: India is a country known for its cultural diversity, with varying languages, traditions, and consumer behaviors across different regions. Implementing CRM allows businesses to tailor their approach to each demographic, ensuring cultural sensitivity and relevance in their interactions.

2. Building Trust and Loyalty: Trust plays a crucial role in Indian business relationships. By maintaining a comprehensive CRM system, businesses can track customer interactions, preferences, and feedback. This enables them to provide personalized services, address grievances promptly, and foster long-term trust and loyalty among Indian consumers.

3. Understanding Customer Needs: The Indian market is vast and dynamic, with diverse consumer needs and preferences. CRM tools help businesses analyze customer data, identify patterns, and anticipate market trends. This understanding enables companies to tailor their products or services to meet the specific demands of Indian consumers, thus gaining a competitive edge.

4. Enhancing Customer Satisfaction: In a rapidly evolving market like India, customer satisfaction is paramount. CRM facilitates efficient communication and resolution of customer queries, ensuring a seamless and satisfactory experience. Satisfied customers are more likely to become brand advocates and contribute to positive word-of-mouth publicity, essential for business growth in India.

5. Adapting to Regulatory Requirements: India has unique regulatory requirements and compliance standards that businesses must adhere to. A robust CRM system can help in managing customer data securely, ensuring compliance with data protection laws such as the Personal Data Protection Bill. This minimizes the risk of legal issues and strengthens the company's reputation in the Indian market.

6. Driving Sales and Revenue: By maintaining a centralized database of customer information and purchase history, CRM enables businesses to implement targeted marketing campaigns and upselling strategies. This, in turn, boosts sales and revenue generation opportunities in the Indian market.

7. Competitive Advantage: In a competitive business environment like India, CRM can serve as a strategic tool for differentiation. Companies that prioritize customer relationships and invest in CRM technologies stand out by delivering superior customer experiences. This not only helps in acquiring new customers but also in retaining existing ones, thereby establishing a competitive advantage in the Indian market.

10.13 QUESTIONS:

1. Explain the importance of marketing in business?
2. What is marketing mix and its components?
3. Explain the steps in developing a comprehensive marketing strategy.
4. Explain Digital Marketing and Online Presence?
5. Write short notes on importance of digital marketing?
6. Explain Brand Building and Customer Relationship Management?
7. Explain the importance of customer relationship management?

CHAPTER ELEVEN

ROLE OF TECHNOLOGY IN GROWTH

11.1 ROLE OF TECHNOLOGY

The role of technology in fostering business growth is paramount, especially in the context of setting up a business in India, a country with a burgeoning entrepreneurial landscape and a rapidly evolving digital infrastructure. In recent years, technology has emerged as a catalyst for innovation, efficiency, and scalability, offering unprecedented opportunities for both startups and established enterprises to thrive in the dynamic Indian market.

Role of Technology in Growth

One of the key ways technology fuels business growth in India is through enhanced connectivity and accessibility. With the widespread adoption of smartphones and the proliferation of high-speed internet connectivity, businesses can reach and engage with customers across the vast expanse of the country, transcending geographical barriers and tapping into previously untapped markets. Digital platforms, social media channels, and e-commerce marketplaces provide avenues for businesses to showcase their products or services, interact with customers in real-time, and facilitate seamless transactions, thereby expanding their reach and driving sales growth.

Moreover, technology enables businesses to streamline operations and improve efficiency through automation, data analytics, and cloud-based solutions. Whether it's automating routine tasks, optimizing supply chain management, or leveraging data insights for informed decision-making, technology empowers businesses to operate more efficiently, reduce costs, and enhance productivity. This is particularly important for startups and small businesses in India, where resource constraints often pose significant challenges. By leveraging technology, these businesses can level the playing field, compete more effectively, and accelerate their growth trajectory.

Technology plays an important role in fostering innovation and driving competitive advantage. India's vibrant startup ecosystem is fueled by technological innovation across diverse sectors, ranging from fintech and healthcare to e-commerce and agritech. Emerging technologies such as artificial intelligence, machine learning, blockchain, and the Internet of Things (IoT) are revolutionizing traditional business models, enabling startups to disrupt industries, introduce novel solutions, and capture market opportunities. By embracing innovation and staying abreast of technological trends, businesses can differentiate themselves, stay ahead of the curve, and carve out a niche in India's dynamic business landscape.

Furthermore, technology facilitates collaboration and networking, enabling businesses to forge strategic partnerships, access mentorship and expertise, and tap into funding opportunities. Platforms such as coworking spaces, incubators, accelerators, and online communities provide avenues for entrepreneurs to connect, collaborate, and exchange ideas, fostering a culture of innovation and entrepreneurship in India.

11.2 TRANSFORMATIVE IMPACT OF TECHNOLOGY ON BUSINESSES.

The transformative impact of technology on businesses, particularly in the context of setting up a business in India, is profound and multifaceted. India, as one of the fastest-growing economies globally, offers a fertile ground for businesses, both domestic and foreign, to thrive.

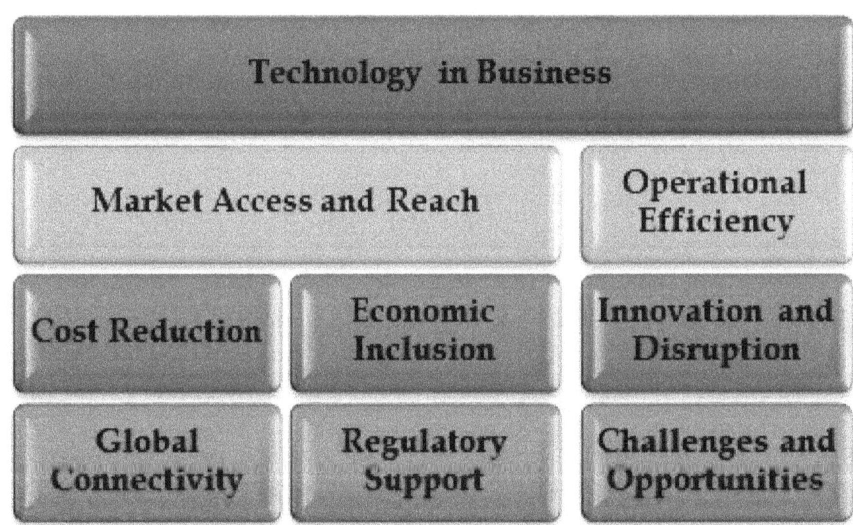

Impacts of Technology in Business

Here's how technology is revolutionizing the business landscape in India:

a. Market Access and Reach: Technology has significantly lowered the barriers to entry for businesses in India. E-commerce platforms, social media, and digital marketing tools allow even small businesses to reach a wide audience across the country, tapping into both urban and rural markets.

a. Operational Efficiency: Automation, AI, and data analytics are enhancing operational efficiency for businesses. This is particularly beneficial in a country like India, where manual processes have historically been prevalent. Implementing technology-driven systems streamlines processes, reduces errors, and improves overall productivity.

c. Cost Reduction: Cloud computing and software-as-a-service (SaaS) solutions enable businesses to access advanced technology without heavy upfront investments. This is especially advantageous for startups and small enterprises, allowing them to leverage powerful tools at a fraction of the cost compared to traditional infrastructure setups.

d. Economic Inclusion: Technology has the potential to drive economic inclusion by providing opportunities to segments of the population previously excluded from the formal economy. Digital payment systems, for example, are empowering small businesses and individuals in rural areas to participate in economic activities and access financial services.

e. Innovation and Disruption: The Indian startup ecosystem is witnessing a surge in innovation across various sectors, fueled by technology. From fintech and edtech to agritech and healthcare, startups are leveraging cutting-edge technology to disrupt traditional industries and address pressing societal challenges.

f. Global Connectivity: Technology enables Indian businesses to connect with global markets seamlessly. E-commerce platforms facilitate cross-border trade, while digital communication tools make it easier to collaborate with international partners and customers. This global connectivity opens up new growth opportunities for businesses of all sizes.

g. Regulatory Support: The Indian government has been actively promoting digitalization and technology adoption through initiatives such as Digital India and Startup India. Regulatory frameworks are evolving to support innovation and entrepreneurship, providing incentives and support mechanisms for technology-driven businesses.

h. Challenges and Opportunities: While technology offers immense opportunities, businesses in India also face challenges such as digital infrastructure gaps, cybersecurity threats, and skill shortages. However, these challenges also present opportunities for businesses to innovate and differentiate themselves by addressing important needs in the market.

Technology is reshaping the business landscape in India, offering unprecedented opportunities for growth, innovation, and economic empowerment. By embracing technology and leveraging its transformative potential, businesses can position themselves for success in the dynamic Indian market.

11.3 EXAMPLES OF TECHNOLOGY-DRIVEN SUCCESS STORIES IN SETTING UP BUSINESSES:

1. Flipkart:

Started as an online bookstore, Flipkart became one of India's largest e-commerce platforms offering a wide range of products.

2. Paytm:

Initially a mobile recharge platform, Paytm diversified its services into digital payments, e-commerce, banking, and financial services.

3. Ola Cabs:

Leveraging technology to connect riders with drivers, Ola disrupted the traditional taxi industry in India.

4. Zomato:

Restaurants registry and food delivery platform that revolutionized the process of ordering food through online.

5. BYJU'S:

An online learning platform that offers personalized educational content through engaging video lessons and interactive quizzes.

6. OYO Rooms: Utilizing technology to streamline hotel bookings and provide standardized accommodation options across India.
7. Swiggy:

Similar to Zomato, Swiggy is a food delivery platform that utilizes technology to connect customers with local restaurants.

8. InMobi:

A global mobile advertising platform, that provides innovative solutions for advertisers and publishers.

9. RedBus:

An online bus ticketing platform that simplifies the process of booking bus tickets across India.

10. Freshworks:

Software-as-a-service (SaaS) company, that offers customer engagement software to business worldwide.

11. Dream11:

A fantasy sports platform that leverages technology to engage sports enthusiasts and provide them with a unique gaming experience.

12. Policybazaar:

An online platform that helps users compares and purchases insurance policies from various providers.

13. BigBasket:

India's largest online grocery platform, that delivers fresh produce and household essentials to customers' doorsteps.

14. Cure.fit:

Health and fitness platform, that offers digital fitness classes, personalized nutrition plans and health consultations.

15. Udaan:

B2B e-commerce platform connects manufacturers, wholesalers, traders and retailers through its online marketplace.

16. Razorpay:

Payment gateway and financial company operates with technology that provides businesses with easy-to-integrate payment solutions.

17. Meesho:

A socio- commerce platform, that enables individuals to start their online businesses by selling products through social media channels.

18. Unacademy:

An online education platform, that offers live classes, interactive sessions and test preparation modules for various competitive exams.

These success stories demonstrate how technology has played a crucial role in transforming various sectors and driving business growth in India.

11.4 E-COMMERCE AND DIGITAL TRANSFORMATION

In recent years, India has witnessed a remarkable surge in the adoption of e-commerce and digital transformation, reshaping the landscape of how businesses are established and operated in the country. This paradigm shift has been driven by technological advancements, changing consumer behaviors, and supportive government policies aimed at fostering a condusive environment for digital entrepreneurship.

E-commerce, characterized by the buying and selling of goods and services online, has emerged as a game-changer for businesses looking to reach a wider audience and streamline their operations. With the proliferation of smartphones and affordable internet connectivity, millions of Indians now have access to online shopping platforms, creating a vast market waiting to be tapped. This presents a lucrative opportunity for entrepreneurs to set up businesses with minimal physical infrastructure and leverage digital channels to market their products or services.

Furthermore, the digital transformation wave sweeping across India has revolutionized various aspects of business operations, from marketing and sales to customer service and supply chain management. By embracing digital tools and technologies such as cloud computing, data analytics, artificial intelligence, and automation, businesses can enhance efficiency, agility, and innovation, thereby gaining a competitive edge in the market.

One of the key drivers behind the rapid growth of e-commerce and digital transformation in India is the government's initiatives to promote digitalization and entrepreneurship. Programs like Digital India and Startup India have been instrumental in creating an ecosystem condusive to the growth of online businesses, offering incentives, subsidies, and regulatory support to startups and small enterprises. Additionally, the implementation of Goods and Services Tax (GST) has streamlined the taxation system, making it easier for businesses to operate across state borders and facilitating seamless e-commerce transactions.

However, while the opportunities presented by e-commerce and digital transformation are immense, businesses in India also face challenges such as cybersecurity threats, digital literacy gaps, infrastructure constraints, and regulatory complexities. Overcoming these hurdles requires concerted efforts from all stakeholders – government, industry bodies, educational institutions, and technology providers – to foster a culture of innovation, collaboration, and continuous learning.

The convergence of e-commerce and digital transformation is reshaping the business landscape in India, offering unprecedented opportunities for entrepreneurs to establish and grow their ventures in the digital realm. By harnessing the power of technology, embracing innovation, and adapting to evolving consumer preferences, businesses can thrive in the dynamic and competitive marketplace of the digital age.

11.5 ROLE OF E-COMMERCE IN BUSINESS.

E-commerce, or electronic commerce, refers to the buying and selling of goods and services over the internet. It has become a crucial component of modern business operations, offering numerous benefits and playing various roles in facilitating commercial activities.

1. Global Reach: E-commerce allows businesses to reach customers worldwide, breaking down geographical barriers. This expanded reach opens up new markets and opportunities for growth that would be difficult to access through traditional brick-and-mortar stores alone.

2. 24/7 Availability: Unlike physical stores with set operating hours, e-commerce platforms are accessible 24/7, enabling customers to shop at their convenience. This flexibility caters to different time zones and preferences, accommodating a diverse customer base and increasing sales potential.

3. Cost Efficiency: E-commerce often requires lower operational costs compared to traditional retail setups. Businesses can save on expenses such as rent, utilities, and staffing. Additionally, online marketing and advertising campaigns tend to be more cost-effective than traditional methods like print or television ads.

4. Enhanced Customer Experience: E-commerce platforms provide a streamlined shopping experience, allowing customers to browse products, compare prices, read reviews, and make purchases with ease. Personalization features, such as product recommendations based on past purchases, further enhance the customer experience and increase satisfaction.

5. Data-driven Insights: E-commerce platforms generate vast amounts of data, including customer demographics, purchasing behavior, and preferences. By analyzing this data, businesses can gain valuable insights into market trends, customer needs, and areas for improvement. These insights inform strategic decision-making and help optimize marketing strategies, product offerings, and overall business operations.

6. Scalability: E-commerce offers scalability, allowing businesses to easily expand their operations as demand grows. Whether it's adding new products, entering new markets, or accommodating increased website traffic, e-commerce platforms can scale to meet evolving business needs without significant infrastructure investments.

7. Inventory Management: E-commerce platforms facilitate efficient inventory management through real-time tracking and automated systems. This helps businesses minimize stockouts, reduce excess inventory, and optimize supply chain operations, ultimately improving overall efficiency and profitability.

8. Seamless Integration: E-commerce can be seamlessly integrated with other business systems, such as customer relationship management (CRM), inventory management, and accounting software. This integration streamlines processes, eliminates manual data entry errors, and enhances overall operational efficiency.

Overall, e-commerce plays an important role in modern business by enabling global reach, enhancing customer experiences, driving cost efficiencies, providing valuable insights, and facilitating scalability and integration. As technology continues to advance, e-commerce is expected to further evolve and reshape the landscape of commerce.

11.6 PROCESS OF DIGITAL TRANSFORMATION.

Digital transformation in the context of setting up a business involves leveraging digital technologies to streamline operations, enhance customer experiences, and drive growth.

STEP-BY-STEP GUIDE TO THE PROCESS OF TRANSFORMATION:

1. Assessment of Current State: Understand the current state of your business processes, technology infrastructure, and digital capabilities. Identify areas that need improvement or digitization.
2. Define Goals and Objectives: Determine what you want to achieve through digital transformation. This could include improving efficiency, reducing costs, reaching new markets, or enhancing customer engagement.
3. Develop a Digital Strategy: Create a comprehensive digital strategy that aligns with your business goals. This may involve adopting cloud computing, implementing data analytics, enhancing cybersecurity measures, or leveraging emerging technologies like AI and IoT.
4. Invest in Infrastructure: Upgrade your technology infrastructure to support digital initiatives. This may include investing in high-speed internet connectivity, cloud services, software applications, and hardware devices.
5. Data Management: Develop a robust data management strategy to collect, store, and analyze data effectively. Ensure compliance with data protection regulations such as the General Data Protection Regulation (GDPR) and India's Personal Data Protection Bill.
6. Customer Experience Enhancement: Focus on improving customer experiences through digital channels. This could involve developing a user-friendly website, implementing e-commerce capabilities, or launching mobile apps.
7. Employee Training and Upskilling: Provide training and upskilling opportunities to your employees to ensure they have the necessary digital skills to adapt to new technologies and processes.
8. Partnerships and Collaborations: Collaborate with technology partners, startups, and industry experts to accelerate your digital transformation journey. This could involve outsourcing certain functions or forming strategic alliances.
9. Cybersecurity Measures: Implement robust cybersecurity measures to protect your business and customer data from cyber threats. This may include firewalls, encryption, multi-factor authentication, and regular security audits.
10. Compliance and Regulation: Stay updated with regulatory requirements related to digital business operations in India. Ensure compliance with laws such as the Information Technology Act, 2000, and the Goods and Services Tax (GST) regime.
11. Continuous Improvement: Digital transformation is an ongoing process. Continuously monitor and evaluate the effectiveness of your digital initiatives, and make adjustments as needed to stay competitive and relevant in the market.

By following these steps, businesses can successfully navigate the process of digital transformation in India and position themselves for long-term success in the digital age.

11.7 CYBERSECURITY MEASURES FOR BUSINESS PROTECTION

In the contemporary landscape of business operations, cybersecurity measures have become an indispensable aspect of ensuring the protection and continuity of business operations. This holds particularly true in the context of setting up a business in India, where the digital ecosystem is rapidly evolving, presenting both opportunities and challenges. As businesses embrace digitalization to enhance efficiency and connectivity, they also become increasingly vulnerable to cyber threats such as data breaches, ransomware attacks, and identity theft.

To safeguard their interests and maintain the trust of stakeholders, businesses setting up in India must prioritize robust cybersecurity measures from the outset. One fundamental aspect is the implementation of strong access controls and authentication mechanisms to prevent unauthorized access to sensitive data and systems. This involves the use of multi-factor authentication, encryption techniques, and regular password updates to fortify defenses against potential intrusions.

Furthermore, investing in cutting-edge cybersecurity technologies such as intrusion detection systems, firewalls, and antivirus software is imperative for identifying and mitigating cyber threats in real-time. These technologies serve as the first line of defense against malicious activities and provide businesses with the necessary visibility into their IT infrastructure to proactively address vulnerabilities.

In addition to technological solutions, fostering a culture of cybersecurity awareness among employees is equally vital. Educating staff members about the risks associated with cyber threats and providing comprehensive training on best practices for data protection and safe online behavior can significantly reduce the likelihood of security breaches resulting from human error or negligence.

Moreover, compliance with relevant data protection regulations such as the Personal Data Protection Bill (PDPB) in India is non-negotiable for businesses operating within the country. Adhering to these regulations not only demonstrates a commitment to protecting customer privacy but also helps mitigate legal and financial repercussions arising from non-compliance.

Collaboration with cybersecurity experts and government agencies can further enhance the resilience of businesses against evolving cyber threats. Engaging in information sharing initiatives, participating in cyber threat intelligence programs, and staying abreast of emerging cybersecurity trends and best practices are essential components of a proactive cybersecurity strategy.

Adopting a multi-faceted approach encompassing technological solutions, employee awareness programs, regulatory compliance, and collaborative partnerships, businesses can effectively mitigate cyber risks and thrive in the dynamic business environment of India.

11.8 IMPORTANCE OF CYBERSECURITY FOR BUSINESSES.

Cybersecurity is of paramount importance for businesses established in India, just as it is for businesses worldwide. Here's a detailed overview of why cybersecurity is important for Indian businesses:

1. Protection of Sensitive Data: Businesses in India, like those elsewhere, handle sensitive data such as customer information, financial records, and intellectual property. Effective cybersecurity measures safeguard this data from theft, unauthorized access, or manipulation. With stringent data protection laws like the Personal Data Protection Bill (PDPB) in the pipeline, Indian businesses face increasing pressure to secure sensitive information.
2. Regulatory Compliance: Compliance with cybersecurity regulations is vital for Indian businesses to avoid penalties, legal liabilities, and reputational damage. Regulatory bodies like the Reserve Bank of India (RBI) and the Ministry of Electronics and Information Technology (MeitY) have established guidelines and frameworks for cybersecurity, such as the RBI's Cyber Security Framework for Banks.
3. Mitigation of Cyber Threats: Indian businesses are vulnerable to various cyber threats, including malware, ransomware, phishing attacks, and insider threats. Cybersecurity measures such as firewalls, antivirus software, encryption, and employee training help mitigate these risks, ensuring business continuity and minimizing financial losses.

4. Protection of Online Transactions: With the rapid digitization of India's economy, businesses conduct a significant portion of their transactions online. Cybersecurity safeguards are essential to secure e-commerce platforms, online banking systems, and digital payment gateways from fraud and cyberattacks, thereby fostering trust among consumers.

5. Safeguarding important Infrastructure: Important infrastructure sectors such as energy, transportation, healthcare, and finance are prime targets for cyberattacks due to their economic and societal importance. Robust cybersecurity measures are necessary to protect these sectors from cyber threats that could disrupt essential services and undermine national security.

6. Prevention of Cyber Espionage: Indian businesses, particularly those involved in sectors like defense, aerospace, and technology, are at risk of cyber espionage conducted by state-sponsored actors or corporate rivals seeking to steal proprietary information or gain a competitive advantage. Strong cybersecurity defenses help detect and deter such espionage activities.

7. Preservation of Brand Reputation: A cyber breach can severely damage a business's reputation, leading to loss of customer trust, negative publicity, and decreased market share. Investing in cybersecurity not only protects sensitive data but also preserves brand reputation and customer loyalty, essential for long-term success in India's competitive business landscape.

8. Support for Digital Transformation: As Indian businesses embrace digital transformation initiatives to remain competitive and innovative; cybersecurity becomes integral to the success of these initiatives. By integrating cybersecurity into their digital strategies, businesses can unlock the full potential of technologies like cloud computing, Internet of Things (IoT), and artificial intelligence while minimizing security risks.

11.9 MEASURES TO PROTECT AGAINST CYBER THREATS.

Setting up a business in India, like in any other part of the world, requires robust measures to protect against cyber threats. India, with its rapidly growing digital infrastructure, is increasingly becoming a target for cybercriminals. Measures to protect against cyber threats:

1. Implement Robust Cybersecurity Policies: Develop comprehensive cybersecurity policies that encompass all aspects of the business operations, including data protection, network security, employee training, incident response, etc.

2. Regular Security Audits and Risk Assessments: Conduct regular security audits and risk assessments to identify vulnerabilities and weaknesses in the IT infrastructure. This helps in understanding potential threats and taking proactive measures to mitigate them.

3. Secure Network Infrastructure: Ensure that the network infrastructure is secure by implementing firewalls, intrusion detection and prevention systems, VPNs, and other security measures to protect against unauthorized access and data breaches.

4. Data Encryption: Encrypt sensitive data both in transit and at rest to prevent unauthorized access. Use strong encryption algorithms and protocols to secure data stored on servers, databases, and other devices.

5. Strong Authentication Mechanisms: Implement multi-factor authentication (MFA) for accessing critical systems and applications. This adds an extra layer of security beyond just passwords and helps prevent unauthorized access, even if passwords are compromised.

6. Regular Software Updates and Patch Management: Keep all software, operating systems, and applications up to date with the latest security patches. Vulnerabilities in software are often exploited by cyber attackers, and timely patching can help prevent such exploits.

7. Employee Training and Awareness: Conduct regular cybersecurity awareness training programs for employees to educate them about potential threats such as phishing attacks, social engineering, malware, etc. Employees should be trained to recognize and report suspicious activities.

8. Secure Remote Access: With the increasing trend of remote work, secure remote access to corporate networks is essential. Use secure VPNs and other technologies to ensure that remote workers can access company resources securely.
9. Incident Response Plan: Develop and regularly update an incident response plan to effectively respond to cyber incidents such as data breaches, ransomware attacks, etc. This plan should outline roles and responsibilities, escalation procedures, and steps to contain and mitigate the impact of the incident.
10. Compliance with Regulations: Ensure compliance with relevant cybersecurity regulations and standards such as the Information Technology (IT) Act, 2000, and the Personal Data Protection Bill, 2019, once enacted. Compliance helps in maintaining the trust of customers and stakeholders and avoids potential legal consequences.
11. Engage Cybersecurity Professionals: Consider hiring cybersecurity professionals or outsourcing cybersecurity services to experienced firms to strengthen the organization's security posture and stay ahead of evolving threats.
12. Backup and Disaster Recovery: Implement regular backup procedures and disaster recovery plans to ensure business continuity in case of cyber incidents or natural disasters. Backup data should be stored securely and tested regularly for reliability.

By implementing these measures, businesses can significantly enhance their cybersecurity posture and minimize the risk of falling victim to cyber threats while setting up operations in India.

11.10 DATA ANALYTICS FOR INFORMED DECISION MAKING

Setting up a business in India can be a lucrative venture, given the country's rapidly growing economy and large consumer base. Data analytics can play a important role in making informed decisions throughout the process.

HOW TO UTILIZE DATA ANALYTICS FOR SETTING UP A BUSINESS:

1. Market Research:

1. Use data analytics tools to analyze market trends, consumer behavior, and preferences in various sectors and regions of India.
2. Utilize demographic data to identify target markets and understand their needs and purchasing power.
3. Analyze competitor data to identify gaps in the market and areas where the business can differentiate itself.

2. Location Analysis:

1. Utilize geographic data and demographic information to identify optimal locations for setting up the business, such as areas with high foot traffic or underserved markets.
2. Analyze factors such as proximity to suppliers, competitors, transportation hubs, and target customer demographics.

3. Regulatory Compliance:

1. Use data analytics to stay updated on regulatory requirements and compliance standards for setting up a business in India.
2. Analyze legal and regulatory data to ensure that the business operations adhere to all applicable laws and regulations.

4. Financial Planning:

1. Utilize financial data and predictive analytics to forecast revenue, expenses, and cash flow for the business.
2. Conduct sensitivity analysis to assess the potential impact of various economic scenarios on the business's financial performance.

5. Customer Insights:

1. Use data analytics to gather insights into customer preferences, behavior, and satisfaction levels.
2. Implement customer relationship management (CRM) systems to track interactions with customers and personalize marketing strategies.

6. Supply Chain Optimization:

1. Utilize data analytics to optimize the supply chain, including sourcing, procurement, inventory management, and distribution.
2. Analyze historical data to identify inefficiencies and areas for improvement in the supply chain processes.

7. Marketing and Advertising:

1. Use data analytics to optimize the marketing and advertising strategies, including digital marketing campaigns, social media engagement, and targeted advertising.
2. Analyze customer data to create personalized marketing messages and promotions that resonate with the target audience.

8. Talent Acquisition:

1. Utilize data analytics for talent acquisition and workforce planning, including identifying skill gaps, predicting future staffing needs, and optimizing recruitment processes.
2. Analyze employee data to improve retention rates, employee satisfaction, and overall organizational performance.

By leveraging data analytics throughout the process of setting up a business in India, one can make ainformed decisions that increase the chances of success and profitability in this dynamic market.

11.11 ROLE OF DATA ANALYTICS IN BUSINESS DECISION-MAKING.

Data analytics plays an important role in modern business decision-making processes.
DATA ANALYTICS SIGNIFICANCE:

1. Informed Decision Making: Data analytics provides businesses with valuable insights derived from analyzing large datasets. These insights help decision-makers understand trends, patterns, and correlations within their operations, market, and customer behavior. By leveraging data analytics, organizations can make more informed decisions rather than relying solely on intuition or past experiences.

2. Predictive Analytics: Advanced data analytics techniques enable businesses to forecast future trends and outcomes based on historical data. Predictive analytics models can anticipate customer preferences, market fluctuations, and potential risks, allowing organizations to proactively address challenges and seize opportunities.

3. Optimizing Operations: Data analytics can optimize various aspects of business operations, including supply chain management, resource allocation, and production processes. By analyzing operational data, organizations can

identify inefficiencies, streamline workflows, and reduce costs while enhancing productivity and quality.

4. Enhancing Customer Experience: Understanding customer behavior is essential for delivering personalized experiences and fostering customer loyalty. Data analytics enables businesses to segment their customer base, identify preferences, and tailor products, services, and marketing strategies accordingly. This leads to improved customer satisfaction and retention.

5. Risk Management: Data analytics helps businesses identify and mitigate risks effectively. By analyzing historical and real-time data, organizations can detect potential threats such as fraud, cybersecurity breaches, and market volatility. This proactive approach enables businesses to implement risk mitigation strategies and safeguard their assets and reputation.

6. Market Intelligence: Data analytics provides valuable insights into market trends, competitor activities, and consumer sentiment. By monitoring social media, online reviews, and industry reports, businesses can stay ahead of the competition, identify emerging opportunities, and adapt their strategies to meet evolving market demands.

7. Measuring Performance: Data analytics enables businesses to track key performance indicators (KPIs) and evaluate the effectiveness of their strategies and initiatives. By setting benchmarks and analyzing performance metrics, organizations can identify areas for improvement, allocate resources efficiently, and drive continuous growth and innovation.

8. Strategic Planning: Data-driven insights empower businesses to develop and refine their strategic plans. By analyzing market data, consumer behavior, and internal performance metrics, organizations can make informed decisions about market entry, product development, and expansion strategies, ensuring long-term sustainability and competitiveness.

Overall, data analytics has become indispensable for modern businesses seeking to gain a competitive edge, drive innovation, and achieve sustainable growth in today's data-driven economy.

11.12 EXAMPLES OF HOW DATA ANALYTICS CAN BE LEVERAGED.

Examples of how data analytics can be leveraged across various industries and DOMAINS:

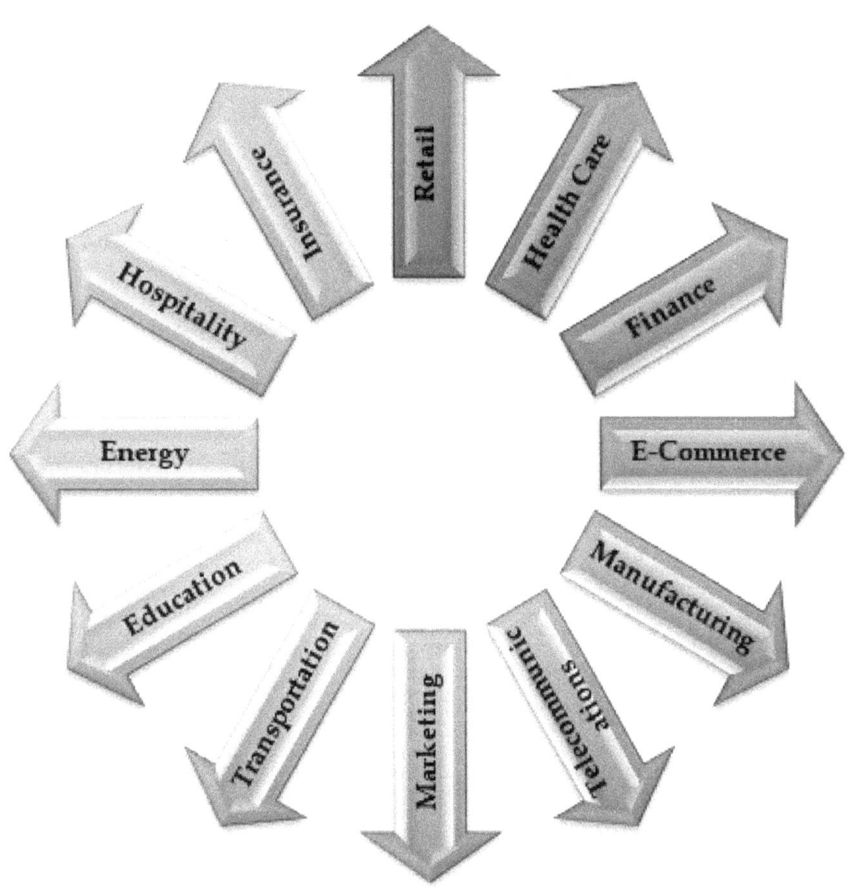

Data analytics in Different Domains

1. Retail: Analyzing customer purchase history helps to personalize recommendations and promotions.
2. Healthcare: Predictive analytics to forecast patient admission rates and optimize staffing levels accordingly.
3. Finance: Detecting fraudulent activities through anomaly detection algorithms applied to transaction data.
4. E-commerce: Analyzing website traffic patterns to optimize product placement and improve user experience.
5. Manufacturing: Predictive maintenance using sensor data to anticipate equipment failures and minimize downtime.
6. Telecommunications: Analyzing call detail records to identify customer churn factors and implement retention strategies.
7. Marketing: testing of effectiveness of after and before different advertising campaigns and messaging strategies.
8. Transportation: Route optimization using historical traffic data to minimize fuel consumption and delivery times.
9. Education: Analyzing student performance data to identify at-risk students and provide targeted interventions.
10. Energy: Optimizing energy usage through smart grid analytics and demand forecasting.
11. Hospitality: Analyzing guest feedback data to improve service quality and guest satisfaction.
12. Insurance: Predictive modeling to assess risk profiles and determine optimal pricing strategies.
13. Supply Chain: Inventory optimization through demand forecasting and supply chain analytics.
14. Real Estate: Market trend analysis to identify investment opportunities and pricing strategies.

15. Human Resources: Employee turnover prediction to develop retention strategies and improve workforce planning.
16. Sports: Performance analytics to optimize team strategies and player recruitment.
17. Cybersecurity: Identifying and mitigating security threats through advanced threat detection algorithms.
18. Pharmaceuticals: Drug discovery and development optimization through data-driven approaches.
19. Environmental Science: Analyzing environmental sensor data to monitor pollution levels and inform policy decisions.
20. Government: Analyzing citizen data to improve public service delivery and policy formulation.

These examples illustrate the diverse range of applications for data analytics across various industries, demonstrating its importance in driving insights and decision-making.

11.13 QUESTIONS:

1. Explain the Role of Technology in Business Growth?
2. Explain E-commerce and Digital Transformation?
3. Explain the role of e-commerce in business?
4. Write a short note on process of digital transformation.
5. Importance of cybersecurity for businesses. Explain?
6. What are the measures to protect against cyber threats?
7. Explain the role of data analytics in business decision-making.

CHAPTER TWELVE

CORPORATE SOCIAL RESPONSIBILITY

12.1 COPRPORATE SOCIAL RESPONSIBILITY (CSR)

Csr is an important consideration for businesses setting up operations in India. The concept of CSR in India has been formalized through legislation mandating certain companies to allocate a portion of their profits towards socially beneficial activities.

1. Legal Requirements: As per the Companies Act, 2013, certain categories of companies meeting specified financial thresholds are required to spend at least 2% of their average net profits of the preceding three years on CSR activities. This mandate applies to companies with a net worth of INR 500 crore or more, or turnover of INR 1000 crore or more, or a net profit of INR 5 crore or more.

2. 2. Areas of Focus: The law provides a broad framework for CSR activities, including eradicating hunger and poverty, promoting education, gender equality, environmental sustainability, and healthcare. Companies have the flexibility to choose the specific areas they want to focus on based on their priorities and the needs of the communities they operate in.

3. Implementation: Companies are required to establish a CSR committee comprising the board of directors, which formulates and monitors CSR policies and activities. The CSR activities should be aligned with the company's business and expertise, ensuring maximum impact and sustainability.

4. Reporting and Disclosure: Companies need to disclose their CSR policies and activities in their annual reports, outlining the initiatives undertaken, amount spent, and the impact achieved. Transparency and accountability are essential in demonstrating compliance with CSR obligations.

5. Partnerships and Collaboration: Collaborating with local NGOs, government agencies, and other stakeholders can enhance the effectiveness and reach of CSR initiatives. Engaging with the community and understanding their needs is important for designing impactful programs.

6. Long-Term Sustainability: Sustainable development and long-term impact should be the focus of CSR initiatives. Companies should strive to create programs that not only address immediate needs but also contribute to the socio-economic development of the communities in the long run.

7. Innovation and Scalability: Encouraging innovation and scalability in CSR initiatives can lead to more efficient and impactful solutions. Leveraging technology and best practices can help in reaching larger populations and addressing complex social challenges

12.2 CORPORATE SOCIAL RESPONSIBILITY (CSR) DEFINITION

Corporate social responsibility (CSR) is a concept that has been defined and interpreted by various authors and scholars over time.

Definitions provided by different authors:

1. Archie B. Carroll: Carroll is known for his CSR pyramid model, which encompasses four types of responsibilities: economic, legal, ethical, and philanthropic. He defines CSR as the "economic, legal, ethical, and discretionary expectations that society has of organizations at a given point in time."

2. Milton Friedman: Friedman is known for his controversial stance on CSR. He argued that the only social responsibility of a business is to increase its profits. According to him, "the social responsibility of business is to increase its profits."

3. Peter Drucker: Drucker, a management guru, emphasized the importance of social responsibility in business. He defined CSR as "doing what is right, fair, and just."

4. Carroll and Buchholtz: Carroll collaborated with Ann K. Buchholtz to further expand on the concept of CSR. They define it as "the social responsibility of business encompasses the economic, legal, ethical, and discretionary (philanthropic) expectations that society has of organizations at a given point in time."

5. Philip Kotler and Nancy Lee: Kotler and Lee emphasize the strategic aspect of CSR. They define it as "a commitment to improve community well-being through discretionary business practices and contributions of corporate resources."

6. Sethi: Sethi offers a broader definition, stating that CSR is "the decision-making and implementation process that guides all company activities in the protection and promotion of international human rights, labor and environmental standards, and compliance with legal requirements within its operations and in its relations to the societies and communities in which it operates."

7. Carroll and Shabana: In their book "The Business Case for Corporate Social Responsibility: A Review of Concepts, Research, and Practice," Carroll and Shabana define CSR as "a multi-dimensional construct representing the corporate obligations to meet or exceed the ethical, legal, commercial, and public expectations that society has of business."

These definitions highlight the multifaceted nature of CSR, encompassing economic, legal, ethical, and philanthropic responsibilities that businesses have towards society.

Under the Companies Act 2013, corporate social responsibility (CSR) refers to the responsibility of a company to operate in a manner that promotes the well-being of society, beyond maximizing profits for shareholders. Specifically, Section 135 of the Companies Act 2013 mandates certain classes of companies to spend a specified portion of their profits towards CSR activities. These activities typically focus on areas such as education, health, poverty alleviation, environmental sustainability, and rural development, among others. The Act also requires companies to establish a CSR committee, develop a CSR policy, and report on their CSR initiatives in their annual financial statements. Failure to comply with these provisions may result in penalties or other legal consequences for the company. Therefore, under the Companies Act 2013, CSR is an integral aspect of corporate governance and business conduct for companies operating in India.

12.3 IMPACT OF CSR ON BUSINESS REPUTATION

Corporate Social Responsibility (CSR) has become increasingly important in shaping the reputation of businesses in India, as it has in many other parts of the world.

IMPACT OF CSR ON BUSINESS REPUTATION:

1. Enhanced Reputation: Companies that actively engage in CSR initiatives tend to enjoy a better reputation among consumers, investors, and other stakeholders. When businesses demonstrate a commitment to social causes such as education, healthcare, environmental sustainability, or poverty alleviation, they are perceived as socially responsible entities contributing positively to society.

2. Consumer Perception: In India, where consumers are becoming more socially conscious, CSR initiatives can significantly influence purchasing decisions. Consumers are more likely to support brands that align with their

values and demonstrate a sense of social responsibility. This can lead to increased customer loyalty and positive word-of-mouth advertising.

3. Attracting and Retaining Talent: A strong CSR program can also help businesses attract and retain top talent. Many employees, particularly the younger generation, prefer to work for companies that are socially responsible and contribute to making a positive impact on society. CSR initiatives can contribute to employee morale, satisfaction, and overall engagement.

4. Investor Confidence: Investors are increasingly considering CSR practices when making investment decisions. Companies with robust CSR programs are often seen as more stable and trustworthy, which can attract investment and improve access to capital markets. Additionally, some investors have specific criteria related to environmental, social, and governance (ESG) factors, and companies with strong CSR initiatives may have a competitive advantage in accessing capital from these investors.

5. Regulatory Compliance and Stakeholder Expectations: In recent years, the Indian government has introduced regulations mandating certain companies to spend a percentage of their profits on CSR activities. Compliance with these regulations is essential to maintain a positive reputation and avoid any potential legal or regulatory issues. Furthermore, stakeholders, including customers, employees, communities, and civil society organizations, increasingly expect companies to demonstrate their commitment to CSR.

6. Mitigating Risks: Engaging in CSR can help businesses mitigate certain risks, such as reputational risks associated with unethical practices or negative environmental impacts. By proactively addressing social and environmental issues, companies can prevent or minimize potential backlash from stakeholders and protect their reputation in the long term.

7. Competitive Advantage: In a competitive market like India, where numerous companies operate in various industries, CSR can serve as a differentiator. Companies that go above and beyond in their CSR efforts can stand out from competitors, attract more customers, and build stronger relationships with stakeholders.

12.4 ETHICAL BEHAVIOR IN BUSINESS

Emphasizing the importance of ethical behavior in business , especially in India, is important for several reasons:

1. Building Trust: Ethical behavior fosters trust between businesses, customers, employees, and other stakeholders. In India, where relationships play a significant role in business dealings, trust is paramount for long-term success.

2. Legal Compliance: Adhering to ethical standards ensures compliance with Indian laws and regulations. Non-compliance can lead to legal repercussions, tarnishing the company's reputation and resulting in financial penalties.

3. Enhancing Reputation: Businesses known for ethical practices enjoy a positive reputation, which can attract customers, investors, and talented employees. In a competitive market like India, a good reputation can be a significant differentiator.

4. Sustainable Growth: Ethical behavior contributes to sustainable business growth by fostering long-term relationships and loyalty among stakeholders. Unethical practices may yield short-term gains but often lead to negative consequences in the long run.

5. Social Responsibility: Indian society values businesses that contribute positively to the community. Ethical behavior demonstrates a commitment to social responsibility, which can enhance the company's standing and create goodwill among consumers.

6. Attracting Investment: Ethical companies are more likely to attract investment from socially responsible investors, both domestically and internationally. With India's growing economy, attracting investment is important for business expansion and development.

7. Employee Morale and Productivity: Ethical business practices create a positive work environment, boosting employee morale and productivity. Employees are more likely to remain loyal to companies that uphold ethical

standards, reducing turnover and recruitment costs.

8. Mitigating Risks: Ethical behavior helps mitigate various risks, including legal, financial, and reputational risks. By conducting business ethically, companies can avoid scandals, lawsuits, and damage to their brand image.

9. Setting Industry Standards: Ethical businesses often set industry standards and influence the behavior of competitors. In India, where certain industries may have a history of unethical practices, leading by example can drive positive change across the sector.

10. Contributing to National Development: Ethical businesses contribute to the overall development of India by promoting fair competition, supporting sustainable development goals, and adhering to ethical labor practices.

Emphasizing ethical behavior in Indian business is not just a moral imperative but also a strategic business decision. By prioritizing ethics, businesses can build trust, enhance their reputation, foster sustainable growth, and contribute positively to society and the economy as a whole.

12.5 ETHICAL CHALLENGES AND SOLUTIONS.

Setting up a business in India comes with its own set of ethical challenges, many of which are common across various industries and sectors.

ETHICAL CHALLENGES FACED BY BUSINESSES IN INDIA ALONG WITH POTENTIAL SOLUTIONS:

1. Corruption: Corruption is often cited as one of the most significant ethical challenges in India. Bribery, kickbacks, and facilitation payments are still prevalent in many sectors, making it difficult for businesses to operate ethically.

Solution: Implement a strict zero-tolerance policy towards corruption within the organization. Train employees on ethical conduct and provide channels for reporting unethical behavior anonymously. Establishing transparent processes and complying with anti-corruption laws can help mitigate this challenge.

2. Compliance with Regulations: India has a complex regulatory environment, and staying compliant with various laws and regulations can be challenging for businesses. Non-compliance can lead to legal and ethical issues.

Solution: Invest in robust legal and compliance teams to ensure that the business adheres to all relevant regulations. Conduct regular audits to identify and address any compliance gaps. Building strong relationships with regulatory authorities can also help navigate the regulatory landscape more effectively.

3. Labor Practices: Ensuring fair labor practices, such as providing safe working conditions, fair wages, and respecting employee rights, can be a challenge in India, particularly in industries like manufacturing and construction.

Solution: Implement and enforce strict labor policies that adhere to national and international labor standards. Conduct regular inspections of workplace conditions and address any issues promptly. Providing training and education to employees on their rights can also help promote ethical labor practices.

4. Environmental Impact: With rapid industrialization and urbanization, businesses in India face increasing pressure to minimize their environmental footprint. Pollution, resource depletion, and waste management are significant ethical concerns.

Solution: Adopt environmentally sustainable practices and technologies to reduce carbon emissions, minimize waste generation, and conserve natural resources. Implementing environmental management systems and obtaining relevant certifications can demonstrate the business's commitment to environmental responsibility.

5. Social Responsibility: Businesses are increasingly expected to contribute positively to society beyond just generating profits. Issues such as community development, education, and healthcare access are important ethical considerations.

Solution: Develop corporate social responsibility (CSR) initiatives that align with the company's values and address relevant social issues. Engage with local communities through partnerships and outreach programs.

Transparently communicate CSR efforts to stakeholders to build trust and credibility.

6. Fair Competition: Unfair business practices, such as monopolistic behavior, price fixing, or deceptive marketing, can undermine fair competition and harm consumers.

Solution: Commit to fair and transparent business practices that comply with competition laws. Avoid engaging in anti-competitive behavior and ensure that marketing and advertising campaigns are honest and truthful. Supporting initiatives that promote fair competition and consumer rights can also contribute to ethical business conduct.

12.6 ENVIRONMENTAL SUSTAINABILITY IN BUSINESS

Setting up a business with a focus on environmental sustainability in India requires consideration of various factors and adherence to relevant regulations.

1. Legal Compliance: Ensure compliance with environmental laws and regulations applicable in India. The Environmental Impact Assessment (EIA) Notification, 2006, and subsequent amendments, is a crucial regulation that governs the environmental clearance process for various projects.

2. Renewable Energy: Incorporate renewable energy sources into your business operations where feasible. This could involve installing solar panels, wind turbines, or using biomass energy for power generation to reduce reliance on fossil fuels.

3. Resource Efficiency: Implement measures to minimize resource consumption and waste generation. This includes adopting energy-efficient technologies, optimizing water usage, and reducing, reusing, and recycling materials wherever possible.

4. Green Supply Chain: Work with suppliers and partners who prioritize environmental sustainability. Encourage the adoption of eco-friendly practices throughout the supply chain, such as sourcing sustainably produced raw materials and reducing transportation-related emissions.

5. Green Buildings: If you're constructing or leasing office space, consider green building certifications such as LEED (Leadership in Energy and Environmental Design) or GRIHA (Green Rating for Integrated Habitat Assessment) to ensure energy efficiency, water conservation, and overall environmental performance of the building.

6. Waste Management: Develop and implement a comprehensive waste management plan to minimize waste generation and ensure proper disposal or recycling of waste materials. Comply with regulations related to hazardous waste management, if applicable.

7. Environmental Awareness: Promote environmental awareness and sustainability practices among employees, customers, and stakeholders. Conduct training programs, organize awareness campaigns, and encourage eco-friendly behaviors in the workplace.

8. Community Engagement: Engage with local communities and stakeholders to understand their environmental concerns and ensure that your business activities do not adversely impact the surrounding environment. Consider investing in community development projects that contribute to environmental conservation and sustainable livelihoods.

9. Monitoring and Reporting: Establish mechanisms for monitoring environmental performance and regularly report on key metrics such as energy consumption, greenhouse gas emissions, water usage, and waste generation. Use this data to identify opportunities for improvement and track progress towards sustainability goals.

10. Continuous Improvement: Commit to continuous improvement in environmental performance by setting targets, conducting periodic reviews, and implementing measures to enhance sustainability across all aspects of your business operations.

By integrating environmental sustainability into your business practices from the outset, you can not only minimize negative environmental impacts but also create long-term value for your business, stakeholders, and society as a whole.

12.7 ROLE OF BUSINESSES IN ENVIRONMENTAL SUSTAINABILITY.

The role of businesses in environmental sustainability in India is paramount, given the country's rapidly growing economy and its significant environmental challenges.

1. Resource Management: Businesses in India have a important role in managing resources efficiently. This includes reducing waste generation, optimizing energy and water consumption, and promoting recycling and reuses practices. Adopting sustainable practices in resource management not only benefits the environment but also improves cost-efficiency for businesses in the long run.
2. Green Technologies and Innovation: Indian businesses can drive environmental sustainability through the adoption and development of green technologies and innovations. This includes investing in renewable energy sources such as solar and wind power, developing energy-efficient manufacturing processes, and utilizing eco-friendly materials and packaging.
3. Corporate Social Responsibility (CSR): CSR initiatives play a significant role in promoting environmental sustainability among businesses in India. Many companies allocate funds and resources towards environmental conservation projects, such as afforestation, water conservation, and waste management programs. By integrating CSR into their business models, companies can contribute positively to both society and the environment.
4. Compliance and Regulation: Businesses must adhere to environmental regulations and standards set by the government. Compliance ensures that businesses operate within environmentally responsible parameters, minimizing their impact on ecosystems and natural resources. Additionally, businesses can proactively engage with policymakers to advocate for stronger environmental policies and regulations.
5. Sustainable Supply Chains: Indian businesses can promote environmental sustainability by implementing sustainable practices throughout their supply chains. This includes working with suppliers who adhere to ethical and environmentally responsible practices, reducing carbon emissions from transportation and logistics, and promoting fair labor practices.
6. Consumer Awareness and Education: Businesses play a important role in raising consumer awareness about environmental issues and promoting sustainable consumption patterns. Through marketing campaigns, product labeling, and educational initiatives, businesses can empower consumers to make environmentally conscious choices and support sustainable products and services.
7. Collaboration and Partnerships: Collaboration among businesses, government agencies, non-profit organizations, and research institutions is essential for driving collective action towards environmental sustainability. By forming partnerships, sharing best practices, and collaborating on innovative solutions, stakeholders can address complex environmental challenges more effectively.

Overall, businesses in India have a significant responsibility to integrate environmental sustainability into their operations and contribute to the country's efforts towards a greener and more sustainable future. By adopting sustainable practices, investing in green technologies, and collaborating with stakeholders, businesses can play a important role in mitigating environmental degradation and promoting sustainable development in India.

12.8 GREEN PRACTICES AND THEIR BENEFITS.

Setting up a business in India with a focus on green practices can be advantageous in numerous ways, both for the environment and for the success of the business.

1. Renewable Energy Integration: Utilizing renewable energy sources such as solar, wind, or hydroelectric power for the business operations can significantly reduce carbon emissions and dependence on fossil fuels. In India, there are various government incentives and subsidies available for businesses adopting renewable energy solutions.

2. Energy Efficiency: Implementing energy-efficient technologies and practices in the business operations can lead to cost savings through reduced energy consumption. This includes using energy-efficient lighting, HVAC systems, and appliances, as well as optimizing processes to minimize energy waste.

3. Waste Reduction and Recycling: Implementing waste reduction strategies and establishing recycling programs can help minimize the environmental impact of the business operations. This not only reduces landfill waste but also conserves natural resources by recycling materials for reuse.

4. Sustainable Supply Chain: Partnering with suppliers who follow sustainable practices can help reduce the environmental footprint of the business's supply chain. This includes sourcing raw materials responsibly, minimizing transportation emissions, and supporting ethical labor practices.

5. Green Building Design: Designing or retrofitting the business premises to meet green building standards can enhance energy efficiency, indoor air quality, and overall sustainability. Features such as efficient insulation, natural lighting, and water-saving fixtures can contribute to long-term cost savings and environmental benefits.

6. Promotion of Eco-Friendly Products and Services: Offering eco-friendly products or services can attract environmentally conscious consumers and differentiate the business in the market. Highlighting the sustainability benefits of the offerings can help build brand reputation and customer loyalty.

7. Community Engagement and Environmental Initiatives:

Engaging with local communities and participating in environmental initiatives can demonstrate the commitment to corporate social responsibility. This can include organizing tree planting drives, participating in clean-up campaigns, or supporting environmental education programs.

BENEFITS OF ADOPTING GREEN PRACTICES:

1. Cost Savings: Implementing green practices can lead to significant cost savings in the long run through reduced energy and resource consumption, as well as potential tax incentives and subsidies offered by the government.

2. Competitive Advantage: Differentiating the business through its commitment to sustainability can attract environmentally conscious consumers and investors who prioritize ethical and eco*friendly businesses.

3. Regulatory Compliance: As environmental regulations become stricter worldwide, adopting green practices can ensure compliance with existing and future environmental laws and regulations, reducing the risk of fines or penalties.

4. Enhanced Brand Image: Demonstrating environmental stewardship can enhance the brand's reputation and credibility, fostering trust and loyalty among customers, employees, and stakeholders.

5. Long-Term Sustainability:By investing in green practices, businesses can contribute to the long-term sustainability of the environment and society, ensuring a healthier planet for future generations.

12.9 BUILDING A POSITIVE CORPORATE IMAGE

For building a positive corporate image, when setting up a business requires a strategic approach. Considering cultural nuances, local regulations, societal expectations will pave way for better image building.

STEPS TO ESTABLISH A POSITIVE CORPORATE IMAGE:

1. Understanding Local Culture and Values: India is a diverse country with rich cultural heritage. Understanding and respecting the local customs, traditions, and values is important. Showcasing cultural sensitivity in the business practices can help build trust and credibility among the local population.

2. Compliance with Regulations: Ensure compliance with all relevant laws, regulations, and policies governing business operations in India. This includes obtaining necessary permits, licenses, and registrations.

Demonstrating commitment to legal and ethical business conduct enhances the corporate image.

3. Corporate Social Responsibility (CSR): Engage in CSR initiatives that benefit the community and address social issues prevalent in India. This could involve supporting education, healthcare, environmental sustainability, or other causes aligned with local needs. Being socially responsible enhances the reputation and fosters goodwill.

4. Transparency and Integrity: Maintain transparency in the business dealings and demonstrate integrity in all interactions. Uphold high ethical standards and adhere to best practices in corporate governance. Building a reputation for honesty and reliability is essential for long-term success in India.

5. Local Partnerships and Alliances: Collaborate with local partners, suppliers, and stakeholders to demonstrate the commitment to the Indian market. Building strong relationships with local entities can facilitate smoother business operations and foster a positive perception of the company.

6. Employment Practices: Treat the employees fairly and with respect. Provide opportunities for skill development, career advancement, and a safe working environment. Demonstrating a commitment to employee welfare enhances the reputation as a responsible employer.

7. Communication and Branding: Develop a communication strategy that resonates with the Indian audience. Tailor the messaging to reflect cultural sensitivities and preferences. Invest in branding efforts that convey the company's values, vision, and commitment to the Indian market.

8. Customer Satisfaction: Prioritize customer satisfaction and strive to exceed expectations in product quality, service delivery, and after-sales support. Positive word-of-mouth from satisfied customers can significantly enhance the corporate image in India.

9. Adaptability and Flexibility: Be adaptable and flexible in the approach to business in India. Embrace cultural differences and be open to feedback and suggestions from local stakeholders. Demonstrating a willingness to learn and evolve can help to earn respect and credibility.

10. Long-Term Commitment: Show the commitment to the Indian market by investing in long-term growth and development initiatives. Avoid short-term, opportunistic strategies that may damage the corporate image. Building trust and credibility takes time but is essential for sustainable success in India.

12.10 STRATEGIES FOR BUILDING AND MAINTAINING POSITIVE CORPORATE IMAGE

Building and maintaining a positive corporate image in India, or any other country, requires a strategic approach that aligns with cultural sensitivities, societal expectations, and business ethics.

1. Social Responsibility Initiatives: Engage in corporate social responsibility (CSR) activities that address local community needs. This could include initiatives related to education, healthcare, environmental sustainability, or rural development. Actively involving employees in these initiatives can enhance their sense of belonging and pride in the organization.

2. Cultural Sensitivity: Understand and respect India's diverse cultures, languages, and customs. Tailor marketing campaigns and communication strategies to resonate with different regional audiences. Avoid actions or statements that could be perceived as disrespectful or insensitive to cultural sensitivities.

3. Transparency and Ethics: Practice transparency in business operations and adhere to high ethical standards. Uphold integrity in dealings with stakeholders, including customers, employees, suppliers, and government agencies. Any unethical behavior can quickly tarnish a company's reputation in India.

4. Quality Products and Services: Deliver high-quality products or services that meet or exceed customer expectations. Consistently focus on innovation and improvement to stay competitive in the market. Positive word-of-mouth from satisfied customers can significantly enhance corporate image.

5. Employee Welfare: Prioritize employee well-being by providing a safe and inclusive work environment, fair compensation, opportunities for skill development, and work-life balance. Employee satisfaction translates into

higher productivity and better customer service, contributing to a positive corporate image.

6. Engagement with Government and Regulatory Bodies: Maintain proactive engagement with government authorities and regulatory bodies. Comply with all applicable laws and regulations while also advocating for policies that promote business growth and societal welfare.

7. Effective Communication: Communicate openly and transparently with stakeholders through various channels, including traditional media, social media, and corporate websites. Respond promptly to inquiries, feedback, and concerns to demonstrate accountability and build trust.

8. Brand Building: Invest in brand-building activities that emphasize the company's values, vision, and contributions to society. Leverage endorsements from reputable individuals or organizations to enhance credibility and visibility.

9. Crisis Management Preparedness: Develop robust crisis management protocols to effectively handle any unforeseen events or controversies. Timely and responsible resolution of crises can mitigate reputational damage and strengthen trust in the brand.

10. Continuous Monitoring and Feedback: Regularly monitor public perception through surveys, social media monitoring, and feedback mechanisms. Actively address any negative feedback or misconceptions to prevent reputational damage from spreading.

12.11 LINK BETWEEN CORPORATE IMAGE AND BUSINESS SUCCESS

The corporate image plays an important role in determining business success.
Link between corporate image and business success:

1. Consumer Perception: A positive corporate image enhances consumer perception. In a diverse and competitive market like India, where consumers have numerous options, a strong corporate image can differentiate a company from its competitors. Consumers are more likely to trust and engage with companies that have a positive image, leading to increased sales and market share.

2. Brand Loyalty: Building a reputable corporate image fosters brand loyalty among consumers. In India, where brand loyalty is often influenced by trust and cultural factors, a favorable corporate image can lead to long-term customer relationships. Loyal customers are more likely to repeat purchases and recommend the brand to others, contributing to sustainable business growth.

3. Investor Confidence: A positive corporate image not only attracts customers but also investors. In India's dynamic business environment, investors seek companies with strong reputations for reliability, transparency, and ethical business practices. A favorable corporate image can facilitate access to capital, drive stock performance, and attract strategic partnerships, fueling business expansion and innovation.

4. Employee Engagement: A company's corporate image also impacts employee engagement and retention. In India, where the workforce is diverse and talented, employees are increasingly drawn to organizations with a positive image that aligns with their values and aspirations. A reputable corporate image enhances employee morale, productivity, and loyalty, reducing turnover costs and fostering a positive work culture condusive to innovation and success.

5. Government Relations: Maintaining a positive corporate image is crucial for navigating regulatory and governmental relations in India. Companies with strong reputations are more likely to garner support from policymakers, secure favorable policies, and mitigate regulatory risks. A favorable corporate image enhances a company's standing within the community and stakeholders, facilitating smoother business operations and expansion opportunities.

6. Crisis Management: A well-established corporate image serves as a buffer during times of crisis. In India's dynamic socio-political landscape, companies may face various challenges such as public scrutiny, regulatory changes, or unforeseen emergencies. A positive corporate image built on trust, integrity, and responsiveness can

help companies' weather crises, maintain stakeholder confidence, and emerge stronger from adversity.

12.12 QUESTIONS:

1. Explain the impact of CSR on business reputation.
2. What do you mean by ethical behavior in business?
3. Explain the ethical challenges and solutions.
4. Write short note on Environmental Sustainability in Business?
5. Explain green practices and their benefits.
6. Explain the strategies for building and maintaining a positive corporate image?
7. What is the link between corporate image and business success?

CHAPTER THIRTEEN

GLOBAL BUSINESS EXPANSION

13.1 INTERNATIONAL TRADE AND BUSINESS

International trade is the exchange of goods, services, and capital across borders, fostering economic interdependence and connecting nations in a global marketplace. This practice has been a cornerstone of economic development for centuries, offering a myriad of benefits while presenting challenges that require strategic management.

ADVANTAGES AND CHALLENGES OF INTERNATIONAL TRADE

13.1.1 BENEFITS OF INTERNATIONAL TRADE:

1. Economic Growth: International trade stimulates economic growth by providing access to larger markets. Nations can specialize in the production of goods and services in which they have a comparative advantage, leading to increased efficiency and productivity.
2. Expanded Market Access: Businesses gain access to a broader customer base, allowing them to sell their products and services in foreign markets. This diversification can reduce dependency on a single market and enhance revenue streams.
3. Resource Utilization: International trade enables the efficient allocation of resources. Countries can focus on producing goods and services for which they have abundant resources or specialized skills, leading to increased overall efficiency.
4. Technological Transfer: Trade facilitates the flow of technology and innovation across borders. Companies can adopt and adapt technologies developed elsewhere, leading to improved productivity and competitiveness.
5. Job Creation: Increased international trade can contribute to job creation as businesses expand to meet growing demand, fostering employment opportunities and reducing unemployment rates.
6. Diversity and Choice: Consumers benefit from a wider array of goods and services, fostering competition and driving innovation. This diversity enhances consumer choices and quality of life.

13.1.2 CHALLENGES OF INTERNATIONAL TRADE:

1. Political and Regulatory Barriers: Governments may impose trade barriers, such as tariffs and quotas, for protectionist reasons. These barriers can hinder market access and create uncertainties for businesses.
2. Currency Fluctuations: Exchange rate volatility poses risks for businesses engaged in international trade. Sudden changes in currency values can impact the cost of goods, pricing strategies, and overall profitability.
3. Cultural Differences: Cultural variations across borders can pose challenges in communication, negotiation, and marketing. Understanding and adapting to diverse cultural norms is important for successful international business relationships.
4. Supply Chain Disruptions: Global supply chains are susceptible to disruptions due to geopolitical events, natural disasters, or economic crises. Businesses must develop resilient supply chain strategies to mitigate these risks.

5. Intellectual Property Concerns: Protecting intellectual property becomes complex in international trade. Differences in legal frameworks and enforcement mechanisms can lead to the unauthorized use and infringement of intellectual property rights.
6. Environmental and Ethical Considerations: International trade may contribute to environmental degradation and raise ethical concerns, particularly in industries with lax regulations. Balancing economic interests with sustainable and ethical practices is essential for responsible international trade.

13.2 UNDERSTANDING THE GLOBAL MARKETS

In an era defined by interconnected economies and rapid technological advancements, understanding global markets is paramount for individuals, businesses, and policymakers alike. The intricate web of international trade, finance, and communication has transformed the world into a closely-knit global village, where events in one corner can send ripples across the entire economic landscape. Recognizing the importance of comprehending global markets is not merely an academic pursuit but a strategic imperative for navigating the complexities of our contemporary world.

One of the primary reasons to emphasize the significance of understanding global markets lies in the profound impact they have on economic growth and prosperity. Nations are no longer isolated entities; their fortunes are interlinked with the ebbs and flows of the global economic tide. For businesses, the ability to grasp market dynamics on a global scale is a prerequisite for sustainable success. Whether it be anticipating consumer preferences, identifying emerging trends, or mitigating risks associated with currency fluctuations, a nuanced understanding of global markets empowers businesses to thrive in an environment characterized by constant change.

Furthermore, the interconnected nature of global markets underscores the need for effective international cooperation and diplomacy. Political leaders and policymakers must be well-versed in the intricacies of global trade agreements, financial systems, and geopolitical dynamics to make informed decisions that promote national interests while fostering collaboration on the international stage. Failure to comprehend the global economic landscape can lead to missed opportunities, diplomatic tensions, and economic instability.

Individuals, too, stand to benefit from a comprehensive understanding of global markets. In an age where information travels at the speed of light, financial decisions made on a local scale can have far-reaching consequences. Whether it's investment choices, career paths, or personal financial planning, an awareness of global market trends and developments is important for making informed and strategic decisions that align with one's aspirations and goals.

13.2.1 IMPORTANCE OF UNDERSTANDING GLOBAL MARKETS

1. Economic Interdependence: Globalization has made economies deeply interconnected. Events in one part of the world can have significant ripple effects across borders. Understanding global markets helps individuals, businesses, and governments navigate these interconnected relationships.
2. Diversification Opportunities: Access to global markets provides opportunities for diversification, spreading risk across different regions, industries, and asset classes. This is important for investors seeking to optimize returns while minimizing risk.
3. Market Expansion: For businesses, understanding global markets opens doors to new opportunities for expansion. With a broader market reach, companies can tap into new customer segments, access cheaper resources, and benefit from economies of scale.
4. Competitive Advantage: In a globalized marketplace, competitors can emerge from any corner of the world. Understanding global markets allows businesses to stay ahead by anticipating market trends, identifying emerging competitors, and adapting strategies accordingly.

5. Policy Implications: Government policies and regulations in one country can impact markets worldwide. For policymakers, a nuanced understanding of global markets is essential for crafting effective economic policies, managing trade relations, and addressing global challenges such as climate change and pandemics.

6. Cultural Sensitivity: Global markets are not just about numbers; they involve diverse cultures, traditions, and consumer behaviors. Understanding these cultural nuances is vital for effective marketing strategies and building strong customer relationships.

7. Technological Innovation: Innovation often transcends borders, with technology driving rapid changes in global markets. Keeping abreast of technological advancements and their impact on various industries is important for staying competitive in the global marketplace.

13.3 EXPANDING BUSINESS OPERATIONS GLOBALLY

Expanding business operations globally is a strategic move that can open up new markets, increase revenue streams, and enhance the overall competitiveness of a company. However, venturing into the global arena requires careful planning, thorough research, and a clear understanding of the complexities involved.

STEPS INVOLVED IN THE PROCESS OF GLOBAL BUSINESS EXPANSION:

1. Market Research and Analysis: Conducting comprehensive market research is the foundational step in global expansion. It involves understanding the target market's demographics, economic conditions, cultural nuances, legal requirements, and competitive landscape. This market research provides valuable insights that help in making informed decisions and adapting business strategies to suit the global market.

2. Legal and Regulatory Compliance: Every country has its own set of laws, regulations, and compliance requirements. It is important to navigate and understand these intricacies to ensure the business operates legally and ethically in the new market. This may involve obtaining necessary permits, licenses, and adhering to local labor laws and taxation regulations.

3. Risk Assessment and Mitigation: Identifying and assessing potential risks associated with global expansion is essential. These risks may include currency fluctuations, geopolitical instability, cultural misunderstandings, and supply chain disruptions. Developing a robust risk management strategy helps in mitigating these challenges and ensuring a smoother transition into the global market.

4. Financial Planning: Adequate financial planning is imperative for successful global expansion. This includes budgeting for initial setup costs, ongoing operational expenses, and potential unforeseen challenges. Establishing a clear financial model helps in managing resources efficiently and ensures sustainability in the new market.

5. Adaptation of Products and Services: Tailoring products and services to meet the specific needs and preferences of the target market is important for acceptance and success. This may involve product modifications, adjusting pricing strategies, or even developing entirely new offerings based on local demand and cultural considerations.

6. Establishing a Strong Local Presence: Building a local presence is the key to gaining trust and credibility in a new market. This can be achieved through partnerships, establishing local offices, hiring local talent, and actively engaging with the community. Localizing marketing efforts and communication materials also contribute to building a strong brand presence.

7. Supply Chain Management: Efficient supply chain management is vital for the timely delivery of products and services. Understanding local logistics, customs procedures, and building strong relationships with local suppliers and distributors are important components of successful global supply chain management.

8. Cultural Sensitivity and Communication: Cultural differences can significantly impact business relationships. It's essential to invest in cultural sensitivity training for employees and create communication strategies that resonate with the local audience. This helps in building positive relationships and avoiding misunderstandings that could hinder business success.

9. Monitoring and Adaptation: Once the business is operational in the global market, continuous monitoring and adaptation are necessary. Regularly reassessing market conditions, consumer preferences, and the competitive

landscape enable the company to stay agile and responsive to changes, ensuring sustained success in the global arena.

13.4 STEPS INVOLVED IN GLOBAL BUSINESS EXPANSION.

Expanding a business globally involves a series of strategic steps to ensure success.
STEPS INVOLVED IN GLOBAL BUSINESS EXPANSION:
1. Market Research and Analysis:

a. Identify potential markets for expansion.
b. Analyze market conditions, trends, and demand.
c. Assess competition, regulatory environment, and cultural factors.
d. Evaluate the economic stability and political situation of target countries.

2. Strategic Planning:

a. Define clear objectives and goals for expansion.
b. Develop a comprehensive business plan outlining strategies, timelines, and resource allocation.
c. Determine the mode of entry (e.g., exporting, licensing, joint venture, wholly -owned subsidiary).

3. Legal and Regulatory Compliance:

a. Understand and comply with local laws, regulations, and business practices.
b. Obtain necessary permits, licenses, visas, and certifications.
c. Establish legal entities and structures in accordance with local requirements.

4. Financial Planning:

a. Assess the financial feasibility of expansion.
b. Develop a budget for initial setup costs, ongoing operations, and contingencies.
c. Secure funding through internal resources, external investors, loans, or grants.

5. Localization and Cultural Adaptation:

a. Customize products, services, and marketing strategies to fit local preferences and cultural norms.
b. Adapt branding, messaging, and communication strategies for different markets.
c. Hire local talent or work with local partners to better understand the target market.

6. Supply Chain and Logistics:

a. Establish efficient supply chain networks to ensure timely delivery of goods or services.
b. Identify reliable suppliers, distributors, and logistics partners.
c. Optimize inventory management and transportation logistics to minimize costs and delays.

7. Marketing and Promotion:

a. Develop a localized marketing strategy to reach target customers.
b. Utilize various marketing channels, including digital, print, and social media.
c. Build brand awareness and credibility through advertising, promotions, and public relations efforts.

8. Human Resources Management:

a. Recruit and train local employees with the necessary skills and cultural understanding.
b. Develop HR policies and practices compliant with local labor laws.
c. Foster a diverse and inclusive workplace culture that promotes employee engagement and retention.

9. Risk Management:

a. Identify potential risks and develop mitigation strategies.
b. Establish crisis management protocols to address unforeseen challenges.
c. Secure appropriate insurance coverage for various business risks (e.g., political, legal, operational).

10. Monitoring and Evaluation:

a. Track key performance indicators (KPIs) to measure the success of expansion efforts.
b. Conduct regular performance reviews and adjust strategies as needed.
c. Solicit feedback from customers, employees, and stakeholders to continuously improve operations.

By following these steps diligently and adapting to the unique challenges of each market, businesses can successfully expand their operations globally and achieve sustainable growth.

13.5 MARKET ENTRY STRATEGIES AND CULTURAL CONSIDERATIONS

Expanding a business globally requires careful consideration of market entry strategies and cultural factors.
1. Market Entry Strategies:

a. Exporting: This involves selling products or services directly to customers in a foreign market. It's relatively low-risk and requires less investment initially. However, it may limit control over distribution and marketing.
b. Licensing and Franchising: This strategy involves granting permission to use the company's intellectual property (licensing) or business model (franchising) to a foreign entity. It allows for rapid market entry with minimal investment but may lead to a loss of control over brand image and quality.
c. Joint Ventures and Strategic Alliances:

Partnering with local businesses can provide valuable insights into the foreign market while sharing risks and costs. However, it requires careful selection of partners and potential conflicts over decision-making.

a. Direct Investment: Establishing wholly-owned subsidiaries or acquiring existing businesses in the foreign market provides maximum control but involves high investment and greater risk.

2. Cultural Considerations:

a. Language and Communication: Understanding the local language is important for effective communication with customers, employees, and stakeholders. Translating marketing materials and adapting communication styles can enhance engagement.
b. Social Norms and Customs: Cultural differences in social norms, etiquette, and customs can significantly impact business interactions. It's essential to respect and adapt to local practices to build trust and relationships.
c. Consumer Behavior: Cultural values, preferences, and buying habits vary across regions. Conducting thorough market research helps in understanding consumer behavior and tailoring products or services accordingly.

d. Business Etiquette: Proper business etiquette varies globally, including aspects such as greeting rituals, negotiation styles, and decision-making processes. Adhering to local customs demonstrates respect and enhances business relationships.

e. Legal and Regulatory Environment: Legal systems and regulations differ across countries, affecting various aspects of business operations, including intellectual property rights, taxation, and employment laws. Complying with local regulations is essential to avoid legal issues.

f. Work Culture: Understanding work culture norms such as hierarchy, teamwork, and work-life balance are important for managing employees effectively and fostering a productive work environment.

g. Socio-Economic Factors: Economic conditions, income levels, and social structures influence consumer purchasing power and market demand. Adapting pricing strategies and product offerings based on socio-economic factors can optimize market penetration.

13.6 CROSS-CULTURAL MANAGEMENT CHALLENGES

Cross-cultural management poses significant challenges for businesses expanding globally.

1. Communication Barrier: Different cultures have distinct communication styles, norms, and languages. Misinterpretation or misunderstanding due to language barriers can hinder effective communication within the organization and with external stakeholders.

2. Cultural Differences: Each culture has its own values, beliefs, and norms. These differences can lead to misunderstandings, conflicts, or inefficiencies in the workplace, affecting teamwork, decision-making, and overall productivity.

3. Leadership and Management Style: Leadership and management practices vary across cultures. What may be considered effective leadership in one culture might not be perceived similarly in another. Leaders must adapt their styles to accommodate diverse cultural expectations and preferences.

4. Employee Motivation and Engagement: Cultural differences influence what motivates and engages employees. Recognition rewards, and incentives that work well in one culture may not be as effective in another. Understanding cultural nuances is crucial for fostering employee engagement and motivation.

5. Workplace Etiquette and Customs: Customs related to greetings, meetings, and interpersonal interactions differ across cultures. Failure to adhere to these customs can lead to discomfort or offense among employees and external partners.

6. Decision-Making Processes: Decision-making processes vary across cultures, ranging from hierarchical to consensus-based approaches. Businesses operating in multiple cultural contexts must navigate these differences to ensure efficient decision-making and alignment with organizational goals.

7. Legal and Regulatory Compliance: Legal and regulatory frameworks differ across countries, requiring businesses to understand and comply with various laws and regulations. Failure to do so can result in legal issues, fines, or reputational damage.

8. Managing Diversity and Inclusion: Global expansion increases workforce diversity, requiring organizations to promote inclusivity and create a supportive environment for employees from diverse cultural backgrounds. Failure to manage diversity effectively can lead to discrimination, bias, or a lack of cohesion within the workforce.

9. Cross-Cultural Team Dynamics: Managing teams composed of members from different cultural backgrounds requires special attention to communication, conflict resolution, and collaboration. Cultural differences can lead to misunderstandings or tensions within teams if not managed effectively.

10. Adapting Products and Services: Cultural differences influence consumer preferences, behaviors, and purchasing patterns. Businesses must tailor their products, services, and marketing strategies to suit the cultural context of target markets to ensure market acceptance and success.

13.7 CHALLENGES AND STRATEGIES IN MANAGING DIVERSE TEAMS.

Managing diverse teams in global expansion presents both opportunities and challenges.
Challenges:

1. Cultural Differences: Cultural nuances can lead to misunderstandings, miscommunications, and clashes in work styles, values, and norms.
2. Language Barriers: Language differences can hinder effective communication and collaboration within the team.
3. Time Zone Variations: Coordinating meetings, deadlines, and project updates across different time zones can be challenging and may lead to delays and inefficiencies.
4. Different Work Ethics: Diverse teams may have varying work ethics, expectations, and approaches to problem-solving and decision-making.
5. Conflict Resolution: Addressing conflicts arising from cultural misunderstandings or differences in opinions requires sensitivity and effective conflict resolution strategies.
6. Inclusivity and Belonging: Ensuring all team members feel valued included, and a sense of belonging can be challenging, particularly in multicultural environments.

Strategies:

1. Cultural Sensitivity Training: Provide cultural sensitivity training to all team members to enhance understanding and appreciation of diverse cultural backgrounds, norms, and practices.
2. Clear Communication Channels: Establish clear communication channels and protocols to mitigate language barriers, such as providing language support or using translation tools when necessary.
3. Flexible Work Arrangements: Implement flexible work arrangements to accommodate different time zones and schedules, allowing team members to work asynchronously when needed.
4. Embrace Diversity: Foster a culture of inclusivity and diversity where different perspectives and ideas are valued and celebrated.
5. Cross-Cultural Team Building: Organize team-building activities and initiatives that promote cross-cultural understanding, collaboration, and cohesion.
6. Effective Leadership: Provide strong leadership that promotes fairness, equality, and respect for all team members, regardless of their cultural background.
7. Regular Feedback and Check-ins: Schedule regular check-ins and provide constructive feedback to ensure everyone is aligned and on track, addressing any issues or concerns promptly.
8. Customized Approaches: Tailor management approaches, processes, and strategies to accommodate the specific needs and preferences of diverse team members.
9. Conflict Resolution Mechanisms: Establish clear and effective conflict resolution mechanisms to address any conflicts or misunderstandings that may arise, emphasizing open communication and mutual respect.
10. Continuous Learning and Adaptation: Encourage a culture of continuous learning and adaptation, where team members are encouraged to learn from each other's diverse perspectives and experiences.

13.8 IMPORTANCE OF CULTURAL SENSITIVITY.

Highlighting the importance of cultural sensitivity in global expansion is paramount for the success of any organization venturing into new markets.
REASONS WHY CULTURAL SENSITIVITY IS IMPORTANT:

1. Respect for Diversity: Different cultures have unique customs, traditions, and values. Being culturally sensitive demonstrates respect for diversity and fosters positive relationships with local communities.
2. Avoiding Offense: Without cultural sensitivity, businesses risk inadvertently offending local populations through misunderstandings or inappropriate behavior. This can damage reputation and hinder business growth.
3. Effective Communication: Cultural sensitivity enhances communication by ensuring messages are tailored to resonate with local audiences. This leads to clearer understanding and stronger connections with customers and partners.
4. Building Trust: Cultural sensitivity builds trust by showing that a company acknowledges and respects the cultural norms and practices of the communities it operates in. Trust is important for long-term success and sustainable growth.
5. Adapting Products and Services: Understanding cultural nuances enables businesses to adapt their products and services to better meet the needs and preferences of diverse markets. This increases the likelihood of acceptance and success.
6. Navigating Legal and Regulatory Differences: Cultural sensitivity helps businesses navigate complex legal and regulatory landscapes in different countries. Understanding cultural norms can prevent unintentional breaches of local laws or customs.
7. Employee Engagement and Retention: Promoting cultural sensitivity within the organization fosters an inclusive and supportive work environment. Employees are more likely to feel valued and engaged, leading to higher retention rates and productivity.

13.9 REGULATIONS GOVERNING IMPORT AND EXPORT ACTIVITIES.

Expanding globally involves navigating various regulations governing import and export activities. These regulations can vary significantly from one country to another and are subject to change due to geopolitical shifts, trade agreements, and local laws.

1. Customs Regulations: Each country has its own customs regulations governing the import and export of goods. These regulations may include requirements for documentation, tariffs, duties, and import/export restrictions.
2. Tariffs and Duties: Tariffs are taxes imposed by governments on imported goods, while duties refer to fees paid on imported or exported goods. Understanding the tariff and duty rates in the target market is important for pricing strategies and overall cost calculations.
3. Trade Agreements: Many countries participate in regional or bilateral trade agreements that can affect import and export regulations. These agreements may lower tariffs or provide other trade incentives between participating countries
4. Documentation Requirements: Import and export activities typically require extensive documentation, including invoices, packing lists, certificates of origin, and export/import licenses. Ensuring compliance with documentation requirements is essential to avoid delays or penalties.
5. Product Regulations and Standards: Different countries have varying product regulations and standards related to safety, quality, labeling, and packaging. Businesses must ensure their products meet the regulatory requirements of the target market.
6. Export Controls: Certain goods, technologies, and services may be subject to export controls due to national security concerns or international agreements. Export controls may include restrictions on exporting specific products or technologies to certain countries or entities.
7. Sanctions and Embargoes: Businesses need to be aware of sanctions and embargoes imposed by their home country or international bodies on specific countries or individuals. Engaging in trade with sanctioned entities can lead to severe legal consequences.

8. Transportation and Logistics: International shipping involves complex transportation and logistics considerations, including choosing appropriate shipping methods, complying with packaging requirements, and understanding Incoterms (international commercial terms) for defining responsibilities between buyers and sellers.

9. Intellectual Property Rights: Protecting intellectual property rights (IPR) is important when expanding globally. Businesses should be aware of the IPR regulations in different countries and take steps to safeguard their trademarks, patents, copyrights, and trade secrets.

10. Local Regulations and Cultural Considerations: Beyond national regulations, businesses must also consider local regulations and cultural norms in the target market. This may include language requirements, labeling preferences, and business practices.

13.10 COMPLIANCE REQUIREMENTS FOR GLOBAL TRADE.

Compliance requirements for global trade encompass a range of regulations and standards that businesses must adhere to when engaging in cross-border transactions. These requirements are established by various governmental bodies, international organizations, and industry associations to ensure the legality, safety, and ethical conduct of international trade activities.

COMPLIANCE REQUIREMENTS FOR GLOBAL TRADE:

1. Customs Regulations: Customs regulations govern the movement of goods across international borders. Importers and exporters must comply with customs requirements related to documentation, valuation, classification, and duties/taxes. Non-compliance can result in delays, fines, or seizure of goods.

2. Export Controls: Export control regulations restrict the export of certain goods, technologies, and services that have potential military, security, or dual-use applications. Exporters must obtain appropriate licenses and comply with export control laws to prevent unauthorized transfers of controlled items.

3. Sanctions Compliance: Sanctions are imposed by governments to restrict trade with specific countries, entities, or individuals for various reasons, such as national security, human rights violations, or terrorism. Businesses must screen their partners, customers, and transactions against sanctions lists to ensure compliance and avoid penalties.

4. Anti-Money Laundering (AML) and Counter-Terrorism Financing (CTF): AML and CTF regulations aim to prevent the use of international trade for illicit financial activities, such as money laundering and terrorist financing. Businesses are required to implement due diligence measures, customer identification procedures, and transaction monitoring to detect and report suspicious activities.

5. Trade Compliance Management Systems: Many companies establish trade compliance management systems to ensure adherence to regulatory requirements and mitigate compliance risks. These systems typically involve policies, procedures, training, and technology tools for monitoring and managing trade compliance activities.

6. Product Safety and Standards: Products traded globally must comply with applicable safety, quality, and technical standards to protect consumers and meet regulatory requirements in target markets. Compliance with product standards often involves testing, certification, labeling, and documentation procedures.

7. Environmental Regulations: Environmental regulations may impact global trade through restrictions on the import/export of certain goods, such as hazardous materials or endangered species, as well as requirements for sustainable practices in manufacturing and supply chain operations.

8. Data Privacy and Security: International trade involves the transfer of sensitive information across borders, requiring compliance with data privacy and security regulations, such as the General Data Protection Regulation (GDPR) in the European Union. Businesses must ensure the lawful processing and protection of personal data during cross-border transactions.

9. Ethical and Corporate Social Responsibility (CSR) Standards: Companies are increasingly expected to uphold ethical and CSR standards in their global trade practices, addressing issues such as labor rights, human trafficking,

corruption, and environmental sustainability.

10. Documentation and Record-Keeping: Accurate documentation and record-keeping are essential for demonstrating compliance with regulatory requirements in global trade. Businesses must maintain records of transactions, contracts, licenses, certifications, and compliance activities for auditing and reporting purposes.

13.11 QUESTIONS:

1. What are the ADVANTAGES AND CHALLENGES OF INTERNATIONAL TRADE?
2. Explain the importance of understanding global markets.
3. What are the steps involved in global business expansion?
4. Explain the market entry strategies and cultural considerations?
5. What are the challenges and strategies in managing diverse teams?
6. What is the importance of cultural sensitivity?
7. Explain the regulations governing import and export activities?

CHAPTER FOURTEEN

START-UP IN INDIA

14.1 BUSINESS ORGANISATION

A business organization serves as the backbone of the global economy, driving innovation, creating employment opportunities, and facilitating the exchange of goods and services. Whether a small entrepreneurial venture or a multinational corporation, these entities play an important role in shaping the economic landscape.

A business organization is a structured entity formed with the primary objective of achieving specific goals and objectives, often centered on profitability and sustainable growth. The organizational structure, management hierarchy, and operational processes are meticulously designed to streamline activities, optimize resources, and foster efficiency.

In this dynamic and interconnected world, business organizations adapt to ever-changing market conditions, technological advancements, and consumer preferences, making strategic decisions to remain competitive and resilient.

14.2 TYPES OF BUSINESS ORGANISATION

1. Sole Proprietorship:

This is the simplest form of business organization where a single individual owns and manages the business. The owner has unlimited liability and is personally responsible for all the debts and liabilities of the business.

1. Partnership:

A partnership is formed by two or more individuals who agree to share profits and losses. Partnerships can be either general partnerships or limited partnerships, where liability varies among partners.

3. Limited Liability Partnership (LLP):

An LLP is a hybrid form of business organization that combines the flexibility of a partnership with the limited liability feature of a company. Partners have limited liability, and the business is a separate legal entity.

4. Private Limited Company:

A private limited company is a separate legal entity with limited liability for its shareholders. It is required to have a minimum of two directors and two shareholders and cannot offer its shares to the public.

5. Public Limited Company:

A public limited company is similar to a private limited company but can offer its shares to the public. It must have a minimum of seven shareholders and three directors.

6. One Person Company (OPC):

Introduced to support sole proprietors, an OPC allows a single person to form a company with limited liability.

7. Cooperative Societies:

Cooperative societies are formed by a group of individuals with common economic or social objectives. Members actively participate in decision-making, and profits are distributed based on the level of participation.

8. Multinational Corporations (MNCs):

Many multinational corporations have a significant presence in India, operating in diverse sectors such as IT, manufacturing, pharmaceuticals, and more.

9. Non-Governmental Organizations (NGOs):

NGOs are typically formed for charitable, social, or environmental purposes.They operate as non-profit entities and often focus on social development and welfare activities.

10. Startups:

India has a thriving startup ecosystem, with numerous innovative and technology-driven companies emerging in sectors such as e-commerce, fintech, healthtech, and more. These are just a few examples, and the business landscape in India is continually evolving with changes in regulations and market trends. The choice of business organization depends on factors such as the nature of the business, scale of operations, and liability considerations.

14.3 FACTORS GOVERNING SELECTION OF AN ORGANISATION

Selecting a suitable form of organization is an important decision that profoundly influences the success and efficiency of any enterprise. The organizational structure serves as the framework that defines roles, responsibilities, and communication channels within a company. In essence, it determines how tasks are divided, authority is delegated, and information flows. The right organizational form aligns with the company's goals, industry dynamics, and operational needs, fostering a condusive environment for growth and adaptability. This selection process involves a thoughtful analysis of factors such as size, nature of the business, corporate culture, and market dynamics. In this context, understanding the various forms of organization and their implications is paramount to making informed decisions that will shape the organization's trajectory.

1. NATURE OF BUSINESS: The type of business one is engaged in significantly influences the choice of organization. For instance, a small retail business may opt for a different structure than a high-tech startup.

2. OWNERSHIP STRUCTURE: Consider whether one want sole ownership, partnership, or multiple stakeholders in the business.

3. LIABILITY: Evaluate the level of personal liability one is willing to bear. Sole proprietorships and partnerships have unlimited liability, while companies offer limited liability.

4. CAPITAL REQUIREMENTS: Different business structures have varying capital requirements. Companies, for example, can raise capital through the sale of stocks.

5. TAX IMPLICATIONS: Assess the tax implications of different business structures, as taxation varies for sole proprietorships, partnerships, and companies.

6. MANAGEMENT CONTROL: Determine how much control one want over decision-making. In a sole proprietorship, one have full control, whereas companies involve a board of directors.

7. EASE OF FORMATION: Consider the simplicity or complexity of forming the business entity. Sole proprietorships and partnerships are generally easier to establish than companies.

8. CONTINUITY OF EXISTENCE: Evaluate how long one wants the business to exist. Companies have perpetual existence, while partnerships may dissolve with changes in ownership.

9. TRANSFERABILITY OF OWNERSHIP: if the ability to transfer ownership is important, companies offer the advantage of easily transferring shares.

10. REGULATORY COMPLIANCE: Different business structures have varying regulatory requirements. Be aware of the legal obligations associated with each type

11. ACCESS TO FINANCING: Consider the ease of accessing financing options. Companies often have more options, including issuing bonds and stocks.
12. RISK TOLERANCE: Assess the risk tolerance, as some structures expose personal assets to business liabilities more than others.
13. FLEXIBILITY: Examine the flexibility of the organizational structure. Sole proprietorships and partnerships can adapt more easily to changes.
14. CREDIBILITY AND PERCEPTION: The type of organization can impact how customers, suppliers, and investors perceive the business.
15. EXIT STRATEGY: Consider the exit strategy. Some structures make it easier to sell or transfer the business.
16. COST OF FORMATION AND MAINTENANCE: Evaluate the costs associated with forming and maintaining the chosen business structure, including registration fees and ongoing compliance costs.
17. LOCATION:The geographical location of the business may influence the choice of organization due to regional regulations and market conditions.
18. INDUSTRY STANDARDS: In some industries, certain types of business structures are more common or preferable.
19. EMPLOYEE INCENTIVES: Consider the ability to offer employee incentives such as stock options, which is more feasible in a corporate structure.
20. SOCIAL AND ENVIRONMENTAL IMPACT: Increasingly, businesses are considering their social and environmental impact. Certain structures may align better with sustainability goals or social enterprises.

When selecting a business organization, it's essential to carefully weigh these factors to align the structure with the business goals and circumstances.

14.4 DEFINITION OF A STARTUP

A startup is a newly established business or company, typically in the early stages of its development, with a focus on introducing innovative products, services, or business models to the market. Startups are often characterized by their pursuit of high growth and scalability, as well as their willingness to take risks and challenge established norms in order to disrupt existing industries or create new ones.

In India, a startup is typically defined as a newly established business venture that aims to address a unique problem or meet a specific market demand through innovation, technology, or a differentiated business model. The Government of India, through its various policies and initiatives, provides a broader perspective on startups, considering entities that are less than 10 years old and have an annual turnover below a specified threshold. These enterprises often operate in sectors such as technology, e-commerce, healthcare, and finance, leveraging disruptive ideas and cutting-edge technologies. Startups in India benefit from a supportive ecosystem that includes angel investors, venture capitalists, and government schemes like the 'Startup India' initiative, which offers incentives, funding, and mentorship to foster entrepreneurship and fuel economic growth. The dynamic nature of the startup landscape in India reflects a spirit of innovation and resilience, driving the country's aspirations to become a global hub for entrepreneurial endeavors.

IMPORTANT FEATURES OF STARTUPS INCLUDE:

1. Innovation: Startups are known for their emphasis on innovation, whether it's in terms of technology, business processes, or the products/services they offer.
2. Scalability: Startups aim to grow rapidly and achieve scalability, meaning they can expand their operations efficiently as they acquire more customers or users.

3. High Risk-High Reward: Startups often operate in an environment of uncertainty and are willing to take significant risks in the hope of achieving substantial rewards.

4. Entrepreneurial Spirit: Startups are typically founded by entrepreneurs who are driven by a vision and are willing to work hard to bring their ideas to fruition.

5. Limited Resources: Startups often begin with limited financial resources and a small team, requiring them to be resourceful and efficient in their operations.

6. Focus on Market Niche: Startups often identify and target specific market niches, aiming to meet the unique needs or solve specific problems for their target audience.

Startups play a crucial role in driving economic growth, fostering innovation, and creating employment opportunities. They are commonly associated with the technology sector, but startups can emerge in various industries, including healthcare, finance, agriculture, and more. The journey of a startup involves various stages, including ideation, development, fundraising, market entry, and, ideally, growth and sustainability.

14.5 STARTUP INTRODUCTION

India has become a thriving hub for startups, fostering a dynamic ecosystem driven by innovation, technology, and a burgeoning entrepreneurial spirit. With a population of over 1.4 billion people and a rapidly growing economy, India presents a vast market and diverse opportunities for startups across various sectors.

1. Vibrant Ecosystem: India boasts a vibrant startup ecosystem, with numerous incubators, accelerators, and co-working spaces supporting entrepreneurs. Cities like Bengaluru, Mumbai, Delhi, and Hyderabad have emerged as key hubs, hosting a plethora of startups ranging from technology and e-commerce to healthcare and renewable energy.

2. Government Initiatives: The Indian government has introduced several initiatives to promote entrepreneurship and facilitate the growth of startups. Programs like "Startup India" aim to provide a condusive environment, offering tax benefits, funding support, and regulatory simplifications.

3. Tech-driven Innovation: Technology has been a driving force behind many successful startups in India. The country has witnessed significant advancements in areas such as artificial intelligence, blockchain, fintech, and e-commerce, fostering innovation and disruption across industries.

4. Young Demographic: India has a youthful demographic, with a large percentage of the population under 35 years old. This demographic dividend contributes to a dynamic workforce and a consumer base that is receptive to new ideas, products, and services.

5. Funding Landscape:The startup ecosystem in India has seen a surge in funding from venture capitalists, angel investors, and even international investors. This funding influx has fueled the growth of startups, enabling them to scale operations, conduct research and development, and explore new markets.

6. Diverse Sectors: Startups in India span various sectors, including but not limited to e-commerce, healthtech, edtech, agritech, cleantech, and fintech. This diversity showcases the adaptability and resilience of Indian entrepreneurs in addressing a wide range of challenges.

7. Social Impact: Many startups in India are not only focused on profitability but also on creating a positive social impact. Social enterprises addressing issues such as healthcare accessibility, education, and sustainable development are gaining prominence.

8. Global Recognition: Indian startups have gained international recognition, with some achieving unicorn status (valuation of over $1 billion). This global acknowledgment has positioned India as a formidable player in the global startup landscape.

The startup scene in India is dynamic, evolving, and full of potential. Entrepreneurs are leveraging the country's diverse resources, technological prowess, and supportive ecosystem to build innovative solutions, making India a key player in the global startup arena.

14.6 EVOLUTION OF A STARTUP

The evolution of startups in India has been a dynamic journey, marked by significant changes and growth over the years.

Brief overview of the key phases in the evolution of startups in India:

1. Early Years (Pre-2000s):

a. Before the 2000s, the startup ecosystem in India was relatively nascent.
b. Limited access to capital and a risk-averse environment were significant challenges.
c. A few success stories, such as Infosys and Wipro, inspired the emergence of tech-focused entrepreneurs.

2. Dotcom. Boom (Late 1990s - Early 2000s):

a. The dotcom boom saw the rise of internet-focused startups.
b. Though many startups failed during the dotcom bust, it laid the groundwork for a more robust ecosystem by introducing the concept of entrepreneurship.

3. Post-Liberalization Era (Early 2000s):

a. Economic liberalization in the early 2000s led to increased foreign investment and a more condusive environment for startups.
b. This period saw the emergence of companies like Flipkart (2007) and Naukri.com (1997), pioneers in e-commerce and online job portals, respectively.

4. Rise of E-Commerce (2010s):

a. The 2010s witnessed the rapid growth of e-commerce startups, including Flipkart, Snapdeal, and Paytm.
b. Increased internet penetration and the growing popularity of smartphones fueled the growth of online businesses.

5. Government Initiatives (2015 Onward):

a. The Indian government launched initiatives like 'Startup India' in 2015 to support and foster entrepreneurship.
b. Policy changes aimed at easing regulatory hurdles and promoting innovation contributed to the growth of startups.

6. Emergence of Unicorns (2010s - Present):

a. The Indian startup ecosystem has produced several unicorns (startups with a valuation of $1 billion or more), such as Ola, Zomato, and BYJU'S.
b. These success stories have attracted attention from investors and further fueled the growth of the ecosystem.

7. Diversity of Sectors (2010s - Present):

a. While technology and e-commerce continue to be dominant, startups in various sectors have gained traction, including fintech, healthtech, edtech, and agritech.
b. This diversification reflects the maturation of the ecosystem and the recognition of opportunities in different industries.

8. Global Recognition (2020s - Present):

a.   Indian startups gained global recognition, with several expanding their presence internationally.
b.   Increased interest from global investors and collaborations with international companies has further boosted the ecosystem.

9. Challenges and Adaptations (Ongoing):

a.   The Indian startup ecosystem faces challenges such as regulatory complexities, funding concerns, and market competition.
b.   Startups continue to adapt to changing market dynamics, leveraging technology and innovation to address evolving consumer needs.

The evolution of startups in India is a testament to the resilience and adaptability of entrepreneurs in navigating challenges and seizing opportunities in a rapidly changing business landscape.

14.7 STARTUP LANDSCAPE IN INDIA

India has been experiencing a vibrant and dynamic startup ecosystem. However, that the startup landscape is highly dynamic and subject to change.

IMPORTANT ASPECTS OF THE STARTUP LANDSCAPE IN INDIA:

1.   Government Initiatives: The Indian government has been actively supporting the startup ecosystem through initiatives like Startup India. These initiatives aim to provide financial support, regulatory ease, and fostering innovation.
2.   Investment Climate: India has seen significant investments in its startup ecosystem. Both domestic and international investors are showing interest, and there has been a rise in venture capital funding. Key sectors attracting investments include technology, e-commerce, fintech, health tech, and renewable energy.
3.   Unicorn Growth: India has witnessed the emergence of several unicorn startups, valued at over a billion dollars. These companies span various industries such as e-commerce (Flipkart, Paytm), fintech (PhonePe, Razorpay), edtech (Byju's), and more.
4.   Technology and Innovation: The technology sector continues to be a driving force behind many startups. Artificial intelligence, machine learning, blockchain, and other cutting-edge technologies are being leveraged for innovative solutions across different industries.
5.   E-commerce and Consumer Services: E-commerce platforms, food delivery services, and other consumer-oriented startups have gained widespread popularity. Companies like Flipkart, Amazon India, Zomato, and Swiggy are prominent players in this space.
6.   Fintech: The fintech sector in India has seen significant growth, with startups focusing on digital payments, lending, insurance, and wealth management. Companies like Paytm, PhonePe, and PolicyBazaar are notable examples.
7.   Healthcare and Medtech: The COVID-19 pandemic has accelerated innovation in the healthcare sector. Telemedicine, healthtech, and medtech startups have gained traction, addressing various aspects of healthcare delivery.
8.   Edtech: The education technology sector has seen a surge in demand, especially with the shift towards online learning. Platforms like Byju's, Unacademy, and Vedantu have seen rapid growth.
9.   Sustainability and CleanTech: There is a growing interest in sustainable and clean technology solutions. Startups focusing on renewable energy, waste management, and environmentally friendly practices are gaining attention.

10. Challenges: While the startup ecosystem in India is thriving, challenges such as regulatory hurdles, access to funding, and competition remain. The economic impact of external factors, such as the COVID-19 pandemic, can also influence the startup landscape.

14.8 STARTUP INDIA POLICY

The Startup India initiative is a flagship initiative of the Government of India, launched in 2016, with the aim of fostering entrepreneurship and promoting innovation.

The Startup India Action Plan, launched by the Indian government in January 2016, aims to foster a condusive environment for the growth of startups in the country. The plan focuses on promoting entrepreneurship, innovation, and job creation. It includes various initiatives to simplify regulatory processes, provide financial support, and offer mentorship to startups.

To boost funding for startups, the government has established a fund of funds with a corpus of Rs 10,000 crore to support early-stage ventures. The plan also introduces tax benefits for startups, including a three-year exemption from income tax and a simplified capital gains tax structure.

In addition, the Startup India Hub serves as a single-point contact for all startup-related queries and assistance. The plan encourages industry-academia partnerships, innovation in public procurement, and incubation centers to nurture new ideas. It also promotes skill development through various programs and initiatives.

Overall, the Startup India Action Plan strives to create a thriving ecosystem that empowers entrepreneurs, facilitates innovation, and contributes to economic growth by positioning India as a global hub for startups.

IMPORTANT FEATURES AND COMPONENTS OF THE STARTUP INDIA POLICY

1. Definition of Startups: The policy defines startups as entities that are up to 10 years old from the date of incorporation and are working towards innovation, development, deployment, or commercialization of new products, processes, or services driven by technology or intellectual property.

2. Registration Process: Startups can register on the Startup India portal to avail of various benefits. The registration process involves self-certification and does not require any formal documentation.

3. Tax Benefits: Startups can avail of income tax exemptions for the first three consecutive assessment years, provided they are recognized by the Department of Industrial Policy and Promotion (DPIIT).

4. Fund of Funds for Startups (FFS): The government has established a Fund of Funds for Startups with a corpus to provide financial support to startups. It aims to promote the development and growth of innovation-driven enterprises.

5. Simplification of Compliance: Startups are given a 3-year exemption from labor and environmental laws inspection. They are also allowed to self-certify compliance with nine labor and three environmental laws.

6. Fast-Track Patent Examination: Startups can avail of fast-track examination of patent applications. This helps in expediting the process of obtaining patents for their innovations.

7. Innovation Hub and Learning Program: The government has introduced various initiatives to create a condusive environment for learning and innovation, including innovation hubs, mentorship programs, and incubators.

8. Ease of Winding up: To provide an exit option to unsuccessful startups, the government has simplified the process of closing down a business.

9. Networking and Collaboration: The initiative encourages collaboration between startups and industry, academia, and other stakeholders. It aims to create a network of incubators, accelerators, and industry bodies.

14.9 FUNDING SUPPORT AND INCENTIVES

India has been taking various initiatives to support and promote startups through funding support and incentives.

IMPORTANT MEASURES AND SCHEMES AIMED AT FOSTERING THE STARTUP ECOSYSTEM IN INDIA:

1. Startup India Initiative: Launched by the Government of India, this initiative aims to build a strong ecosystem for nurturing innovation and startups. Provides various benefits, including tax exemptions, self-certification, and a simplified compliance process.

2. Fund of Funds for Startups (FFS): Under the Startup India Action Plan, the government established a fund with a corpus of INR 10,000 crores to provide funding support to startups.

3. Credit Guarantee Fund for Startups (CGFS): A scheme to facilitate funding to startups by offering credit guarantees to banks and financial institutions.

4. Tax Benefits: Startups are eligible for a tax holiday for the first three consecutive years out of their first ten years since incorporation. Capital gains from the sale of residential property can be invested in startups to avail tax exemptions.

5. Angel Tax Exemption: Angel investors investing in startups are exempted from the angel tax to promote early stage funding.

6. Research and Development (R&D) Incentives: Various incentives are provided to encourage research and development activities in startups.

7. State Specific Initiatives: Several states in India have launched their own startup policies, providing additional support and incentives to startups.

8. Ease of Doing Business: Efforts have been made to simplify regulations and reduce bureaucratic hurdles to make it easier for startups to operate.

9. Networking and Collaboration Platforms: Initiatives like incubators, accelerators, and co*working spaces have been set up to provide startups with the necessary infrastructure, mentoring, and networking opportunities.

10. Public Procurement Norms: Preference may be given to startups in government procurement processes to boost their participation in government projects.

14.10 INDIAN STATES WITH STARTUP POLICIES

Several Indian states have implemented startup policies to promote and support the growth of startups in their regions. These policies often include incentives, funding support, infrastructure development, and other measures to create a condusive environment for startup activities.

STATES WITH NOTABLE STARTUP POLICIES INCLUDE:

1. Karnataka:

Karnataka, particularly Bengaluru, is known as the startup hub of India. The state has implemented various policies and initiatives to support the startup ecosystem, including the Karnataka Startup Policy.

2. Telangana:

The Telangana government has launched the "Telangana State Innovation Policy" to encourage innovation and entrepreneurship. Hyderabad, the state's capital, is home to a growing number of startups.

3. Maharashtra:

The Maharashtra State Innovation Society and the Maharashtra State Innovation Council are involved in promoting innovation and startups in the state. Mumbai, Pune, and Nagpur are key startup hubs in Maharashtra.

4. Gujarat:

Gujarat has implemented the Gujarat Startup and Innovation Policy to boost entrepreneurship and innovation in the state. Cities like Ahmedabad and Gandhinagar are witnessing increased startup activity.

5. Tamil Nadu:

The Tamil Nadu Startup and Innovation Policy aim to create an environment that fosters innovation and supports startups. Chennai, the capital, is a prominent hub for technology startups.

6. Rajasthan:

The Rajasthan Startup Policy focuses on creating a condusive ecosystem for startups. The state government has taken steps to support innovation and entrepreneurship.

7. Uttar Pradesh:

Uttar Pradesh has launched the Uttar Pradesh Startup Policy to promote startups and create a favorable environment for entrepreneurs. Noida and Lucknow are emerging as startup hubs in the state.

8. Kerala:

Kerala has initiatives like the Kerala Startup Mission (KSUM) to nurture startups. The state government has implemented policies to support entrepreneurship and innovation.

9. Andhra Pradesh:

Andhra Pradesh has introduced various policies, including the Andhra Pradesh Innovation and Startup Policy, to boost the startup ecosystem in the state.

10. Haryana:

The Haryana Enterprise Promotion Policy aims to promote entrepreneurship and startups in the state. Gurugram and other cities in Haryana have seen the emergence of startups.

14.11 EXEMPTIONS FORSTARTUPS

In India, there are various exemptions and benefits available for startups to promote entrepreneurship and innovation. The Government of India has introduced several initiatives and policies to support startups.

EXEMPTIONS AND BENEFITS THAT STARTUPS IN INDIA CAN AVAIL:

1. Startup India Recognition: Startups can apply for recognition under the Startup India initiative to avail various benefits. To be eligible, a startup should be incorporated as a private limited company or registered as a partnership firm or a limited liability partnership (LLP). The recognition provides benefits such as tax exemptions, self-certification, and access to various government schemes.

2. Income Tax Exemption: Eligible startups can avail income tax exemption for a specified period. The Finance Act of 2016 introduced Section 80-IAC, which provides a 100% tax deduction on profits for three consecutive

assessment years out of seven years.

3. Angel Tax Exemption: Angel tax is the tax on capital raised by unlisted companies through the issue of shares at a price higher than their fair market value. The government has made efforts to address the concerns around angel tax for startups and has introduced exemptions for eligible startups.

4. Capital Gains Tax Exemption: Exemptions on capital gains tax are available for startups. If a startup sells a residential property and invests the capital gains in funding a startup, it can be exempt from capital gains tax.

5. Research and Development (R&D) Grants: Startups engaged in research and development activities can access grants and funds provided by government agencies to support innovation and technology development.

6. Customs Duty Exemption: Startups can benefit from customs duty exemption on the import of specified goods for the development, testing, or use of technology.

7. Public Procurement Relaxation: Startups are given relaxation in the eligibility criteria and prior experience requirements for participating in government tenders and procurement processes.

8. Faster Exit for Startups: The government has introduced simpler and faster exit mechanisms for startups to wind up their operations.

14.12 LIFE CYCLE OF A STARTUP

The life cycle of a startup in India, like in any other country, typically involves several stages. These stages can vary in duration and intensity, and not all startups follow the same path. However, a general framework can be outlined:

1. Idea Generation: This is the initial stage where entrepreneurs come up with a business idea. It could be based on a problem they want to solve or an opportunity they identify in the market.

2. Market Research: Before diving into the business, founders need to conduct thorough market research to validate their idea. This involves understanding the target audience, competition, and potential demand for the product or service.

3. Business Planning: Once the idea is validated, founders create a detailed business plan. This includes defining the business model, revenue streams, marketing strategy, and operational plan.

4. Formation and Registration: The startup needs to be legally registered. This involves choosing a business structure (Private Limited Company, LLP, etc.), obtaining necessary licenses, and adhering to regulatory requirements.

5. Seed Stage / Funding: In the early stages, founders often use personal savings or contributions from friends and family. They may also seek seed funding from angel investors or venture capitalists to develop a prototype or launch the product.

6. Product Development: With funding in place, the startup focuses on developing a minimum viable product (MVP) or a prototype. This stage involves iterative testing and refinement.

7. Launch: The startup officially launches its product or service in the market. This involves marketing, creating awareness, and attracting the first set of customers.

8. Early Growth: This phase sees increasing customer acquisition, product improvement based on user feedback, and possibly expanding the team.

9. Scaling: The startup scales its operations, which may involve expanding into new markets, increasing production capacity, or enhancing the product/service offering. Additional rounds of funding might be sought for scaling.

10. Maturity: The startup reaches a point where it has established a stable market presence, a solid customer base, and sustainable revenue streams. It may continue to innovate and evolve but at a more stable pace.

11. Sustainability or Exit: The startup aims for long-term sustainability, profitability, and possibly an exit strategy. Exit options could include going public through an IPO, mergers and acquisitions, or strategic partnerships.

It's important to note that not all startups follow this linear path, and challenges can arise at any stage. Some startups may face setbacks, pivot their business model, or even shut down. Adaptability and resilience are important for navigating the dynamic startup landscape. Additionally, government policies, economic conditions, and industry trends can influence the trajectory of a startup in India.

14.13 IMPORTANT POINTS FOR A STARTUP

Starting a startup in India involves navigating various challenges and opportunities.
LIST OF IMPORTANT POINTS FOR A STARTUP:
1. Market Research:

1. Conduct thorough market research to understand the demand for the product or service.
2. Identify the target audience and their needs.
3. Analyze competitors and market trends.

2. Business Plan:

1. Develop a comprehensive business plan outlining the goals, target market, revenue model, and marketing strategy.
2. Include financial projections and funding requirements.

3. Legal Structure:

1. Choose an appropriate legal structure for the business (Private Limited Company, LLP, etc.).
2. Register your business with the Ministry of Corporate Affairs (MCA).

4. Compliance and Registration:

1. Ensure compliance with taxation and regulatory requirements.
2. Obtain necessary licenses and permits.

5. Funding: Explore various funding options, including bootstrapping, angel investors, venture capitalists, or government schemes.
6. Technology and Innovation:

1. Leverage technology to enhance the product or service.
2. Focus on innovation to stay competitive in the market.

7. Digital Presence:

1. Establish a strong online presence through a website and social media.
2. Utilize digital marketing strategies to reach a wider audience.

8. Team Building:

1. Assemble a skilled and motivated team.
2. Define roles and responsibilities clearly.

9. Networking:

1. Build a strong network within the industry.
2. Attend relevant events, conferences, and meet ups.

10. Customer Feedback:

1. Gather and value customer feedback.
2. Continuously improve the product or service based on customer needs.

11. Cyber security: Prioritize cyber security to protect the business and customer data.
12. Adaptability:

1. Be adaptable to market changes and customer feedback.
2. Embrace a culture of continuous improvement.

13. Scalability:

1. Plan for scalability right from the beginning.
2. Ensure the infrastructure and processes can handle growth.

14. Government Schemes: Explore government schemes and incentives for startups, such as Startup India.
15. Intellectual Property (IP) Protection: Secure the intellectual property through patents, trademarks, or copyrights.
16. Social Responsibility:

1. Consider incorporating social responsibility into the business model.
2. CSR (Corporate Social Responsibility) initiatives can enhance the brand image.

17. Financial Management:

1. Maintain robust financial management practices.
2. Monitor cash flow and expenses closely.

18. Exit Strategy:

1. Develop an exit strategy, even if it's not an immediate concern.
2. Understand potential exit options like acquisition or IPO.

14.14 FINANCING OPTIONS AVAILABLE FOR STARTUP

FINANCING OPTIONS AVAILABLE FOR STARTUP

Financing options for startups can vary depending on factors such as the industry, stage of development, and the specific needs of the business.

List of financing options available for startups:

1. Bootstrapping: Bootstrapping involves using personal savings, revenue generated by the business, or funds from friends and family to start and grow the business.

ADVANTAGES: Maintaining full control, avoiding debt, and keeping ownership.

DISADVANTAGES: Limited resources, slower growth.

2. Angel Investors: Angel investors are individuals who provide capital in exchange for equity or convertible debt in early-stage startups.

ADVANTAGES: Quick access to capital, mentorship and expertise.

DISADVANTAGES: Loss of some control and ownership.

3. Venture Capital (VC): Venture capitalists are professional groups that manage pooled funds from various investors and invest in startups with high growth potential.

ADVANTAGES: Significant funding, access to networks and expertise.

DISADVANTAGES: Loss of control, stringent criteria for investment.

4. Crowdfunding: Crowdfunding platforms allow startups to raise small amounts of money from a large number of people. This can be done through rewards-based crowdfunding, equity crowdfunding, or debt crowdfunding.

ADVANTAGES: Access to a broad investor base, validation of product or idea.

DISADVANTAGES: Time-consuming, may not raise large amounts.

5. Bank Loans: Traditional bank loans involve borrowing a fixed amount of money with agreed-upon interest rates and repayment terms.

ADVANTAGES: Relatively low interest rates (compared to other debt options), predictable repayment schedule.

DISADVANTAGES: Strict eligibility criteria, may require collateral as security.

6. Government Grants and Subsidies: Some governments offer grants, subsidies, or low-interest loans to support startups in specific industries or regions.

ADVANTAGES: Non-dilutive funding, government support.

DISADVANTAGES: Highly competitive, may have specific eligibility criteria.

7. Corporate Sponsorship or Partnerships: Corporations may provide funding or resources to startups in exchange for strategic partnerships or access to innovative technologies.

ADVANTAGES: Financial support, access to industry expertise and resources.

DISADVANTAGES: May involve giving up some control or intellectual property.

8. Incubators and Accelerators: These programs offer funding, mentorship, and resources in exchange for equity. They often culminate in a demo day where startups pitch to investors.

ADVANTAGES: Mentorship, networking opportunities, support services.

DISADVANTAGES: Equity dilution, competitive application process.

9. Convertible Notes: Convertible notes are a form of short-term debt that can convert into equity during a future funding round.

ADVANTAGES: Quick access to capital, defers valuation until a later date.

DISADVANTAGES: Complex terms, potential for dilution.

10. Initial Coin Offerings (ICOs) and Security Token Offerings (STOs): Blockchain-based fundraising methods where startups issue tokens or coins to investors in exchange for capital.

ADVANTAGES: Access to a global pool of investors, potential for rapid fundraising.

DISADVANTAGES: Regulatory uncertainties, volatility.

It's essential for startups to carefully consider their financing needs, business model, and long-term goals when choosing the most suitable financing option or combination of options.

14.17 VENTURE CAPITAL FINANCING

Venture capital (VC) financing is a popular method for startups to raise funds, fuel growth, and expand their operations. In India, the startup ecosystem has been growing rapidly, and there are various avenues for securing venture capital funding.

IMPORTANT ASPECTS OF VENTURE CAPITAL FINANCING FOR STARTUPS:

1. Understand the Venture Capital Landscape in India:

a. Familiarize yourself with the key venture capital firms in India. Some prominent ones include Sequoia Capital India, Accel Partners India, Nexus Venture Partners, and Light speed India.

b. Different Venture capital firms may focus on specific sectors or stages of startups, so research which ones align with your business.

2. Prepare a Strong Business Plan:

a.   Develop a comprehensive business plan that outlines your startup's mission, market potential, revenue model, and growth strategy.
b.   Highlight key metrics and milestones that demonstrate your business's viability and potential for scalability.

3. Build a Solid Team:

a.   Investors often look for a strong and capable founding team. Showcase the skills, expertise, and experience of your team members in your pitch.

4. Create a Pitch Deck

a.   Craft a compelling pitch deck that summarizes your business, market opportunity, competitive landscape, financial projections, and funding requirements.
b.   Be concise, clear, and visually appealing in your presentation.

5. Identify the Right Venture capital Firms:

c.   Choose venture capital firms that align with your startup's industry, stage, and vision.
d.   Network with entrepreneurs who have received funding from these firms to gain insights and recommendations.

6. Network and Attend Events:

a.   Attend startup events, conferences, and networking sessions to connect with potential investors and build relationships.
b.   Platforms like TiE (The Indus Entrepreneurs) and startup incubators/accelerators can be valuable for networking.

7. Engage with Angel Investors:

a.   Angel investors often play a crucial role in early stage funding. Connect with individuals who have a track record of investing in startups similar to yours.

8. Understand the Term Sheet:

a.   Once a Venture capital firm expresses interest, you will typically receive a term sheet. Understand its terms, including valuation, ownership stake, and rights granted to the investors.

9. Due Diligence:

a.   Be prepared for thorough due diligence by the Venture capital firm. This may involve legal, financial, and operational reviews of your startup.

10. Negotiate and Close the Deal:

a.   Engage in negotiations to ensure that the terms are favorable for both parties.
b.   Seek legal advice to understand the implications of the agreement before finalizing the deal.

11. Post Funding Relationship:

a. Foster a positive and collaborative relationship with your investors. Regularly communicate progress and challenges.

Venture capital financing is not the only option for startups, and entrepreneurs should consider other funding sources like government grants, angel investors, crowd funding, or bootstrapping based on their specific needs and circumstances.

14.18 INITIAL PUBLIC OFFERING (IPO)

Initiating an Initial Public Offering (IPO) for a startup in India involves several steps and considerations.
1. Preparation:

a. Financial Preparation: Ensure that the financial statements are in order. This includes audited financial statements, balance sheets, profit and loss statements, and cash flow statements.
b. Legal Compliance: Ensure compliance with all regulatory requirements. This may include legal due diligence, resolving any outstanding legal issues, and obtaining necessary approvals.
c. Business Plan: Prepare a comprehensive business plan that outlines the company's vision, mission, financials, and growth prospects.

2. Engage Professionals:

a. Underwriters: Select underwriters to manage the IPO process. They will help with pricing, marketing, and distributing the shares.
b. Legal Advisors: Consult legal experts to ensure compliance with all regulatory requirements.
c. Financial Advisors: Seek advice from financial advisors for valuing the company and determining the IPO size.

3. Due Diligence:

a. Financial Due Diligence: Conduct a thorough review of the financial records to identify any discrepancies or potential issues.
b. Legal Due Diligence: Review all legal aspects of the business to identify and resolve any legal issues.

4. Regulatory Compliance:

a. SEBI Approval: The Securities and Exchange Board of India (SEBI) regulates IPOs. Obtain approval from SEBI by submitting the necessary documents and complying with their guidelines.

5. Drafting the Red Herring Prospectus (RHP):

a. Red Herring Prospectus: This document contains all essential information about the company and the IPO. It is circulated to potential investors.

6. Roadshows and Marketing:
Roadshows: Organize roadshows to generate interest among potential investors. This involves presenting the business to institutional investors.
7. Book Building:

Price Discovery: Determine the issue price through a process known as book building, where investors bid for shares within a specified price range.

8. Listing:

a. Listing Application: Submit an application for listing on the stock exchange, where one wishes to list the shares.
b. Allotment and Refund: Allot shares to investors based on the bids received. Refund excess money to unsuccessful bidders.

9. Post IPO Compliance:

a. Listing Agreement: Comply with the listing agreement requirements of the stock exchange.
b. Continuous Disclosure: Keep the market updated on any material developments through regular disclosures.

10. Monitoring PostIPO Performance:

a. Shareholder Relations: Establish effective communication with shareholders and the investment community.
b. Quarterly and Annual Reports: Continue to provide regular financial reports to the public.

11. Important Considerations:

a. Market Conditions: Monitor market conditions and choose an opportune time for the IPO.
b. Valuation: Determine a reasonable valuation for the company.
c. Lock in Periods: Understand the lock in periods for promoters and major shareholders.

14.19 CROWDFUNDING

Crowd funding can be a viable option for raising funds for a startup in India.

STEPS IN CROWDFUNDING PROCESS:

1. Choose the Right Platform: Identify crowdfunding platforms that operate in India and are suitable for your type of business. Some popular crowdfunding platforms include Ketto, Milaap, Wishberry, and FuelADream.

2. Set Clear Goals: Clearly define your funding goals. Outline how much money you need, how you plan to use it, and the timeline for achieving your objectives. Transparency is important in gaining the trust of potential backers.

3. Create an Engaging Campaign: Craft a compelling campaign story. Explain your startup idea, its unique selling points, and the impact it can have. Use visuals, videos, and info graphics to make your campaign more engaging.

4. Offer Attractive Rewards: Many crowd funding campaigns provide backers with rewards based on their level of contribution. Ensure that the rewards are appealing and relevant to your project. This can motivate people to contribute more.

5. Marketing and Promotion: A successful crowd funding campaign requires effective marketing. Utilize social media, email newsletters, and other online channels to create awareness about your campaign. Engage with potential backers and keep them updated on your progress.

6. Legal Compliance: Understand the legal and regulatory requirements for crowd funding in India. Ensure that your campaign complies with all relevant laws, and consider seeking legal advice if needed.

7. Build a Network: Leverage your existing network and reach out to friends, family, colleagues, and acquaintances to support your campaign. A strong initial backing can create momentum and attract more contributors.

8. Regular Updates: Keep your backers informed with regular updates. Share the progress of your startup, milestones achieved, and any challenges faced. Transparency builds trust and encourages continued support.

9. Prepare for Challenges: Crowd funding can be unpredictable, and campaigns may face challenges. Be prepared to adapt your strategy, address concerns, and communicate openly with your backers.

10. Follow Through: If your campaign is successful, ensure that you fulfill your promises and deliver rewards on time. Keep your backers informed about the development of your startup even after the campaign concludes.

Remember that crowd funding success often depends on effective communication, a compelling story, and an engaged audience. Tailor your approach to your specific industry and target audience to maximize your chances of reaching your funding goals.

14.20 INCUBATOR FOR A STARTUP

Starting a business incubator in India can be a rewarding venture, given the country's growing startup ecosystem.

STEPS TO ESTABLISH A SUCCESSFUL STARTUP INCUBATOR:

1. Market Research: Identify the industry or sector one want to focus on. Research the demand, trends, and potential for startups in that sector in India.

2. Legal Structure: Choose a legal structure for the incubator, such as a nonprofit organization, for-profit entity, or a partnership. Ensure compliance with rules and regulations of the Government of India.

3. Location: Select a strategic location that is easily accessible for startups and has the necessary infrastructure and resources.

4. Partnerships: Build partnerships with government bodies, educational institutions, corporations, and other organizations to enhance the incubator's network and resources.

5. Facilities: Provide well-equipped office spaces, meeting rooms, and common areas. Ensure high speed internet connectivity and other essential amenities.

6. Mentorship Programs: Develop mentorship programs by bringing experienced professionals, entrepreneurs, and industry experts on board to guide and advise startups.

7. Networking Events: Organize networking events, workshops, and seminars to connect startups with potential investors, customers, and partners.

8. Funding Support: Establish connections with investors, venture capitalists, and angel investors who can provide funding to startups within the incubator.

9. Training and Workshops: Offer training programs and workshops on various aspects of entrepreneurship, including business development, marketing, finance, and technology.

10. Selection Criteria: Define clear criteria for selecting startups into the incubator. Consider factors such as innovation, market potential, and the team's capabilities.

11. Monitoring and Evaluation: Implement a system for monitoring and evaluating the progress of startups within the incubator. Provide feedback and assistance when necessary.

12. Legal and Administrative Support: Provide legal and administrative support to startups, helping them with registration, compliance, and other regulatory requirements.

13. Brand Building: Build a strong brand for the incubator to attract high quality startups, mentors, and investors. Highlight success stories and achievements.

14. Exit Strategies: Develop exit strategies for startups that successfully graduate from the incubator, ensuring a smooth transition into the broader business environment.

15. Technology Infrastructure: Ensure that startups have access to the latest technology and tools necessary for their development and growth.

16. Government Initiatives: Stay informed about government initiatives and incentives for startups in India, and helps the incubated startups take advantage of these programs.

14.21 MUDRA BANK

The Micro Units Development and Refinance Agency (MUDRA) Bank is an initiative launched by the Government of India. MUDRA was established in April 2015 to provide financial support and assistance to small and micro enterprises in the country. The primary goal of MUDRA is to promote entrepreneurship and generate employment opportunities.

FEATURES OF MUDRA BANK:

1. Refinancing Facility: MUDRA does not directly lend to small businesses. Instead, it refinances microfinance institutions, banks, and non-banking financial institutions that extend credit to micro-enterprises.
2. Three Categories of Loans: MUDRA provides loans under three categories, known as "Shishu," "Kishor," and "Tarun," based on the stage of growth and funding requirements of the micro-enterprises. Shishu covers loans up to Rs. 50,000, Kishor covers loans between Rs. 50,001 and Rs. 5,00,000, and Tarun covers loans between Rs. 5,00,001 and Rs. 10,00,000.
3. Financial Inclusion: MUDRA aims to bring the unbanked and underbanked population into the formal financial system. It facilitates the flow of credit to small businesses that may have difficulty accessing traditional banking services.
4. Interest Rates: Interest rates for MUDRA loans are determined by the lending institutions, but the government provides guidelines to ensure that these rates remain affordable for small borrowers.
5. MUDRA Card: Borrowers may be issued a MUDRA Card, which is a credit card-like instrument that can be used to withdraw funds or make purchases related to their business needs.

14.22 SUCCESSFUL STARTUP IN INDIA.

1. Paytm: A mobile commerce platform offering digital wallet services.
2. Ola: One of the largest ride-sharing platforms in India.
3. Flipkart: An e-commerce giant, acquired by Walmart in 2018.
4. Swiggy: A food delivery platform that connects customers with local restaurants.
5. Zomato: A restaurant discovery and food delivery platform.
6. Byju's: An edtech company offering online learning services.
7. OYO: A hospitality company that provides budget accommodation.
8. Razorpay: A fintech company offering payment solutions to businesses.
9. Udaan: A B2B e-commerce platform connecting small businesses.
10. Unacademy: An edtech platform for online learning and tutoring.
11. Cure.fit: A health and fitness platform offering a range of services.
12. Rivigo: A technology-enabled logistics company.
13. InMobi: A mobile advertising platform.
14. Freshworks: A SaaS company providing customer engagement software.
15. Nykaa: An e-commerce platform focused on beauty and wellness products.
16. Grofers: An online grocery delivery service.
17. PolicyBazaar: An online insurance aggregator.
18. PhonePe: A digital payments platform.
19. Delhivery: A logistics and supply chain services company.
20. Dream11: An online fantasy sports platform.
21. Meesho: A social commerce platform connecting sellers with buyers.
22. Innovaccer: A healthcare technology company.
23. BlackBuck: A logistics platform for trucking services.
24. UpGrad: An online higher education platform.
25. Cred: A fintech platform focused on credit card bill payments.

14.23 QUESTIONS:

1. What are the factors which govern the choice of a business organization?
2. Why would you prefer a Limited Liability Partnership compared to a Private Limited Company?
3. Distinguish between a sole proprietorship and partnership?
4. In which form of business organization, the owner is personally liable for all the debts of the business?
5. What are the advantages of partnership compared to a private limited company?
6. Why would you prefer One Person Company (OPC) compared to a Sole Proprietorship?
7. Define a Startup and trace the evolution of start-ups in India.
8. What are the highlights of the Startup Policy of the Government of India.?
9. What are the tax exemptions available to Startups in India?
10. Describe the different forms of Debt and Equity Financing which can be raised by Startups.

CHAPTER FIFTEEN

NOT-FOR-PROFIT ORGANIZATION

15.1 FORMATION AND REGISTRATION OF NGO'S

The formation and registration of NonGovernmental Organizations (NGOs) in India are governed by the legal framework established by the government.

15.1.1 FORMATION OF NGOS:

1. Define the Purpose and Mission: Clearly define the objectives and mission of the NGO. Determine the cause or issues the organization will address.

2. Choose a Structure: NGOs in India can take different legal forms, such as trusts, societies, or Section 8 companies. The choice depends on the nature and scale of activities.

a. Trust: Governed by the Indian Trusts Act, suitable for charitable activities.
b. Society: Governed by the Societies Registration Act, suitable for promotion of science, literature, fine arts, education, and charitable activities.
c. Section 8 Company: Governed by the Companies Act, 2013, and is a not-for-profit entity. Suitable for promotion of commerce, art, science, sports, education, research, social welfare, religion, charity, protection of the environment, etc.

3. Name Selection: Choose a unique and meaningful name for the NGO. Check the availability of the chosen name with the Registrar of Societies or the Ministry of Corporate Affairs (for Section 8 companies).

15.1.2 REGISTRATION PROCESS:

For Trusts:
1. Draft and prepare a trust deed outlining the aims, objectives, rules, and regulations of the trust.
2. Execution of Trust Deed: The trust deed must be signed by the trustees and registered with the local sub-registrar office.
For Societies:
1. Draft and prepare the Memorandum of Association and Rules & Regulations of the society.
2. Application for Registration: Submit the application, along with the required documents, to the Registrar of Societies in the respective state.
For Section 8 Companies:
1. Name Approval: Apply for name availability through the Ministry of Corporate Affairs (MCA) website.
2. Prepare Memorandum and Articles of Association: Draft the Memorandum and Articles of Association according to the guidelines provided for Section 8 companies.
3. Application for License: Apply for a license under Section 8 of the Companies Act, 2013.

4. Incorporation: Once the license is granted, apply for the ncorporation of the company with the MCA.

15.1.3 COMMON STEPS FOR ALL:

1. PAN and TAN: Obtain a Permanent Account Number (PAN) and Tax Deduction and Collection Account Number (TAN) for the NGO.

2. Bank Account: Open a bank account in the name of the NGO using the registration documents and PAN.

3. 12A and 80G Registration: Apply for 12A registration for tax exemptions. Also, consider obtaining 80G certification for donor benefits.

4. Compliance: Comply with ongoing reporting requirements and file annual returns with the relevant authorities.

15.2 FORMATION AND REGISTRATION OF SECTION 8 COMPANIES

15.2.1 SECTION 8 COMPANY – DEFINITION

Section 8 of the Companies Act, 2013, pertains to the formation of companies with charitable objects, non-profit objectives, or for the promotion of commerce, art, science, sports, education, research, social welfare, religion, and other similar activities. These companies are commonly known as Section 8 companies.

A Section 8 company is essentially a not-for-profit organization that is allowed to use its profits or income solely for promoting its objectives. These companies have certain benefits, such as tax exemptions and reduced compliance requirements. They are typically formed with the primary purpose of promoting charitable activities, and any profits generated are ploughed back into the organization to further its objectives.

A Section 8 Company refers to a type of company defined under Section 8 of the Companies Act, 2013. These companies are established for promoting commerce, art, science, sports, education, research, social welfare, religion, charity, protection of the environment, or any other charitable objectives. They are non-profit entities, and any profits generated are used for promoting the company's objectives.

15.2.2 FEATURES OF SECTION 8 COMPANIES

1. Objective: Section 8 companies are established with the primary objective of promoting commerce, art, science, sports, education, research, social welfare, religion, charity, protection of the environment, or any other similar object. The profits, if any, are utilized for promoting these objectives.
2. No Profit Distribution: The income and profits of Section 8 company cannot be distributed among its members. Any income generated must be used solely for the promotion of its objectives.
3. Limited Liability: Members of a Section 8 company have limited liability. This means that the personal assets of the members are generally not at risk for the company's debts or liabilities.
4. Incorporation Process: To incorporate a Section 8 company, the promoters need to apply to the Registrar of Companies (RoC) for a license under Section 8 of the Companies Act. The application should be accompanied by the company's memorandum and articles of association.
5. Name: The name of a Section 8 company usually ends with the words "Foundation," "Association," "Society," "Council," "Club," "Charity," "Institute," "Organization," or other similar terms.
6. Board of Directors: Section 8 companies must have a minimum of three directors. These directors are responsible for the management and administration of the company.
7. Tax Exemptions: Section 8 companies are eligible for various tax exemptions, including exemption from income tax on their income and donations.
8. Annual Compliance: Like any other type of company, Section 8 companies are required to comply with annual filing requirements, such as filing financial statements and annual returns with the RoC.

15.2.3 STEPS FOR THE FORMATION AND REGISTRATION OF SECTION 8 COMPANIES

1. Name Reservation: Choose a unique name for the company, keeping in mind the guidelines for company names. The name should not resemble any existing company's name. Apply for name reservation through the Ministry of Corporate Affairs (MCA) portal.

2. Drafting of Memorandum and Articles of Association: Draft the Memorandum of Association (MOA) and Articles of Association (AOA) in compliance with the Companies Act, 2013. These documents define the company's objectives and rules governing its internal affairs.

3. Application for License: Prepare and submit the application for a license to the Regional Director (RD) of the Ministry of Corporate Affairs. This license is necessary for forming a Section 8 Company.The application should include the MOA, AOA, and other necessary documents.

4. Approval of License: The RD will review the application, and if satisfied, grant the license. The approval process may involve some back-and-forth communication for any necessary clarifications or modifications.

5. Incorporation Process:

a. Once the license is obtained, the company needs to apply for incorporation with the Registrar of Companies (RoC).
b. Submit the necessary documents, including the license, MOA, AOA, and other required information.
c. The RoC will issue a Certificate of Incorporation upon successful verification of documents.

6. Tax Registration:

a. After incorporation, obtain a Permanent Account Number (PAN) for the company.
b. Apply for Tax Deduction and Collection Account Number (TAN) for deducting and remitting TDS, if applicable.

7. Goods and Services Tax (GST) Registration: If the annual turnover of the Section 8 Company exceeds the prescribed limit, register for GST.

8. Bank Account: Open a bank account in the name of the company.

9. Compliance and Reporting: Comply with the ongoing regulatory requirements, including filing annual returns and other necessary documents with the RoC.

15.2.4 SECTION 8 COMPANIES - EXEMPTIONS

Section 8 companies enjoy certain exemptions and privileges to encourage their activities for the promotion of arts, science, commerce, education, research, social welfare, religion, charity, protection of the environment, or any other similar object.

EXEMPTIONS AND PRIVILEGES FOR SECTION 8 COMPANIES INCLUDE:

1. No Requirement for the Use of the Word "Limited" or "Private Limited": Section 8 companies are not required to use the words "Limited" or "Private Limited" as part of their name.
2. Ease of Alteration of Objects: Section 8 companies have greater flexibility in altering their objects as compared to other types of companies. They can alter their objects by passing a special resolution.
3. Simplified Compliance: Section 8 companies have certain exemptions from compliance with certain provisions of the Companies Act that are applicable to other companies. For example, they may have less stringent requirements regarding the holding of annual general meetings and board meetings.

4. Tax Benefits: Section 8 companies may enjoy certain tax benefits, particularly in terms of exemptions on income earned for promoting charitable purposes.

5. Exemption from Stamp Duty: Some states in India may grant exemptions or reductions in stamp duty for transactions involving Section 8 companies.

It's important to note that while Section 8 companies enjoy several exemptions and privileges, they are also subject to certain regulatory requirements to ensure that they operate for the specified charitable or non-profit purposes. These companies must use their income and profits solely for promoting their objectives, and any surplus generated cannot be distributed among the members but must be ploughed back into the company's activities.

15.2.5 REQUIREMENTS OF SECTION 8 COMPANY

Section 8 Companies are regulated under the Companies Act, 2013. These are non-profit organizations that are formed for promoting commerce, art, science, sports, education, research, social welfare, religion, charity, protection of the environment, or any other charitable objectives.

GENERAL REQUIREMENTS FOR SETTING UP A SECTION 8 COMPANIES:

1. Minimum Members: For a Section 8 Company, a minimum of two individuals is required to act as promoters.

2. Minimum Directors: The Company must have a minimum of two directors.

3. Digital Signature Certificate (DSC): Directors must obtain a Digital Signature Certificate (DSC), which is necessary for filing electronic documents with the Ministry of Corporate Affairs (MCA).

4. Director Identification Number (DIN): All directors must have a Director Identification Number (DIN) issued by the Ministry of Corporate Affairs.

5. Name Approval: Apply for and obtain approval for the proposed name of the company from the Registrar of Companies (RoC).

6. Memorandum and Articles of Association: Draft the Memorandum of Association (MOA) and Articles of Association (AOA) for the company. These documents define the objectives and rules for the company.

7. License from the Central Government: Section 8 Companies require a license from the Central Government. The application for the license is submitted to the Regional Director of the Ministry of Corporate Affairs.

8. Declaration of Charitable Objects: The MOA of the company must include a declaration of charitable objects, and the company must ensure that its income and property are used solely for promoting its objects.

9. No Dividends: Section 8 Companies are prohibited from distributing dividends to their members.

10. Utilization of Profits: Any profits earned by the company must be utilized solely for promoting its charitable objects, and no portion of the profits should be distributed among its members.

11. Annual Compliance: Section 8 Companies must comply with the annual filing requirements of the MCA, including filing annual returns and financial statements.

12. Audit: The accounts of the company must be audited annually by a qualified auditor.

15.2.6 APPLICATION FOR INCORPORATION OF SECTION 8 COMPANIES:

Step 1: Obtain Digital Signature Certificate (DSC):

Directors' DSC: Obtain Digital Signature Certificates for all proposed directors. This is mandatory for filing documents online with the Ministry of Corporate Affairs (MCA).

Step 2: Obtain Director Identification Number (DIN):

DIN Application: Apply for DIN for all proposed directors through the SPICe+ Form (part of the integrated incorporation process).

Step 3: Name Approval:

Name Reservation: Choose a unique name for the Section 8 company and apply for name reservation through the RUN (Reserve Unique Name) form on the MCA portal.

Step 4: Prepare Incorporation Documents:

Draft Memorandum and Articles of Association (MOA & AOA): Prepare the MOA and AOA according to the guidelines provided in the Companies Act, 2013. Ensure compliance with Section 8 regulations.

Step 5: SPICe+ Form:

Fill SPICe+ Form: Complete the SPICe+ (Simplified Proforma for Incorporating Company Electronically) form on the MCA portal. It is an integrated form for name reservation, company incorporation, and applying for PAN/TAN.

1. Attach the necessary documents, including MOA, AOA, and address proof.
2. Declare compliance with Section 8 regulations.

Step 6: Submission and Fee Payment:

1. Submit Form: Upload the SPICe+ form along with the required documents on the MCA portal.
2. Payment of Fees: Pay the applicable fees for company incorporation through the online payment mode.

Step 7: Certificate of Incorporation:

1. Verification: The Registrar of Companies (RoC) will verify the submitted documents.
2. Certificate Issuance: Once approved, the RoC will issue the Certificate of Incorporation. The company is now officially incorporated.

Step 8: Apply for PAN and TAN:

1. Apply for PAN: Once incorporated, apply for a Permanent Account Number (PAN) for the company.
2. Apply for TAN: Apply for a Tax Deduction and Collection Account Number (TAN) for the company.

15.3 TRUST

The Indian Trusts Act of 1882 is a comprehensive legislative framework that governs the creation and administration of trusts in India. Trusts play an important role in the legal landscape, providing a mechanism for individuals to manage and distribute their assets for the benefit of beneficiaries. At the heart of the Indian Trusts Act is the concept of trust, which rests on the foundation of trustworthiness, confidence, and fiduciary responsibility.

Trust, under the Indian Trusts Act, is a legal relationship where a person (known as the settlor) transfers property to another person (known as the trustee) with the intention that the property be held for the benefit of certain individuals or for a charitable purpose. The act recognizes the significance of trust in facilitating organized wealth management and ensuring that the interests of the beneficiaries are protected.

Trust is built on the principles of faith and confidence. The settlor places trust in the trustee to manage the trust property in accordance with the terms specified in the trust deed. The trustee, in turn, is duty-bound to act in the best interests of the beneficiaries, exhibiting a high standard of care, diligence, and loyalty. This fiduciary relationship is central to the functioning of trusts and underscores the importance of trust in the legal landscape.

The Indian Trusts Act incorporates various provisions that delineate the rights, duties, and responsibilities of the settlor, trustee, and beneficiaries. It outlines the conditions under which a trust is deemed valid, the powers of the trustee, and the circumstances under which a trust can be terminated. These provisions are designed to instill confidence in the trust mechanism and provide a legal framework that ensures the proper execution of the settlor's intentions.

Trust, as envisaged by the Indian Trusts Act, is not merely a legal concept but also a social contract. It reflects the societal recognition of the need for a mechanism that allows individuals to allocate and preserve their assets for the benefit of their chosen beneficiaries. Trust, therefore, becomes a cornerstone in fostering financial planning, charitable endeavors, and the overall well-being of the community.

Trust under the Indian Trusts Act embodies the spirit of confidence, responsibility, and faith. It is a legal instrument that facilitates the organized management of assets while upholding the interests of the beneficiaries. The act provides a robust framework that not only governs the legal intricacies of trusts but also underscores the importance of trust in fostering social and economic development.

15.3.1 OBJECTIVES OF A TRUST

A trust is a legal entity that can be established for various purposes, and it typically involves the creation of a trust deed that outlines its objectives, rules, and regulations. The primary objective of a trust is to serve the welfare of the public or a particular section of the public.

1. Charitable and Religious Purposes:

Many trusts in India are formed with the objective of advancing charitable activities, such as providing education, healthcare, relief to the poor, and other social welfare initiatives.

Some trusts may have religious objectives, supporting the maintenance of temples, religious institutions, and related activities.

2. Education and Skill Development: Trusts may be established to promote education by setting up schools, colleges, vocational training centers, or scholarship programs to support students in need.

3. Healthcare and Medical Services: Trusts can focus on providing medical facilities, organizing health camps, and supporting healthcare infrastructure, especially in underserved areas.

4. Poverty Alleviation: Objectives may include the upliftment of the economically disadvantaged through poverty alleviation programs, vocational training, and employment generation initiatives.

5. Environmental Conservation: Trusts may be formed to address environmental issues, such as promoting sustainable practices, wildlife conservation, and ecological balance.

6. Cultural and Artistic Activities: Some trusts aim to promote culture, arts, and heritage by supporting artists, organizing cultural events, and preserving traditional art forms.

7. Women's Empowerment: Trusts may focus on empowering women by supporting initiatives related to education, skill development, and health.

8. Agricultural and Rural Development: Objectives may include promoting sustainable agriculture, rural development, and improving the socio-economic conditions of rural communities.

9. Scientific Research and Innovation: Trusts may support scientific research and innovation by funding research projects, providing scholarships, and establishing research institutions.

10. Social Justice and Human Rights: Some trusts work towards promoting social justice, human rights, and equality by supporting legal aid, advocacy, and awareness programs.

15.3.2 PERSONS WHO CAN CREATE A TRUST

Creating a trust typically involves the involvement of specific individuals or entities that play key roles in the establishment and administration of the trust. The parties involved in creating a trust:

1. Settlor: The settlor is the person who creates the trust by transferring assets or property to the trust. The settlor decides the terms and conditions of the trust, including the beneficiaries and the trustees.

2. Trustees: Trustees are individuals or entities appointed by the settlor to manage and administer the trust on behalf of the beneficiaries. Trustees have a fiduciary duty to act in the best interests of the beneficiaries and follow the terms of the trust deed.

3. Beneficiaries: Beneficiaries are individuals or groups who are intended to benefit from the trust. The settlor specifies the beneficiaries and their respective interests in the trust property in the trust deed.

4. Trust Protector (if applicable): In some cases, a trust protector may be appointed to oversee the administration of the trust. This individual has the authority to ensure that the trustees are acting in accordance with the terms of the trust.

5. Legal Advisor: While not a mandatory party, seeking legal advice is crucial when creating a trust in India. A legal advisor can help draft the trust deed, ensure compliance with relevant laws, and provide guidance on the legal implications of the trust.

6. Registration Authority: Trusts in India are governed by the Indian Trusts Act, 1882. While the registration of a trust is not mandatory, it is advisable to register it with the local registrar of trusts. The registration process involves submitting the trust deed and related documents.

15.3.3 DIFFERENCES BETWEEN A PUBLIC AND PRIVATE TRUST

trusts are broadly categorized into two types: public trusts and private trusts. The primary differences between these two types of trusts lie in their purpose, administration, and the beneficiaries they serve. Distinctions between public trust and private trust:

1. Purpose:

Public Trusts: These trusts are established for charitable or public purposes, such as the advancement of education, relief of poverty, medical relief, and other similar objectives that benefit the general public or a particular community.

Private Trusts: These trusts are created for the benefit of specific individuals or families, and their purposes are usually personal or familial in nature, such as the maintenance and welfare of family members.

2. Beneficiaries:

Public Trusts: The beneficiaries of public trusts are the general public or a specific community. These trusts aim to serve a broader societal interest rather than the interests of specific individuals or families.

Private Trusts: The beneficiaries of private trusts are specific individuals or families mentioned in the trust deed. The benefits are generally confined to the named beneficiaries, and the trust is not intended to serve the public at large.

3. Administration and Control:

Public Trusts: Public trusts are subject to more stringent regulations and oversight by the government authorities to ensure that they fulfill their charitable or public objectives. The administration of public trusts is often more transparent, and compliance with legal requirements is closely monitored.

Private Trusts. Private trusts, while subject to certain legal provisions, may have more flexibility in their administration. They are usually managed by trustees as per the terms specified in the trust deed, and there may be less external scrutiny compared to public trusts.

4. Registration and Compliance:

Public Trusts: Public trusts typically need to be registered with the relevant state authority, such as the Charity Commissioner's office. They are required to comply with regulatory requirements to maintain their charitable status.

Private Trusts: Private trusts may also be registered, but the level of regulatory scrutiny and compliance requirements are generally less stringent compared to public trusts. Private trusts may have more flexibility in their internal management structures.

5. Taxation:

Public Trusts: Public trusts may qualify for certain tax benefits and exemptions under Indian tax laws, as they are engaged in charitable activities that benefit the public.

Private Trusts: Private trusts may not necessarily enjoy the same tax benefits as public trusts, and the tax implications would depend on the specific nature of the trust and its activities.

15.3.4 EXEMPTIONS AVAILABLE TO TRUSTS

Trusts are subject to various provisions under the Income Tax Act, 1961. The exemptions available to trusts depend on their nature, purpose, and compliance with the relevant regulations.

EXEMPTIONS AVAILABLE TO TRUSTS:

1. Income Exemption under Section 10(23C):

1. Educational Institutions: Trusts that manage educational institutions and meet certain conditions are eligible for exemption under Section 10(23C)(iiiab).
2. Hospitals and Medical Institutions: Trusts managing hospitals and medical institutions can be eligible for exemption under Section 10(23C)(iiiae).

2. Charitable and Religious Trusts:

1. Income of trusts formed for charitable or religious purposes may be exempt under Section 11, subject to certain conditions. However, the income should be applied for charitable or religious purposes in India.
2. If the income is not fully applied or accumulated, it is taxable under Section 11(1)(a) or 11(1)(b) as the case may be.

3. Specific Funds and Institutions: Various provisions under Section 10 provide exemptions for specific funds or institutions, such as the National Defence Fund, Prime Minister's National Relief Fund, etc.

4. Exemption for Political Parties: Political parties are exempted from paying income tax on their income under Section 13A, subject to certain conditions.

5. Exemption for Specific Trusts: Certain trusts established for specific purposes, such as research, scientific, or literary purposes, may be eligible for exemptions under Section 10(21).

6. Exemptions for Mutual Funds: Mutual funds registered with the Securities and Exchange Board of India (SEBI) and meeting certain conditions may be eligible for exemptions under Section 10(23D).

7. Exemptions for Venture Capital Companies: Venture capital companies registered with SEBI can be eligible for exemptions under Section 10(23FB).

15.3.5 FORMATION OF A TRUST

The formation of a trust involves certain legal processes and adherence to specific regulations. A trust is a legal arrangement in which a person (settlor) transfers property to another person or entity (trustee) for the benefit of a third party (beneficiary).

STEPS INVOLVED IN FORMING A TRUST:

1. Settlor's Intent: The process begins with the settlor expressing the intention to create a trust for a lawful purpose.

2. Identify Trustees and Beneficiaries: The settlor needs to identify the individuals or entities who will act as trustees to manage the trust property and the beneficiaries who will benefit from the trust.

3. Drafting the Trust Deed: A trust deed is a legal document that outlines the terms and conditions of the trust. The deed must include details such as the trust's name, its objectives, the powers and duties of the trustees, and the benefits accruing to the beneficiaries.

4. Stamp Duty: The trust deed must be executed on non-judicial stamp paper of appropriate value, as per the stamp duty laws of the respective state where the trust is being created. The amount of stamp duty varies from state to state.

5. Registration: While it is not mandatory to register a trust, registering it can provide certain advantages, such as establishing the validity of the trust and making it more credible. To register, the trust deed should be submitted to the office of the local Sub-Registrar of Assurances.

6. Pan Card and Bank Account: Obtain a PAN (Permanent Account Number) for the trust from the Income Tax Department. Use the PAN to open a bank account in the name of the trust.

7. Tax Registration: Depending on the nature of the trust and its activities, it may need to register for income tax and other relevant taxes. Consult with a tax professional to ensure compliance.

8. Compliance with Applicable Laws: Ensure compliance with all relevant laws, including the Indian Trusts Act, 1882, and any state-specific trust laws.

9. Administration and Compliance: The trustees must manage the trust property in accordance with the terms of the trust deed and fulfill their fiduciary duties. Regular compliance with tax and regulatory requirements is essential.

15.3.6 TRUST DEED

In India, a trust deed is a legal document that establishes and governs the operation of a trust. A trust is a legal arrangement where a person (settlor) transfers property to another person or entity (trustee) to hold and manage for the benefit of a third party (beneficiary). The trust deed outlines the terms and conditions under which the trust operates, including the powers and responsibilities of the trustee, the rights of the beneficiaries, and the objectives of the trust.

CONTENTS OF A TRUST DEED:

1. Name and Details:

a.   The full name and address of the settlor(s).
b.   The full name and address of the trustee(s).

2. Trust Property:

a.   A detailed description of the property/assets being transferred to the trust.
b.   Any specific conditions or restrictions on the use of the trust property.

3. Objectives/Purpose:

a.   The specific objectives or purposes for which the trust is created.
b.   The intended beneficiaries of the trust.

4. Powers of Trustee:

a.   The powers granted to the trustee for managing and administering the trust.
b.   Any limitations or restrictions on the trustee's powers.

5. Duration of the Trust:

a.   Whether the trust is revocable or irrevocable.

b.   If revocable, the conditions under which it can be revoked.

6. Appointment of Successor Trustee: The procedure for appointing a successor trustee in case the original trustee is unable or unwilling to act.

7. Distribution of Assets:

a.   The rules and conditions for distributing the trust assets to the beneficiaries.
b.   Any specific instructions regarding the timing and manner of distribution.

8. Governing Law: The laws of the state or jurisdiction that will govern the trust.

9. Amendment and Termination:

a.   Procedures for amending the trust deed if necessary.
b.   Conditions under which the trust can be terminated.

10. Miscellaneous Clauses: Any other relevant clauses, such as dispute resolution mechanisms or confidentiality provisions.

It is important to note that the specific requirements and regulations related to trust deeds may vary across different states in India. Therefore, individuals creating a trust or drafting a trust deed should seek legal advice to ensure compliance with applicable laws. Registration of the trust deed may be required in certain states for it to be legally valid and enforceable.

15.4 SOCIETY

The Societies Registration Act, 1860, is an act passed by the British Indian government during the colonial era, and it continues to be in force in many parts of India. The act provides for the registration of societies for various literary, scientific, and charitable purposes.

15.4.1 BRIEF OVERVIEW OF THE DEFINITION OF SOCIETIES

1. Definition of Society: According to the Societies Registration Act, 1860, a society is defined as an organized group of individuals who come together for pursuing common goals or objectives, such as the promotion of literature, science, fine arts, the diffusion of useful knowledge, the foundation or maintenance of libraries, or public museums, and more.

2. Registration of Societies: The primary purpose of the act is to facilitate the registration of such societies to give them a legal recognition and certain privileges.

3. Requirements for Registration:For a group of individuals to be considered a society under this act, they need to have at least seven members. These members can collectively form a governing body or a managing committee.

4. Objects of the Society:The society must have defined objectives or aims, and these objectives should fall within the purview of the act. Common purposes include the promotion of literature, science, fine arts, education, and charitable activities.

5. Legal Personality: Once registered, a society gains legal recognition as a separate legal entity apart from its individual members. This implies that the society can enter into contracts, own property, and sue or be sued in its own name.

6. Maintenance of Accounts: Registered societies are required to maintain proper accounts and submit annual reports of their activities to the registering authority.

7. Amendment of Rules and Regulations: Societies are allowed to make alterations to their rules and regulations, subject to the provisions of the act.

The Societies Registration Act, 1860, is still applicable in many regions; different states in India might have made amendments to it or might have their own state-specific acts regulating societies.

15.4.2 Society - Advantages and Disadvantages

society is often used to refer to a group of individuals who come together for a common purpose, interest, or objective. These societies can take various forms, such as cultural societies, educational societies, charitable societies, housing societies, and more.

15.4.3 ADVANTAGES AND DISADVANTAGES OF SOCIETAL ORGANIZATIONS:

ADVANTAGES:

1. Collective Action:Societies provide a platform for individuals with similar interests or goals to come together and collectively work towards achieving common objectives. This allows for more impactful and coordinated efforts.
2. Community Building: Societies contribute to the sense of community and belonging. Members often share common values and interests, fostering a supportive environment.
3. Resource Pooling: Members of a society can pool their resources, whether it is financial, intellectual, or physical, to achieve goals that may be challenging for individuals to accomplish on their own.
4. Knowledge Sharing: Societies facilitate the exchange of knowledge and expertise among members. This can lead to a broader understanding of specific subjects and the development of skills.
5. Advocacy and Representation: Societies often act as advocates for their members, representing their interests to external entities such as the government or other organizations. This can be particularly important for marginalized or specific interest groups.

DISADVANTAGES:

1. Bureaucracy: Like any organized structure, societies can become bureaucratic, leading to inefficiencies, delays, and a focus on processes rather than objectives.
2. Conflict of Interest: Differences in opinions and conflicting interests among members can arise, leading to internal disputes and challenges in decision-making.
3. Limited Scope: Societies may sometimes have a limited reach and impact, especially if they are small or lack the resources to address broader issues.
4. Dependency on Leadership: The effectiveness of a society often depends on the quality of its leadership. If leadership is weak or corrupt, it can lead to the failure of the society's objectives.
5. Financial Constraints: Many societies, especially non-profit ones, face financial constraints. Relying on donations or membership fees might limit the scope of their activities.

Societies play an important role in bringing people together for common causes; they also face challenges that need to be managed effectively for sustained success. The advantages and disadvantages may vary depending on the type and purpose of the society in question.

15.4.4 FORMATION OF A SOCIETY

The Societies Registration Act, 1860 is an act of the Indian Parliament that provides for the registration of societies in India. Societies can be formed for various purposes such as the promotion of literature, science, fine arts, education, and charitable activities.

The process for the formation of societies under the Societies Registration Act, 1860:

1. Eligibility Criteria:

a. A society can be formed by a group of individuals who come together for a common, lawful purpose.
b. There must be a minimum of seven individuals to form a society. There is no upper limit on the number of members.

2. Selection of Members:

a. Individuals interested in forming a society should come together and decide on the objectives and aims of the society.
b. A memorandum of association and rules and regulations of the society should be prepared. These documents should contain details about the society's name, objectives, governing body, and other relevant information.

3. Application for Registration:

a. The governing body or members designated for the management of the society should apply for registration by submitting the memorandum of association, rules, and regulations to the Registrar of Societies.
b. The application should be signed by at least seven members of the governing body.

4. Documents Required: The following documents are typically required for registration:

a. Memorandum of Association (MOA)
b. Rules and Regulations of the Society
c. List of members of the governing body
d. An affidavit from the president or secretary of the society

5. Registration Process:

a. The Registrar of Societies reviews the documents and, if satisfied, registers the society.
b. Once registered, the society becomes a legal entity, and a certificate of registration is issued.

6. Post-Registration Formalities:

a. The society can then opens a bank account, acquire property, and enter into contracts in its own name.
b. Annual returns and audited accounts must be submitted to the Registrar of Societies.

7. Amendments to Rules and Regulations: Any changes to the rules and regulations of the society should be intimated to the Registrar within a specified period.

15.4.5 REGISTRATION OF A SOCIETY

The Societies Registration Act, 1860 is an Indian law that governs the registration of societies (nonprofit organizations) in India. If you wish to register a society under this act, you need to follow certain procedures. Please note that the process may vary slightly from state to state, as the act is implemented by state governments.
GENERAL OVERVIEW OF THE REGISTRATION PROCESS:
1. Formation of the Memorandum of Association (MOA) and Rules & Regulations:

a. Draft a Memorandum of Association (MOA) and Rules & Regulations for your society. The MOA typically includes the name of the society, its objectives, and details of its members.
b. The Rules & Regulations should outline the internal functioning of the society, including membership criteria, the structure of the governing body, and the process for meetings.

2. Members' Meeting:

a. Hold a meeting of the founding members to adopt the MOA and Rules & Regulations.
b. The members should pass a resolution to register the society under the Societies Registration Act, 1860.

3. Application for Registration:

a. Prepare an application for registration in the prescribed format. The application should include the MOA, Rules & Regulations, and a list of members of the governing body.
b. The application must be signed by at least seven members who were present at the meeting.

4. Submission to the Registrar:

a. Submit the application, along with the required documents and the prescribed fee, to the Registrar of Societies in the concerned state.
b. The Registrar may require additional information or documentation, so be prepared to fulfill any such requests.

5. Inspection and Approval:

a. The Registrar will examine the documents and may conduct an inspection.
b. If satisfied, the Registrar will issue a Certificate of Registration. This certificate is evidence that the society is legally registered under the Societies Registration Act, 1860.

6. Certificate of Registration: Once the registration is complete, the society can operate legally and carry out its objectives.

15.5 TAX EXEMPTION TO NGOS.

In India, non-governmental organizations (NGOs) that meet certain criteria are eligible for tax exemptions under the Income Tax Act. The relevant sections of the Income Tax Act that provide for tax exemptions to NGOs are Section 11, Section 12A, and Section 80G.

1. Section 11:

This section deals with income derived from property held for charitable or religious purposes. If an NGO's income is applied towards the objects of the organization and it meets the conditions specified in Section 11, such income may be exempt from taxation.

2. Section 12A:

NGOs seeking tax exemptions must be registered under Section 12A of the Income Tax Act. This registration is a one-time process and is essential for claiming tax benefits. It certifies that the NGO exists for genuine charitable or religious purposes.

3. Section 80G:

Donors to registered NGOs can avail of deductions under Section 80G of the Income Tax Act. This section allows individuals and organizations to claim deductions for donations made to eligible NGOs. NGOs must obtain and prominently display an 80G certificate to avail of this benefit.

15.6 QUESTIONS:

1. What are the characteristics of a Section 8 Company? Can it be merged with any other company?
2. List five exemptions available to a Section 8 Company.?
3. What is a Trust? Who can create a Trust?
4. Differentiate between a settlor, trustee and beneficiary.
5. Distinguish between a Public Trust and Private Trust.?

CHAPTER SIXTEEN

REGISTRATION AND LICENSES

Registration and licenses play an important role in the regulatory framework of India, serving as essential components to ensure the smooth functioning of various activities across diverse sectors. In a country as vast and diverse as India, the need for a structured and organized system to monitor and govern different operations becomes paramount. Registration and licenses act as the gateway for individuals and entities to participate in specific activities while adhering to legal norms and standards.

The Indian government has instituted a comprehensive system of registration and licensing to streamline and regulate various sectors such as business, healthcare, education, transportation, and more. This framework aims to establish accountability, protect public interests, and maintain the overall integrity of the economic and social fabric of the nation.

For businesses, the process of obtaining registration and licenses is a fundamental step towards legal compliance and operational legitimacy. Whether it's a small enterprise or a large corporation, entities are required to register under applicable laws and obtain licenses to operate within the defined legal parameters. This not only ensures fair business practices but also provides a level playing field for all participants in the market.

In the healthcare sector, registration of medical professionals, clinics, and hospitals is important to guarantee the delivery of quality healthcare services. Licensing ensures that healthcare providers meet prescribed standards, ensuring the safety and well-being of patients. Similarly, educational institutions are mandated to undergo registration and licensing processes to maintain educational standards and uphold the quality of education imparted to students.

In the realm of transportation, licenses are imperative for individuals operating vehicles, ensuring that drivers are qualified and adhere to traffic rules. Additionally, licenses for businesses involved in transportation, such as logistics and courier services, are essential to regulate the movement of goods and services efficiently.

The legal framework governing registration and licenses in India is dynamic, with periodic updates and amendments to keep pace with evolving societal needs and economic trends. This adaptability reflects the government's commitment to fostering a condusive environment for growth and development while safeguarding the interests of its citizens.

16.1 TYPES OF REGISTRATION AND LICENSES CONCEPTS:

1. Registration:

Registration is the process of officially recording information with a regulatory authority. It provides legal recognition to an individual or entity engaged in a particular activity.

Purpose: Registration ensures accountability, facilitates monitoring, and enables the government to regulate activities effectively.

2. Licenses:

A license is a formal permission granted by a competent authority to engage in a specific activity, business, or profession.

Purpose: Licenses are issued to ensure that individuals or entities comply with specific standards, regulations, and safety measures. They also help in maintaining quality and preventing unlawful practices.

3. Types of Registrations and Licenses:

1. Business Registration: Entities need to register their businesses with the appropriate authorities. This includes obtaining a PAN (Permanent Account Number) and
2. TAN (Tax Deduction and Collection Account Number).
3. GST Registration: Goods and Services Tax (GST) registration is mandatory for businesses with a specified turnover, enabling them to collect and remit taxes.
4. Professional Licenses: Certain professions, such as doctors, lawyers, and chartered accountants, require professionals to obtain licenses from relevant regulatory bodies.
5. Trade Licenses: Local municipal authorities issue trade licenses to businesses, ensuring that they comply with local regulations and safety standards.
6. Environmental Clearances: Industries that have potential environmental impact need to obtain clearances from environmental authorities.
7. Food License: Food businesses must obtain licenses from the Food Safety and Standards Authority of India (FSSAI) to ensure the safety and quality of food products.
8. ImportExport Licenses: Businesses involved in international trade require licenses from the Directorate General of Foreign Trade (DGFT).
9. Intellectual Property Registration: Individuals and businesses can protect their intellectual property through registrations like patents, trademarks, and copyrights.

4. Legal Framework:

1. Companies Act, 2013: Governs the registration and functioning of companies in India.
2. Goods and Services Tax (GST) Act: Regulates the indirect taxation system in India.
3. FSSAI Act: Ensures food safety and quality standards.
4. Trade Marks Act, 1999: Governs the registration and protection of trademarks.
5. Income Tax Act, 1961: Deals with taxrelated registrations and compliances.

5. Compliance and Renewals:

Once registered or licensed, entities must adhere to ongoing compliance requirements and renew licenses as per the specified intervals.

Understanding the intricacies of registration and licensing is essential for individuals and businesses to operate legally in India. It promotes a business friendly environment, protects consumers, and contributes to the overall growth and development of the economy.

16.2 BUSINESS ENTITY REGISTRATION: MANDATORY REGISTRATION

Business entity registration is a fundamental and mandatory step for any aspiring entrepreneur or company looking to operate in India. This process is not only a legal requirement but also a crucial aspect that lays the foundation for the smooth functioning and legitimacy of a business. The regulatory framework for business registration in India is primarily governed by the Ministry of Corporate Affairs, ensuring that businesses comply with the statutory provisions outlined in the Companies Act, 2013.

The process of business entity registration in India involves several steps, depending on the type of business structure chosen by the entrepreneur. The most common business structures include Sole Proprietorship, Partnership, Limited Liability Partnership (LLP), and Private Limited Company. Each structure has its own set of advantages, disadvantages, and legal requirements, making it essential for entrepreneurs to choose the one that aligns with their business goals and vision.

Sole Proprietorship is the simplest form of business entity, where a single individual owns and manages the business. However, it lacks a distinct legal identity, and the owner is personally liable for business debts. Partnership, on the other hand, involves two or more individuals forming a business with shared responsibilities and profits. Limited Liability Partnership (LLP) offers a balance by combining the simplicity of a partnership with limited liability protection for its partners.

Private Limited Company, one of the most popular business structures, provides a separate legal identity to the business, protecting the personal assets of its shareholders. The registration process involves obtaining a Director Identification Number (DIN) and Digital Signature Certificate (DSC) for the directors, choosing a unique company name, and filing the necessary documents with the Registrar of Companies (RoC).

Mandatory business registration not only ensures legal compliance but also offers several benefits. It enhances the credibility of the business, making it easier to attract investors, enter into contracts, and engage in various business transactions. Moreover, registered businesses gain access to various government schemes, subsidies, and incentives, fostering their growth and development.

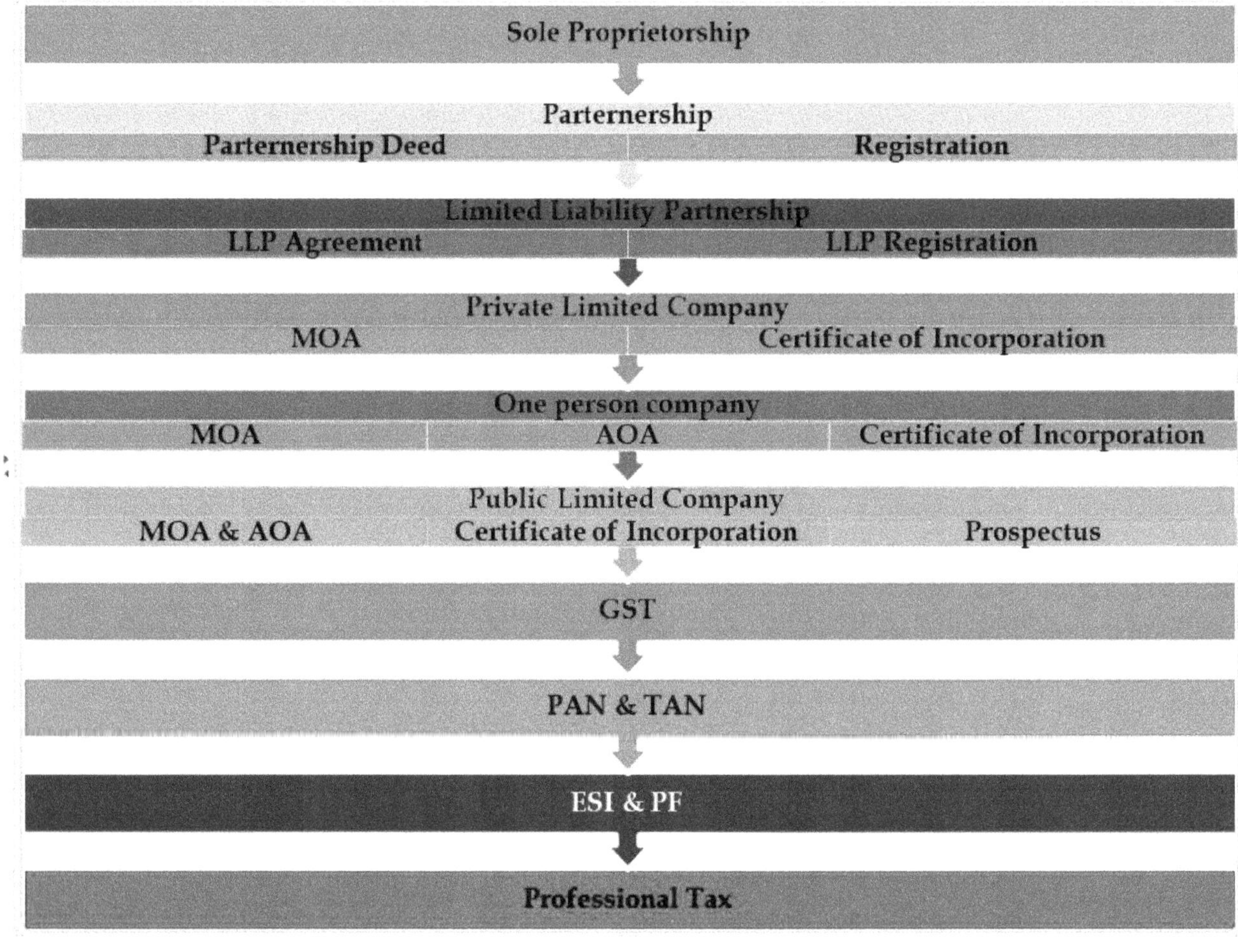

Types of Business Entities

Types of business entities and their mandatory registrations:

1. Sole Proprietorship: No specific registration is required. However, obtaining a Shops and Establishments Act license may be necessary.

2. Partnership Firm:

a. Partnership Deed: A written agreement among partners.
b. Registration with the Registrar of Firms: Although not mandatory, registration provides legal benefits.

3. Limited Liability Partnership (LLP):

a. LLP Agreement: Drafting an agreement specifying the rights and duties of partners.
b. LLP Registration: File the incorporation documents with the Ministry of Corporate Affairs (MCA).

4. Private Limited Company:

a. Memorandum of Association (MOA) and Articles of Association (AOA): Draft and file with the MCA.
b. Certificate of Incorporation: Obtain from the MCA.

5. One Person Company (OPC):

a. MOA and AOA: Draft and file with the MCA.
b. Certificate of Incorporation: Obtain from the MCA.

6. Public Limited Company:

a. MOA and AOA: Draft and file with the MCA.
b. Certificate of Incorporation: Obtain from the MCA.
c. Prospectus: Required if the company intends to issue shares to the public.

7. GST Registration: Goods and Services Tax (GST) registration is mandatory for businesses with a certain turnover threshold.

8. PAN and TAN: Permanent Account Number (PAN) and Tax Deduction and Collection Account Number (TAN) are required for tax purposes.

9. ESI and PF Registration: For businesses employing a certain number of employees, registration under the Employee State Insurance (ESI) Act and the Provident Fund (PF) Act is mandatory.

10. Professional Tax Registration: Some states in India require businesses to register for professional tax.

It's important to note that the specific requirements may vary based on the nature of the business, its location, and the applicable laws. It is advisable to consult with a legal professional or a chartered accountant to ensure compliance with all mandatory registrations and regulations.

Additionally, the Ministry of Corporate Affairs (MCA) website is a valuable resource for the latest information and procedures related to business registrations.Business entity registration is an important step for entrepreneurs in India, serving as the gateway to a legitimate and regulated business environment. It not only establishes the legal identity of the business but also facilitates its growth, sustainability, and compliance with the regulatory framework.

Entrepreneurs are advised to seek professional guidance or to consult with a legal professional or a chartered accountant to ensure compliance with all mandatory registrations and regulations and to navigate the complexities of business registration and choose the most suitable structure for their ventures. the Ministry of Corporate Affairs (MCA) website is a valuable resource for the latest information and procedures related to business registrations.

16.3 PERMANENT ACCOUNT NUMBER (PAN)

The Permanent Account Number (PAN) is a unique alphanumeric identification code issued by the Income Tax Department to individuals, companies, and entities. Introduced in 1972, PAN serves as a vital tool for the government to track financial transactions and ensure tax compliance. This 10-character code, which is unique to each PAN holder, is an essential requirement for various financial activities, including filing income tax returns, opening a bank account, conducting large transactions, and even for certain employment purposes.

The structure of a PAN comprises five components: the first five characters are letters, the next four are numbers, and the final character is again a letter. The initial three characters represent a sequence of alphabets, indicating the series and jurisdiction of the issuing authority. The fourth character signifies the status of the PAN holder – whether an individual, company, or another entity. The fifth character is the first letter of the holder's last name, and the subsequent four digits form a unique numerical identifier.

Obtaining a PAN is a straightforward process for Indian residents and entities, involving the submission of an application form along with the necessary supporting documents. Non-residents may also apply for a PAN if they engage in financial transactions in India. The application can be made online through the official website of the Income Tax Department or at designated PAN facilitation centers.

The significance of PAN extends beyond tax-related activities. It is an integral component of the government's initiatives to promote transparency and curb black money. With the increasing digitization of financial transactions, the PAN has become even more important in ensuring traceability and accountability in the financial system.

The Permanent Account Number in India plays an important role in the country's taxation and financial systems. Its unique alphanumeric code facilitates the identification and monitoring of individuals and entities, contributing to greater transparency and compliance in financial transactions. Whether for tax purposes or other financial activities, possessing a PAN is a fundamental requirement for residents and entities operating within the Indian economic landscape.

16.3.1 SIGNIFICANCE OF PAN

The Permanent Account Number (PAN) holds significant importance in India for various financial and tax-related purposes.

1. Identification: PAN serves as a unique identification number for individuals, families, and businesses. It helps in tracking financial transactions and preventing tax evasion.
2. Income Tax Filing: PAN is mandatory for filing income tax returns in India. Individuals and entities earning taxable income need to provide their PAN while filing tax returns.
3. Financial Transactions: PAN is required for various financial transactions such as opening a bank account, making large transactions, investing in financial instruments like mutual funds, and buying or selling immovable property.
4. Bank Transactions: PAN is essential for opening a bank account, whether it's a savings account or a fixed deposit. It is also necessary for high-value transactions, and the bank may ask for PAN details for various banking operations.
5. Credit Card Application: When applying for a credit card, individuals need to provide their PAN details. This helps financial institutions verify the creditworthiness of the applicant.
6. Property Transactions: PAN is mandatory for property transactions such as buying or selling real estate. Both the buyer and the seller are required to provide their PAN details for the transaction to be legally valid.
7. Business Transactions: PAN is necessary for businesses and entities for various financial and business transactions. It is used for opening a business bank account, obtaining loans, and conducting other financial activities.
8. Tax Deduction at Source (TDS): PAN is required for any transaction on which TDS is applicable. This ensures that the government can track and verify the taxes deducted and deposited by individuals and businesses.
9. Foreign Exchange Transactions: PAN is necessary for foreign exchange transactions exceeding a specified limit, as mandated by the Reserve Bank of India (RBI).
10. GST Registration: PAN is required for the Goods and Services Tax (GST) registration for businesses. It is a key identification number for businesses involved in the supply of goods and services.

PAN plays an important role in the Indian financial system, helping the government track financial transactions, curb tax evasion, and ensure compliance with various financial and legal regulations.

16.3.2 APPLICATION AND REGISTRATION OF PAN

PAN, or Permanent Account Number, is a unique 10digit alphanumeric identifier issued by the Income Tax Department in India. It is used for various financial transactions and is mandatory for several activities such as filing income tax returns, opening a bank account, and conducting highvalue financial transactions.

APPLICATION PROCESS FOR PAN

Online Application:

1. Visit the NSDL or UTIITSL Website: National Securities Depository Limited (NSDL) and UTI Infrastructure Technology and Services Limited (UTIITSL) are the two authorized entities to process PAN applications.

2. Access the PAN Application Form (Form 49A or Form 49AA): Form 49A is for Indian citizens, while Form 49AA is for foreign nationals and entities.

3. Fill in the Form: Provide accurate details such as name, date of birth, address, etc. Attach necessary documents like proof of identity, address, and photographs as required.

4. Payment of Fees: Pay the prescribed fee for PAN application.

the fee for Indian citizens is Rs. 110, while it is Rs. 1,020 for foreign citizens.

5. Submission: Submit the application online. After successful submission, one will receive an acknowledgment containing a 15digit acknowledgment number.

6. Document Submission: Print the acknowledgment, sign it, affix photographs, and send it along with necessary documents to the NSDL or UTIITSL address within 15 days.

7. Tracking Application Status: one can track the status of the PAN application online using the acknowledgment number.

Offline Application:

1. Visit PAN Application Centers: PAN application forms are available at PAN application centers. These centers can include NSDL TIN facilitation centers, UTIITSL facilitation centers, and some government offices.

2. Fill the Form: Fill the form and attach required documents.

3. Submit the Form: Submit the form along with the documents and fees at the PAN application center.

4. Acknowledgment: After submission, one will receive an acknowledgment with a 15digit acknowledgment number.

5. Tracking Application Status: One can track the status of the PAN application using the acknowledgment number.

PAN Card Dispatch:Once the application is processed and approved, the PAN card is dispatched to the address mentioned in the application form.

IMPORTANT POINTS:

1. The PAN application process can also be done through TINFCs (Tax Information Network Facilitation Centers) and online intermediaries.
2. Ensure that all information provided is accurate to avoid delays or rejection.
3. It is mandatory to quote PAN in specified financial transactions, and it is advisable to link PAN with Aadhaar for seamless verification.

16.3.3 LINKING OF PAN WITH AADHAR

As per Section 139AA, every person who is eligible to obtain Aadhar is required to quote his Aadhar number in the PAN application form with effect from 1st day of July, 2017. If any person does not possess the Aadhar Number but he had applied for the Aadhar card then he can quote Enrolment ID of Aadhar application Form.

In case of an applicant, being a company which has not been registered under the Companies Act, 2013, the application for allotment of a Permanent Account Number may be made in SpiceINC32 specified under subsection (1) of section 7 of the said Act for incorporation of the company.

STEPS FOR LINKING OF PAN WITH AADHAR

1. Online Method:

1. Visit the official Income Tax eFiling website (https://www.incometaxindiaefiling.gov.in/).
2. Find the link or section related to AadhaarPAN linking.
3. Enter the PAN, Aadhaar number, and other required details.
4. Validate the information, and if everything is correct, submit the request.

2. SMS Method:

1. Send an SMS to a designated number from the registered mobile number.
2. The format of the SMS may include details like PAN, Aadhaar number, etc.

3. Offline Method:

1. Visit a PAN Service center or an Aadhaar enrollment center.
2. Fill out the necessary form for linking Aadhaar with PAN.
3. Submit the form along with a copy of the PAN card and Aadhaar card.

4. Through Income Tax Department's Customer Care:

1. Contact the customer care of the Income Tax Department and follow their guidance for linking Aadhaar with PAN.
2. Always make sure to use official and secure channels when providing sensitive information such as PAN and Aadhaar details. Verify the current procedure from official sources to ensure accuracy and compliance with the latest regulations.

16.4 TAX DEDUCTION AND COLLECTION ACCOUNT NUMBER (TAN)

Tax Deduction and Collection Account Number (TAN) is a unique alphanumeric code issued by the Income Tax Department of India to entities responsible for deducting or collecting tax at source. This 10-digit identifier plays an important role in streamlining the taxation process and ensuring compliance with the tax laws of the country.

TAN is primarily used for tracking and monitoring tax transactions related to deductions and collections. It is mandatory for entities such as companies, businesses, and individuals who are required to deduct or collect tax at source to obtain a TAN. This distinctive number is essential for facilitating seamless communication between the deductor or collector and the Income Tax Department.

One of the primary purposes of TAN is to keep a comprehensive record of tax deducted at source (TDS) and tax collected at source (TCS) by various entities. TAN helps in distinguishing between different deductors and collectors, making it easier for tax authorities to identify and verify tax transactions. It also aids in preventing tax evasion and ensures that the government receives its due revenue in a timely and organized manner.

When an entity obtains a TAN, it becomes legally obligated to quote this number in all communication related to TDS and TCS. Whether it's filing TDS/TCS returns, issuing TDS certificates, or conducting any other transaction involving tax deduction or collection, the TAN must be mentioned to ensure accurate tracking and reporting.

Moreover, TAN serves as a means to prevent fraudulent activities related to tax deductions and collections. By assigning a unique identifier to each deductor or collector, the tax authorities can easily cross-verify the information provided in returns and other documents. This enhances the overall transparency and efficiency of the tax system in India.

16.4.1 TAN

TAN stands for Tax Deduction and Collection Account Number. It is a 10-digit alphanumeric number issued by the Income Tax Department to individuals or entities that are required to deduct or collect tax on payments made under various sections of the Income Tax Act. TAN is primarily used for tracking tax payments and ensuring that the tax deducted at source (TDS) is properly accounted for.

16.4.1 PERSON LIABLE TO APPLY FOR TAN

1. Entities Deducting TDS: Any person or entity making payments such as salary, interest, rent, commission, etc., and is required to deduct tax at source is liable to apply for TAN. This includes businesses, companies, and individuals who are required to deduct TDS.
2. Entities Collecting TCS: Persons or entities collecting tax at source (TCS) also need to apply for TAN. TCS is applicable in certain specified transactions, and the collector is required to collect tax from the payer and remit it to the government.
3. Individuals/Entities Required to File TDS/TCS Returns: Any person or entity required to file TDS or TCS returns is mandated obtaining a TAN. This includes submission of quarterly TDS or TCS statements with details of tax deducted or collected.

16.4.2 RELEVANCE OF TAN:

1. Identification: TAN serves as a unique identification number for entities responsible for deducting or collecting tax at source. It helps in the proper identification of taxpayers and ensures that the tax deducted is correctly attributed.
2. TDS Compliance: TAN is important for compliance with TDS provisions. Entities cannot deduct TDS without a valid TAN, and failure to comply with TDS provisions can lead to penalties.
3. TCS Compliance: Similarly, TAN is essential for entities collecting tax at source. It ensures compliance with TCS provisions, and non-compliance may attract penalties.
4. Tracking Transactions: TAN helps in tracking and monitoring transactions where TDS or TCS is applicable. It aids the Income Tax Department in maintaining a record of tax collections at source.
5. Filing Returns: TAN is a prerequisite for filing TDS and TCS returns. It facilitates the submission of accurate and timely returns to the Income Tax Department.

TAN is important for entities involved in deducting or collecting tax at source as it ensures compliance with tax regulations and facilitates proper tracking and reporting of such transactions to the Income Tax Department.

16.5 GOODS AND SERVICES TAX

Goods and Services Tax (GST) in India is a comprehensive indirect tax that was introduced on July 1, 2017, replacing the complex and fragmented tax structure that existed earlier. The implementation of GST marked a significant milestone in the country's economic reforms, aiming to streamline taxation, reduce cascading effects, and create a unified national market.

GST in India is a destination-based tax, meaning that it is levied at the final consumption point. It is a multi-stage tax that is applied at every step of the production and distribution chain, from the manufacturing stage to the final consumer. The tax is designed to be a value-added tax, allowing businesses to claim credit for the tax paid on inputs, which helps in eliminating the tax-on-tax effect.

One of the key features of GST is its dual structure, which involves both the central and state governments. The tax is divided into two components – Central GST (CGST) levied by the Central government and State GST (SGST) levied by the individual states. Additionally, there is an Integrated GST (IGST) for inter-state transactions, collected by the central government.

GST has brought about several advantages for businesses and the economy at large. It has simplified the tax structure, reducing the compliance burden for businesses by replacing multiple indirect taxes with a single tax. This has led to increased efficiency in tax administration and has made it easier for businesses to operate across state borders.

Moreover, GST has facilitated the formalization of the economy by encouraging businesses to register and comply with tax regulations. The transparency and accountability introduced by GST have helped in curbing tax evasion and increasing tax compliance.

However, the implementation of GST has not been without challenges. The initial phase witnessed some teething issues, including technological glitches and compliance complexities. Small and medium enterprises (SMEs) faced challenges in adapting to the new system, but efforts have been made to simplify procedures and address concerns.

GST in India represents a major stride towards a more unified and efficient tax system. While there have been challenges in the initial stages, the long-term benefits in terms of economic growth, simplification of taxation, and enhanced compliance are expected to outweigh the transitional hurdles. As the government continues to refine and improve the GST framework, it is anticipated to play an important role in shaping India's economic landscape.

16.5.1 PROCEDURE FOR GST REGISTRATION

Goods and Services Tax (GST) registration in India is a fundamental requirement for businesses engaging in the supply of goods or services. Enacted on July 1, 2017, GST replaced the complex and multi-layered indirect tax system with a unified tax structure, streamlining the taxation process across the country. This revolutionary tax reform aimed to create a common market, eliminate cascading effects, and enhance the ease of doing business.

To comply with GST regulations, businesses with an aggregate turnover exceeding the prescribed threshold limit must undergo GST registration. The threshold limits may vary for different categories of taxpayers, such as suppliers of goods, service providers, and special category states. Entities that do not meet the turnover criteria may opt for voluntary registration to avail of the benefits and avoid any legal implications.

The GST registration process is predominantly online, facilitating a seamless and efficient procedure for businesses. Applicants are required to submit relevant documents, including proof of business registration, PAN card, proof of address, bank statements, and photographs of the authorized signatory. The registration application is submitted through the GST Common Portal, where applicants receive a unique GST Identification Number (GSTIN) upon successful registration.

Once registered, businesses are obligated to comply with various GST regulations, including filing regular GST returns, maintaining accurate records, and adhering to invoicing requirements. Failure to comply with these obligations may result in penalties and legal consequences.

GST registration brings several advantages to businesses, such as the ability to legally collect and pass on input tax credit, enhancing competitiveness in the market. Additionally, registered businesses contribute to the formalization of the economy and gain credibility in the eyes of customers and stakeholders.

The GST framework in India is dynamic, with periodic updates and amendments to adapt to changing economic scenarios. Businesses are encouraged to stay informed about the latest developments to ensure continuous compliance and leverage the benefits offered by the GST regime.

16.5.2 PROCEDURE FOR GST REGISTRATION

1. Determine Eligibility: Individuals, businesses, and entities engaged in the supply of goods or services with an aggregate turnover exceeding the prescribed threshold are required to register for GST.

2. Online Application: Visit the official GST portal (https://www.gst.gov.in/) and navigate to the 'Services' > 'Registration' section.

3. New Registration: Click on "New Registration" and fill out the necessary details, including the legal name of the business, PAN, email address, and mobile number.

4. Verification Process: After submitting the online application, an acknowledgment with an Application Reference Number (ARN) will be sent to the registered email and mobile number.

5. Submission of Documents: Upload the required documents, including proof of business registration, identity and address proofs of promoters/partners/directors, bank statements, and photographs.

6. Verification by Authorities: The GST authorities will verify the application and documents. If any additional information is required, they may communicate with you.

7. Issue of GSTIN: Once the verification is successful, a Goods and Services Tax Identification Number (GSTIN) will be issued.

8. Certificate of Registration: A Certificate of Registration will be issued in Form GST REG06.

9. Timeline for Registration: The entire registration process usually takes a few working days.

10. Mandatory Registration: GST registration is mandatory for certain businesses, even if their turnover is below the threshold limit. These include interstate suppliers, ecommerce operators, and those liable to pay tax under the reverse charge mechanism.

11. Voluntary Registration: Businesses below the threshold limit can also opt for voluntary registration to avail of input tax credit benefits.

GST registration is an important step for businesses to participate in the modern, unified tax structure of India and contribute to the nation's economic growth.

It's essential to note that the GST registration process may evolve, and the threshold limits could change. Therefore, it is advisable to consult with a tax professional or visit the official GST portal for the latest and most accurate information. Additionally, the documentation requirements may vary based on the type of business entity and the nature of the business.

16.5.3 REGISTRATION UNDER THE SHOP AND ESTABLISHMENT ACT

Registration under the Shops and Establishment Act in India is an important legal requirement for businesses operating within the country. The Shops and Establishment Act, which is a state-specific legislation, aims to regulate the working conditions of employees in commercial establishments, including shops, offices, and other places of business. This legislation is designed to ensure the welfare of workers and to maintain a standardized work environment.

To initiate the process of registration, businesses need to submit an application to the relevant state authorities along with the necessary documentation. The application typically requires details such as the name and address of the establishment, nature of business, number of employees, working hours, and other relevant information. Once the application is processed and approved, the establishment is issued a registration certificate.

The Shops and Establishment Act outlines various provisions related to working hours, weekly offs, holidays, leave policies, and other conditions of service for employees. By registering under this Act, businesses demonstrate their commitment to adhering to these statutory regulations, contributing to a fair and just working environment.

Registration under the Shops and Establishment Act offers several advantages to businesses. It provides legal recognition, establishes compliance with labor laws, and facilitates the resolution of disputes through the proper legal channels. Furthermore, having a valid registration certificate is often a prerequisite for obtaining other licenses and permits, such as the Goods and Services Tax (GST) registration and various trade licenses.

Non-compliance with the Shops and Establishment Act can lead to legal consequences, including fines and penalties. Therefore, it is imperative for businesses to prioritize the registration process and ensure ongoing compliance with the stipulated regulations. Regular audits and updates to the registration details may be required to reflect any changes in the establishment's operations.

16.6 STEPS FOR REGISTERING UNDER THE SHOPS AND ESTABLISHMENT ACT

1. Identify Applicable Law: Determine the Shops and Establishment Act applicable to the business. Each state or union territory has its own Shops and Establishment Act, and one need to comply with the rules and regulations of the respective jurisdiction.
2. Application Form: Obtain the prescribed application form for registration. This form is usually available on the official website of the state's labor department.
3. Provide Information: Fill in the required information in the application form. This information typically includes details about the establishment, such as its name, address, type of business, working hours, number of employees, and other relevant information.
4. Attach Documents: Attach the necessary supporting documents, which may include proof of address (rent agreement or ownership document), details of the employees, and any other documents required by the respective state's labor department.
5. Submit Application: Submit the completed application form along with the supporting documents to the local labor department or the authority designated for such registrations.
6. Payment of Fees: Pay the applicable registration fees. The fee structure may vary depending on factors such as the size of the establishment and the number of employees.
7. Inspection: After the submission of the application, the labor department may conduct an inspection of the premises to verify the details provided in the application.
8. Grant of Certificate: Once the authorities are satisfied with the information and inspection, they will issue the Shops and Establishment registration certificate. This certificate is usually valid for a specific period, and renewal may be required.

Registration under the Shops and Establishment Act in India is a fundamental step for businesses seeking to operate legally and responsibly. It not only ensures compliance with labor laws but also contributes to the overall well-being and dignity of the workforce, fostering a positive and productive work environment.

It's important to note that compliance requirements may differ between states, and it's advisable to check the specific rules and procedures outlined by the labor department of the state or union territory where the business is located. Additionally, changes in the law or procedures may occur, so it's recommended to consult with a professional or legal advisor for the most up to date information.

16.7 REGISTRATION OF MSME's

Micro, Small, and Medium Enterprises (MSMEs) form the backbone of India's economy, contributing significantly to employment generation, industrial production, and overall economic growth. Recognizing the important role played by these enterprises, the Government of India has implemented various initiatives to support and promote their growth, with the MSME registration being an important aspect of this strategy.

MSME registration in India is a streamlined process designed to provide formal recognition and numerous benefits to enterprises falling within the prescribed criteria. The classification of MSMEs is primarily based on investment in plant and machinery or equipment and turnover.

One of the primary advantages of MSME registration is access to various government schemes, subsidies, and incentives. These incentives aim to alleviate financial constraints and encourage the growth and development of MSMEs. Additionally, registered MSMEs often enjoy preferential treatment in government procurement processes, fostering a more condusive business environment.

The registration process itself has been made more accessible through online platforms, reducing bureaucratic hurdles and expediting the entire procedure. Entrepreneurs can typically apply for MSME registration by submitting essential documents, including business PAN, Aadhaar, and other relevant details. The ease of registration aims to encourage more businesses to formalize their operations and avail themselves of the benefits associated with MSME status.

Furthermore, MSME registration fosters a sense of credibility and trust among potential customers, suppliers, and financial institutions. It serves as a mark of authenticity and reliability, potentially opening up new business opportunities and partnerships. Banks and financial institutions are often more willing to extend credit facilities to MSMEs with proper registration, facilitating their financial needs for expansion and working capital.

16.7.1 STEPS FOR MSME REGISTRATION

1. Visit the Udyam Registration Portal: Access the official website for MSME registration, which is the Udyam Registration portal (https://udyamregistration.gov.in/).

2. New Registration: Click on the "For New Entrepreneurs who are not registered yet as MSME" option.

3. Enter Aadhaar Number: Provide the 12-digit Aadhaar number and validate it through the OTP sent to the registered mobile number.

4. Entrepreneur Details: Fill in the required details about the entrepreneur, including name, category, gender, and others.

5. PAN and GST Details: Enter PAN and GST details if applicable. It's important to note that having a PAN and GST is not mandatory for all types of businesses.

6. Business Details: Fill in the details about the enterprise, such as name, type, and location.

7. Bank Account Details: Provide the bank account details for the purpose of registration.

8. NIC Code: Choose the appropriate National Industrial Classification (NIC) code that corresponds to the business activities. You can select multiple codes if needed.

9. Investment and Employment Details: Specify the total amount of investment in plant and machinery or equipment, as well as the number of people employed in the enterprise.

10. Verification and Submission: Review the entered details and submit the application. An OTP will be sent to the registered mobile number for verification.

11. Udyam Registration Certificate: Upon successful verification, one will receive the Udyam Registration Certificate. This certificate is valid for the lifetime of the business entity.

MSME registration in India plays an important role in empowering small and medium enterprises, offering them a platform to thrive in a competitive business landscape. By providing formal recognition, financial incentives, and facilitating easier access to resources, the government aims to create an ecosystem condusive to the sustained growth of MSMEs, thereby contributing significantly to the overall economic development of the country. Entrepreneurs are encouraged to explore the benefits of MSME registration and leverage the support available to build resilient and thriving enterprises.

16.8 CLEARANCE FROM THE POLLUTION CONTROL BOARD

Clearance from the Pollution Control Board (PCB) is an important step for industries and businesses seeking to operate in an environmentally responsible manner. The Pollution Control Board, operating under the Ministry of Environment, Forest and Climate Change, plays a important role in regulating and monitoring activities that have the potential to impact the environment adversely.

To obtain clearance from the Pollution Control Board, businesses are required to adhere to stringent environmental norms and standards set by the regulatory body. The process typically involves a thorough evaluation of the proposed project or operation to assess its potential environmental impact. This assessment encompasses factors such as air and water pollution, noise levels, waste generation, and overall ecological sustainability.

The clearance process involves the submission of detailed project reports, environmental impact assessments, and other relevant documents that outline the measures the business plans to undertake to mitigate and manage its environmental footprint. The Pollution Control Board scrutinizes these submissions to ensure that the proposed project aligns with the existing environmental regulations and guidelines.

The clearance granted by the Pollution Control Board is not only a legal requirement but also a testament to the commitment of the business to operate in an environmentally responsible manner. It signifies that the proposed project has been evaluated thoroughly, and the necessary precautions and safeguards have been put in place to minimize its impact on the environment.

Post-clearance, businesses are often subject to periodic monitoring by the Pollution Control Board to ensure ongoing compliance with environmental norms. Failure to adhere to the stipulated guidelines can result in penalties, suspension, or revocation of the clearance, underscoring the importance of continuous adherence to environmental best practices.

Clearance from the Pollution Control Board is a reflection of the government's commitment to sustainable development and environmental conservation. It serves as a mechanism to strike a balance between industrial growth and ecological well-being, promoting responsible business practices that prioritize environmental sustainability. In essence, obtaining clearance from the Pollution Control Board is not merely a regulatory requirement but a proactive step towards fostering a harmonious coexistence between industrial progress and environmental preservation in India.

16.9 FSSAI REGISTRATION AND LICENSE

The Food Safety and Standards Authority of India (FSSAI) plays a pivotal role in ensuring the safety and quality of food products consumed by the vast and diverse population of the country. Established under the Food Safety and Standards Act, 2006, the FSSAI is an autonomous body that operates under the Ministry of Health and Family Welfare.

FSSAI registration and licensing are essential components of the regulatory framework designed to uphold food safety standards across the food industry in India. The registration and licensing process is designed to cover various businesses involved in the production, processing, distribution, and sale of food products. This comprehensive approach ensures that all players in the food supply chain adhere to the prescribed standards and regulations.

For businesses operating on a small scale or with limited annual turnover, FSSAI registration is mandatory. This registration process involves the submission of basic details and documents related to the nature of the business, its address, and the food products it deals with. Once registered, the business receives a unique 14-digit FSSAI registration number, which must be displayed on the food packages.

On the other hand, larger businesses with higher turnovers are required to obtain an FSSAI license. The licensing process is more rigorous and involves a detailed scrutiny of the food safety management system, infrastructure, and quality control measures implemented by the business. The license is issued for a specific period and must be renewed before expiry.

Obtaining FSSAI registration or license is not just a legal obligation but also a testament to a business's commitment to ensuring the safety and well-being of consumers. It serves as a quality assurance mechanism, instilling confidence among consumers and business partners alike. The FSSAI regularly updates its standards and guidelines to keep pace with advancements in the food industry, ensuring that businesses stay informed and compliant.

Non-compliance with FSSAI regulations can result in penalties, recalls, and even closure of the business. Therefore, it is imperative for food businesses to understand the significance of FSSAI registration and licensing and adhere to the prescribed guidelines. This not only fosters a culture of responsibility but also contributes to the overarching goal of safeguarding public health and promoting a robust and sustainable food industry in India.

1. FSSAI Registration:

a. FSSAI registration is required for small businesses or startups with an annual turnover of up to Rs. 12 lakhs.
b. It is a basic registration and is suitable for smallscale businesses, street food vendors, and petty food manufacturers.
c. The application for registration can be submitted online on the FSSAI website or through the Food Licensing and Registration System (FLRS).

2. FSSAI State License:

a. FSSAI State License is applicable to mediumsized businesses with an annual turnover between Rs. 12 lakhs and Rs. 20 crores.
b. This license is granted by the State Authorities.

3. FSSAI Central License:

a. FSSAI Central License is required for largescale businesses with an annual turnover exceeding Rs. 20 crores.
b. This license is granted by the Central Authority.

16.9.1 STEPS TO OBTAIN FSSAI REGISTRATION OR LICENSE:

1. Visit the FSSAI Website: Go to the official FSSAI website (https://www.fssai.gov.in/).

2. Create an Account: Create an account on the Food Licensing and Registration System (FLRS) by providing the required details.

3. Fill the Application Form: Fill the relevant application form based on the type of license you require (Basic, State, or Central).

4. Submit Documents: Attach the necessary documents, which may include identity proof, address proof, proof of business ownership, food safety management plan, etc.

5. Payment of Fees: Pay the applicable fees online.

6. Inspection (if required): The authorities may conduct an inspection of your premises, especially for State and Central licenses.

7. Issuance of License: Once the application is processed and all requirements are met, the FSSAI license is issued.

FSSAI compliance is important to ensure food safety and adherence to quality standards. Noncompliance can result in penalties, cancellation of the license, or legal action. Therefore, businesses involved in the food industry in India should prioritize obtaining the necessary FSSAI registration or license. It's advisable to consult with FSSAI officials or seek professional assistance for a smooth application process.

16.10 TRADEMARK REGISTRATION AND LICENSING

In the dynamic landscape of commerce and business, trademarks serve as indispensable tools for brand identification and protection. India, with its burgeoning economy and thriving entrepreneurial spirit, recognizes the paramount importance of safeguarding intellectual property rights. The registration and licensing of trademarks in the country play an important role in fostering innovation, ensuring fair competition, and fortifying the foundation of a robust market.

16.10.1 TRADEMARK REGISTRATION:

Trademark registration is a legal process that provides exclusive rights to the owner of a distinctive mark, symbol, logo, or name associated with goods or services. The objective is to prevent unauthorized use and infringement by competitors, thereby safeguarding the reputation and goodwill built by the business. In India, the Trademarks Act of 1999 governs the registration and protection of trademarks, and the process is administered by the Office of the Controller General of Patents, Designs, and Trademarks.

The registration process involves a comprehensive examination of the proposed trademark to ensure its distinctiveness and non-similarity to existing trademarks. Once registered, the trademark owner gains the exclusive right to use the mark in connection with the specified goods or services for a period of ten years, with the option to renew indefinitely.

Trademark Licensing:

Trademark licensing is a strategic arrangement wherein the owner of a trademark (licensor) grants permission to another party (licensee) to use the trademark under specified terms and conditions. This enables businesses to expand their market presence, capitalize on brand recognition, and generate additional revenue streams. The licensing agreement delineates the scope of use, geographical limitations, quality control measures, and the duration of the license.

In India, trademark licensing is subject to certain legal requirements, and it is essential for both parties to adhere to the stipulations set forth in the licensing agreement. Properly drafted agreements help maintain the integrity of the trademark and prevent any dilution of its distinctiveness.

16.10.2 STEPS FOR TRADE MARK REGISTRATION

Registering a trademark in India involves a legal process that grants the owner exclusive rights to use the mark concerning the goods or services for which it is registered.

Steps to register a trademark

1. Identify the Mark: Choose a unique and distinctive mark that represents the goods or services. It could be a word, logo, slogan, or a combination thereof.

2. Conduct a Trademark Search: Before applying for registration, conduct a thorough search to ensure that the chosen mark is not already registered by someone else. One can perform a search on the official website of the Intellectual Property India (IPI) office or seek the assistance of a trademark attorney.

3. Create a User Account: Visit the official website of the Controller General of Patents, Designs, and Trademarks (CGPDTM) at ipindia.gov.in. Create a user account to access the trademark filing system.

4. File an Application: Fill out the trademark application form, known as Form TM-A, either online or offline. Provide details such as the name and address of the applicant, description of the goods/services, and a representation of the mark.

5. Pay the Fees: Pay the prescribed filing fees for the trademark application. The fees may vary depending on the type of applicant (individual, startup, small enterprise, or others) and the mode of filing.

6. Examination by the Trademark Office: After filing, the Trademark Office will examine the application. If there are no objections or oppositions, the trademark will be published in the Trademarks Journal.

7. Opposition Period: After publication, there is a specified period during which third parties can oppose the registration of the trademark. If there are no objections, the trademark proceeds to registration.

8. Registration Certificate: If there are no oppositions or if any opposition are overcome, the Trademark Office will issue a registration certificate. This certificate establishes the exclusive rights to the mark in connection with the specified goods or services.

9. Renewal: Trademark registrations are valid for ten years, after which they can be renewed indefinitely. Make sure to renew the trademark in a timely manner to maintain its validity.

Obtaining a trademark registration in India involves a series of steps. Here is a general overview of the process:

1. Conduct a Trademark Search: Before filing an application, it's important to conduct a thorough search to ensure that the proposed trademark is unique and not already registered or pending registration.

2. Identify the Class of Goods/Services: Trademarks are registered for specific classes of goods or services. Identify the class or classes relevant to the business.

3. Preparation of Trademark Application: Prepare the trademark application with all the required details, including the name and address of the applicant, a representation of the trademark, and a list of goods or services for which registration is sought.

4. Filing the Application: Submit the application to the Trademark Registry. In India, this can be done online through the official website of the Trademark Registry.

5. Examination by the Trademark Office: The Trademark Office examines the application to ensure it complies with legal requirements. If there are any objections, the applicant is given an opportunity to respond.

6. Publication in the Trademark Journal: If the application is accepted, the trademark is published in the Trademark Journal. This allows third parties to oppose the registration within a specified period.

7. Opposition Period: The application is open for opposition for a certain period (usually four months). If there is no opposition, or if opposition is unsuccessful, the trademark proceeds to registration.

8. Registration Certificate: Once the trademark is accepted and there is no opposition, the Trademark Registry issues a Registration Certificate. This certificate is proof of the trademark owner's rights.

9. Renewal of Trademark: Trademarks in India are initially registered for a period of 10 years. After this period, the registration can be renewed indefinitely in successive periods of 10 years.

10. Enforcement of Trademark Rights: After registration, the trademark owner must actively monitor and enforce their rights against unauthorized use by others.

It is advisable to consult with a trademark attorney or agent during this process, as they can provide legal advice, help with the application, and ensure that all requirements are met. The process can take several months to complete, and it's essential to be patient and diligent throughout.

Trademark registration and licensing in India are integral components of the intellectual property landscape, providing a framework for businesses to protect their brands and explore collaborative opportunities. As the Indian economy continues to evolve, the emphasis on trademark rights becomes even more pronounced, fostering an environment condusive to innovation, investment, and fair competition. Businesses navigating the intricacies of trademark registration and licensing contribute not only to their own success but also to the overall growth and vibrancy of the Indian business ecosystem.

16.11 PATENTS REGISTRATION AND LICENSE

In the dynamic landscape of innovation and technological advancement, the protection of intellectual property plays a pivotal role in fostering creativity and economic growth. In India, the legal framework for safeguarding inventions is primarily governed by the Patents Act, 1970. This legislation establishes a comprehensive system for the registration and licensing of patents, aiming to incentivize inventors, encourage research and development, and promote the dissemination of knowledge.

A patent is a legal document granted by the government, conferring exclusive rights to the inventor for a limited period, typically 20 years. This exclusive right enables the inventor to prevent others from making, using, selling, or importing the patented invention without permission. The process of obtaining a patent in India involves a meticulous examination of the invention's novelty, inventive step, and industrial applicability by the Indian Patent Office.

One of the fundamental aspects of the patent system is the registration process. Patent registration is important for inventors seeking legal protection for their innovative ideas and technologies. It involves the submission of a detailed patent application, including a comprehensive description of the invention, along with supporting documentation. The application undergoes a thorough examination process by patent examiners to determine its eligibility for grant.

In addition to registration, the concept of licensing plays a significant role in the utilization and commercialization of patented inventions. Patent licensing involves the transfer of rights from the patent holder to another party, allowing them to use, make, sell, or distribute the patented technology in exchange for a negotiated fee or royalty. Licensing agreements can be beneficial for both parties, as they enable the patent holder to generate revenue from their invention while providing the licensee with access to valuable technologies.

India's patent regime aims to strike a balance between promoting innovation and ensuring that the public benefits from the advancements. Through a well-defined system of registration and licensing, the Indian government encourages inventors to disclose their inventions, contributing to the growth of science and technology in the country.

16.11.1 PATENT REGISTRATION

Registering a patent in India involves a series of steps and adherence to specific regulations. The patent registration process in India is governed by the Indian Patent Act, 1970, and is administered by the Indian Patent Office (IPO), which operates under the Controller General of Patents, Designs & Trade Marks.

PATENT REGISTRATION PROCESS

1. Determine Patentability: Ensure that your invention is eligible for patent protection. Not all inventions can be patented; they must be novel, nonobvious, and industrially applicable.
2. Patent Search: Conduct a thorough patent search to check if a similar invention has already been patented. This step helps in determining the novelty of your invention.
3. Draft a Patent Specification: Prepare a detailed patent specification that includes a description of the invention, its novelty, and how it works. This includes both a provisional and a complete specification.
4. Filing a Patent Application: File a patent application with the Indian Patent Office. You can file either a provisional or a complete application. Filing a provisional application provides a priority date for your invention, allowing you time to prepare a complete specification.
5. Request for Examination: After filing, you must request the examination of your patent application within 48 months (4 years) from the date of filing. If you filed a request for a provisional application, the request for examination must be made within 48 months from the filing date of the provisional application.
6. Publication: The patent application is published after 18 months from the date of filing or the priority date, whichever is earlier.
7. Examination by the Patent Office: The patent office examines the application to ensure that the invention meets the criteria for patentability. You may need to respond to any objections raised by the patent examiner.
8. Grant of Patent: If the patent office is satisfied with the application and any objections have been addressed, a patent is granted. The term of a patent in India is 20 years from the filing date.
9. Renewal/Renewal Fees: Once the patent is granted, it's important to pay the renewal fees to maintain the validity of the patent.

It is advisable to seek professional assistance from a patent agent throughout the patent registration process to ensure compliance with all legal requirements. The process may take several years, and the timeline can vary depending on factors such as the complexity of the invention and the workload at the patent office.

Obtaining a patent registration or license in India involves a series of steps. Here is a general overview of the process:

1. Determine Patentability: Ensure that your invention is eligible for patent protection. Not all inventions can be patented, and there are specific criteria that must be met.

2. Conduct a Patent Search: Perform a thorough patent search to check if a similar invention already exists. This step helps in assessing the novelty of your invention.

3. Drafting the Patent Application: Prepare a detailed and welldrafted patent application. This is an important step, and it's often advisable to seek professional help from a patent agent.

4. Choose the Type of Patent Application: Decide whether to file a provisional or complete patent application. A provisional application is a temporary filing that gives you a priority date, while a complete application provides a detailed description of the invention.

5. File the Patent Application: Submit the patent application to the Indian Patent Office. You can file it online or through physical means. Ensure that you include all the necessary documents and fees.

6. Examination of the Patent Application: The patent application undergoes examination by the Patent Office to determine its patentability. You may be required to respond to any objections raised by the examiner during this stage.

7. Publication of the Application: Once the patent application is accepted, it is published in the Official Journal. This publication allows the public to oppose the grant of the patent within a specified period.

8. Opposition Proceedings: If there are no oppositions or if opposition issues are resolved, the patent is granted. If there is an opposition, a hearing may be scheduled to resolve the matter.

9. Grant of Patent: If there are no further issues or oppositions, the patent is granted, and a certificate of grant is issued.

10. Renewal of the Patent: Maintain the patent by paying the prescribed renewal fees at regular intervals. Failure to pay these fees may result in the patent being revoked.

11. Licensing: If you wish to license your patent to others, you can negotiate licensing agreements with interested parties. This involves setting terms and conditions for the use of your patented invention.

12. Enforcement: If someone infringes on the patent rights, one may take legal action to enforce the rights. This could involve filing a lawsuit for patent infringement.

The process of patents registration and licensing in India is a cornerstone of intellectual property protection, fostering innovation, and contributing to the nation's economic development. As India continues to evolve as a global hub for research and development, the patent system plays an important role in shaping the future of technological progress and promoting a culture of innovation and creativity.

16.12 DESIGN REGISTRATION

Design Registration is an important aspect of intellectual property protection, playing an important role in safeguarding the unique visual aesthetics of various products. Governed by the Designs Act, 2000, the registration process is administered by the Office of the Controller General of Patents, Designs, and Trademarks (CGPDTM) under the Ministry of Commerce and Industry.

A design, in the context of registration, refers to the visual ornamental characteristics embodied in an article. This encompasses shapes, configurations, patterns, or ornamentations applied to an article, either manually or through industrial processes. The primary objective of design registration is to prevent unauthorized replication and imitation of a design, thereby providing legal exclusivity to the registered proprietor.

The process of design registration involves filing an application with the Design Wing of the Indian Patent Office. The application should include representations or drawings of the design, along with a statement highlighting the novelty and originality of the design. The design is examined to ensure it meets the statutory requirements, such as novelty and distinctiveness. Once accepted, the design is published in the official journal, opening a window for third-party oppositions.

The registration is valid for an initial period of ten years, extendable for another five years upon payment of the prescribed fees. It's important to note that the design registration process is distinct from patents and trademarks, as it exclusively focuses on the visual appearance of an article.

Design registration provides the registered proprietor with exclusive rights, preventing others from making, importing, using, or selling the article with the registered design. This legal protection encourages innovation and creativity by rewarding designers for their efforts and investments in creating aesthetically pleasing and unique products.

In the fast-paced world of commerce, where the visual appeal of products often plays an important role in consumer choices, design registration in India serves as a vital tool for businesses to safeguard their investments in creating distinctive and attractive designs. It not only fosters creativity but also contributes to building a culture of respect for intellectual property rights, ultimately benefiting the economy and promoting innovation.

16.12.1 DESIGN REGISTRATION:

1. Preparation:

a. Novelty Search: Before applying for design registration, it's advisable to conduct a novelty search to ensure that the design is unique and hasn't been registered by someone else.
b. Representation of Design: Create clear and accurate representations (drawings, photographs, or samples) of the design.

2. Filing the Application:

a. Application Form: Fill out the application form for design registration (Form-1), which is available on the official website of the Indian Patent Office.
b. Class and Locarno Classification: Specify the class of the product and the Locarno classification under which the design falls.

3. Submission of Documents:

a. Declaration of Priority (if any): If you have filed a design application in a convention country, submit the declaration of priority.
b. Power of Attorney: Submit a Power of Attorney, if applicable.
c. Statement of Novelty: Include a statement of novelty explaining the distinctive features of the design.

4. Examination:

a. Examination Request: File a request for examination within six months from the date of filing.
b. If one fails to do so, the application will be treated as abandoned.

5. Publication: After the examination, if the design is found to be novel and distinctive, it will be published in the Official Designs Journal.

6. Opposition: Third parties have the opportunity to file an opposition against the registration within four months from the date of publication.

7. Registration: If there is no opposition or if the opposition is unsuccessful, the design will be registered, and a certificate of registration will be issued.

8. Renewal: Renew the registration periodically to maintain protection. The first renewal is due after five years from the date of registration.

16.13 QUESTIONS:

1. Discuss the process of acquiring PAN and TAN in India.
2. What are mandatory registrations Discuss?
3. Discus Trade Mark registration?

4. What is the process of registering Patents in India?

5. What is Design registration? Discuss its purpose and registration process in detail.

LIMITED LIABILITY: PARTNERSHIP AND JOINT VENTURE

17.1 LIMITED LIABILITY PARTNERSHIP (LLP)

A Limited Liability Partnership (LLP) is a legal structure for business that combines elements of both a traditional partnership and a corporation. It provides limited liability to its partners, which means that the personal assets of the partners are protected from the debts and liabilities of the LLP. This is a important feature that distinguishes it from a general partnership, where the partners have unlimited personal liability.

In an LLP, each partner is not personally responsible for the actions, debts, or liabilities of the other partners. This limited liability protection allows individual partners to participate in the management and decision-making of the business without being personally held accountable for the actions of their colleagues.

LLPs are often chosen by professionals such as lawyers, accountants, and consultants because they allow for flexibility in management while offering the protection of limited liability. The specific regulations and requirements for forming and operating an LLP can vary by jurisdiction, so it's important for individuals considering this business structure to be aware of and comply with the relevant local laws and regulations.

17.1.2 DEFINITION OF LIMITED LIABILITY PARTNERSHIP (LLP)

Section 2(n) of the Limited Liability Partnership Act, defines Limited Liability Partnership as: "limited liability partnership" means a partnership formed and registered under this Act.

Limited Liability Partnership is governed by Limited Liability Partnership act, 2008. Provisions of erstwhile Indian Partnership act, 1932 are not applicable.

Limited Liability Partnership (LLP) is a type of business structure that combines features of both partnerships and corporations, offering limited liability protection to its partners while maintaining the flexibility and tax benefits of a partnership.

1. Limited Liability Partnership (LLP):

Definition: A business structure where partners enjoy limited personal liability for the company's debts and obligations, similar to shareholders in a corporation, while maintaining the flexibility and pass-through taxation of a partnership.

Author: The concept of LLP has evolved over time and is shaped by various legal scholars and practitioners. There is no single author associated with the term, as it represents a collective development in business law.

2. Limited Liability:

Definition: The legal protection that shields the personal assets of LLP partners from the business debts and liabilities, limiting their financial risk to the amount of their investment in the partnership.

Author: The concept of limited liability has historical roots and has been developed through legal precedents and legislative acts. Authors like William Blackstone, a legal scholar from the 18th century, laid the groundwork for the notion of limited liability.

3. Pass-Through Taxation:

Definition: A taxation method where the LLP itself is not taxed, and profits and losses are passed through to the individual partners, who report the income on their personal tax returns.

Author: The concept of pass-through taxation has been influenced by various tax laws and regulations. Scholars in tax law, such as Boris Bittker and James Eustice, have contributed to the understanding and development of pass-through taxation principles.

4. Flexibility in Management:

Definition: The ability of LLP partners to structure the management and decision-making processes in a manner that suits the needs of the business, without the rigid formalities imposed on corporations.

Author: Authors like Henry Hansmann and Reinier Kraakman, in their work on the theory of the firm, have explored the flexibility in management structures and how different business entities, including LLPs, can adapt to the preferences of their participants.

It's important to note that the development of legal concepts is often a collaborative effort involving lawmakers, legal scholars, and practitioners, and these definitions represent general principles associated with LLPs

17.1.2 LIMITED LIABILITY PARTNERSHIP: NATURE AND CHARACTERISTICS

A Limited Liability Partnership (LLP) is a type of business structure that combines features of both a partnership and a corporation. In India, LLPs are governed by the Limited Liability Partnership Act, 2008.

NATURE AND CHARACTERISTICS OF AN LLP:

1. Separate Legal Entity: An LLP is considered a separate legal entity distinct from its partners. It can enter into contracts, sue, and be sued in its own name.

2. Limited Liability: One of the key features of an LLP is that the liability of partners is limited. Each partner's liability is restricted to the amount of capital contributed by them. Personal assets of the partners are not usually at risk for the LLP's debts and liabilities.

3. Number of Partners: An LLP must have a minimum of two partners. There is no upper limit on the number of partners, and they can be individuals or corporate entities.

4. Formation and Registration: Formation of an LLP involves registering with the Ministry of Corporate Affairs (MCA) in India. The registration process includes filing the necessary documents and complying with regulatory requirements.

5. Perpetual Succession: LLPs have perpetual succession, meaning the death, insolvency, or withdrawal of a partner does not affect the continuity of the LLP. The LLP continues to exist until it is legally dissolved.

6. Management and Decision Making: The management of an LLP is typically done by its partners, but the LLP agreement can define the roles and responsibilities of partners. Decisions are usually made by a consensus, and the LLP agreement can govern matters related to decisionmaking processes.

7. Audit Requirements: LLPs are required to maintain proper books of accounts, and an annual audit is mandatory if the annual turnover exceeds a prescribed limit or if the capital contribution exceeds a specified amount.

8. Taxation: LLPs are taxed as a separate legal entity, and the partners are not personally taxed for the business profits. The LLP is subject to income tax, and partners are taxed on their share of profits.

9. Flexibility: LLPs offer a certain degree of flexibility in terms of internal structure, management, and decisionmaking processes. The LLP agreement can be customized to suit the specific needs of the partners.

10. Compliance Requirements: LLPs need to comply with various statutory and regulatory requirements, including filing annual returns and maintaining proper records.

17.1.3 LIMITED LIABILITY PARTNERSHIP: ADVANTAGES AND DISADVANTAGES

A Limited Liability Partnership (LLP) is a type of business structure that combines elements of a partnership and a corporation. In India, LLPs are governed by the Limited Liability Partnership Act, 2008.

ADVANTAGES OF LLP:

1. Limited Liability: One of the main advantages of an LLP is limited liability. The personal assets of the partners are separate from the assets of the business. This means that the personal assets of the partners are generally protected from the liabilities of the LLP.
2. Flexibility in Management: LLPs provide flexibility in management, allowing partners to organize the internal structure as per their agreement. Partners have the freedom to decide how they want to manage the LLP, which provides for a more adaptable and customized business structure.
3. Ease of Formation and Compliance: Formation of an LLP is relatively simple, and the compliance requirements are less burdensome compared to a private limited company. There is no requirement for a minimum capital contribution, and the filing of annual returns is less complex.
4. Tax Benefits: LLPs are taxed as a partnership, and the income is not taxed at the entity level. Instead, profits and losses are passed through to the individual partners, who report this income on their personal tax returns. This can lead to tax savings, especially if the partners are in lower tax brackets.
5. No Dividend Distribution Tax (DDT): Unlike a private limited company, LLPs are not subject to Dividend Distribution Tax on the distribution of profits to partners.

DISADVANTAGES OF LLP:

1. Limited Capital Infusion: LLPs may face challenges in raising capital as they cannot issue shares to the public. The capital infusion is limited to the contributions made by the partners.
2. Perpetual Succession Limited:LLPs have a limited life, and their existence is dependent on the partners. In case of death, withdrawal, or insolvency of a partner, the LLP may face continuity issues.
3. Regulatory Compliance: While the compliance requirements for LLPs are generally less than those for private limited companies, there are still certain statutory compliances that need to be met. Failure to comply with these requirements can lead to penalties.
4. Complex Dissolution Process: Dissolving an LLP can be a complex process involving compliance with regulatory procedures. This may involve approval from the Registrar of Companies and other authorities, making it more cumbersome than the dissolution of a partnership.
5. Restrictions on Business Activities: LLPs may face restrictions on certain business activities, and they may not be suitable for businesses that require extensive capital investment, such as manufacturing.

17.1.4 LLP - PROCEDURE FOR INCORPORATION

The procedures and requirements for registering a Limited Liability Partnership (LLP)
LLP registration process:

1. Name Reservation:

    a. Choose a unique name for the LLP.
    b. Check the availability of the chosen name on the Ministry of Corporate Affairs (MCA) website.
    c. Once the name is approved, it is reserved for 20 days.

2. Digital Signature Certificate (DSC): Obtain Digital Signature Certificates for the proposed Designated Partners. At least two partners must obtain DSC.
3. Designated Partner Identification Number (DPIN): All designated partners must obtain a DPIN (Designated Partner Identification Number).

4. Documents Preparation: Prepare the necessary documents, including the LLP Agreement. The LLP Agreement defines the mutual rights and duties among the partners and between the LLP and its partners.

5. LLP Incorporation Form: File the LLP incorporation form (Form FiLLiP) with the Registrar of Companies (RoC) along with the necessary documents. Pay the prescribed registration fees based on the contribution of partners.

6. LLP Agreement Submission: File the LLP Agreement (Form 3) within 30 days of the date of incorporation.

7. Certificate of Incorporation: Once the RoC is satisfied with the documents, they will issue a Certificate of Incorporation.

8. PAN and TAN Application: Apply for the Permanent Account Number (PAN) and Tax Deduction and Collection Account Number (TAN) for the LLP.

9. Bank Account Opening: Open a bank account in the name of the LLP using the Certificate of Incorporation and partnership agreement.

10. PostIncorporation Compliance: Comply with the postincorporation requirements, such as filing annual returns and other regulatory filings. LLPs are required to file an annual return (Form 11) and a statement of accounts and solvency (Form 8) with the RoC.

11. Professional Assistance: Engaging the services of a professional, such as a company secretary or chartered accountant, can be beneficial to ensure compliance with all legal requirements.

17.1.5 LLP AGREEMENT

A Limited Liability Partnership (LLP) is a popular form of business structure that combines the flexibility of a partnership with the limited liability feature of a company. An LLP agreement is an important document that outlines the rights, responsibilities, and obligations of the partners in the LLP. The LLP agreement is governed by the Limited Liability Partnership Act, 2008, and it is mandatory for every LLP to have one.

Important points about the LLP agreement:

Mandatory Requirement: Every LLP is required to have an LLP agreement, and it must be filed with the Ministry of Corporate Affairs (MCA) during the incorporation process.

Contents of the Agreement: The LLP agreement typically includes the following information:

a. Name and registered office of the LLP
b. Names and details of partners
c. Contribution of each partner
d. Profitsharing ratio
e. Rights and duties of partners
f. Rules for management and decisionmaking
g. Process for admission or retirement of partners
h. Process for resolution of disputes among partners
a. Provisions for the dissolution of the LLP

1. Amendments to the Agreement:The LLP agreement can be amended by mutual consent of the partners. Any changes to the agreement must be filed with the MCA within 30 days of such amendments.

2. Stamp Duty: The LLP agreement may require stamping based on the Stamp Act applicable in the state where the LLP is registered.

3. Default Provisions: In the absence of specific provisions in the LLP agreement, the default provisions specified in the LLP Act will apply.

4. Professional Assistance: It is advisable to seek professional help, such as a chartered accountant or a company secretary, to draft the LLP agreement to ensure that it complies with legal requirements and adequately reflects the intentions of the partners.
5. Filing with the MCA: The LLP agreement, along with the initial incorporation documents, needs to be filed with the MCA at the time of LLP registration. Subsequent amendments should also be filed promptly.
6. Annual Return: LLPs are required to file an annual return with the MCA, and any changes in the LLP agreement should be updated in the annual return.

It's essential to note that the LLP agreement plays an important role in defining the relationship between partners and managing the affairs of the LLP, so careful consideration and legal advice are recommended during its drafting.

A Limited Liability Partnership (LLP) agreement is a important document that outlines the rights, responsibilities, and obligations of the partners involved in the LLP. The LLP agreement is governed by the Limited Liability Partnership Act, 2008. While specific details may vary based on the preferences of the partners and the nature of the business, the following are typical contents found in an LLP agreement:

1. Name and Address:

a. Full name and address of the LLP.
b. Registered office address.

2. Business Activities: Description of the business activities that the LLP will undertake.

3. Capital Contribution: Details of the capital contribution by each partner should be mentioned including contribution is in the form of cash, property, or services.

4. Profit Sharing and Loss Allocation: Provisions for the distribution of profits and losses among the partners.

5. Management and Decision Making:

a. How the LLP will be managed, including the decisionmaking process.
b. Appointment and powers of designated partners for management and decision making

6. Admission and Withdrawal of Partners:

a. Procedures for admitting new partners.
b. Terms and conditions for withdrawal or retirement of partners.

7. Meetings and Voting:

a. Frequency and procedures for partner meetings.
b. Voting rights and decisionmaking mechanisms.

8. Transfer of Ownership:

a. Conditions under which a partner can transfer their ownership interest.
b. Preemptive rights for existing partners to buy out the interest.

9. Remuneration and Salaries:

a. Terms of remuneration or salaries for partners, if any.

10. Books of Accounts and Auditing:

a. Maintenance of books of accounts and records.
b. Procedures for auditing and financial reporting.

11. Dispute Resolution: Mechanisms for resolving disputes among partners.
12. Dissolution and Winding Up:

a. Conditions and procedures for the dissolution of the LLP.
b. Distribution of assets in the event of dissolution.

13. Indemnity and Liability: Indemnification provisions to protect partners from certain liabilities.

14. Miscellaneous Provisions: Miscellaneous clauses such as force majeure, confidentiality, noncompete, etc.

It's important to note that the LLP agreement is a flexible document, and partners have the freedom to customize it based on their specific needs and requirements.

ANNUAL COMPLIANCES OF LLP

Limited Liability Partnerships (LLPs) are required to comply with various annual statutory requirements to ensure proper governance and transparency.

1. Annual Return Filing (Form 11): LLPs are required to file Form 11 annually. This form contains details such as the number of partners, changes in the management, and details of the registered office.

2. Financial Statements (Form 8): LLPs must file Form 8, which includes the Statement of Account & Solvency and the Annual Return. This needs to be filed within 30 days from the end of six months of the financial year.

3. Income Tax Return (ITR): LLPs are required to file income tax returns annually. The due date for filing LLP tax returns is generally July 31st, but it can be extended. LLPs are also required to get their accounts audited if their turnover exceeds a specified limit.

4. Audit of Accounts: LLPs with a turnover exceeding a prescribed limit (currently Rs. 40 lakhs for business and Rs. 25 lakhs for professionals) or contribution exceeding Rs. 25 lakhs are required to get their accounts audited by a qualified Chartered Accountant.

5. Annual General Meeting (AGM): Unlike companies, LLPs are not explicitly required to hold an AGM. However, they must discuss and finalize their accounts and file the necessary returns within the specified deadlines.

6. DIN and DPIN: Ensure that the Designated Partners have a valid Director Identification Number (DIN) and Designated Partner Identification Number (DPIN). In case of any changes, these need to be updated with the Ministry of Corporate Affairs (MCA).

7. Update Changes: LLPs need to promptly inform the Registrar of Companies (RoC) about any changes in the LLP agreement, change in partners, or any other significant changes in the LLP structure.

8. Penalty and Late Fees: LLPs should ensure timely filing of all required documents to avoid penalties and late fees imposed by the Registrar.

9. Maintaining Books of Accounts: LLPs are required to maintain proper books of accounts at their registered office.secretary or a chartered accountant can help ensure compliance with all regulatory requirements.

17.2 BUSINESS COLLABORATION

Business collaborations play an important role in the contemporary landscape of commerce, fostering synergies and driving innovation across industries. In an era marked by rapid technological advancements and globalization, the notion of going it alone has given way to strategic partnerships, alliances, and collaborations that enable organizations to navigate the complexities of the business world more effectively.

Collaborations come in various forms, ranging from joint ventures and strategic alliances to partnerships and co-development agreements. These arrangements allow companies to pool resources, share expertise, and leverage each other's strengths to achieve common goals. By combining complementary skill sets and resources, businesses can accelerate product development, enter new markets, and enhance their competitive edge.

One of the main advantages of business collaborations is the ability to tap into diverse perspectives and ideas. Partnering with other entities brings fresh insights and approaches, fostering a culture of creativity and innovation. This cross-pollination of ideas often results in the development of cutting-edge solutions and services that may not have been possible through individual efforts.

Furthermore, collaborations provide a means for businesses to mitigate risks and navigate uncertainties. Shared responsibilities and joint decision-making enable companies to pool their expertise and resources, spreading the burden of challenges and uncertainties that may arise in the business environment. This collaborative risk-sharing approach can enhance resilience and adaptability in the face of unforeseen circumstances.

In the context of globalization, collaborations also facilitate market entry and expansion. Local partners can offer valuable insights into unfamiliar markets, navigate regulatory landscapes, and establish relationships with key stakeholders. This is particularly important in industries where local knowledge and cultural understanding are paramount for success.

While collaborations present numerous benefits, they also require effective communication, mutual trust, and a shared vision. Clear agreements, transparent communication channels, and well-defined roles and responsibilities are essential for the success of any collaborative endeavor. Additionally, companies must be mindful of potential challenges, such as differences in corporate cultures, conflicting interests, and the need for ongoing commitment to maintaining the partnership's success.

Business collaborations represent a cornerstone of modern business strategy. As organizations seek to thrive in a dynamic and interconnected global economy, strategic partnerships and alliances provide a pathway to innovation, resilience, and sustained growth. The ability to navigate the complexities of collaboration while capitalizing on shared strengths and resources is a hallmark of successful businesses in today's interconnected world.

17.2.1 BUSINESS COLLABORATION - DEFINITIONS

Business collaboration refers to the strategic alliance or partnership between two or more entities with the aim of achieving common goals, such as mutual growth, innovation, or market expansion.

DEFINITIONS OF BUSINESS COLLABORATION:

1. "Collaboration is a key driver of overall business success. It is the process of two or more people or organizations working together to complete a task or achieve a goal." - Ken Blanchard

2. "Business collaboration is a strategic relationship formed between two or more entities to achieve a common business objective through the sharing of resources, risks, and rewards." - Gary Hamel

3. "Collaboration is a mindset that involves individuals and organizations actively working together to create shared value, innovation, and success." - Rosabeth Moss Kanter

4. "Business collaboration is the art of thinking, planning, and working together to achieve shared objectives. It's about leveraging collective intelligence and resources for mutual benefit." - Stephen Covey

5. "Collaboration is the fuel that allows common people to achieve uncommon results in business. It is the synergy of different perspectives and skills coming together for a greater purpose." - Andrew Carnegie

6. "Business collaboration is a strategic dance where partners synchronize their steps to achieve a harmonious and mutually beneficial performance in the marketplace." - Peter Drucker

7. "Collaboration is not just about doing more; it's about creating something greater than the sum of its parts. It involves shared goals, open communication, and a commitment to collective success." - Margaret Heffernan

17.2.2 BUSINESS COLLABORATIONS - FEATURES

Business collaboration refers to the process of individuals or entities working together to achieve shared goals or objectives. This collaborative effort can take various forms and may involve different levels of coordination and integration.

FEATURES OF BUSINESS COLLABORATIONS:

1. Joint Effort: Business collaboration involves a joint effort where multiple parties pool their resources, expertise, and efforts to accomplish a common objective. This can include organizations, teams, or individuals working together to achieve mutual benefits.
2. Shared Goals: Collaboration in business is characterized by a shared vision or common goals that participants aim to accomplish collectively. This alignment of objectives helps in fostering a sense of unity and purpose among collaborators.
3. Mutual Benefit: Successful business collaboration typically results in mutual benefits for all parties involved. This can include increased efficiency, cost savings, access to new markets, enhanced innovation, or improved overall performance.
4. Communication and Information Sharing: Effective communication is an important component of business collaboration. It involves sharing information, ideas, and feedback among collaborators to ensure that everyone is on the same page and can contribute to the collaborative effort.
5. Flexibility and Adaptability: Collaboration often requires flexibility and adaptability as partners may need to adjust their strategies or processes to accommodate the changing dynamics of the collaboration. Being open to new ideas and responsive to evolving circumstances is key.
6. Technology Integration: In the modern business landscape, technology plays a vital role in enabling collaboration. Collaborative tools, communication platforms, and project management software help facilitate seamless interaction and coordination among participants, especially in geographically dispersed teams.
7. Trust and Relationship Building: Building trust is essential in business collaboration. Trustworthy relationships among collaborators create a foundation for effective teamwork, as individuals and organizations feel confident in each other's abilities and commitment to the collaboration.
8. Risk and Reward Sharing: Business collaboration often involves sharing risks and rewards. Participants may share the costs, responsibilities, and potential benefits associated with the collaborative venture, creating a more equitable distribution of both the burdens and benefits.
9. Strategic Alliances: Collaborations can take the form of strategic alliances, where organizations come together to leverage each other's strengths and resources to gain a competitive advantage. This can include partnerships, joint ventures, or other forms of strategic cooperation.
10. Continuous Improvement: Business collaboration is an ongoing process that may require continuous improvement. Regular evaluation, feedback, and adaptation are necessary to ensure that the collaboration remains effective and aligned with the changing needs of the involved parties.

17.2.3 TYPES OF BUSINESS COLLABORATIONS

Business collaboration refers to the strategic partnership or cooperation between two or more entities, typically organizations or businesses, with the aim of achieving mutual benefits. These collaborations can take various forms and serve different purposes, ranging from expanding market reach to sharing resources and expertise.

TYPES OF BUSINESS COLLABORATION:

1. Joint Ventures (JVs):

a. A joint venture is a business arrangement in which two or more companies come together to create a new entity, sharing ownership, control, and profits.
b. Types: Equity Joint Ventures, Cooperative Joint Ventures, and Contractual Joint Ventures.

2. Strategic Alliances:

a. Strategic alliances involve collaboration between independent entities for a specific project or objective, without forming a new, separate entity.

b. Types: Marketing alliances, distribution alliances, research and development alliances, etc.

3. Technology Transfer Agreements:

a. These collaborations involve the sharing or licensing of technology, intellectual property, or knowhow between two organizations.
b. Types: Licensing agreements, research and development partnerships, and technology sharing agreements.

4. Supply Chain Collaboration:

a. Collaboration in the supply chain involves partnerships between different companies at various stages of the production or distribution process.
b. Types: Supplier collaborations, distributor collaborations, and logistics partnerships.

5. Research and Development (R&D) Partnerships:

a. Entities collaborate on research and development activities to leverage each other's capabilities and resources for innovation.
b. Types: Consortia, collaborative research agreements, and industryacademia partnerships.

6. PublicPrivate Partnerships (PPPs):

a. Partnerships between government bodies and private enterprises to jointly fund, implement, and manage projects that serve a public interest.
b. Types: Infrastructure development projects, healthcare partnerships, and education initiatives.

7. Franchising:

a. A business collaboration where one party (franchisor) grants another party (franchisee) the right to use its business model, brand, and processes in exchange for fees or royalties.
b. Types: Product franchising, business format franchising, and manufacturing franchising.

8. Mergers and Acquisitions (M&A):

a. While not strictly collaboration, M&A activities involve the integration of two companies, combining their assets and operations.
b. Types: Mergers (integration of equals) and acquisitions (one company acquiring another).

9. Collaborative Marketing:

a. Businesses collaborate on marketing efforts to promote each other's products or services, often through joint campaigns or cobranded initiatives.
b. Types: Comarketing agreements, sponsorship collaborations, and crosspromotions.

Business collaborations are influenced by the legal and regulatory environment, industryspecific dynamics, and the objectives of the participating entities. The choice of collaboration type depends on factors such as the goals of the partnership, the nature of the industry, and the complementary strengths of the collaborating entities.

17.3 JOINT VENTURES - MEANING

A joint venture in India, like in many other countries, refers to a business arrangement where two or more parties come together to collaborate and pool their resources to achieve a specific business objective. In the context of India, a joint venture typically involves a foreign company partnering with an Indian company to engage in a mutually beneficial business venture.

Important points about joint ventures include:

1. Partnership:

It involves a partnership between two or more entities, which can be companies, individuals, or a combination of both.

1. Shared Control and Ownership:

Each party in the joint venture maintains a certain degree of control and ownership over the venture. The level of control and ownership is usually defined in the joint venture agreement.

3. Common Business Objective:

The parties join forces to pursue a common business objective, such as entering a new market, developing a new product, or leveraging each other's expertise.

4. Risk and Reward Sharing:

Risks, as well as rewards, are typically shared among the parties involved. This sharing arrangement is agreed upon in the joint venture agreement.

5. Legal Structure:

In India, joint ventures can take various legal forms, such as a separate legal entity (e.g., a company or a limited liability partnership) or a contractual arrangement. The choice of structure depends on the nature of the venture and the preferences of the parties involved.

6. Regulatory Compliance:

Foreign companies engaging in joint ventures in India need to comply with the foreign direct investment (FDI) regulations and other applicable laws.

7. Joint Venture Agreement:

The terms and conditions of the joint venture are usually outlined in a formal agreement. This document specifies the roles and responsibilities of each party, the investment contributions, profit-sharing mechanisms, dispute resolution processes, and other important details.

Joint ventures can be advantageous as they allow companies to leverage each other's strengths, share risks and costs, and access new markets. However, successful joint ventures require careful planning, clear communication, and a well-drafted joint venture agreement to address potential challenges and ensure a smooth collaboration.

17.3.1 JOINT VENTURE ADVANTAGES AND DISADVANTAGES

A joint venture (JV) refers to a business arrangement where two or more parties come together to collaborate and form a new entity to achieve a common business objective. Joint ventures can have several advantages and disadvantages, and these can vary based on the specific circumstances of the venture.

ADVANTAGES OF JOINT VENTURES:

1. Shared Risks and Responsibilities:

Risks and responsibilities are shared among the partners, which can be particularly beneficial in complex or high-risk projects.

2. Access to Local Expertise:

A local partner can provide valuable insights into the Indian market, including knowledge of local regulations, culture, and business practices.

3. Cost Sharing:

Partners can pool their resources, leading to cost efficiencies in terms of capital, technology, and human resources.

4. Market Entry:

Joint ventures can serve as an effective means for foreign companies to enter the Indian market by leveraging the local partner's established network.

5. Government Approvals:

In some industries, obtaining government approvals may be easier with a local partner, as it demonstrates a commitment to working in collaboration with Indian entities.

6. Technology Transfer:

Joint ventures facilitate the transfer of technology between partners, allowing for the exchange of skills and knowledge.

DISADVANTAGES:

1. Conflict of Interest: Differing business cultures, objectives, or strategies among partners may lead to conflicts that can impact the success of the joint venture.

2. Shared Profits: Profits must be shared among the partners, potentially reducing the overall financial gain for each individual entity.

3. Dependency on Partner: The success of the joint venture depends on the performance and reliability of the partners. If one partner fails to meet expectations, it can affect the entire venture.

4. Complex Decision-Making: Decision-making can be complex and time-consuming, especially when partners have different views on key business matters.

5. Regulatory Challenges: Navigating through India's regulatory landscape can be challenging, and compliance with local laws and regulations may pose difficulties for foreign partners.

6. Exit Challenges: Exiting a joint venture can be challenging, especially if there are disagreements between partners or if the regulatory environment makes it difficult.

Before entering into a joint venture, it is important for the parties involved conducting thorough due diligence, clearly define roles and responsibilities, and have a well-drafted agreement that addresses potential challenges. Seeking legal and business advice is advisable to ensure compliance with local laws and regulations.

17.3.2 TYPES OF JOINT VENTURES

Joint ventures are popular business structures that allow two or more entities to collaborate and share resources, risks, and profits for a specific project or business activity. Joint ventures can take various forms, and the type chosen often depends on the nature of the business and the objectives of the parties involved.

Types of joint ventures:

1. Equity Joint Venture (EJV):

a. In an Equity Joint Venture, partners contribute capital in the form of equity shares.
b. The profits and risks are shared based on the equity participation of each partner.
c. It is a popular choice when both partners want to be actively involved in the management of the venture.

2. Contractual Joint Venture:

a. In a Contractual Joint Venture, the collaboration is based on a contractual agreement that outlines the terms and conditions of the partnership.
b. Partners contribute resources, skills, or services as specified in the contract.
c. This type is often chosen when parties want a flexible arrangement without the need for significant capital investment.

3. Cooperative Joint Venture:

a. A Cooperative Joint Venture involves collaboration between Indian and foreign companies, where both contribute resources and share risks and profits.
b. This structure is often chosen when the partners have complementary skills or technologies.

4. Technology Joint Venture:

a. In a Technology Joint Venture, the collaboration focuses on the development or transfer of technology.
b. This is common in industries where specialized knowledge or technology is a crucial component of the venture.

5. Joint Venture with Indian Government Participation:

a. The government of India sometimes participates in joint ventures, particularly in strategic sectors.
b. This involvement can take various forms, such as equity participation, technology sharing, or resource collaboration.

6. Non-Incorporate Joint Venture:

a. In a NonIncorporate Joint Venture, the collaboration is not a separate legal entity.
b. Partners maintain their individual legal identities and share profits or losses based on the terms agreed upon.

7. Limited Liability Partnership (LLP):

a. LLP is a hybrid form of business that combines elements of a partnership and a company.
b. Partners in an LLP have limited liability, and it offers flexibility in terms of management and operations.

8. Strategic Alliance:

a. While not a formal joint venture structure, a strategic alliance involves collaboration between businesses for mutual benefit.
b. This can include sharing distribution networks, marketing efforts, or research and development activities.

Before entering into a joint venture, it's essential for the parties involved to carefully consider their objectives, responsibilities, and the legal and regulatory framework in India. Seeking professional advice and legal guidance is crucial to ensure a smooth and compliant partnership.

17.3.3 JOINT VENTURES AGREEMENTS

A Joint Venture (JV) is a business arrangement where two or more parties come together to collaborate and share resources, risks, and rewards for a specific project or business activity. Joint ventures are commonly used by companies to enter new markets, access local expertise, and pool resources. In India, the regulatory and legal framework for joint ventures is governed by the Companies Act, 2013, and other applicable laws.

IMPORTANT STEPS FOR DRAFTING A JOINT VENTURE AGREEMENT:

1. Identify the Parties: Clearly specify the names, addresses, and details of the parties involved in the joint venture. This includes the names of the companies or individuals entering into the agreement.

2. Purpose of the Joint Venture: Define the objectives and purpose of the joint venture. Clearly outline the scope of the venture, including the business activities it will engage in.

3. Contributions and Responsibilities: Detail the contributions each party will make to the joint venture, whether it's financial, intellectual property, technology, or other resources. Specify the responsibilities and roles of each party.

4. Ownership Structure: Define the ownership structure of the joint venture, including the percentage of ownership each party holds. This is important for decision-making and profit-sharing.

5. Management and Control: Outline the governance structure, decision-making processes, and management responsibilities. Specify how major decisions will be made and who will have control over key aspects of the joint venture.

6. Confidentiality and Non-Compete Clauses: Include provisions for maintaining confidentiality of sensitive information and restrict the parties from engaging in competing activities during and after the joint venture.

7. Duration and Termination: Specify the duration of the joint venture and conditions under which it can be terminated. Include provisions for dispute resolution and exit mechanisms.

8. Financial Arrangements: Clearly define the financial arrangements, including profit-sharing mechanisms, funding requirements, and the handling of losses.

9. Compliance with Laws: Ensure that the joint venture complies with all applicable laws and regulations in India. Specify the legal jurisdiction for dispute resolution.

10. Dispute Resolution: Include a dispute resolution mechanism, such as arbitration or mediation, to address conflicts that may arise between the parties.

11. Intellectual Property Rights: Address the ownership and use of intellectual property created during the joint venture.

12. Exit Strategy: Plan for the exit of parties from the joint venture, whether it's through a buyout, sale of assets, or other means.

SUCCESSFUL JOINT VENTURES IN INDIA.

1. Maruti Suzuki India Limited:

- Joint Venture: Suzuki Motor Corporation and Government of India
- Industry: Automotive

2. Hindustan Unilever Limited (HUL):

- Joint Venture: Hindustan Petroleum Corporation Limited (HPCL) and Unilever
- Industry: FastMoving Consumer Goods (FMCG)

3. Sony Pictures Networks India:

- Joint Venture: Sony Corporation and Essel Group
- Industry: Media and Entertainment

4. Bharti Walmart Pvt Ltd:

- Joint Venture: Bharti Enterprises and Walmart
- Industry: Retail

5. Tata Starbucks Limited:

- Joint Venture: Tata Global Beverages and Starbucks Corporation
- Industry: Food and Beverage

6. Hero Honda Motors Ltd (Now Hero MotoCorp):

- Joint Venture: Hero Group and Honda Motor Company
- Industry: Automotive

7. Vodafone Idea Limited:

- Joint Venture: Vodafone Group and Aditya Birla Group
- Industry: Telecommunications

8. Tata Sky Limited:

- Joint Venture: Tata Sons and 21st Century Fox
- Industry: DirecttoHome (DTH) television service

9. General Electric (GE) and Wipro Limited:

- Joint Venture: General Electric and Wipro Limited
- Industry: Information Technology and Services

10. Siemens Ltd:

- Joint Venture: Siemens AG and Siemens Ltd (India)
- Industry: Technology and Infrastructure

11. Renault Nissan Automotive India Private Limited:

- Joint Venture: Renault and Nissan
- Industry: Automotive

12. Toyota Kirloskar Motor Private Limited:

- Joint Venture: Toyota Motor Corporation and Kirloskar Group
- Industry: Automotive

13. Mahindra Renault Limited (Now Mahindra & Mahindra):

- Joint Venture: Mahindra & Mahindra and Renault

- Industry: Automotive

14. Ericsson India Private Limited:

- Joint Venture: Ericsson and Redington
- Industry: Telecommunications

15. Samsung India Electronics Private Limited:

- Joint Venture: Samsung and the Government of India
- Industry: Electronics

16. Bajaj Allianz General Insurance Company Limited:

- Joint Venture: Bajaj Finserv Limited and Allianz SE
- Industry: Insurance

17. Hinduja Leyland Finance Limited:

- Joint Venture: Hinduja Group and Ashok Leyland
- Industry: Financial Services

18. Mahindra Susten:

- Joint Venture: Mahindra Group and CLP Holdings
- Industry: Renewable Energy

19. LG Electronics India Pvt Ltd:

- Joint Venture: LG Corporation and Videocon Group
- Industry: Electronics

20. Suzlon Energy Limited:

- Joint Venture: Suzlon Energy and the Government of Karnataka
- Industry: Wind Energy

21. Godrej Hershey Ltd:

- Joint Venture: Godrej Industries and The Hershey Company
- Industry: Food and Beverage

22. Tata Cummins Pvt. Ltd:

- Joint Venture: Tata Motors and Cummins
- Industry: Automotive

23. GSK Consumer Healthcare Ltd:

- Joint Venture: GlaxoSmithKline and Hindustan Unilever Limited
- Industry: Healthcare and FMCG

24. Bosch Chassis Systems India Limited:

- Joint Venture: Bosch Limited and ZF Friedrichshafen AG
- Industry: Automotive

25. Hero Electric Vehicles Pvt Ltd:

- Joint Venture: Hero MotoCorp and Hero Exports
- Industry: Electric Vehicles.

17.5 SPECIAL PURPOSE VEHICLE

Special Purpose Vehicles (SPVs) play an important role in India's economic landscape, particularly in the context of infrastructure development and financing. In the Indian financial and business sectors, SPVs are essentially entities created for a specific project or purpose, designed to isolate risks and facilitate efficient resource management. These entities are commonly used in public-private partnership (PPP) projects and large-scale infrastructure ventures.

In India, the establishment of SPVs is often seen as a strategic approach to mobilize funds, mitigate risks, and ensure the timely execution of complex projects. One of the primary reasons for the adoption of SPVs is their ability to ring-fence assets and liabilities, providing a layer of protection for investors and lenders involved in a particular venture.

SPVs in India are typically set up as separate legal entities, often in the form of special purpose companies (SPCs), trusts, or limited liability partnerships (LLPs). The choice of structure depends on the nature of the project, regulatory requirements, and the preferences of stakeholders involved. These entities serve as conduits for channeling funds, managing project-related activities, and maintaining financial independence from the parent companies or organizations.

The use of SPVs is prevalent in various sectors, including transportation, energy, real estate, and telecommunications. For instance, major infrastructure projects like highways, airports, and power plants often involve the creation of SPVs to streamline funding, enhance project oversight, and allocate risks appropriately among stakeholders.

Furthermore, SPVs contribute to enhancing transparency and accountability in project execution. By isolating the financial and operational aspects of a specific venture, these entities enable a clearer assessment of the project's performance, making it easier to track and manage resources effectively.

However, it is important to note that the success of SPVs in India depends on several factors, including regulatory frameworks, government policies, and the overall economic environment. Authorities need to strike a balance between providing a condusive environment for SPV formation and ensuring adequate safeguards to prevent misuse or malpractices.

17.5.1 SPECIAL PURPOSE VEHICLE - MEANING

The term "Special Purpose Vehicle" (SPV) refers to a legal entity or company that is created for a specific and limited purpose. SPVs are often established to undertake a particular project, transaction, or set of activities, and they are designed to isolate the associated risks from the parent company or other businesses.

CHARACTERISTICS OF A SPECIAL PURPOSE VEHICLE INCLUDE:

1. Limited Purpose: SPVs are created for a specific purpose, such as developing a particular project, raising capital, or holding certain assets. They are not intended to engage in a broad range of business activities.
2. Ring-Fencing of Risks: One of the primary reasons for establishing an SPV is to isolate the risks associated with a specific project or transaction. This helps protect the parent company or other entities from potential financial liabilities related to the SPV's activities.
3. Legal Independence: SPVs are separate legal entities, which mean they have their own legal personality distinct from the entities that create them. This separation helps ensure that the liabilities and obligations of the SPV are generally limited to its own assets.
4. Asset Protection: SPVs are often used to hold and manage specific assets, such as real estate, intellectual property, or financial instruments, without exposing the entire corporate structure to the associated risks.
5. Facilitating Financing: SPVs are commonly used in financing arrangements, especially in infrastructure projects and securitization transactions. They allow for the efficient pooling of funds and the allocation of risks among different investors.
6. Bankruptcy Remote: SPVs are typically structured to be bankruptcy remote, meaning that the financial distress or bankruptcy of the parent company does not automatically impact the SPV. This feature is essential in protecting the interests of investors and creditors involved in the SPV.

Examples of the use of SPVs in India include infrastructure projects, public-private partnerships, and structured finance transactions. By creating a separate legal entity with a focused purpose, businesses can manage risks more effectively and pursue specific projects without exposing the entire organization to potential challenges or uncertainties.

17.5.2 SPECIAL PURPOSE VEHICLE - BENEFITS

A Special Purpose Vehicle (SPV) refers to a separate legal entity created for a specific project or business venture. SPVs are commonly used in various industries and sectors to isolate risks, protect the interests of stakeholders, and facilitate efficient management of projects.

BENEFITS OF SPECIAL PURPOSE VEHICLES:

1. Risk Isolation: One of the primary purposes of an SPV is to isolate the risks associated with a specific project or venture from the rest of the business. This helps in protecting the assets and interests of the parent company and its stakeholders.
2. Financial Structuring: SPVs are often used for financial structuring purposes. They can be set up to raise capital, issue debt or equity, and manage funds separately for a particular project, reducing the financial impact on the parent company.
3. Legal Protection: By creating a separate legal entity, the parent company can limit its liability in case of any legal issues or financial distress related to the project. This can safeguard the parent company's other assets from being affected.
4. Tax Efficiency: SPVs may offer tax advantages, depending on the jurisdiction and the nature of the project. They can be structured in a way that optimizes tax benefits and minimizes tax liabilities for the parent company.
5. Facilitates Collaboration: SPVs are often used in joint ventures and public-private partnerships. They provide a structured and independent platform for collaboration between different entities, allowing for efficient management of shared projects.
6. Enhances Project Management:

Since SPVs are dedicated to specific projects, they allow for focused and efficient management. This can result in better planning, execution, and monitoring of the project, leading to increased chances of success.

7. Funding Flexibility: SPVs can attract funding from various sources, including banks, financial institutions, and private investors. This flexibility in fundraising allows companies to pursue projects that might be financially challenging for the parent company alone.
8. Asset Securitization: SPVs are commonly used for asset securitization, where a company can convert illiquid assets into tradable securities. This can help in unlocking the value of assets and improving liquidity.
9. Regulatory Compliance: SPVs can be structured to comply with specific regulatory requirements related to a project. This ensures that the project operates within the legal framework, reducing regulatory risks.
10. Ease of Exit: In case of a project's completion or if it becomes unviable, the parent company can exit the venture by winding up the SPV without affecting the overall business.

While SPVs offer various benefits, it's essential to carefully plan and structure them to align with the specific goals and needs of the project and the parent company. Consulting legal and financial experts is important to ensuring compliance with regulations and optimizing the advantages of using SPVs.

17.5.3 SPECIAL PURPOSE VEHICLE - FORMATION

A Special Purpose Vehicle (SPV) refers to a legal entity created for a specific project or purpose. SPVs are commonly used in infrastructure and large-scale projects to isolate risks, facilitate financing, and ensure that the project operates independently.

Steps for forming a Special Purpose Vehicle:

1. Identify the Purpose: Define the specific purpose or project for which the SPV is being created. This could be a large infrastructure project, real estate development, or any other venture requiring a separate legal entity.

2. Select the Type of Entity: Choose the appropriate legal structure for the SPV. In India, SPVs are often formed as private limited companies, limited liability partnerships (LLPs), or public limited companies, depending on the nature and scale of the project.

3. Name Reservation: Choose a unique name for the SPV and check its availability with the Ministry of Corporate Affairs (MCA). Once the name is approved, it can be reserved for a certain period.

4. Incorporation: File the necessary documents with the Registrar of Companies (RoC) for the incorporation of the SPV. This typically involves submitting the Memorandum of Association (MOA), Articles of Association (AOA), and other required documents.

5. Capitalization: Determine and allocate the initial capital for the SPV. This could come from equity contributions by promoters or investors.

6. Board of Directors: Appoint the board of directors for the SPV. The composition of the board should comply with the regulatory requirements, and individuals with relevant expertise may be appointed.

7. Obtain Necessary Approvals: Depending on the nature of the project, obtain any required approvals from regulatory bodies or government authorities. This may include environmental clearances, project-specific approvals, etc.

8. Bank Account: Open a separate bank account for the SPV to ensure clear segregation of funds related to the specific project.

9. Compliance with Regulations: Ensure that the SPV complies with all relevant laws, regulations, and taxation requirements. This may include compliance with the Companies Act, 2013, and other applicable laws.

10. Operationalize the SPV: Once all formalities are completed, the SPV can start its operations, managing and executing the specific project for which it was formed.

17.6 QUESTIONS:

1. Explain the characteristics of a Limited Liability Partnership and distinguish it from a private company.
2. What are the benefits of forming a Limited Liability Partnership?
3. What is an LLP Agreement? State the procedure for altering the LLP Agreement.
4. A Limited Liability Partnership wants to change its name. Explain under what factors have to be borne in mind and the procedure for the same.
5. State whether the partners of a Limited Liability Partnership are liable for its debts and if so, under what circumstances.
6. Define a Joint Venture Company. What are its characteristics?
7. . Distinguish between a Joint Venture Company and a Special Purpose Vehicle (SPV)
8. Explain, with reasons, why the concept of Special Purpose Vehicle (SPV) has gained prominence in India in recent times. Quote Examples.

CHAPTER EIGHTEEN

ENVIRONMENTAL LEGISLATIONS IN INDIA

18.1 THE GEOGRAPHICAL INDICATIONS OF GOODS (REGISTRATION AND PROTECTION) ACT, 1999

The Geographical Indications of Goods (Registration and Protection) Act, 1999, is a significant legal framework in India aimed at recognizing and safeguarding the distinctive identity and reputation of goods originating from specific geographical locations. Enacted to comply with the Agreement on Trade-Related Aspects of Intellectual Property Rights (TRIPS) under the World Trade Organization, this legislation has played a important role in protecting the interests of producers and consumers alike.

Geographical indications (GIs) are indications that identify a good as originating from a specific territory, region, or locality, where a particular quality, reputation, or other characteristic of the product is essentially attributable to its geographical origin. The primary objective of the Act is to prevent unauthorized use of such indications, ensuring that consumers can trust the authenticity and quality of goods associated with a particular region.

Under the Geographical Indications Act, a registration system is established, allowing producers of goods with specific geographical indications to obtain legal protection for their products. The registration process involves submitting an application to the Geographical Indications Registry, which examines the application and, upon fulfillment of the necessary criteria, grants the registration. Once registered, the geographical indication becomes a valuable intellectual property right and the registered proprietor gains the exclusive right to use the indication in relation to the goods.

The Act not only provides protection to agricultural and natural goods but also extends its coverage to industrial and manufactured products. This broad scope ensures that a wide range of products, including handicrafts, textiles, and manufactured items, can benefit from the legal recognition and protection offered by the legislation.

18.1.1 OBJECTIVES OF THE GEOGRAPHICAL INDICATIONS OF GOODS (REGISTRATION AND PROTECTION) ACT,

The Geographical Indications of Goods (Registration and Protection) Act, 1999, aims to provide legal protection to goods that have a specific geographical origin and possess qualities, reputation, or characteristics that are essentially attributable to that place of origin. The primary objectives of the Act are as follows:

1. Protection of Geographical Indications (gis): The main objective is to protect the unique qualities and reputation associated with goods originating from a specific geographical location.
2. Preventing Misuse: To prevent unauthorized use of geographical indications in connection with goods not originating from the designated place, which could mislead consumers?
3. Promoting Economic Development: Encouraging the economic development of regions by providing legal protection to products that have a strong connection to their geographical origin.

4. Preservation of Cultural Heritage: Safeguarding the traditional knowledge and cultural heritage associated with the production of specific goods in particular regions

18.1.2 SALIENT FEATURES OF GEOGRAPHICAL INDICATION OF GOODS (REGISTRATION AND PROTECTION) ACT

1. Definition of Geographical Indication: The Act defines a "geographical indication" as an indication that identifies goods as originating from a particular territory, region, or locality, where a given quality, reputation, or other characteristic of the goods is essentially attributable to their geographical origin.

2. Registration of Geographical Indications: Provides for the registration of geographical indications to protect them from unauthorized use. The registration process involves filing an application with the Geographical Indications Registry.

3. Rights Conferred: The registered proprietor of a geographical indication has the exclusive right to use the indication in relation to the goods for which it is registered. Others are prohibited from using a similar indication for goods not originating from the designated place.

4. Duration of Protection: The protection granted to a registered geographical indication is initially for ten years and can be renewed indefinitely for further periods of ten years.

5. Prohibition on Falsification: The Act prohibits the use of any false representation that a good originates from a place with a registered geographical indication.

6. Penalties and Remedies: Provides for penalties and remedies, including injunctions, damages, and the destruction of infringing goods, to address violations of the Act.

7. Enforcement: Establishes a legal framework for the enforcement of the rights conferred by geographical indications, including civil and criminal remedies.

8. International Recognition: The Act enables the protection of geographical indications in foreign countries through international treaties and agreements.

In addition to the registration process, the Geographical Indications Act also includes provisions for the enforcement of rights and penalties for infringement. Unauthorized use of a registered geographical indication is prohibited, and legal remedies, including injunctions and damages, are available to the registered proprietor to protect their rights. This ensures that consumers are not misled and that the economic interests of producers linked to a particular geographical origin are safeguarded.

The Geographical Indications of Goods (Registration and Protection) Act, 1999, stands as an important piece of legislation in India, promoting and protecting the rich diversity of goods originating from various regions. By recognizing the unique qualities and characteristics associated with specific geographical areas, the Act contributes to the preservation of traditional knowledge, fosters rural development, and enhances the overall economic wellbeing of communities tied to the production of geographically indicated goods.

18.2 THE ENVIRONMENT (PROTECTION) ACT, 1986

The Environment (Protection) Act, 1986, stands as an important piece of legislation in India, embodying the nation's commitment to safeguarding and enhancing the environment. Enacted with the primary objective of addressing growing environmental concerns, the Act empowers the government to take necessary measures for the protection and improvement of the environment.

At the time of its inception, India was grappling with the adverse effects of rapid industrialization, urbanization, and deforestation. Recognizing the urgent need for comprehensive environmental protection, the Environment (Protection) Act was enacted to provide a legal framework for the prevention, control, and abatement of environmental pollution.

One of the key features of the Act is its ability to empower the central government to take proactive measures. Section 3 of the Act grants the central government the authority to take necessary steps to protect and improve the quality of the environment, including setting standards for emissions and discharges. This allows for the regulation of industries and activities that have the potential to harm the environment.

The Act further emphasizes the precautionary principle, urging authorities to take preventive action when there is a threat of harm to the environment, even in the absence of scientific certainty. This forward-looking approach reflects the awareness that environmental degradation can have far-reaching consequences on public health, biodiversity, and overall ecological balance.

To facilitate effective implementation, the Environment (Protection) Act establishes the Central Pollution Control Board (CPCB) and State Pollution Control Boards (SPCBs), which play an important roles in monitoring and regulating pollution. These bodies are tasked with enforcing standards, conducting environmental impact assessments, and taking punitive actions against violators.

Over the years, the Act has undergone amendments to keep pace with evolving environmental challenges. It has been instrumental in shaping policies and regulations to combat air and water pollution, hazardous waste management, and the conservation of natural resources.

18.2.1 FEATURES OF THE ENVIRONMENT (PROTECTION) ACT 1986:

1. Objective: The primary objective of the act is to implement the decisions of the United Nations Conference on the Human Environment held in Stockholm in 1972. It aims to protect and improve the environment and prevent hazards to human beings, other living creatures, plants, and property.

2. Authority and Power: The Act empowers the central government to take measures to protect and improve the environment, set standards for emissions and discharge of environmental pollutants, and regulate activities that may cause environmental pollution.

3. Rules and Notifications: The Act enables the central government to frame rules and issue notifications to address specific environmental issues, set standards, and regulate various activities.

4. Environmental Impact Assessment (EIA): The Act provides for the preparation of Environmental Impact Assessments (EIA) for certain projects and activities that may have a significant impact on the environment. This process involves assessing the potential environmental effects before a project is undertaken.

5. Regulation of Hazardous Substances: The Act empowers the central government to regulate and restrict the handling of hazardous substances, including the generation, treatment, and disposal of hazardous wastes.

6. Penalties and Offenses: The Act prescribes penalties for contravention of its provisions. Offenses under the Act can lead to imprisonment or fines, or both, depending on the nature and severity of the violation.

7. Environmental Laboratories: The Act allows for the establishment and recognition of environmental laboratories for the purposes of carrying out analyses of samples.

8. Public Participation: The Act encourages public participation in environmental protection by allowing individuals to file complaints regarding environmental violations.

The Environment (Protection) Act, 1986, symbolizes India's commitment to sustainable development and environmental stewardship. By providing a legal framework for proactive measures, pollution control, and the conservation of natural resources, the Act has played a important role in shaping the country's environmental policies and ensuring a healthier, more sustainable future for generations to come.

18.3 PREVENTION, CONTROL AND ABATEMENT OF ENVIRONMENTAL POLLUTION

India has been working on various initiatives to prevent, control, and abate environmental pollution. Measures and strategies that have been implemented are

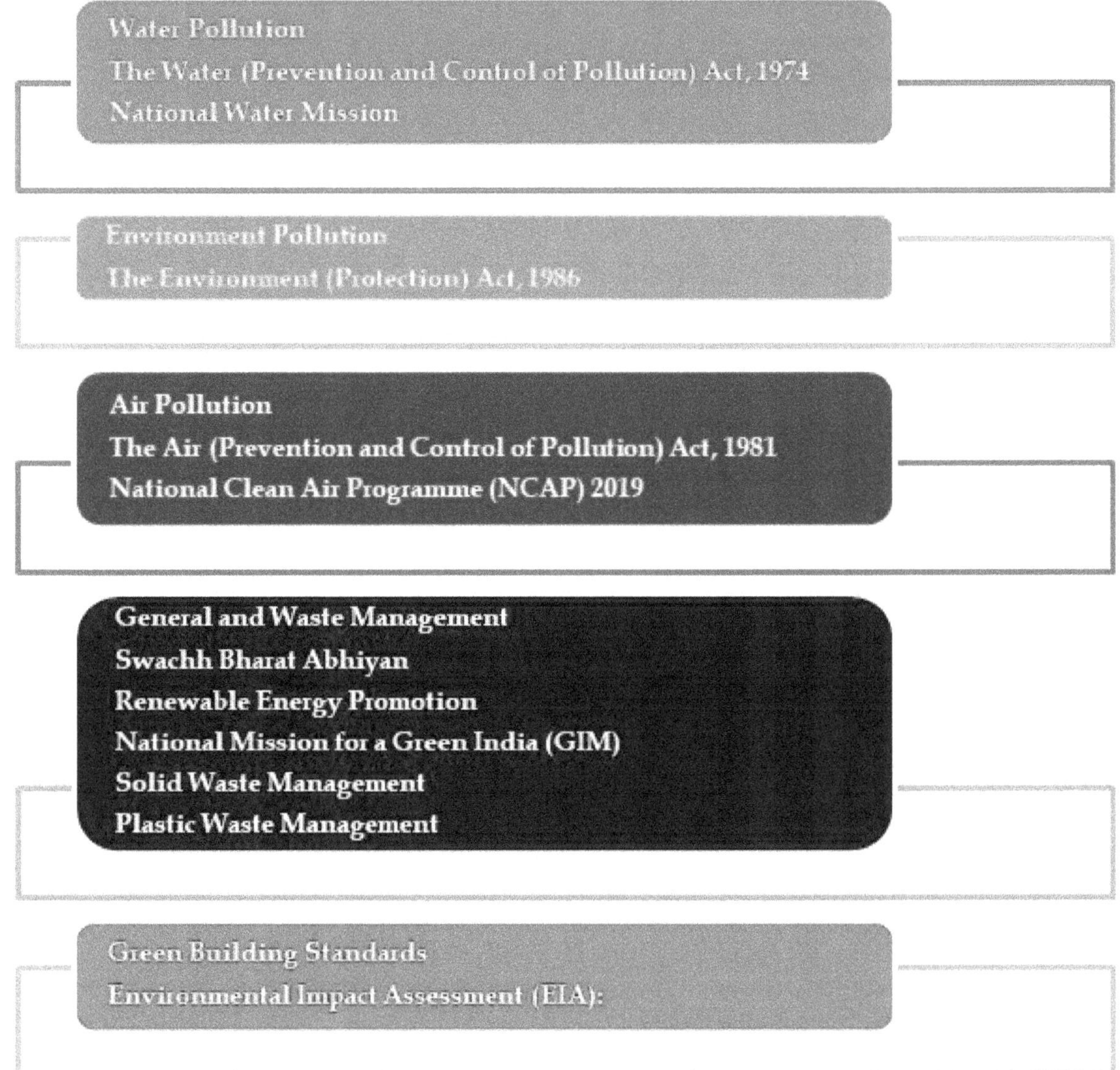

Indian Initiatives to abate Pollution

1. Legislation and Policies:

a. The Air (Prevention and Control of Pollution) Act, 1981: This legislation focuses on preventing and controlling air pollution.
b. The Water (Prevention and Control of Pollution) Act, 1974: This law addresses water pollution issues.
c. The Environment (Protection) Act, 1986: This act empowers the central government to take measures to protect and improve the quality of the environment.

2. National Clean Air Programme (NCAP):

a. Launched in 2019, the NCAP aims to reduce particulate matter (PM) levels by 2030% in 102 cities by 2024.
b. The program emphasizes cityspecific action plans, technology interventions, and public awareness.

3. Swachh Bharat Abhiyan: This nationwide cleanliness campaign includes initiatives to manage solid waste and promote proper waste disposal practices.

4. Renewable Energy Promotion: Promoting renewable energy sources, such as solar and wind power, helps reduce reliance on fossil fuels and lowers air pollution.

5. National Mission for a Green India (GIM): GIM focuses on biodiversity conservation, afforestation, and sustainable management of ecosystems.

6. National Water Mission: Part of the National Action Plan on Climate Change, this mission aims to conserve water, minimize wastage, and ensure equitable distribution.

7. Waste Management:

a. Solid Waste Management Rules (2016): These rules focus on proper waste segregation, recycling, and scientific disposal.
b. Plastic Waste Management Rules (2016): Aimed at reducing the impact of plastic on the environment.

8. Green Building Standards: Promoting ecofriendly construction practices through guidelines like the Green Building Rating System (LEED India).

9. Environmental Impact Assessment (EIA): Projects are required to undergo an EIA before approval to assess their potential environmental impact.

10. Public Awareness and Education: Creating awareness among the public about the importance of environmental conservation and pollution prevention.

18.4 THE WATER (PREVENTION AND CONTROL OF POLLUTION) ACT, 1974

The Water (Prevention and Control of Pollution) Act, 1974 is a key environmental legislation in India that addresses the prevention and control of water pollution. The Act was enacted to empower the central and state pollution control boards to prevent and control water pollution and to maintain or restore the wholesomeness of water.

Features of the Water (Prevention and Control of Pollution) Act, 1974:

1. Objective: The primary objective of the Act is to prevent and control water pollution and to maintain or restore the wholesomeness of water.

2. Constitution of Boards: The Act establishes Central Pollution Control Board (CPCB) at the central level and State Pollution Control Boards (SPCBs) at the state level. These boards are responsible for planning comprehensive programs for the prevention, control, and abatement of water pollution.

3. Powers of the Boards:

a. The boards have been granted powers to collect and disseminate information relating to water pollution.
b. They can collaborate with the central and state governments, industrial and other associations, and carry out investigations and research related to water pollution.

4. Standards for Emission or Discharge:

a. The Act empowers the boards to prescribe standards for the discharge of pollutants into water bodies.
b. Industries and other establishments are required to comply with these standards.

5. Power to Take Samples: The boards have the authority to take samples of water from any stream or well for the purpose of analysis.

6. Prohibition and Restriction on the Use of Stream or Well Water: The Act gives the boards the power to take measures to prohibit the use of stream or well water for certain purposes if it is satisfied that such water is polluted.

7. Penalties: The Act stipulates penalties for contravention of its provisions, including imprisonment and fines.

8. Cognizance of Offenses: The courts can take cognizance of offenses under the Act upon a complaint made by the Pollution Control Board or any officer authorized by it.

9. Coordination with Other Agencies: The Act encourages coordination between the central and state pollution control boards and other relevant agencies involved in environmental protection.

10. Amendments: The Act has undergone amendments over the years to address emerging environmental concerns.

The Water (Prevention and Control of Pollution) Act, 1974, is an important legislative tool in India's efforts to protect and preserve its water resources and combat water pollution. It lays the foundation for regulatory measures and enforcement mechanisms to ensure a cleaner and healthier environment.

18.4.1 THE CENTRAL AND STATE BOARDS FOR PREVENTION AND CONTROL OF WATER POLLUTION

The Central and State Boards for Prevention and Control of Water Pollution play important roles in addressing water pollution issues. These boards are responsible for formulating policies, implementing strategies, and enforcing regulations to prevent and control water pollution. The primary bodies involved are:

1. Central Pollution Control Board (CPCB):

a. The Central Pollution Control Board is the apex regulatory body at the national level.
b. It operates under the Ministry of Environment, Forest and Climate Change (MoEF&CC).
c. CPCB formulates policies and plans for the prevention and control of water pollution.
d. It coordinates the activities of state pollution control boards and provides technical assistance and guidance.

2. State Pollution Control Boards (SPCBs):

a. Each state and union territory in India has its own State Pollution Control Board.
b. SPCBs work under the guidance of the CPCB and are responsible for implementing pollution control measures within their respective jurisdictions.
c. They issue permits, monitor industries, and take necessary actions to ensure compliance with environmental regulations.
d. SPCBs also conduct environmental impact assessments and provide input for the formulation of statespecific pollution control policies.

The Water (Prevention and Control of Pollution) Act, 1974, and its amendments empower these boards to regulate and manage water pollution in India. The Main functions of these boards include setting water quality standards, monitoring water quality, issuing permits to industries, conducting environmental impact assessments, and taking punitive actions against violators.

POWERS AND FUNCTIONS OF BOARDS

CENTRAL BOARD FOR PREVENTION AND CONTROL OF WATER POLLUTION:

1. Policy Formulation: Develop and recommend policies related to water pollution prevention and control at the national level.

2. Standard Setting: Establish water quality standards and guidelines for various water bodies, taking into account different uses of water such as drinking, agriculture, and industrial purposes.

3. Monitoring and Assessment: Monitor water quality across the country through networks of monitoring stations. Assess the impact of pollutants on water bodies and ecosystems.

4. Research and Development: Conduct or support research to understand the sources, effects, and control measures of water pollution.

5. Regulatory Oversight: Enforce regulations related to water pollution. Issues permit and approvals for the industries and projects with potential water pollution that may have impacts.

6. Public Awareness and Education: Raise public awareness about water pollution issues. Educate the public on water conservation and pollution prevention.

7. Coordination: Coordinate with statelevel pollution control boards and other relevant authorities.

STATE BOARDS FOR PREVENTION AND CONTROL OF WATER POLLUTION:

1. Implementation of Policies: Implement national policies and guidelines at the state level.

2. Regulatory Functions: Regulate and monitor activities within the state that may lead to water pollution. Issue permits and approvals based on national standards.

3. Local Monitoring: Establish local monitoring networks to assess water quality in specific regions.

4. Enforcement: Enforce statelevel regulations and take actions against entities violating pollution control measures.

5. Data Collection and Reporting: Collect and maintain data on water quality within the state. Submits report on findings to the central board.

6. Public Engagement: Engage with local communities and industries to promote responsible water management practices.

7. Emergency Response: Develop and implement emergency response plans for water pollution incidents.

THE PREVENTION AND CONTROL OF WATER POLLUTION

The prevention and control of water pollution are governed by various laws and regulations. The primary legislation addressing water pollution in the country is the Water (Prevention and Control of Pollution) Act, 1974. Additionally, the Environment (Protection) Act, 1986, plays a crucial role in regulating and managing environmental issues, including water pollution.

WATER (PREVENTION AND CONTROL OF POLLUTION) ACT, 1974:

1. Central Pollution Control Board (CPCB): The Act establishes the Central Pollution Control Board at the central level and State Pollution Control Boards (SPCBs) at the state level. These boards are responsible for formulating plans and programs for the prevention, control, and abatement of water pollution.

2. Water Quality Standards: The Act empowers the central and state pollution control boards to set water quality standards and prescribe effluent standards for different industries and local bodies.

3. Prohibition on Discharge of Pollutants: The Act prohibits the discharge of pollutants in excess of the standards set by the pollution control boards. Violation of these standards can lead to penalties and legal consequences.

4. Authorization for Discharge: Industries and local bodies are required to obtain authorization from the pollution control boards for discharging pollutants into water bodies. Failure to obtain such authorization can result in penalties.

5. Inspections and Monitoring: The Act provides for the inspection of pollution control facilities and monitoring of effluents to ensure compliance with the prescribed standards.

18.5 ENVIRONMENT (PROTECTION) ACT, 1986:

1. Central Authority: The Environment (Protection) Act, 1986, empowers the central government to take measures to protect and improve the quality of the environment. The Central Pollution Control Board operates under this Act as well.

2. Power to Give Directions: The Act provides the central government with the authority to issue directions to any person, industry, or local authority for the prevention, control, and abatement of environmental pollution.

PENALTIES AND PROCEDURE FOR WATER POLLUTION

Penalties and procedure for water pollution are as follows:

1. Penalties: Violations of the provisions of the Water (Prevention and Control of Pollution) Act, 1974, and the Environment (Protection) Act, 1986, can lead to penalties, fines, and imprisonment. The severity of penalties may vary based on the nature and extent of the violation.

2. Legal Proceedings: Legal proceedings can be initiated against individuals, industries, or authorities found guilty of causing water pollution. This may involve the imposition of fines, closure of non-compliant industries, or other appropriate measures.

3. Civil and Criminal Liability: Apart from administrative penalties, individuals or entities responsible for water pollution may also face civil and criminal liability, depending on the circumstances of the violation.

18.6 THE AIR (PREVENTION AND CONTROL OF POLLUTION) ACT, 1981

The Air (Prevention and Control of Pollution) Act, 1981 is an important environmental legislation in India that aims to prevent and control air pollution. The Act was enacted to address the growing concerns about the deterioration of air quality and its adverse impact on human health and the environment.

FEATURES OF THE AIR ACT:

1. Objective: The primary objective of the Air Act is to prevent, control, and abate air pollution. It empowers the central and state governments to take measures to improve air quality and regulate industrial and vehicular emissions.

2. Regulatory Authorities: The Act establishes the Central Pollution Control Board (CPCB) at the national level and State Pollution Control Boards (SPCBs) at the state level. These boards are responsible for implementing the provisions of the Act and coordinating activities related to pollution control.

3. Standards and Limits: The Act empowers the central and state governments to prescribe standards for emission or discharge of air pollutants into the atmosphere from different sources, including industries and vehicles. These standards set limits on the concentration of pollutants to be released into the air.

4. Consent Mechanism: Industries and other entities that release pollutants into the air are required to obtain consent from the State Pollution Control Board. The consent mechanism ensures that these entities comply with the prescribed standards and take measures to control pollution.

5. Prohibition of Certain Acts: The Act prohibits the use of certain fuels and the operation of certain industrial processes that may lead to air pollution. It also prohibits the letting off of any air pollutant in excess of the standards laid down by the regulatory authorities.

6. Monitoring and Inspection: The Act empowers the pollution control boards to carry out inspections, assess the quality of air, and monitor compliance with the standards. Industries are required to install monitoring equipment and maintain records of emissions.

7. Penalties and Offenses: The Act prescribes penalties for contravention of its provisions. Offenses under the Act may result in fines or imprisonment. Repeat offenses may lead to more severe penalties.

8. Public Awareness: The Act emphasizes the importance of creating awareness among the public about the prevention and control of air pollution. It encourages the promotion of cleaner technologies and practices.

The Air Act, along with other environmental laws, plays a important role in addressing environmental challenges in India. It provides a legal framework for the regulation of air pollution, aiming to protect the environment and public health. It has undergone amendments to strengthen its provisions over the years.

18.6.1 PREVENTION AND CONTROL OF AIR POLLUTION

The prevention and control of air pollution are primarily governed by various central and state boards. The key regulatory bodies involved in this domain are the Central Pollution Control Board (CPCB) at the central level and State Pollution Control Boards (SPCBs) at the state level. These boards have specific powers and functions assigned to them to regulate and monitor air quality.

1. Central Pollution Control Board (CPCB): Powers and Functions are as follows:

a. Formulation of Standards: The CPCB is responsible for formulating standards for the quality of air and implementing these standards across the country.
b. Air Quality Monitoring: It monitors and collects data on air quality at the national level. The CPCB establishes and operates the National Air Quality Monitoring Program (NAMP). Research and Development: Conducting research on pollution control technologies, providing technical assistance, and promoting research and development in the field of air pollution control.
c. Regulatory Measures: Recommending regulatory measures and enforcing environmental laws to control and prevent air pollution. Coordination: Coordinating activities between the central and state pollution control boards, as well as other related agencies.

2. State Pollution Control Boards (SPCBs): Powers and Functions are as follows:

a. Implementation of Standards: Implementing the air quality standards set by the CPCB at the state level.
b. Monitoring and Data Collection: Conducting regular monitoring of air quality within the state and maintaining a database of the collected information.
c. Regulatory Functions: Enforcing regulations and standards related to air pollution control within their respective states.
d. Issuing Permits: Granting consent to operate to industries and other sources of pollution, subject to compliance with specified standards.
e. Research and Development: Promoting research and development activities for effective pollution control measures.

3. District Level Authorities: At the district level, Pollution Control Committees or Boards may be established to oversee and implement pollution control measures within specific regions.

4. Public Awareness and Education: Both the central and state boards are involved in creating awareness among the public regarding the adverse effects of air pollution and the importance of pollution control.

5. Advisory Role: Both the central and state boards play an advisory role, providing guidance to industries, local bodies, and other stakeholders in matters related to air pollution prevention and control.

These boards work in tandem to create a comprehensive regulatory framework for the prevention and control of air pollution in India. They play an important role in formulating policies, setting standards, monitoring air quality, and enforcing regulations to ensure a cleaner and healthier environment.

18.6.2 POWERS AND FUNCTIONS OF THE CENTRAL AND STATE POLLUTION CONTROL BOARD.

The Central Pollution Control Board (CPCB) and State Pollution Control Boards (SPCBs) in India play important roles in environmental governance by formulating and implementing policies to control and prevent pollution. These boards are instrumental in ensuring sustainable development and safeguarding the environment for current and future generations.

CENTRAL POLLUTION CONTROL BOARD (CPCB):

1. Policy Formulation: The CPCB, under the Ministry of Environment, Forest, and Climate Change, is responsible for formulating national policies and strategies for pollution control. It develops guidelines and standards for the prevention and control of pollution across the country.

2. Monitoring and Assessment: The CPCB monitors and assesses the quality of environmental parameters through a network of monitoring stations. It collects data on air, water, and soil quality, providing a comprehensive understanding of the pollution levels and trends nationwide.

3. Research and Development: The board conducts research to identify emerging pollutants and develops innovative technologies for pollution control. It collaborates with scientific institutions and experts to enhance its knowledge base and stay abreast of global best practices.

4. Capacity Building: The CPCB plays an important role in building the capacity of various stakeholders, including government agencies, industries, and the general public. It conducts training programs, workshops, and awareness campaigns to enhance understanding and compliance with pollution control measures.

5. Enforcement of Regulations: The CPCB ensures the implementation of environmental laws and regulations. It has the authority to issue directives, guidelines, and even take legal action against entities violating pollution control norms.

STATE POLLUTION CONTROL BOARDS (SPCBS):

1. Implementation of Policies: SPCBs are responsible for implementing the policies and guidelines formulated by the CPCB at the state level. They tailor national policies to suit local environmental conditions and enforce regulations within their respective jurisdictions.

2. Monitoring and Enforcement: SPCBs monitor pollution levels in their states through their own network of monitoring stations. They conduct regular inspections of industries, construction sites, and other potential sources of pollution. SPCBs also have the authority to issue notices, fines, and closure orders for non-compliance.

3. Issuing Consents: Industries and other establishments must obtain consent from SPCBs before commencing operations. These boards assess the environmental impact of proposed activities and stipulate conditions to mitigate adverse effects. Regular renewals and reviews are conducted to ensure ongoing compliance.

4. Public Awareness: SPCBs play a vital role in raising awareness among the public about the importance of pollution control. They conduct educational programs, workshops, and community engagement initiatives to promote environmental consciousness.

5. Collaboration with Local Bodies: SPCBs collaborate with local authorities and municipal bodies to address specific regional environmental challenges. They work in tandem with other stakeholders to develop and implement solutions tailored to the local context.

The Central and State Pollution Control Boards in India work collaboratively to address the complex issue of pollution. While the CPCB provides national leadership and sets overarching standards, SPCBs execute and enforce these measures at the state level, ensuring a comprehensive and coordinated approach to environmental protection.

18.6.2 PREVENTION AND CONTROL OF AIR POLLUTION

The prevention and control of air pollution are important aspects of environmental stewardship, aiming to safeguard human health, ecological balance, and the overall well-being of our planet. Air pollution, often resulting from anthropogenic activities, industrial processes, and vehicular emissions, poses a significant threat to both the environment and public health. As urbanization and industrialization continue to expand, the need for robust strategies to mitigate air pollution becomes increasingly urgent.

One fundamental approach to preventing air pollution is the implementation of stringent regulations and standards. Governments worldwide must enact and enforce laws that limit emissions from industrial sources, mandate the use of cleaner technologies, and establish emission standards for vehicles. Strict enforcement of these regulations ensures that industries adopt environmentally friendly practices and that vehicles adhere to emission limits, thereby curbing the release of harmful pollutants into the atmosphere.

Promoting sustainable and eco-friendly practices is another essential element in the prevention and control of air pollution. Encouraging the adoption of renewable energy sources, such as solar and wind power, helps reduce reliance on fossil fuels, which are major contributors to air pollution. Additionally, promoting energy efficiency in industries and households minimizes the overall environmental impact and decreases pollutant emissions.

Public awareness and education play an important role in preventing air pollution. By informing communities about the sources and consequences of air pollution, individuals can make informed choices to minimize their carbon footprint. Public support for environmental initiatives, such as tree planting campaigns and waste reduction programs, contributes to the overall efforts in creating a cleaner and healthier atmosphere.

Investment in research and development of innovative technologies is important for the prevention and control of air pollution. The development of advanced air quality monitoring systems, emission reduction technologies, and sustainable transportation solutions can significantly contribute to minimizing the impact of human activities on air quality. Governments, industries, and research institutions must collaborate to foster the creation and implementation of cutting-edge technologies that address the root causes of air pollution.

The prevention and control of air pollution require a multifaceted approach involving regulatory measures, sustainable practices, public awareness, and technological advancements. As global awareness of environmental issues continues to grow, it is imperative that societies around the world prioritize and implement strategies to protect the air we breathe for current and future generations. Only through collective and sustained efforts can we hope to achieve a world where clean and breathable air is a reality for everyone.

18.6.3 PREVENTION AND CONTROL MEASURES:

1. National Ambient Air Quality Standards (NAAQS): India has set NAAQS to regulate the permissible levels of air pollutants. These standards cover pollutants such as particulate matter (PM10 and PM2.5), sulfur dioxide (SO2), nitrogen dioxide (NO2), carbon monoxide (CO), ozone (O3), ammonia (NH3), and lead.

2. Emission Standards for Industries: Various industries are required to adhere to emission standards set by the Central Pollution Control Board (CPCB) for controlling air pollutants. These standards vary for different industries.

3. Vehicular Emission Norms: The government has implemented Bharat Stage (BS) emission norms for vehicles to control vehicular pollution. Stricter norms are periodically introduced to promote cleaner fuel and reduce emissions.

4. Renewable Energy Promotion: Encouraging the use of renewable energy sources like solar and wind power helps reduce reliance on fossil fuels, contributing to lower air pollution.

5. Green Cover and Afforestation: Increasing green cover and promoting afforestation are important steps in combating air pollution. Trees act as natural filters and absorb pollutants.

6. Public Awareness and Education: Creating awareness among the public regarding the harmful effects of air pollution and promoting eco friendly practices is essential for prevention.

18.6.4 PENALTIES AND PROCEDURES

1. Consent Mechanism: Industries are required to obtain consent from pollution control boards for operation. Violation of consent conditions can lead to penalties.

2. Legal Actions: Noncompliance with emission standards and environmental regulations can result in legal actions, including fines and closure orders.

3. Polluter Pays Principle: The polluter pays principle is applied, meaning that those responsible for pollution bear the costs of measures to prevent, control, and reduce pollution.

4. Environmental Impact Assessment (EIA): Industries and development projects must undergo an EIA to assess their potential environmental impact. Failure to comply with EIA regulations can lead to penalties.

5. CPCB and State Pollution Control Boards: These bodies have the authority to take legal actions against polluters and can issue closure orders, fines, or initiate legal proceedings.

6. Court Interventions: Courts may intervene in cases of severe environmental violations, issuing directives and penalties to offenders.

18.7 QUESTIONS:

1. Write a detailed note on Geographical Indication of Goods (Registration and Protection) Act 1999. ?
2. Discuss the provisions of Water (Prevention and Control of Pollution) Act, 1974 applicable to setting up of business in India.
3. What are the key features of The Air (Prevention and Control of Pollution) Act, 1981?
4. Discuss aims and objectives of Environment Protection Act, 1986
5. Explain the Prevention and Control of Air Pollution - Penalties and Procedure.

CHAPTER NINETEEN

NAVIGATING CHALLENGES AND RISKS

19.1 GOVERNMENT POLICIES AND CHANGES

Setting up a business in India involves navigating various government policies, regulations, and changes.

1. Company Registration: Businesses in India need to register with the Ministry of Corporate Affairs (MCA) under the Companies Act, 2013. The registration process varies based on the type of company (private limited, public limited, LLP, etc.).
2. Foreign Direct Investment (FDI): India has liberalized its FDI policies in recent years, allowing for increased foreign investment in various sectors. However, certain sectors still have restrictions or require government approval.
3. Goods and Services Tax (GST): India has a unified tax regime called GST, which replaced multiple indirect taxes. Understanding GST rates and compliance is crucial for businesses operating in India.
4. Labour Laws: India has numerous labor laws governing aspects such as wages, working conditions, employee benefits, etc. Businesses must comply with these laws, which can vary based on the state and industry.
5. Environmental Regulations: Businesses need to adhere to environmental laws and obtain necessary clearances, especially for industries with potential environmental impacts.
6. Intellectual Property Rights (IPR): Protecting intellectual property is essential. India has robust laws for patents, trademarks, copyrights, and designs. Registering trademarks and patents can safeguard business interests.
7. Ease of Doing Business Reforms: The Indian government has been implementing various reforms to improve the ease of doing business in the country. This includes simplifying procedures for company registration, obtaining permits/licenses, and reducing bureaucratic hurdles.
8. Digital India Initiatives: India is promoting digitalization across sectors, offering opportunities for businesses to leverage technology. Initiatives like Digital India aim to create a digitally empowered society and provide a condusive environment for digital businesses.
9. Startup India Initiative: The Indian government launched the Startup India initiative to support startups and foster entrepreneurship. It includes incentives such as tax benefits, funding support, and simplification of regulations for startups.
10. Sector-specific Regulations: Certain industries may have specific regulations and policies that businesses need to comply with. For example, healthcare, pharmaceuticals, finance, and telecommunications have their own set of regulations.
11. Customs and Import/Export Regulations: Understanding customs duties, import/export regulations, and trade policies is important for businesses engaged in international trade.
12. State-specific Policies: While there are federal laws and regulations, each Indian state may have its own policies and incentives to attract investment and promote business development.

19.2 POLICY RISKS

Setting up a business in India can offer significant opportunities due to its large market, growing economy, and skilled workforce. However, like any other country, India also has its share of policy risks that entrepreneurs and investors need to be aware of.

Policy risks in setting up a business include:

1. Regulatory Environment: India has a complex regulatory environment with numerous laws, regulations, and bureaucratic procedures at the national, state, and local levels. Navigating through these regulations can be time-consuming and challenging for businesses, especially for foreign investors unfamiliar with the Indian legal system.
2. Taxation: India's taxation system is often seen as complicated and can pose challenges for businesses. Corporate tax rates, indirect taxes such as Goods and Services Tax (GST), and compliance requirements may vary based on the type of business and industry sector.
3. Government Policies: Changes in government policies and regulations can impact businesses significantly. Shifts in economic policies, trade regulations, foreign investment norms, and sector-specific policies can affect business operations and profitability.
4. Bureaucracy and Corruption: Bureaucratic red tape and corruption are persistent challenges in India. Dealing with bureaucratic delays, inefficiencies, and demands for bribes can hinder business operations and increase costs.
5. Labour Laws: India has a complex framework of labour laws that govern aspects such as wages, working conditions, industrial relations, and employment termination. Compliance with these laws can be challenging for businesses and may require careful planning and legal advice.
6. Infrastructure Constraints: Despite significant improvements in recent years, India still faces infrastructure challenges such as inadequate power supply, transportation bottlenecks, and limited access to quality healthcare and education facilities. These constraints can impact the efficiency and cost-effectiveness of business operations.
7. Political Instability: India's political landscape can be unpredictable, with changes in government and policy priorities potentially affecting businesses. Political instability, protests, and regional tensions can create uncertainties for investors and impact business confidence.
8. Intellectual Property Rights (IPR) Protection: Intellectual property rights enforcement in India has historically been weak, leading to concerns about piracy, counterfeiting, and inadequate protection of patents, trademarks, and copyrights. Businesses need to take proactive measures to safeguard their intellectual property rights in India.
9. Environmental Regulations: Increasing environmental awareness and stricter regulations in India require businesses to comply with environmental standards and obtain necessary permits for activities that may have environmental impacts. Non-compliance can lead to fines, legal liabilities, and reputational damage.

19.3 POLITICAL STABILITY

Political stability is an essential factor to consider when setting up a business in any country, including India.

OVERVIEW OF POLITICAL STABILITY IN INDIA:

1. Democratic System: India is the world's largest democracy with a robust political system. Since gaining independence in 1947, India has maintained a democratic form of government, ensuring regular elections at national, state, and local levels.
2. Political Parties: India has a multi-party system, with several political parties representing diverse ideologies and interests. While this diversity can lead to occasional political disagreements and debates, it also ensures a system of checks and balances.
3. Policy Continuity: Despite changes in government, India generally maintains continuity in its economic policies. Successive governments have pursued economic liberalization, privatization, and globalization, albeit with

varying degrees of emphasis.

4. Investor-Friendly Policies: In recent years, the Indian government has been focusing on improving the ease of doing business and attracting foreign investment. Reforms such as the Goods and Services Tax (GST) and initiatives like Make in India aim to create a more condusive environment for businesses.

5. Regional Variations: While the central government plays a significant role, India's federal structure means that political stability can vary across states. It's essential to consider regional political dynamics and regulatory environments when planning business operations.

6. Challenges: Despite progress, India still faces challenges related to bureaucratic red tape, corruption, and occasional political unrest. These factors can impact the ease of doing business and require careful navigation by investors.

7. Stakeholder Engagement: Engaging with local stakeholders, including government officials, industry associations, and community leaders, can help businesses navigate political complexities and build strong relationships.

Overall, while India offers significant opportunities for business growth, it's essential to conduct thorough research, assess risks, and stay informed about political developments to make informed decisions and mitigate potential challenges.

19.4 COMPLIANCE AND LEGAL CHALLENGES

Setting up a business in India can be a lucrative venture given its growing economy, but it also presents various compliance and legal challenges that businesses need to navigate.

1. Company Registration: Businesses need to register their company under the appropriate legal structure, such as a Private Limited Company, Public Limited Company, Limited Liability Partnership (LLP), etc. This involves adhering to the Companies Act, 2013, and fulfilling various requirements such as obtaining Director Identification Number (DIN), Digital Signature Certificate (DSC), etc.

2. Foreign Direct Investment (FDI) Regulations: For foreign investors, understanding FDI regulations is important . Certain sectors have restrictions on the percentage of foreign equity allowed, and compliance with these regulations is essential.

3. Taxation: India has a complex tax regime comprising direct and indirect taxes. Understanding and complying with tax laws, such as Goods and Services Tax (GST), income tax, withholding tax, etc., is essential to avoid penalties and legal issues.

4. Labour Laws: India has numerous labour laws governing aspects such as minimum wages, working hours, employee bencfits, etc. Compliance with these laws is necessary to avoid legal disputes and penalties.

5. Intellectual Property Rights (IPR): Protecting intellectual property is important for businesses. Understanding and complying with laws related to trademarks, copyrights, patents, etc., is important to safeguard intellectual assets.

6. Regulatory Compliance: Depending on the industry, businesses may need to adhere to sector-specific regulations and obtain necessary licenses and permits from regulatory authorities.

7. Environmental Regulations: Businesses need to comply with environmental regulations to ensure sustainable operations. Obtaining environmental clearances and adhering to pollution control norms are essential.

8. Contractual Agreements: Businesses need to draft and execute various contractual agreements, such as employment contracts, lease agreements, vendor contracts, etc., ensuring compliance with relevant laws and regulations.

9. Compliance Reporting: Regular compliance reporting to regulatory authorities is necessary to maintain legal status and avoid penalties.

10. Data Protection and Privacy Laws: With the advent of digitalization, businesses need to comply with data protection and privacy laws such as the Personal Data Protection Bill, 2019, to ensure the security and privacy of

customer data.

11. Corporate Governance: Ensuring proper corporate governance practices and compliance with corporate governance norms is essential, especially for publicly listed companies.

19.5 RESOLVING DISPUTES

Resolving disputes during setting up a business in India is important for smooth operations and long-term success. Methods commonly used for dispute resolution:

1. Negotiation and Mediation: Often, disputes can be resolved amicably through negotiation or mediation. This involves discussions between the parties involved, sometimes facilitated by a neutral third party (mediator), to reach a mutually acceptable solution.
2. Arbitration: Arbitration is a popular alternative to litigation in India. Parties agree to submit their dispute to an arbitrator or a panel of arbitrators who then make a binding decision. Arbitration can be faster, more flexible, and less formal than court proceedings.
3. Litigation: If other methods fail, businesses may resort to litigation, i.e., taking the matter to court. India has a well-established legal system, but court proceedings can be lengthy and costly. However, sometimes litigation is unavoidable, especially for matters involving complex legal issues or significant sums of money.
4. Alternative Dispute Resolution (ADR) Mechanisms: Apart from mediation and arbitration, there are other ADR mechanisms like conciliation, expert determination, and mini-trials, which businesses can explore for resolving disputes efficiently.
5. Institutional Arbitration: Parties may choose to resolve their disputes through institutional arbitration conducted by organizations like the Indian Council of Arbitration (ICA), the International Chamber of Commerce (ICC), or the London Court of International Arbitration (LCIA) India.
6. Statutory Bodies and Regulatory Authorities: Depending on the nature of the dispute, parties may need to engage with specific statutory bodies or regulatory authorities relevant to their industry sector. These bodies often have dispute resolution mechanisms in place.
7. Legal Counsel: It's advisable for businesses to seek legal counsel early on when a dispute arises. A skilled attorney with expertise in Indian business law can provide guidance on the most suitable dispute resolution method and represent the business's interests throughout the process.

19.6 ANTI-CORRUPTION MEASURES

Setting up a business requires adherence to various anti-corruption measures to ensure compliance with legal and ethical standards.

IMPORTANT MEASURES TO CONSIDER:

1. Understand Anti-Corruption Laws: Familiarize oneself with relevant anti-corruption laws in India, such as the Prevention of Corruption Act, 1988, and the Foreign Corrupt Practices Act (FCPA).
2. Transparent Business Practices: Establish transparent business practices and maintain accurate financial records. Transparency helps in preventing corrupt practices and builds trust with stakeholders.
3. Implement Compliance Programs: Develop and implement robust compliance programs that include anti-corruption policies, procedures, and training for employees. Ensure that employees understand the consequences of engaging in corrupt activities.
4. Due Diligence: Conduct thorough due diligence on business partners, suppliers, and intermediaries to ensure they comply with anti-corruption laws and ethical standards. Verify their reputation and integrity before entering into

any agreements.

5. Implement Internal Controls: Implement internal controls and risk management systems to detect and prevent corruption within the organization. This may include segregation of duties, regular audits, and whistleblower mechanisms.
6. Third-Party Monitoring: Monitor the activities of third parties, such as agents, distributors, and consultants, to prevent bribery and corruption in business dealings. Implement contracts with clear anti-corruption clauses and conduct periodic reviews of their activities.
7. Government Interface: Exercise caution when dealing with government officials and agencies. Ensure that all interactions with government entities are conducted transparently and in compliance with applicable laws and regulations.
8. Reporting Mechanisms: Establish effective reporting mechanisms for employees to report suspected cases of corruption anonymously and without fear of retaliation. Investigate all reports promptly and take appropriate action.
9. Engage Legal Counsel: Seek guidance from legal counsel with expertise in anti-corruption laws to ensure compliance with relevant regulations and to mitigate legal risks associated with corrupt practices.
10. Corporate Culture: Foster a corporate culture that promotes integrity, ethics, and compliance with anti-corruption laws. Lead by example and encourage ethical behavior at all levels of the organization.

By adhering to these anti-corruption measures, businesses can mitigate risks, uphold their reputation, and contribute to a fair and transparent business environment in India.

19.7 CULTURAL AND SOCIAL CHALLENGES

Setting up a business in India can be both rewarding and challenging due to various cultural and social factors. Challenges include:

1. Bureaucracy and Red Tape: India's bureaucratic system can be complex and slow-moving, leading to delays and frustration in obtaining permits, licenses, and approvals required for starting a business.
2. Corruption: Corruption is still prevalent in many sectors in India, which can pose challenges for businesses, especially smaller enterprises, in navigating regulatory processes and obtaining necessary approvals.
3. Cultural Diversity: India is a highly diverse country with multiple languages, religions, and cultural practices. Understanding and navigating this diversity, especially in terms of consumer preferences and business practices, can be challenging for businesses operating across different regions.
4. Labour Relations: India has complex labor laws, and maintaining good relations with employees while adhering to these laws can be challenging. Additionally, strikes and labor unrest are not uncommon and can disrupt business operations.
5. Infrastructure: While India has made significant strides in improving its infrastructure, there are still challenges in terms of inadequate transportation, power, and telecommunications infrastructure, particularly in rural areas.
6. Market Entry Barriers: Entry into the Indian market can be challenging due to regulatory barriers, restrictions on foreign investment in certain sectors, and competition from established local players.
7. Cultural Etiquette: Understanding and respecting cultural norms and etiquette is important for business success in India. Building relationships based on trust and respect takes time and effort.
8. Social Responsibility and Sustainability: Increasingly, consumers and stakeholders in India are demanding businesses to be socially responsible and sustainable. Meeting these expectations while remaining profitable can be a challenge for businesses.
9. Gender Dynamics: While progress has been made, gender dynamics can still present challenges in the workplace, particularly in terms of gender bias and unequal opportunities for women.

10. Digital Divide: While India is experiencing rapid digital transformation, there is still a significant digital divide between urban and rural areas. Businesses need to consider this disparity while formulating their marketing and distribution strategies.

Despite these challenges, India offers immense opportunities for businesses due to its large and growing consumer market, burgeoning middle class, and increasing economic liberalization. Success in India requires patience, adaptability, and a deep understanding of the local culture and business environment.

19.8 BUILDING CROSS-CULTURAL TEAMS

Building cross-cultural teams for setting up a business in India requires careful consideration and planning to ensure effective communication, collaboration, and productivity.
STEPS TO BUILD SUCCESSFUL CROSS-CULTURAL TEAMS:

1. Understand Cultural Differences: Start by researching and understanding the cultural nuances of both the home country and India. Recognize differences in communication styles, work ethics, hierarchy, decision-making processes, and attitudes towards authority.
2. Diversity in Hiring: Embrace diversity in the hiring process. Look for team members who have experience working in multicultural environments or have a strong understanding of Indian culture. This diversity will bring different perspectives and insights to the team.
3. Cultural Sensitivity Training: Provide cultural sensitivity training to all team members, including those from India and those from other countries. This training should cover topics such as communication styles, cultural norms, religious practices, and social etiquette.
4. Clear Communication Channels: Establish clear communication channels within the team. Encourage open dialogue and create a culture where team members feel comfortable expressing their thoughts and ideas, regardless of cultural background.
5. Assign Cultural Ambassadors: Designate cultural ambassadors within the team who can act as bridges between different cultural groups. These ambassadors can help facilitate understanding, resolve conflicts, and promote inclusivity.
6. Set Common Goals and Expectations: Clearly define the goals, expectations, and roles of each team member. Ensure that everyone understands their responsibilities and how they contribute to the overall success of the business.
7. Promote Cross-Cultural Collaboration: Encourage cross-cultural collaboration by creating opportunities for team members to work together on projects, share knowledge, and learn from each other's experiences.
8. Respect Cultural Holidays and Practices: Be mindful of cultural holidays and practices observed in India and accommodate them in the team's schedule and operations. Show respect for cultural differences and avoid scheduling important meetings or deadlines during these times.
9. Foster a Positive Work Environment: Create a positive work environment that celebrates diversity and inclusion. Encourage teamwork, mutual respect, and appreciation for different cultural perspectives.
10. Regular Feedback and Evaluation: Provide regular feedback and evaluation to the team members, focusing on both individual performance and team dynamics. Address any cultural misunderstandings or conflicts promptly and constructively.

19.9 COMMUNITY ENGAGEMENT

Community engagement plays a significant role in setting up a business

1. Local Support and Acceptance: Engaging with the local community helps in gaining their support and acceptance, which is vital for the success of any business venture. This involves understanding the needs and preferences of the community and aligning business practices accordingly.
2. Building Relationships: Establishing relationships with community leaders, influencers, and stakeholders can provide valuable insights into the local market dynamics, regulatory environment, and potential challenges. These relationships can also help in navigating bureaucratic hurdles and gaining access to resources.
3. Cultural Sensitivity: India is a diverse country with multiple languages, cultures, and customs. Engaging with the local community helps in understanding and respecting cultural sensitivities, which is essential for building trust and rapport.
4. Employment Opportunities: Involving the community in the hiring process can create employment opportunities and contribute to local economic development. This can be particularly impactful in rural areas or regions with high unemployment rates.
5. Environmental and Social Responsibility: Businesses need to consider the environmental and social impact of their operations. Engaging with the local community allows businesses to address concerns related to environmental sustainability, social responsibility, and corporate citizenship.
6. Conflict Resolution: Inevitably, conflicts may arise between businesses and local communities over issues such as land acquisition, environmental pollution, or labor practices. Effective community engagement strategies can help in resolving conflicts through dialogue, negotiation, and compromise.
7. CSR Initiatives: Corporate Social Responsibility (CSR) initiatives can be tailored to address the specific needs of the local community. This could include funding education programs, healthcare facilities, or infrastructure development projects.
8. Market Access: Local communities often serve as important market segments for businesses. Engaging with these communities can help in understanding consumer behavior, preferences, and purchasing power, thereby facilitating market access and penetration.

Community engagement is not just a moral imperative but also a strategic necessity for businesses setting up operations in India. By actively involving and collaborating with the local community, businesses can build strong relationships, mitigate risks, and create sustainable value for both the company and the community.

19.10 QUESTIONS:

1. What are the Government Policies and Changes in setting up of business in India?
2. Explain the policy risk for business setup?
3. Explain the political stability a key factor for setting up of business in India?
4. Write a short note on Resolving Disputes for a business set up??
5. What is Anti-Corruption Measures?
6. Explain Cultural and Social Challenges for setting up business in India?
7. Write a brief note on Building Cross-Cultural Teams?

Appendices

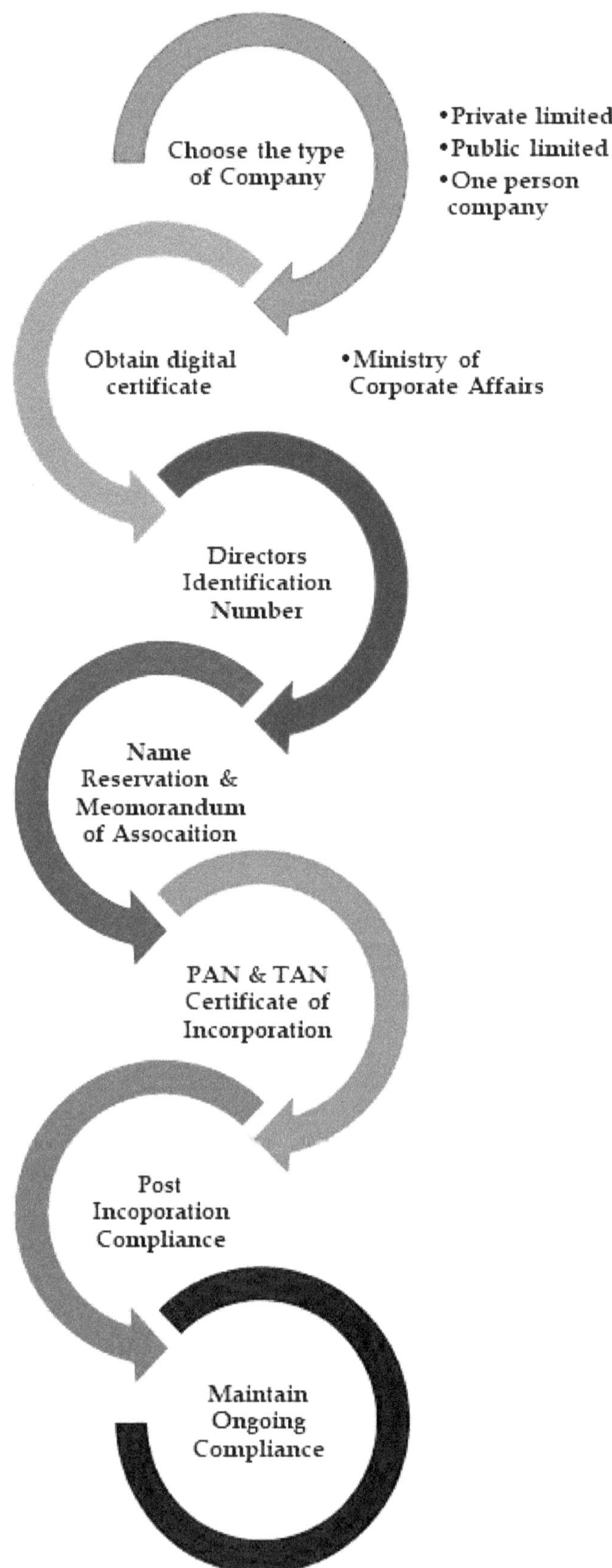

Steps in Setting Up of Business Entities in India

USEFUL RESOURCES AND CONTACTS

Setting up a business in India can be a rewarding venture, but it's important to have the right resources and contacts to navigate through the legal, financial, and administrative aspects.

1. Invest India: Invest India is the national investment promotion and facilitation agency of India. They provide comprehensive support to investors, including information on policies, regulatory framework, and assistance in setting up businesses. Website: [investindia.gov.in](https://www.investindia.gov.in/)
2. Ministry of Corporate Affairs (MCA): MCA governs corporate affairs in India through the Companies Act, and it's responsible for the registration and regulation of companies. Their website provides guidance on company registration procedures and compliance requirements. Website: [mca.gov.in](https://www.mca.gov.in/)
3. Startup India: Startup India is a flagship initiative of the Government of India aimed at promoting entrepreneurship and supporting startups. They offer various benefits and schemes for startups, including tax exemptions and funding opportunities. Website: [startupindia.gov.in](https://www.startupindia.gov.in/)
4. Local Chamber of Commerce: Each state and major city in India has its own Chamber of Commerce, which provides support and resources for businesses, including networking opportunities, industry insights, and advocacy. Examples include the Federation of Indian Chambers of Commerce & Industry (FICCI) and the Confederation of Indian Industry (CII).
5. Chartered Accountants and Legal Firms: Hiring a local chartered accountant (CA) and legal firm can be invaluable for navigating through tax regulations, company laws, and compliance requirements in India. They can also assist with company registration, drafting legal documents, and ongoing financial management.
6. Local Business Consultants: Engaging with local business consultants or advisors who have experience in setting up businesses in India can provide valuable insights and assistance tailored to the specific industry and location.
7. Banking Institutions: Establishing a business bank account is essential for conducting financial transactions. Major banks in India such as State Bank of India (SBI), ICICI Bank, and HDFC Bank offer specialized services for businesses and can provide guidance on financial matters.
8. Trade Associations: Depending on the industry, joining relevant trade associations can provide access to industry-specific resources, networking opportunities, and market insights.
9. Government Agencies: Apart from Invest India and MCA, various government departments and agencies at the state and central levels offer support and information for businesses. Examples include the Department for Promotion of Industry and Internal Trade (DPIIT) and state-specific industrial development corporations.
10. Online Portals and Forums: Online platforms like LinkedIn groups, business forums, and industry-specific portals can be useful for networking, seeking advice, and staying updated on the latest trends and regulations in the Indian business landscape.

GOVERNMENT AGENCIES AND ITS ADDRESSES

1. Ministry of Corporate Affairs (MCA), Shastri Bhawan, Dr. Rajendra Prasad Road, New Delhi - 110001
2. Department for Promotion of Industry and Internal Trade (DPIIT), Udyog Bhawan, New Delhi - 110011
3. Reserve Bank of India (RBI), Central Office Building, Shahid Bhagat Singh Marg, Fort, Mumbai - 400001
4. Securities and Exchange Board of India (SEBI), SEBI Bhavan, Plot No.C4-A, G Block, Bandra Kurla Complex, Bandra (E), Mumbai - 400051
5. Central Board of Indirect Taxes and Customs (CBIC), North Block, New Delhi - 110001
6. Goods and Services Tax Network (GSTN), East Wing, 4th Floor, World Mark - 1, Aerocity, New Delhi - 110037
7. Directorate General of Foreign Trade (DGFT), Udyog Bhawan, New Delhi - 110011

8. National Small Industries Corporation (NSIC), NSIC Bhawan, Okhla Industrial Estate, New Delhi - 110020

9. Export Credit Guarantee Corporation of India (ECGC), Express Towers, 10th Floor, Nariman Point, Mumbai - 400021

10. National Stock Exchange of India (NSE), Exchange Plaza, Bandra Kurla Complex, Bandra (East), Mumbai - 400051

11. Bombay Stock Exchange (BSE), Phiroze Jeejeebhoy Towers, Dalal Street, Mumbai - 400001

12. Central Board of Direct Taxes (CBDT), North Block, New Delhi - 110001

13. National Payments Corporation of India (NPCI), 1001A, B wing, 10th Floor, The Capital, Bandra Kurla Complex, Mumbai - 400051

14. Telecom Regulatory Authority of India (TRAI), Mahanagar Doorsanchar Bhawan, Jawaharlal Nehru Marg (Old Minto Road), New Delhi - 110002

15. Food Safety and Standards Authority of India (FSSAI), FDA Bhawan, Kotla Road, New Delhi - 110002

16. National Highways Authority of India (NHAI), G 5&6, Sector-10, Dwarka, New Delhi - 110075

17. Bureau of Indian Standards (BIS), Manak Bhawan, 9 Bahadur Shah Zafar Marg, New Delhi - 110002

18. Central Electricity Regulatory Commission (CERC), Ground Floor (Front Side), Chanderlok Building, 36, Janpath, New Delhi - 110001

19. Directorate General of Civil Aviation (DGCA), Opposite Safdarjung Airport, New Delhi - 110003

20. Central Pollution Control Board (CPCB), Parivesh Bhawan, CBD-cum-Office Complex, East Arjun Nagar, Delhi - 110032

BUSINESS SUPPORT ORGANISATION

1. Confederation of Indian Industry (CII) - National Headquarters: New Delhi

2. Federation of Indian Chambers of Commerce & Industry (FICCI) - National Headquarters: New Delhi

3. Associated Chambers of Commerce and Industry of India (ASSOCHAM) - National Headquarters: New Delhi

4. National Small Industries Corporation (NSIC) - National Headquarters: New Delhi

5. Small Industries Development Bank of India (SIDBI) - National Headquarters: Lucknow

6. Indian Angel Network (IAN) - Offices in multiple cities including Delhi, Mumbai, Bengaluru

7. TiE (The Indus Entrepreneurs) - Offices in multiple cities including Delhi-NCR, Mumbai, Bengaluru

8. Startup India - Government initiative, New Delhi

9. Invest India - Government initiative, New Delhi

10. Indian Institute of Technology (IIT) Incubators - Multiple locations across India

11. Indian Institute of Management (IIM) Incubators - Multiple locations across India

12. State Industrial Development Corporations (SIDC) - Various states have their own corporations

13. National Institute for Entrepreneurship and Small Business Development (NIESBUD) - National Headquarters: Noida

14. Indian Institute of Entrepreneurship (IIE) - National Headquarters: Guwahati

15. National Entrepreneurship Network (NEN) - Offices in multiple cities including Mumbai, Bengaluru, Chennai

16. Indian Chamber of Commerce (ICC) - Offices in multiple cities including Kolkata, Mumbai, New Delhi

17. Export Promotion Councils - Various councils for different industries, located in major cities

18. Technology Business Incubators (TBI) - Various institutions across India

19. Business Accelerators - Various private accelerators in major cities

20. MSME Development Institutes - Located in various cities across India, under the Ministry of MSME

CHECK LIST FOR SETTING UP OF BUSINESS IN INDIA

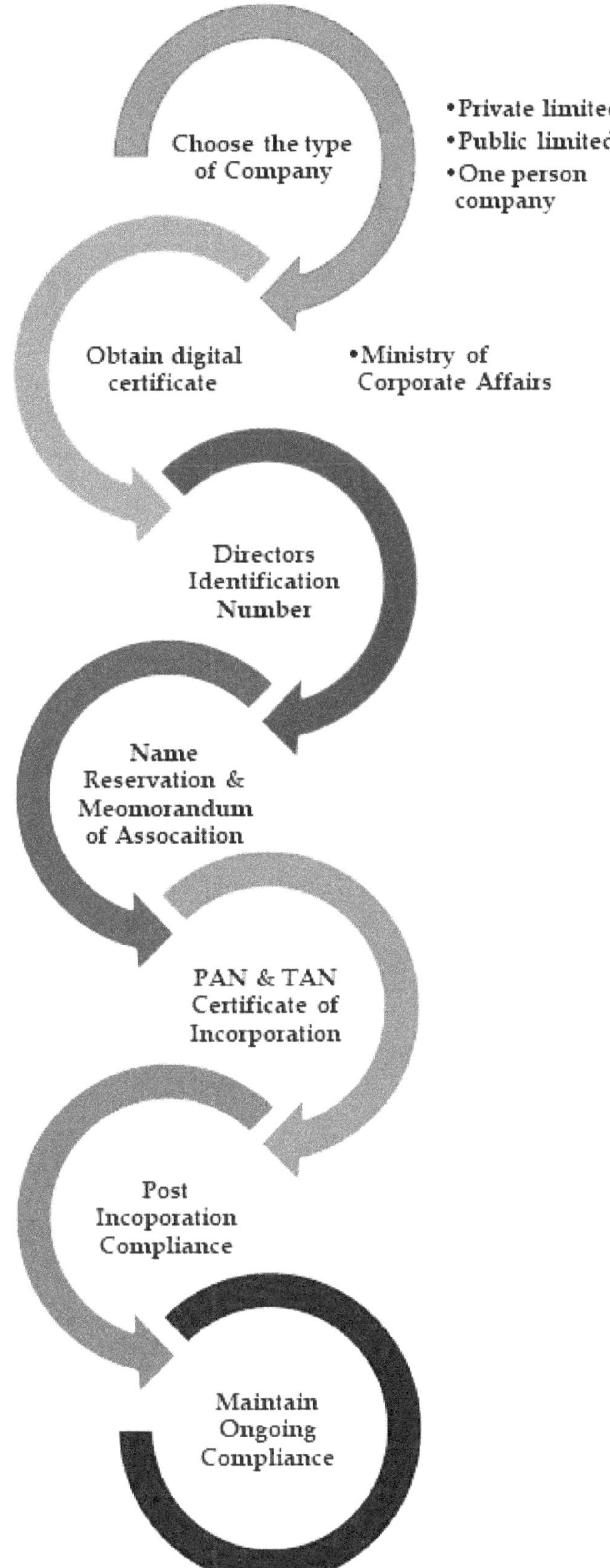

Choose the type of Company
• Private limited
• Public limited
• One person company
Obtain digital certificate
• Ministry of Corporate Affairs
Directors Identification Number
Name Reservation & Meomorandum of Assocaition
PAN & TAN Certificate of Incorporation
Post Incoporation Compliance
Maintain Ongoing Compliance

I. STEPS IN SETTING UP A BUSINESS IN INDIA

1. Determine Business Structure: Decide on the legal structure of the business (e.g., sole proprietorship, partnership, limited liability partnership (LLP), private limited company, etc.).

2. Register Business Name:

a. Choose a unique name for the business and ensure its availability.

b. Register the business name with the Registrar of Companies (RoC) if it's a company.

3. Obtain Director Identification Number (DIN): If forming a company, obtain DIN for all directors.

4. Obtain Digital Signature Certificate (DSC): Obtain DSC for signing necessary documents electronically.

5. Register for Goods and Services Tax (GST): Obtain GST registration if the business turnover exceeds the threshold limit.

6. Open a Business Bank Account: Open a bank account in the name of the business entity.

7. Obtain Permanent Account Number (PAN): Apply for PAN from the Income Tax Department.

8. Register for Tax Deduction at Source (TDS): If applicable, register for TDS with the Income Tax Department.

9. Register for Employees' Provident Fund (EPF) and Employees' State Insurance (ESI): If the business has employees, register for EPF and ESI.

10. Obtain Import Export Code (IEC) (if applicable): If the business involves importing or exporting goods, obtain IEC from the Directorate General of Foreign Trade (DGFT).

11. Business Licenses and Permits: Obtain necessary licenses and permits required for the specific industry and location.

12. Labor Compliance: Ensure compliance with labor laws regarding minimum wages, working hours, and employment contracts.

13. Environmental Clearances (if applicable): Obtain necessary clearances if the business activities impact the environment.

14. Trademark Registration: Consider registering the business name, logo, or any unique identifiers as trademarks to protect the brand.

15. Compliance with Local Regulations: Familiarize with local regulations and compliance requirements specific to the business location.

16. Insurance: Consider obtaining insurance coverage such as business liability insurance, property insurance, and health insurance for employees.

17. Document Filing and Compliance: Ensure timely filing of required documents and compliance with regulatory obligations.

18. Accounting and Record-Keeping: Set up accounting systems and maintain accurate records of financial transactions.

19. Establish Physical Presence (if applicable): Secure office space or establish a physical presence as per the business requirements.

20. Employment Contracts and HR Policies: Develop employment contracts and HR policies compliant with Indian labor laws.

21. Local Network and Partnerships: Build a network of local contacts, suppliers, and partners to support the business operations.

22. Market Research and Business Plan: Conduct market research and develop a comprehensive business plan outlining the objectives, target market, and growth strategy.

23. Compliance with Foreign Direct Investment (FDI) Regulations (if applicable): If the business involves foreign investment, ensure compliance with FDI regulations and reporting requirements.

24. Seek Professional Assistance: Consider seeking assistance from legal, accounting, or consulting professionals to navigate the complexities of setting up a business in India.

25. Stay Informed: Stay updated with changes in regulations and compliance requirements affecting the business.

STEPS IN SETTING UP A BUSINESS IN INDIA

Setting of business in India involves several steps, and the process can vary depending on the type of business entity

1. Market Research: Understand the market you're entering, including demand, competition, and regulatory environment.
2. Choose a Business Structure: Decide on the type of business entity you want to form. Common options include:

   a. Sole Proprietorship
   b. Partnership
   c. Limited Liability Partnership (LLP)
   d. Private Limited Company (PLC)
   e. Public Limited Company (PLC)

3. Register Your Business:

   a. For Sole Proprietorship: You may need to register with your local municipality or obtain a Shops & Establishment License.
   b. For Partnership: Create a Partnership Deed and register it with the Registrar of Firms.
   c. For LLP: Register with the Ministry of Corporate Affairs (MCA) through the LLP portal.
   d. For Companies: Register with the Registrar of Companies (ROC) through the MCA portal.

4. Obtain Necessary Licenses and Permits: Depending on your business activities and industry, you may need to obtain specific licenses and permits from regulatory authorities. Some common ones include:

   a. GST Registration (Goods and Services Tax)
   b. Shop and Establishment License
   c. Trade License
   d. FSSAI License (for food-related businesses)
   e. Environmental Clearances
   f. Import-Export Code (IEC)

5. Open a Business Bank Account:Once your business is registered, open a separate bank account in the name of your business entity.
6. Comply with Taxation Requirements: Understand your tax obligations, including income tax, GST, and any other applicable taxes. Obtain a Permanent Account Number (PAN) and Tax Deduction and Collection Account Number (TAN) if required.
7. Register for Employee Provident Fund (EPF) and Employee State Insurance (ESI): If you have employees, you'll need to register for EPF and ESI contributions.
8. Setup Accounting and Bookkeeping: Establish accounting systems and procedures to track your financial transactions.
9. Secure Intellectual Property Rights: If applicable, protect your intellectual property through trademarks, copyrights, or patents.
10. Hire Employees (if needed): Comply with labor laws and regulations when hiring employees. Maintain necessary

documentation such as employment contracts, offer letters, and employee handbooks.

11. Obtain Necessary Insurances: Consider getting business insurance such as liability insurance, property insurance, and health insurance for employees.

12. Setup Physical Infrastructure (if required): Arrange for office space, equipment, and utilities as per your business needs.

13. Compliance with Local Regulations: Ensure ongoing compliance with all local, state, and national regulations relevant to your business.

14. Market Your Business products and services: Develop a marketing plan to promote your products or services and attract customers.

15. Stay Informed: Stay updated with changes in regulations, tax laws, and market trends that may affect your business.

IMPORTANT DOCUMENTS

Setting up a business in India involves several legal and administrative procedures.

1. Business Plan: While not a legal requirement, having a detailed business plan is essential for outlining the business objectives, strategies, financial projections, and market analysis.

2. Identity Proof of Directors/Partners:

a. Aadhaar Card (for Indian nationals)
b. Passport (for foreign nationals)
c. PAN Card (Permanent Account Number)

3. Address Proof of Directors/Partners:

a. Aadhaar Card
b. Passport
c. Voter ID
d. Utility Bills (electricity, water, or gas bills)

4. Proof of Registered Office Address:

a. Rental Agreement or Sale Deed
b. Utility Bills of the premises
c. No Objection Certificate (NOC) from the property owner

5. Memorandum of Association (MOA) and Articles of Association (AOA): These documents define the constitution and structure of the company, including its objectives, powers, and internal regulations.

6. Certificate of Incorporation: Issued by the Ministry of Corporate Affairs (MCA) once the company is registered.

7. Tax-related Documents:

a. Permanent Account Number (PAN) for the company
b. Tax Identification Number (TIN)
c. Goods and Services Tax (GST) registration (if applicable)

8. Bank Account Opening Documents:

a. Board Resolution authorizing the opening of a bank account
b. Copy of Certificate of Incorporation
c. PAN Card of the company
d. Address proof of the company

9. Employer Identification Number (EIN): Required if business plan to hire employees.

10. Trademark Registration (Optional): If entity wishes to protect the brand name or logo, entity can register for a trademark.

11. Licenses and Permits: Depending on the nature of the business, entity may need specific licenses and permits from local or central government authorities.

12. Share Certificates: Issued to shareholders to signify their ownership in the company.

13. GST Returns: If the business is registered under GST, need to file regular GST returns.

14. Import-Export Code (IEC): Required if entity plan to engage in import/export activities.

15. Other Industry-Specific Documents: Certain industries may have specific regulatory requirements, so entity may need additional documents based on the nature of the business.

GLOSSARY OF TERMS

1. Business Structure:

- Sole Proprietorship: A business owned and operated by a single individual. The owner has unlimited liability and is personally responsible for all business debts.
- Partnership: A business structure where two or more individuals manage and operate a business in accordance with the terms and objectives set out in a Partnership Deed.
- Private Limited Company: A legal entity where the liability of the members is limited to the extent of their shares in the company.
- Public Limited Company: A company whose shares are traded on the stock exchange and can be purchased by the public.

2. Company Registration:

- Registrar of Companies (RoC): The government office responsible for the registration of companies in India.
- Memorandum of Association (MoA): A legal document that outlines the company's objectives and its relationship with shareholders.
- Articles of Association (AoA): A document that defines the internal rules and regulations for the company's operation.

3. Business Registration:

- Goods and Services Tax (GST): A unified tax system in India that replaced various indirect taxes. Business entities need to register for GST.
- Permanent Account Number (PAN): A unique identification number issued by the Income Tax Department for tax purposes.
- Tax Identification Number (TIN): A unique number assigned to businesses for tracking their transactions for tax purposes.

4. Foreign Direct Investment (FDI):

- Foreign Exchange Management Act (FEMA): Legislation that regulates foreign exchange transactions in India.
- Automatic Route: A method of FDI where foreign investors do not require prior approval from the government.

5. Compliance and Regulatory Terms:

- Compliance: Adhering to the laws and regulations governing businesses in India.
- Registrar of Companies (RoC): Government body overseeing company registration and compliance.
- Annual General Meeting (AGM): A mandatory yearly meeting of a company's shareholders.

6. Intellectual Property Rights (IPR):

- Trademark: A symbol, word, or words legally registered or established by use as representing a company.
- Patent: Exclusive rights granted to an inventor for their invention.
- Copyright: Protection provided to the authors of original works.

7. Labour Laws:

- Employees' Provident Fund (EPF): A social security scheme for employees.
- Employees' State Insurance (ESI): A self*financing social security and health insurance scheme for Indian workers.

8. Environmental and Safety Compliance:

- Environmental Impact Assessment (EIA): An evaluation of the potential environmental effects of a project.
- Occupational Safety and Health (OSH) Act: Legislation aimed at ensuring a safe and healthy working environment.

9. Startup Ecosystem:

- Department for Promotion of Industry and Internal Trade (DPIIT): Government department promoting and regulating industrial growth.
- Incubator: Organizations supporting the development of startups by providing resources and services.

10. Local Business Environment:
* Special Economic Zone (SEZ): Geographical regions with economic regulations different from the rest of the country, designed to attract foreign investment.

CASE STUDIES OF SUCCESSFUL BUSINESSES IN INDIA

1. Reliance Industries Limited (RIL)
Overview:RIL is a conglomerate with interests in petrochemicals, refining, oil, and gas exploration. It has successfully diversified into telecommunications with Jio.
Lessons Learned: The key lesson is strategic diversification. RIL leveraged its core competency in energy to enter new sectors like telecommunications, which paid off immensely.
Overcoming Challenges: RIL faced challenges during the initial phase of Jio due to intense competition. However, by offering disruptive pricing and focusing on infrastructure, they overcame challenges to become a dominant player

in the telecom industry.

2. Tata Consultancy Services (TCS)

Overview: TCS is a global IT services, consulting, and business solutions organization.

Lessons Learned:Continuous innovation and a focus on adapting to global technological trends have been crucial. TCS invested heavily in research and development, staying ahead in areas like artificial intelligence, cloud computing, and cybersecurity.

Overcoming Challenges: Initially, TCS faced skepticism with the outsourcing model. However, by showcasing the benefits of outsourcing and building strong client relationships, TCS overcame these challenges.

3. Hindustan Unilever Limited (HUL)

Overview: HUL is a consumer goods company with a wide range of products.

Lessons Learned: Understanding and catering to diverse consumer needs is important. HUL adapted its products to local preferences, ensuring a strong market presence.

Overcoming Challenges: Economic fluctuations and changing consumer behaviors presented challenges. HUL's ability to quickly adapt marketing strategies and product portfolios helped them navigate these challenges successfully.

4. Infosys

Overview: Infosys is a multinational IT services company.

Lessons Learned: Building a strong organizational culture focused on innovation and client satisfaction is essential. Infosys emphasized employee training and development, fostering a culture of continuous improvement.

Overcoming Challenges: During the dot-com bubble burst, Infosys faced challenges due to a decline in IT spending. However, their focus on cost-efficiency, quality delivery, and exploring new markets helped them recover.

5. Bharti Airtel

Overview: Bharti Airtel is a leading telecommunications company.

Lessons Learned: Investing in cutting-edge technology and understanding the dynamic telecom market has been crucial for Airtel. The company constantly adapted to changing consumer demands and emerging technologies.

Overcoming Challenges: Intense competition and regulatory hurdles posed challenges. Airtel's strategic partnerships, innovative service offerings, and regulatory compliance strategies helped them overcome obstacles.

6. Adani Group

Overview: Adani Group is a conglomerate with interests in sectors like energy, logistics, agribusiness, and more.

Lessons Learned: Diversification of multiple sectors and strategic acquisitions has been pivotal. Adani Group's ability to identify growth opportunities and enter emerging markets contributed to its success.

Overcoming Challenges: Environmental concerns and protests against projects posed challenges. Adani Group focused on sustainability, corporate social responsibility, and engaged the stakeholders to address these concerns.

7. Maruti Suzuki India Limited

Overview: Maruti Suzuki is a leading automobile manufacturer.

Lessons Learned: Understanding the Indian automotive market and providing value for money products have been key lessons. Maruti Suzuki focused on fuel efficiency, affordability, and continuous product innovation.

Overcoming Challenges: The economic downturn and changing consumer preferences presented challenges. Maruti Suzuki adapted its product lineup, introduced new models, and invested in marketing to maintain its market share.

8. Flipkart

Overview: Flipkart is one of India's largest e-commerce platforms.

Lessons Learned: Early adoption of e-commerce trends and a customer-centric approach have been vital. Flipkart focused on user experience, offering a wide range of products, and building a robust delivery network.

Overcoming Challenges: Intense competition in the e-commerce space and logistical challenges were obstacles. Flipkart's strategic partnerships, innovative marketing, and investment in logistics helped them overcome these challenges.

9. Asian Paints

Overview:Asian Paints is a leading paint manufacturing company.

Lessons Learned: Innovation in product offerings and understanding consumer preferences are key lessons. Asian Paints introduced a variety of paints, catered to different market segments, and embraced eco-friendly products.

Overcoming Challenges: Fluctuations in raw material prices and market competition were challenges. Asian Paints focused on operational efficiency, cost optimization, and strategic pricing to mitigate these challenges.

10. Ola Cabs

Overview: Ola is a major player in the ride-hailing industry in India.

Lessons Learned: Understanding local market dynamics and rapid adaptation to technological advancements have been critical. Ola embraced digital payment systems, expanded into multiple cities, and diversified into food delivery services.

Overcoming Challenges:Regulatory challenges and competition from global players were obstacles. Ola collaborated with local authorities, invested in driver-partner welfare, and offered innovative services to differentiate itself.

These case studies highlight the importance of strategic planning, innovation, adaptability, and a customer-centric approach for businesses to thrive in the dynamic Indian market. Each success story also involves overcoming unique challenges through resilience, strategic decision-making, and a commitment to meeting evolving consumer needs.

SUCCESS STORIES OF FOREIGN COMPANIES IN INDIA

1. Microsoft:

Strategy for Success: Microsoft entered India with a long-term vision, focusing on adapting its products to the local market. The company invested in local talent, establishing research and development centers to address specific Indian needs. Collaborations with local businesses and government bodies further helped in customizing solutions. They also adopted a flexible pricing strategy to make their products more accessible to a diverse market.

Impact on Local Communities: Microsoft's presence has significantly contributed to skill development in the technology sector. Through various educational initiatives and partnerships with universities, they have enhanced the employability of the local workforce. Additionally, Microsoft's CSR programs have focused on digital literacy and empowerment, making technology accessible to rural and underprivileged communities.

2. Samsung:

Strategy for Success: Samsung strategically entered India with a comprehensive product portfolio catering to various price points. They understood the importance of localization, establishing manufacturing units to assemble products within the country. Focusing on innovation and quality, Samsung gained consumer trust, and aggressive marketing campaigns helped establish a strong brand presence.

Impact on Local Communities: Samsung's manufacturing units have not only created job opportunities but also boosted the growth of ancillary industries. The company actively engages in community development projects, supporting education and healthcare initiatives. Their commitment to sustainable practices has also positively influenced the local environment.

3. Coca-Cola:

Strategy for Success: Coca-Cola's success in India can be attributed to its deep understanding of local tastes and preferences. They introduced a range of products tailored to the Indian palate and invested in a robust distribution network. Collaborating with local bottling partners, Coca-Cola ensured efficient supply chain management and affordability.

Impact on Local Communities: Coca-Cola's presence has generated employment in both urban and rural areas through its bottling plants. The company has also initiated water conservation and community development projects, positively impacting local ecosystems and communities. Through its CSR initiatives, Coca-Cola has focused on education, health, and water stewardship.

4. Toyota:

Strategy for Success: Toyota's success in India stems from its commitment to quality and innovation. The company strategically localized its product lineup to meet the demands of the Indian market. Emphasizing sustainability, Toyota introduced hybrid models and engaged in collaborations for the development of eco-friendly technologies.

Impact on Local Communities: Toyota's manufacturing plants have created job opportunities and stimulated economic growth in the regions where they operate. The company has invested in skill development programs, contributing to the overall advancement of the local workforce. Additionally, Toyota has been involved in community welfare projects, focusing on healthcare and education.

5. Amazon:

Strategy for Success: Amazon's entry into India was marked by an understanding of the unique challenges posed by the diverse market. The company invested heavily in building a robust logistics network and adopting innovative technologies for efficient delivery. Amazon also introduced localized features like vernacular language support and diverse payment options.

Impact on Local Communities: Amazon's presence has had a significant impact on the e-commerce ecosystem in India, creating opportunities for small businesses and entrepreneurs. The company's initiatives like Amazon Cares focus on education, healthcare, and skill development, positively influencing local communities.

6. IKEA:

Strategy for Success: IKEA's success in India lies in its commitment to understanding local consumer behavior. The company adapted its product range to suit Indian tastes and preferences while maintaining its core values of affordability and sustainability. Establishing a strong online and offline presence, IKEA ensured accessibility to a wide range of consumers.

Impact on Local Communities: IKEA's entry into India has resulted in job creation across various functions, from manufacturing to retail. The company's commitment to sustainable sourcing and production practices has had a positive impact on local ecosystems. Additionally, IKEA's community initiatives focus on education, livelihood, and women's empowerment.

7. Google:

Strategy for Success: Google's success in India can be attributed to its focus on localization and adapting its services to suit the diverse linguistic and cultural landscape. The company has collaborated with local developers and businesses, fostering innovation. Google's Android operating system has become a dominant player in the Indian smartphone market.

Impact on Local Communities: Google's initiatives in India have led to the growth of the digital ecosystem, providing opportunities for local developers and entrepreneurs. The company's educational programs and partnerships have enhanced digital literacy, contributing to skill development in the country.

8. *Unilever:*

Strategy for Success: Unilever's success in India is grounded in its ability to understand and cater to the diverse consumer needs. The company introduced a wide range of products at various price points, focusing on affordability and quality. Unilever also invested in local research and development to create products specifically tailored to Indian preferences.

Impact on Local Communities: Unilever's manufacturing units and distribution networks have contributed significantly to local economies by generating employment and supporting ancillary industries. The company's sustainability initiatives, such as water conservation and waste reduction, have had a positive impact on the environment and local communities.

9. *Siemens:*

Strategy for Success: Siemens entered India with a focus on providing innovative solutions in the fields of energy, healthcare, and infrastructure. The company established strong partnerships with local businesses and government bodies, contributing to the development of important sectors. Siemens emphasized technology transfer and skill development.

Impact on Local Communities: Siemens' projects in India have not only created job opportunities but also advanced technology and infrastructure development. The company's commitment to corporate social responsibility includes initiatives in education, healthcare, and environmental conservation, positively impacting local communities.

10. *Apple:*

Strategy for Success: Apple's success in India is attributed to its brand appeal and a targeted approach to marketing premium products. The company adopted a phased entry strategy, gradually expanding its product offerings. Apple also invested in local manufacturing units, supporting the 'Make in India' initiative.

Impact on Local Communities: Apple's manufacturing units have contributed to job creation and skill development in the country. The company's focus on environmental sustainability has influenced local suppliers and manufacturers to adopt eco-friendly practices. Additionally, Apple's initiatives in education and skill development have positively impacted local communities.

The success stories of these foreign companies in India underscore the importance of adapting to local nuances, investing in localization, and actively engaging with the community. Beyond economic growth, these companies have played an important role in skill development, job creation, and community welfare. The strategies employed by these companies serve as valuable lessons for businesses looking to navigate diverse markets successfully. By aligning with local needs and contributing to community development, foreign companies can establish themselves as integral contributors to the growth and prosperity of the regions they operate in.

IV.   SYLLABUS COVERED FOR MASTER OF COMMERCE (M.COM.,)

UNIT I: Startups in India

Types of business organisations –Factors governing selection of an organisation - Startups – Evolution – Definition of a Startup – Startup landscape in India – Startup India policy – Funding support and incentives – Indian states with Startup policies – Exemptions forstartups – Life cycle of a Startup – Important points for Startups – Financing options available for Startups – Equity financing – Debt financing – Venture capital financing – IPO – Crowd funding – Incubators - Mudra banks –Successful Startups in India.

UNIT II: Not-for-Profit Organisations

Formation and registration of NGOs – Section 8 Company – Definition – Features – Exemptions – Requirements of Section 8 Company – Application for incorporation – Trust: Objectives of a trust – Persons who can create a trust – Differences between a Public and private trust – Exemptions available to trusts – Formation of a trust – Trust Deed –Society – Advantages – Disadvantages – Formation of a society – Tax exemption to NGOs.

UNIT III: Limited Liability Partnership and Joint Venture

Limited Liability Partnership: Definition – Nature and characteristics – Advantages and disadvantages – Procedure for incorporation – LLP agreement – Annual compliances of LLP-Business collaboration: Definition – Types –Joint venture: Advantages and disadvantages – Types – Joint venture agreement - Successful joint ventures in India– Special Purpose Vehicle – Meaning – Benefits – Formation.

UNIT IV: Registration and Licenses

Registration and Licenses: Introduction – Business entity registration – Mandatory registration – PAN – Significance – Application and registration of PAN – Linking of PAN with Aadhar –TAN – Persons liable to apply for TAN – Relevance of TAN – Procedure to apply for TAN –GST: Procedure for registration – Registration under Shops and Establishment Act –MSME registration – Clearance from Pollution Control Board – FSSAI registration and license – Trade mark, Patent and Design registration.

UNIT V: Environmental Legislations in India

Geographical Indication of Goods (Registration and Protection) Act, 1999: Objectives, Salient Features - The Environmental Protection Act, 1986: Prevention, control and abatement of environmental pollution - The Water (Prevention And Control of Pollution)Act, 1974: The Central and State Boards for Prevention and Control of Water Pollution - Powers and Functions of Boards - Prevention and Control of Water Pollution - Penalties and Procedure- The Air (Prevention and Control of Pollution) Act, 1981: Central and State Boards for The Prevention and Control of Air Pollution – Powers and Functions - Prevention and Control of Air Pollution - Penalties and Procedure.